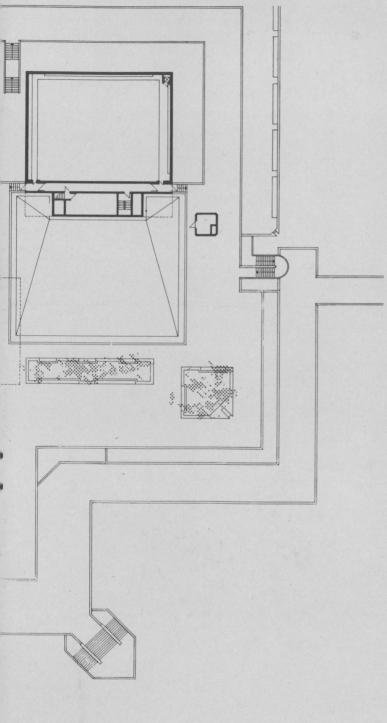

This, the seventh volume in the Revels History
of Drama in English, traces the development of
British drama from the late nineteenth century
to the present day. It follows the many upheavals
of this modern period which have brought about
radical change in the theatre, leading to new
ideas and techniques in acting, directing and
theatre building, as well as in the drama itself.

Beginning with the social and literary context,
including the national, repertory and little
theatre movements, the influence of cinema,
radio and television, and increasing political
militancy, the book moves on to a detailed
consideration of the actors and theatres of the
period. The changing nature of the stage is
analysed, with its many styles of presentation —
from variety and music hall, the West End,
Stratford and the Old Vic, to the fringe and the
birth of the National Theatre; and the
discussion ranges over the dominance of such
actor-managers as Irving and Tree, the great
innovators like Grein, Poel and Granville
Barker, the influence of the director, and the
styles of the great actors, including Gielgud and
Olivier. Finally, there is a chronological study of
dramatists and their plays — from Shaw, Synge
and O'Casey to Beckett, Osborne, Pinter and the
'new drama'. A chronological table, substantial
bibliography and illustrations from contemporary
sources are provided.

There are twenty-nine half-tone plates.

*Hugh Hunt is Emeritus Professor of Drama at the
University of Manchester; Kenneth Richards is
Professor of Drama at the University of
Manchester; John Russell Taylor is Professor in
the Cinema Division of the School of Performing
Arts at the University of Southern California.*

*Jacket illustrations: Janet Suzman as Cleopatra
in the Royal Shakespeare Company's production of*
Antony and Cleopatra (*Photo: Reg Wilson*).

The *Revels*
History of Drama
in English

GENERAL EDITOR
T. W. Craik

The *Revels* History of Drama in English

VOLUME VII 1880 to the Present Day

Hugh Hunt, Kenneth Richards
John Russell Taylor

LONDON
Methuen & Co Ltd
Barnes & Noble Books
NEW YORK

First published in 1978 by
Methuen & Co Ltd
11 New Fetter Lane, London EC4P 4EE

ISBN 0 416 13080 1 (hardbound)
ISBN 0 416 81390 9 (paperback)

and by Barnes & Noble Books
10 East 53rd Street
New York NY *10022*

ISBN 0-06-473247-9 (hardbound)
ISBN 0-06-473248-7 (paperback)

© 1978 Hugh Hunt, Kenneth Richards, John Russell Taylor

Printed in Great Britain by
Richard Clay (The Chaucer Press) Ltd
Bungay, Suffolk

Contents

vi Contents

viii Contents

List of illustrations

Plates

Section one   *between pages 50 and 51*

x   List of illustrations

Endpapers

Plan of the Olivier Theatre. Denys Lasdun and Partners

Acknowledgements

The authors and publishers would like to thank the following for permission
to reproduce the illustrations appearing in this book:
The Tate Gallery for No. 5
John Vickers for Nos. 24 and 25
The Harvard Theatre Collection for Nos. 26, 27 and 28 (Angus McBean
Photographs)
The National Theatre for No. 29 (Dave King photograph) and Architects:
Denys Lasdun and Partners for the endpapers

Preface

This volume of *The Revels History of Drama in English* carries the history from 1880 to the present time, beginning where Volume VI (published in 1975) left off. Besides a survey of the leading dramatists' work, it includes accounts of the principal actors and directors, the development of the theatre, and the effects of social changes on the drama; the relationship of the theatrical drama to new artistic forms – the film and the radio and television drama – is also discussed.

The chronological table has been prepared by the present General Editor with the assistance of the contributors and of Mr Peter Lewis of Durham University.

It is with great regret that we record the death in 1977 of Professor Clifford Leech, the original General Editor. Professor Leech conceived the idea of the series and gathered together the original team of contributors.

Of the three volumes still to appear, Volume II (1500–1576) will be edited by the present General Editor. Volumes I (Medieval Drama) and IV (1616–1660) will be edited by Dr Lois D. Potter of Leicester University.

T. W. Craik

Date	Historical events	Theatrical events	Non-dramatic literary events
1878		Irving assumes management at Lyceum with Ellen Terry as leading lady; Phelps d.	
1879		Hare–Kendal management at St James's; Irving's Shylock; Comédie-Française visits London; Fechter d.	
1880		Bancrofts assume management at Haymarket; Rotterdamers visit London; Ibsen's *Pillars of Society* given morning performance at Gaiety Theatre	Hardy, *The Trumpet Major*; Meredith, *The Tragic Comedians*
1881		Irving acts Othello and Iago alternately with Booth; D'Oyly Carte opens Savoy with Gilbert and Sullivan, *Patience*; Poel gives presentation of *Hamlet* in 1603 Quarto version; Meiningen visits London	James, *The Portrait of a Lady*; Mark Rutherford, *Autobiography*; Wilde, *Poems*
1882		Irving's Romeo and Benedick; William Archer's *English Dramatists of Today* published	
1883	Fabian Society formed	Frank Benson's Shakespeare Company formed; Irving's first American tour	Nietzsche, *Thus Spake Zarathustra*
1884		Irving's Malvolio	Mark Twain, *Huckleberry Finn*; Huysmans, *A rebours*
1885		Music Hall Artists' Association formed; Tommaso Salvini acts in London; Irving's *Faust*; George Edwardes forms partnership with John Hollingshead at the Gaiety	Rider Haggard, *King Solomon's Mines*; Meredith, *Diana of the Crossways*; Zola, *Germinal*
1886	Gladstone's first Home Rule Bill defeated	Frank Benson starts thirty-year-long control of annual Stratford festivals	Gissing, *Demos*; Hardy, *The Mayor of Casterbridge*; James, *The Bostonians*; Kipling, *Departmental Ditties*; Stevenson, *Dr Jekyll and Mr Hyde*

First performance of notable plays written in English (excluding American plays)	Births and deaths of notable playwrights	Theatrical events in Europe and the USA
		Ibsen, *A Doll's House*
A. W. Pinero, *The Money-Spinner*	S. O'Casey b.	Coquelin, *L'Art et le comédien*, published
A. W. Pinero, *The Squire*	L. Abercrombie b.; P. Colum b.; S. Houghton b.	Ibsen, *Ghosts*
H. A. Jones, *The Silver King* (with H. A. Herman); O. Wilde, *Vera, or the Nihilists* (New York)		Becque, *Les Corbeaux*; Ibsen, *An Enemy of the People*
	H. Brighouse b.; St J. Ervine b.	
H. A. Jones, *Saints and Sinners, Breaking a Butterfly*; A. W. Pinero, *The Profligate*		Ibsen, *The Wild Duck*
W. S. Gilbert and A. Sullivan, *The Mikado*; A. W. Pinero, *The Magistrate*		Adelaide Ristori retires
A. W. Pinero, *The Hobby Horse, The Schoolmistress*	T. S. Eliot b.; L. Robinson b.; B. Travers b.; C. Williams b.	

Date	Historical events	Theatrical events	Non-dramatic literary events
1887	International Copyright Act	Tree assumes management at Haymarket	Conan Doyle, *A Study in Scarlet*; Hardy, *The Woodlanders*
1888		William Archer's *Masks or Faces?*; William Archer's translations of *Pillars of Society, An Enemy of the People, Ghosts*; Irving's second *Macbeth*	Doughty, *Travels in Arabia Deserta*; Kipling, *Plain Tales from the Hills*; Stevenson and Osbourne, *The Wrong Box*
1889		Théâtre Libre visits London; first English production of Ibsen's *A Doll's House*	Barrie, *A Window in Thrums*; Jerome, *Three Men in a Boat*
1890		Alexander assumes management at St James's; Dion Boucicault d.	Booth, *In Darkest England*; W. James, *Principles of Psychology*; Wilde, *The Picture of Dorian Gray*
1891	American Copyright Act	J. T. Grein's Independent Theatre Society founded: produces Ibsen's *Ghosts*; British Actors' Association formed; Shaw's *The Quintessence of Ibsenism* published; Barry Sullivan d.	Conan Doyle, *The Adventures of Sherlock Holmes*; Hardy, *Tess of the D'Urbervilles*; Gissing, *New Grub Street*
1892	First Labour MP (Keir Hardie) elected	Independent Theatre Society produces Shaw's *Widowers' Houses*; Irving's Lear	Kipling, *Barrack-Room Ballads*
1893		Daly's Theatre opened; Irving's production of Tennyson's *Becket*; Tree's production of Wilde's *Woman of No Importance*; Pinero's *The Second Mrs Tanqueray* with Mrs Patrick Campbell at St James's	
1894		William Poel's Elizabethan Stage Society formed	Grossmith, *The Diary of a Nobody*; Anthony Hope, *The Prisoner of Zenda*; Moore, *Esther Waters*

First performance of notable plays written in English (excluding American plays)	Births and deaths of notable playwrights	Theatrical events in Europe and the USA
W. S. Gilbert and A. Sullivan, *Ruddigore*; A. W. Pinero, *Dandy Dick*		Strindberg, *The Father*; A. Antoine founds Théâtre Libre, Paris
W. S. Gilbert and A. Sullivan, *The Yeomen of the Guard*	J. Bridie (O. H. Mavor) b.	O'Neill b.
W. S. Gilbert and A. Sullivan, *The Gondoliers*; H. A. Jones, *Wealth*, *The Middleman*	M. MacLiammoir b.	Strindberg, *Miss Julie*; O. Brahm founds Freie Bühne, Berlin
H. A. Jones, *Judah*; A. W. Pinero, *The Cabinet Minister*		Ibsen, *Hedda Gabler*; Maeterlinck, *Les Aveugles*; Salvini retires
J. M. Barrie, *Richard Savage*; A. W. Pinero, *The Times*; O. Wilde, *The Duchess of Padua*		
J. M. Barrie, *Walker, London*; G. B. Shaw, *Widowers' Houses*; B. Thomas, *Charley's Aunt*; O. Wilde, *Lady Windermere's Fan, Salome*		Hauptmann, *The Weavers*
W. S. Gilbert and A. Sullivan, *Utopia Limited*; H. A. Jones, *The Tempter*; A. W. Pinero, *The Second Mrs Tanqueray*; A. Tennyson, *Becket* (written 1879); O. Wilde, *A Woman of No Importance*	Dorothy L. Sayers b.	*The Execution of Mary Queen of Scots* (film, Edison); Steele MacKaye designs Spectatorium for Chicago (not completed)
J. M. Barrie, *The Professor's Love Story*; H. A. Jones, *The Case of Rebellious Susan*; G. B. Shaw, *Arms and the Man*	J. B. Priestley b.	Wedekind, *Earth Spirit*

Date	Historical events	Theatrical events	Non-dramatic literary events
1895		Irving knighted; Bernhardt and Duse act in London; Théâtre de l'Œuvre visits London; Wilde's *The Importance of Being Earnest* at St James's; Tree's production of *Trilby*; Forbes-Robertson's Romeo; Pinero's *The Notorious Mrs Ebbsmith* with Mrs Patrick Campbell at Garrick	Crane, *The Red Badge of Courage*; Hardy, *Jude the Obscure*; Wells, *The Time Machine*; Yeats, *Poems*
1896		Irving's *Cymbeline* and *Richard III*; Augustus Harris d.	Conrad, *An Outcast of the Islands*; Housman, *A Shropshire Lad*
1897		Bancroft knighted; Forbes-Robertson's Hamlet; Her Majesty's Theatre opened under Tree's management	Conrad, *The Nigger of the Narcissus*; James, *What Maisie Knew*; Wells, *The Invisible Man*
1898		Forbes-Robertson's Macbeth; Irish Literary Theatre formed by Yeats, Martyn and Lady Gregory; Tree's *Julius Ceasar*	Hewlett, *The Forest Lovers*; Shaw, *The Perfect Wagnerite*; Wilde, *The Ballad of Reading Gaol*
1899		Wyndham's Theatre opened; Irving sells Lyceum lease to the Lyceum Theatre Company; Incorporated Stage Society formed; Martin-Harvey's Sidney Carton in *The Only Way*; Augustin Daly d.	Freud, *The Interpretation of Dreams*; Hornung, *The Amateur Cracksman*; James, *The Awkward Age*; Yeats, *The Wind Among the Reeds*
1900		Japanese Company at Coronet Theatre; Tree's *A Midsummer Night's Dream*	Conrad, *Lord Jim*; Wells, *Love and Mr Lewisham*
1901	Death of Queen Victoria; Edward VII accedes	Apollo Theatre opened; Irving's Coriolanus; Poel first produces *Everyman*	Butler, *Erewhon Revisited*; W. James, *The Varieties of Religious Experience*; Mann, *Buddenbrooks*
1902	Education Act	Wyndham knighted; Irving leaves Lyceum; Tree's *Merry Wives of Windsor*; Forbes-Robertson's *Othello*	Bennett, *The Grand Babylon Hotel*; Gide, *L'Immoraliste*; James, *The Wings of the Dove*; Mason, *The Four Feathers*

First performance of notable plays written in English (excluding American plays)	Births and deaths of notable playwrights	Theatrical events in Europe and the USA
H. James, *Guy Domville*; A. W. Pinero, *The Notorious Mrs Ebbsmith*, *The Benefit of the Doubt*; O. Wilde, *An Ideal Husband*, *The Importance of Being Earnest*	Dodie Smith (C. L. Anthony) b.	*The Arrival of the Paris Express* (film, Lumières); Steele MacKaye's Scenitorium opens
W. S. Gilbert and A. Sullivan, *The Grand Duke*; H. A. Jones, *Michael and his Lost Angel*	J. R. Ackerley b.; R. C. Sherriff b.; Enid Bagnold b.	Artaud b.; Chekhov, *The Seagull*; Jarry, *Ubu roi*; Rossi d.
J. M. Barrie, *The Little Minister*; H. A. Jones, *The Liars*; G. B. Shaw, *The Devil's Disciple*		Chekhov, *Uncle Vanya*; Rostand, *Cyrano de Bergerac*
A. W. Pinero, *Trelawny of the 'Wells'*		Stanislavsky and Nemirovich-Danchenko found Moscow Art Theatre; Brecht b.
E. Martyn, *The Heather Field*; F. Wills, *The Only Way*; W. B. Yeats, *The Countess Cathleen*	N. Coward b.	Ibsen, *When We Dead Awaken*; Appia, *Music and Staging*, published
S. Houghton, *The Younger Generation*; H. A. Jones, *Mrs Dane's Defence*; G. B. Shaw, *You Never Can Tell*	O. Wilde d.	*Jeanne d'Arc* (film, Méliès)
H. G. Barker, *The Marrying of Anne Leete*; S. Phillips, *Herod*; A. W. Pinero, *Iris*	D. Johnson b.	Chekhov, *The Three Sisters*
J. M. Barrie, *The Admirable Crichton, Quality Street*; S. Phillips, *Paolo and Francesca*		Gorký, *The Lower Depths*

Date	Historical events	Theatrical events	Non-dramatic literary events
1903	Emmeline Pankhurst founds Women's Social and Political Union	New Theatre opened; Tree's *Richard II*	Butler, *The Way of All Flesh*; Conrad, *Typhoon*; James, *The Ambassadors*; G. E. Moore, *Principia Ethica*
1904		Barker–Vedrenne Repertory starts at Court Theatre; Abbey Theatre opened; Tree founds Academy of Dramatic Art (later RADA); Granville Barker and Archer, *Scheme and Estimates for a National Theatre* (published privately)	Bradley, *Shakespearean Tragedy*; Chesterton, *The Napoleon of Notting Hill*; Conrad, *Nostromo*; Hudson, *Green Mansions*; James, *The Golden Bowl*
1905		Aldwych Theatre opened; Scala Theatre opened; Tree starts annual Shakespeare Festival at Her Majesty's; Court Theatre production of Shaw's *Man and Superman*; Craig's *The Art of the Theatre* published; Irving d. Actors' Union formed	Forster, *Where Angels Fear to Tread*; Baroness Orczy, *The Scarlet Pimpernel*; Wilde, *De Profundis*
1906		Variety Artists' Federation established; Tree's *Antony and Cleopatra*; Reinhardt's production of *A Midsummer Night's Dream*	Barrie, *Peter Pan in Kensington Gardens*; Galsworthy, *The Man of Property*; E. Nesbit, *The Railway Children*; Wallace, *The Four Just Men*
1907		*Playboy* riots at Abbey Theatre; Mrs Patrick Campbell's *Hedda Gabler* at Court Theatre; Shaw's *Caesar and Cleopatra* with Forbes-Robertson at the Savoy; Queen's Theatre opened	Conrad, *The Secret Agent*; Forster, *The Longest Journey*; Gosse, *Father and Son*
1908		Manchester Repertory, started (1907) by Miss Horniman, moves to Gaiety Theatre; Craig starts *The Mask* in Florence	Bennett, *The Old Wives' Tale*; Davies, *The Autobiography of a Super-Tramp*; Grahame, *The Wind in the Willows*
1909		Scottish Repertory Theatre established by Arthur Wareing; Beerbohm Tree knighted	Florence M. Barclay, *The Rosary*; John Buchan, *Prester John*; Wells, *Ann Veronica*, *Tono Bungay*

First performance of notable plays written in English (excluding American plays)	Births and deaths of notable playwrights	Theatrical events in Europe and the USA
J. M. Synge, *The Shadow of the Glen*	W. Greenwood b.	
J. M. Barrie, *Peter Pan*; G. B. Shaw, *Candida, John Bull's Other Island*; J. M. Synge, *Riders to the Sea*; W. B. Yeats, *The Shadowy Waters*		Chekhov, *The Cherry Orchard*; Chekhov d.
H. G. Barker, *The Voysey Inheritance*; St J. Hankin, *The Return of the Prodigal*; G. B. Shaw, *Major Barbara, Man and Superman, The Philanderer*; J. M. Synge, *The Well of the Saints*	G. Greene b.; E. Williams b.	Meyerhold assumes charge of Moscow Art Theatre Studio; Reinhardt produces *A Midsummer Night's Dream* at his Neues Theater (opened 1903)
J. Galsworthy, *The Silver Box*; Lady Gregory, *The Gaol Gate, Hyacinth Halvey*; St J. Hankin, *The Charity that Began at Home*; A. W. Pinero, *His House in Order*; G. B. Shaw, *The Doctor's Dilemma*	S. Beckett b.	Ibsen d.
H. G. Barker, *Waste*; Lady Gregory, *The Rising of the Moon*; St J. Hankin, *The Cassilis Engagement*; W. S. Maugham, *Lady Frederick, Mrs Dot, Jack Straw*; J. M. Synge, *The Tinker's Wedding, The Playboy of the Western World*	C. Fry b.; L. MacNeice b.; J. M. Synge d.	Strindberg and Falk found Intima Teatern, Stockholm; Strindberg, *A Dream Play*
J. M. Barrie, *What Every Woman Knows*; Lady Gregory, *The Workhouse Ward*; A. W. Pinero, *The Thunderbolt*; L. Robinson, *The Clancy Name*; G. B. Shaw, *Getting Married*	N. C. Hunter b.	Strindberg, *The Ghost Sonata*
Elizabeth Baker, *Chains*; J. Galsworthy, *Strife*	J. Davidson d.; St J. Hankin d.; G. Savory b.	Molnár, *Liliom*; Diaghilev Company in Paris; Coquelin d.; Modjeska d.

Date	Historical events	Theatrical events	Non-dramatic literary events
1910	George V accedes	Poel's *Two Gentlemen of Verona* in Tree's Shakespeare Festival	Bennett, *Clayhanger*; Forster, *Howards End*; Wells, *The History of Mr Polly*; Yeats, *The Green Helmet and other Poems*
1911	Parliament Act – powers of the House of Lords diminished; outbreak of strikes	George Alexander knighted; Liverpool Repertory Theatre started; Diaghilev Company in London	Beerbohm, *Zuleika Dobson*; Chesterton, *The Innocence of Father Brown*; Conrad, *Under Western Eyes*; Munro, *The Chronicles of Clovis*
1912		Reinhardt's London production of *Oedipus* with Martin-Harvey; Barker's productions at the Savoy of *The Winter's Tale* and *Twelfth Night*	Bentley, *Trent's Last Case*
1913		Barry Jackson starts Birmingham Repertory Theatre; Craig's *Towards a New Theatre* published; Forbes-Robertson retires	Alain-Fournier, *Le Grand Meaulnes*; Lawrence, *Sons and Lovers*; Mackenzie, *Sinister Street* (Vol. II, 1914); Mann, *Death in Venice*; Proust, *A la recherche du temps perdu* (to 1927)
1914	First World War begins	Shaw's *Pygmalion* at His Majesty's with Tree and Mrs Patrick Campbell; Lilian Baylis starts Old Vic; Barker's *A Midsummer Night's Dream*	Joyce, *Dubliners*; Yeats, *Responsibilities*
1915		Lewis Waller d.; George Edwardes d.	Brooke, *1914 and other Poems*; Conrad, *Victory*; Ford, *The Good Soldier*; Lawrence, *The Rainbow*; Maugham, *Of Human Bondage*
1916	Entertainments Department of Armed Forces started; Entertainments Tax introduced; Easter Rising in Dublin	Benson knighted	Joyce, *A Portrait of the Artist as a Young Man*; Jung, *Psychology of the Unconscious*
1917		Beerbohm Tree d.	Eliot, *Prufrock and Other Observations*; Edward Thomas, *Poems*; Yeats, *The Wild Swans at Coole*

First performance of notable plays written in English (excluding American plays)	*Births and deaths of notable playwrights*	*Theatrical events in Europe and the USA*
H. G. Barker, *The Madras House*; J. Galsworthy, *Justice*; G. B. Shaw, *Misalliance*		Meyerhold produces Molière's *Dom Juan* at Alexandrinsky Theatre; Reinhardt produces *Oedipus Rex* (Vienna) with arena staging; Genet b.
St J. Ervine, *Mixed Marriage*	W. Browne b.; W. S. Gilbert d.; T. Rattigan b.	
S. Houghton, *Hindle Wakes*; G. B. Shaw, *Pygmalion*; Githa Sowerby, *Rutherford and Son*		Ionesco b.; Craig produces *Hamlet* at Moscow Art Theatre; Strindberg d.
St J. Ervine, *Jane Clegg*; J. Galsworthy, *The Fugitive*; G. B. Shaw, *Androcles and the Lion*	S. Houghton d.	Copeau founds Théâtre du Vieux-Colombier
H. A. Jones, *The Lie* (in New York; in London 1923)	S. Grundy d.	Meyerhold opens Studio in Moscow; Andreyev, *He Who Gets Slapped*; Tennessee Williams b.
H. Brighouse, *Hobson's Choice* (New York); St J. Ervine, *John Ferguson*; W. S. Maugham, *Our Betters*	J. Whiting b.	Charles Frohman d.
J. M. Barrie, *A Kiss for Cinderella*; L. Robinson, *The Whiteheaded Boy*		Salvini d.
J. M. Barrie, *Dear Brutus*		Kaiser, *Gas* I (II, 1920); Pirandello, *So It Is, If You Think So*

Date	Historical events	Theatrical events	Non-dramatic literary events
1918	Armistice signed	Alexander d.; Playfair leases Lyric Theatre, Hammersmith; Cochran assumes management of the London Pavilion (to 1931)	Firbank, *Valmouth*; Strachey, *Eminent Victorians*
1919		Wyndham d.; Bridges Adams succeeds Benson as director of Shakespeare Memorial Theatre; Actors' Association re-formed as trade union; British Drama League formed; Du Maurier leases Wyndham's Theatre	Daisy Ashford, *The Young Visiters*; Barbellion, *The Journal of a Disappointed Man*; Hardy, *Collected Poems*; Sassoon, *War Poems*
1920	Unemployment grows	*The Beggar's Opera*, Lyric Theatre, Hammersmith	Eliot, *The Sacred Wood*; Fry, *Vision and Design*; Lawrence, *Women in Love*; Sinclair Lewis, *Main Street*; Pound, *Hugh Selwyn Mauberley*; Yeats, *Michael Robartes and the Dancer*
1921	The dole introduced; Anglo-Irish Treaty		Huxley, *Chrome Yellow*; Strachey, *Queen Victoria*
1922	British Broadcasting Company licensed	Barry Jackson presents *The Immortal Hour*, Regent Theatre	Eliot, *The Waste Land*; Joyce, *Ulysses*; Edith Sitwell, *Façade*
1923		Charlot presents Coward's *London Calling* with Gertrude Lawrence; first seasons of Fagan's Oxford Repertory Theatre and Gray's Festival Theatre, Cambridge; James Agate becomes dramatic critic of *The Sunday Times* (to 1947)	Huxley, *Antic Hay*; Rilke, *Duino Elegies*
1924		Gielgud's Romeo, Regent Theatre; Edith Evans's Millamant in *The Way of the World*, Lyric Theatre, Hammersmith; Sybil Thorndike in *Saint Joan*, New Theatre; first of the Aldwych farces (to 1927)	Forster, *A Passage to India*; Hulme, *Speculations*; M. Kennedy, *The Constant Nymph*; Mann, *The Magic Mountain*; M. Webb, *Precious Bane*; Wodehouse, *The Inimitable Jeeves*

First performance of notable plays written in English (excluding American plays)	Births and deaths of notable playwrights	Theatrical events in Europe and the USA
W. S. Maugham, *Caesar's Wife*; A. W. Pinero, *The Freaks*; L. Robinson, *The Lost Leader*	G. Cooper b.	Theatre Guild established in New York; Mayakovsky, *Mystery-Bouffe*; Pirandello, *The Rules of the Game*; Toller, *Masses and Men*; Wedekind d.
N. Coward, *I'll Leave It to You*; W. S. Maugham, *Home and Away*, *The Circle*	N. F. Simpson b.	
J. M. Barrie, *Mary Rose*; J. Galsworthy, *The Skin Game*; G. B. Shaw, *Heartbreak House* (written 1916)		O'Neill, *The Emperor Jones*
G. B. Shaw, *Back to Methuselah*	P. Ustinov b.	Bakst designs *The Sleeping Princess*; Capek, *R.U.R.*; Pirandello, *Six Characters in Search of an Author*
J. M. Barrie, *Shall We Join the Ladies?*; N. Coward, *The Young Idea*; J. Galsworthy, *Loyalties*; S. O'Casey, *The Shadow of a Gunman*; A. W. Pinero, *The Enchanted Cottage*		O'Neill, *The Hairy Ape*; Stanislavsky begins tour of Europe and USA (to 1924); Pirandello, *Enrico IV*
N. Coward, *The Vortex, Fallen Angels*; J. E. Flecker, *Hassan*; F. Lonsdale, *Aren't We All?*; G. B. Shaw, *Saint Joan*	B. Behan b.; E. Martyn d.; J. Mortimer b.; J. Saunders b.	Rice, *The Adding Machine*
N. Coward, *Easy Virtue, Hay Fever*; A. Dukes, *The Man with a Load of Mischief*; S. O'Casey, *Juno and the Paycock*	R. Bolt b.; D. Campion b.	

Date	Historical events	Theatrical events	Non-dramatic literary events
1925		Barrymore's Hamlet, Haymarket Theatre; *Hamlet* in modern dress, Kingsway Theatre; Komisarjevsky directs Chekhov's plays, Barnes Theatre; the Gate Theatre Club opens	Fitzgerald, *The Great Gatsby*; Kafka, *The Trial*; A. Loos, *Gentlemen Prefer Blondes*; V. Woolf, *Mrs Dalloway*
1926	General Strike; British Broadcasting Corporation incorporated under Royal Charter	Shakespeare Memorial Theatre destroyed by fire; Theatre Managers' Association formed	A. Christie, *The Murder of Roger Ackroyd*; Gide, *Les Faux-Monnayeurs*; Hemingway, *The Sun Also Rises*; Kafka, *The Castle*; T. E. Lawrence, *The Seven Pillars of Wisdom*
1927		Arts Theatre Club opens; Granville Barker's *Prefaces to Shakespeare*, Vol. I, published	Forster, *Aspects of the Novel*; T. F. Powys, *Mr Weston's Good Wine*; V. Woolf, *To the Lighthouse*
1928		Fortune and Piccadilly Theatres built; Ellen Terry d.	Hardy, *Winter Words*; Huxley, *Point Counter Point*; Lawrence, *Lady Chatterley's Lover*; Remarque, *All Quiet on the Western Front*; Sassoon, *Memoirs of a Fox-Hunting Man*; Waugh, *Decline and Fall*; V. Woolf, *Orlando*
1929	Wall Street stock exchange crashes	Harcourt Williams director of Old Vic Company; Gielgud joins Old Vic and plays Oberon and Richard II; Savoy Theatre rebuilt; British Actors' Equity formed; first Malvern Festival season (to 1933)	Aldington, *Death of a Hero*; Faulkner, *The Sound and the Fury*; Graves, *Goodbye to All That*; Hemingway, *A Farewell to Arms*; Priestley, *The Good Companions*
1930		Gielgud's first Hamlet, Old Vic and Queen's Theatre; Coward author/director/actor *Private Lives*, Phoenix Theatre	Jeans, *The Mysterious Universe*; W. Lewis, *The Apes of God*; Eliot, *Ash Wednesday*; Empson, *Seven Types of Ambiguity*

First performance of notable plays written in English (excluding American plays)	Births and deaths of notable playwrights	Theatrical events in Europe and the USA
F. Lonsdale, *The Last of Mrs Cheyney, On Approval*; B. Travers, *Cuckoo in the Nest*		Pirandello opens his Theatre of Art, Rome
J. R. Ackerley, *The Prisoners of War*; J. Galsworthy, *Escape*; W. S. Maugham, *The Letter, The Constant Wife*; S. O'Casey, *The Plough and the Stars*; B. Travers, *Rookery Nook*	A. Owen b.; P. Shaffer b.; F. Marcus b.	
B. Travers, *Thark*	D. Turner b.	
W. S. Maugham, *The Sacred Flame*; S. O'Casey, *The Silver Tassie*; R. C. Sherriff, *Journey's End*; J. Van Druten, *Young Woodley*; E. Williams, *Glamour*	Ann Jellicoe b.; D. Mercer b.	Brecht, *The Threepenny Opera*; Albee b.
N. Coward, *Private Lives*; F. Lonsdale, *Canaries Sometimes Sing*; G. B. Shaw, *The Apple Cart*	H. A. Jones d.; H. Livings b.	First talking films marketed
R. Besier, *The Barretts of Wimpole Street*; J. Bridie, *The Anatomist, Tobias and the Angel, Jonah and the Whale*; W. S. Maugham, *The Breadwinner*; R. C. Sherriff, *Badger's Green*; E. Williams, *A Murder Has Been Arranged*	J. Arden b.; J. Osborne b.; H. Pinter b.; C. Exton b.	Michel Saint-Denis re-forms Théâtre du Vieux-Colombier as Compagnie des Quinze; Brecht, *Mahagonny*

Date	Historical events	Theatrical events	Non-dramatic literary events
1931	Unemployment reaches 2½ million	Sadler's Wells Theatre rebuilt; Compagnie des Quinze, New Theatre; Sybil Thorndike created DBE	Cronin, *Hatter's Castle*; Powell, *The Afternoon Men*; Williams, *The Place of the Lion*; V. Woolf, *The Waves*
1932		Gielgud and Peggy Ashcroft in *Richard of Bordeaux*, New Theatre; new Shakespeare Memorial Theatre opens	S. Gibbons, *Cold Comfort Farm*; Huxley, *Brave New World*; Morgan, *The Fountain*; Saint-Exupéry, *Vol de Nuit*
1933		Guthrie's first season as director of Old Vic Company; Saint-Denis directs Gielgud in *Noah*, New Theatre; Open Air Theatre, Regent's Park, begins operations; Guthrie resigns as director of Old Vic Company	Greenwood, *Love on the Dole*; Hilton, *Lost Horizon*; Malraux, *La Condition humaine*
1934		Gielgud's second Hamlet, New Theatre; Devlin's Lear, Westminster Theatre; Maurice Evans's Richard II, Old Vic	Graves, *I, Claudius*; D. Thomas, *18 Poems*; Waugh, *A Handful of Dust*
1935		Gielgud and Olivier alternate as Romeo and Mercutio, New Theatre; first of Ivor Novello's musicals at Drury Lane (to 1945)	E. Bowen, *The House in Paris*; I. Compton-Burnett, *A House and its Head*; Isherwood, *Mr Norris Changes Trains*
1936	Left Book Club founded; Spanish Civil War; television introduced on BBC services (discontinued 1939); George VI accedes	Guthrie reappointed director of Old Vic Company; Edith Evans's Rosalind in *As You Like It*, Old Vic	Huxley, *Eyeless in Gaza*
1937		Olivier and Richardson join Old Vic Company; Olivier plays Hamlet, Coriolanus, Macbeth, Henry V; Guthrie's production of *Hamlet* at Elsinore; Lilian Baylis d.; Johnston Forbes-Robertson d.	Tolkien, *The Hobbit*; Orwell, *The Road to Wigan Pier*; Jones, *In Parenthesis*

First performance of notable plays written in English (excluding American plays)	Births and deaths of notable playwrights	Theatrical events in Europe and the USA
N. Coward, *Cavalcade*; D. Johnson, *The Moon in the Yellow River*; J. B. Priestley and E. Knoblock, *The Good Companions*	J. Hopkins b.	O'Neill, *Mourning Becomes Electra*
N. Coward, *Design for Living*; Gordon Daviot, *Richard of Bordeaux*; W. S. Maugham, *For Services Rendered*; J. B. Priestley, *Dangerous Corner*; G. B. Shaw, *Too True to be Good*	Lady Gregory d.; P. Terson b.; A. Wesker b.; T. Stoppard b.; C. Wood b.	Okhlopkov becomes director of the Realistic Theatre, Moscow (to 1938); Artaud, *Manifeste du théâtre de la cruauté*, published
W. H. Auden, *The Dance of Death*; J. Bridie, *A Sleeping Clergyman*; W. S. Maugham, *Sheppey*; J. B. Priestley, *Laburnum Grove*	J. Galsworthy d.; J. Orton b.; D. Storey b.	Lorca, *Blood Wedding*
L. Housman, *Victoria Regina*; S. O'Casey, *Within the Gates*; J. B. Priestley, *Eden End*	A. W. Pinero d.	Cocteau, *La Machine infernale*
W. H. Auden and C. Isherwood, *The Dog Beneath the Skin*; T. S. Eliot, *Murder in the Cathedral*; W. Greenwood (with R. Gow), *Love on the Dole*; I. Novello, *Glamorous Night*; E. Williams, *Night Must Fall*	E. Bond b.	Anderson, *Winterset*; Giraudoux, *La Guerre de Troie n'aura pas lieu*
W. H. Auden and C. Isherwood, *The Ascent of F6*; J. M. Barrie, *The Boy David*; I. Novello, *Careless Rapture*; J. B. Priestley, *Bees on the Boatdeck*; T. Rattigan, *French Without Tears*; G. B. Shaw, *The Millionairess*; C. Williams, *Thomas Cranmer of Canterbury*	D. Rudkin b.; S. Gray b.	Lorca, *The House of Bernarda Alba*
St J. Ervine, *Robert's Wife*; L. MacNeice, *Out of the Picture*; J. B. Priestley, *Time and the Conways, I Have Been Here Before*; G. Savory, *George and Margaret*; Dorothy L. Sayers, *The Zeal of Thy House*	J. M. Barrie d.	

Date	Historical events	Theatrical events	Non-dramatic literary events
1938	Republic of Ireland; Munich Crisis	Gielgud's Queen's Theatre seasons (to 1939) (Saint-Denis directs *The Three Sisters*, Gielgud directs *The Importance of Being Earnest*, Edith Evans plays Lady Bracknell)	Beckett, *Murphy*; Greene, *Brighton Rock*; Sartre, *La Nausée*
1939	Second World War begins	CEMA and ENSA formed; Benson d.	Cary, *Mister Johnson*; Isherwood, *Goodbye to Berlin*; Joyce, *Finnegans Wake*; O'Brien, *At Swim-Two-Birds*; Steinbeck, *The Grapes of Wrath*
1940		Granville Barker directs Gielgud in *King Lear*, Old Vic; Wolfit launches Shakespeare seasons, Kingsway Theatre; Mrs Patrick Campbell d.	Chandler, *Farewell, My Lovely*; Greene, *The Power and the Glory*; Hemingway, *For Whom the Bell Tolls*; Wright, *Native Son*
1941		Old Vic Company moves to Burnley; Old Vic Theatre bombed; first CEMA tour of Old Vic Company (to 1944)	Cary, *Herself Surprised*; Woolf, *Between the Acts*
1942		Clunes takes lease of Arts Theatre Club	Camus, *L'Étranger*, *The Myth of Sisyphus*; Cary, *To Be A Pilgrim*
1943		Joan Littlewood's Theatre Workshop founded in Manchester	
1944		Old Vic Company opens at New Theatre (Richardson's Peer Gynt, Olivier's Richard III); Citizens' Theatre, Glasgow, founded; Wolfit's Lear, Kingsway Theatre; Martin-Harvey d.; Giclgud's Haymarket Theatre season	Cary, *The Horse's Mouth*; Eliot, *Four Quartets*; Hartley, *The Shrimp and the Anemone*

First performance of notable plays written in English (excluding American plays)	Births and deaths of notable playwrights	Theatrical events in Europe and the USA
W. H. Auden and C. Isherwood, *On the Frontier*; C. Fry, *The Boy With a Cart*; J. B. Priestley, *When We Are Married, Music at Night*; Dodie Smith, *Dear Octopus*; S. Spender, *Trial of a Judge*; C. Williams, *The House by the Stable*; E. Williams, *The Corn is Green*	L. Abercrombie d.; D. Hare b.	Wilder, *Our Town*; Artaud, *Le Théâtre et son double*, published
J. Bridie, *What Say They?*; N. Coward, *This Happy Breed*; T. S. Eliot, *The Family Reunion*; I. Novello, *The Dancing Years*; J. B. Priestley, *Johnson over Jordan*; Dorothy L. Sayers, *The Devil to Pay*; G. B. Shaw, *In Good King Charles's Golden Days*; C. Williams, *Judgment at Chelmsford, Seed of Adam*	A. Ayckbourn b.; Shelagh Delaney b.	
J. B. Priestley, *The Long Mirror*		First theatre-in-the-round playhouse built at University of Washington, Seattle
	H. Williams b.	Brecht, *Mother Courage* (written)
T. Rattigan, *Flare Path*; P. Ustinov, *House of Regrets*	H. Brenton b.	Anouilh, *Antigone*; Wilder, *The Skin of our Teeth*
J. Bridie, *Mr Bolfry*; S. O'Casey, *Red Roses for Me*; J. B. Priestley, *Desert Highway, They Came to a City*; T. Rattigan, *While the Sun Shines*	L. Binyon d.	Brecht, *Life of Galileo, The Good Woman of Setzwan*; Rodgers and Hammerstein, *Oklahoma!*; Sartre, *Les Mouches*
J. Bridie, *The Forrigan Reel*; T. Rattigan, *Love in Idleness*; P. Ustinov, *The Banbury Nose*		Sartre, *Huis clos*; T. Williams, *The Glass Menagerie*

Date	Historical events	Theatrical events	Non-dramatic literary events
1945	Welfare State legislation begins	Richardson's Falstaff, Olivier's Oedipus, New Theatre	Green, *Loving*; Orwell, *Animal Farm*; Waugh, *Brideshead Revisited*; Williams, *All Hallows' Eve*
1946	Atom bomb exploded on Hiroshima; hostilities end; BBC resumes television service	Barry Jackson appointed director of Shakespeare Memorial Theatre (Brook directs *Love's Labour's Lost*; Gielgud directs *Much Ado About Nothing*); Old Vic School and Young Vic founded; Bristol Old Vic founded; Arts Council of Great Britain incorporated under Royal Charter; first Edinburgh Festival; Edith Evans created DBE; Granville Barker d.	Hersey, *Hiroshima*
1947		Joint Council of National Theatre and Old Vic formed; Richardson and Olivier knighted; Helpmann and Margaret Rawlings in Benthall's production of *The White Devil*, Duchess Theatre; Harold Hobson becomes dramatic critic of *The Sunday Times* (to 1976)	Camus, *La Peste*; Lowry, *Under the Volcano*; Moravia, *The Woman of Rome*; Sartre, *What Is Literature?*
1948	Local Government Act	Guthrie directs *The Three Estates*, Edinburgh Festival	Greene, *The Heart of the Matter*; Kinsey, *Sexual Behaviour in the Human Male*; Mailer, *The Naked and the Dead*; Mann, *Dr Faustus*; Paton, *Cry, the Beloved Country*; Waugh, *The Loved One*
1949		National Theatre Act; Olivier, Richardson and Burrell leave Old Vic; Quayle succeeds Jackson, Stratford-on-Avon; Olivier directs *A Streetcar Named Desire*, Aldwych Theatre; *Love's Labour's Lost* with Redgrave as Berowne, New Theatre	Orwell, *Nineteen Eighty-Four*; Wilson, *The Wrong Set*

First performance of notable plays written in English (excluding American plays)	Births and deaths of notable playwrights	Theatrical events in Europe and the USA
J. Bridie, *Lancelot*; R. Duncan, *This Way to the Tomb*; I. Novello, *Perchance to Dream*; S. O'Casey, *Purple Dust*; J. B. Priestley, *An Inspector Calls*; C. Williams, *The House of the Octopus*; E. Williams, *The Wind of Heaven*; P. Yates, *The Assassin*	C. Williams d.	Camus, *Caligula*
N. Coward, *Peace in Our Time*; C. Fry, *A Phoenix Too Frequent*; M. MacLiammoir, *Ill Met By Moonlight*; T. Rattigan, *The Winslow Boy*	H. Granville Barker d.	O'Neill, *The Iceman Cometh*; J.-L. Barrault and M. Renaud form Compagnie Renaud–Barrault
J. Bridie, *Dr Angelus, It Depends What You Mean, John Knox*; J. B. Priestley, *The Linden Tree*; E. Williams, *Trespass*		Genet, *Les Bonnes*; T. Williams, *A Streetcar Named Desire*
C. Fry, *Thor, with Angels, The Firstborn, The Lady's Not for Burning*; T. Rattigan, *The Browning Version*; P. Ustinov, *The Indifferent Shepherd*	G. Bottomley d.	Artaud d.
J. Bridie, *Daphne Laureola*; T. S. Eliot, *The Cocktail Party*; I. Novello, *King's Rhapsody*; S. O'Casey, *Cock a Doodle Dandy*		Miller, *Death of a Salesman*; Brecht founds Berliner Ensemble, gives first performance of *Mother Courage*

Date	Historical events	Theatrical events	Non-dramatic literary events
1950		Redgrave's Hamlet, New Theatre and Elsinore; Old Vic rebuilt; Hunt, Devine, Saint-Denis, Byam Shaw as directors of Old Vic Company	
1951	Festival of Britain	National Theatre foundation stone laid; Saint-Denis, Devine and Byam Shaw resign from Old Vic Company; Old Vic Centre, School and Young Vic disbanded; Guthrie directs Wolfit in *Tamburlaine the Great*, Old Vic; Brook directs *The Winter's Tale*, Stratford-on-Avon and London; Novello d.; Cochran d.	Beckett, *Molloy, Malone meurt*; Greene, *The End of the Affair*; Powell, *A Question of Upbringing*; Salinger, *The Catcher in the Rye*; Snow, *The Masters*
1952	Elizabeth II accedes	Gielgud and Scofield in *Venice Preserved*, Lyric Theatre, Hammersmith; Tennent Productions Ltd's management of Lyric Theatre, Hammersmith (to 1963)	Hemingway, *The Old Man and the Sea*; D. Lessing, *Martha Quest*; Waugh, *Men at Arms*; Wilson, *Hemlock and After*
1953		Theatre Workshop leases Theatre Royal, Stratford East; Benthall succeeds Hunt at Old Vic	Beckett, *The Unnameable*; Bellow, *The Adventures of Augie March*; Wain, *Hurry on Down*
1954	Hydrogen bomb exploded; Commercial Television Act	Kenneth Tynan becomes dramatic critic of *The Observer* (to 1958); Dylan Thomas, *Under Milk Wood* (broadcast)	Amis, *Lucky Jim*; Golding, *Lord of the Flies*; D. Lessing, *A Proper Marriage*; I. Murdoch, *Under the Net*; Tolkien, *The Lord of the Rings* (to 1956)
1955	Independent Television services commence	Brook directs Olivier in *Titus Andronicus*, Stratford-on-Avon and London	Donleavy, *The Ginger Man*; Golding, *The Inheritors*; Larkin, *The Less Deceived*; Nabokov, *Lolita*; Waugh, *Officers and Gentlemen*

First performance of notable plays written in English (excluding American plays)	Births and deaths of notable playwrights	Theatrical events in Europe and the USA
J. Bridie, *Mr Gillie*, *The Queen's Comedy*; C. Fry, *Venus Observed*, *Ring Round the Moon*; F. Lonsdale, *The Way Things Go*; T. Rattigan, *Who is Sylvia?*; G. B. Shaw, *Far-Fetched Fables*; R. C. Sherriff, *Home at Seven*	G. B. Shaw d.	Ionesco, *La Cantatrice chauve*
C. Fry, *A Sleep of Prisoners*; N. C. Hunter, *Waters of the Moon*; P. Ustinov, *The Love of Four Colonels*, *The Moment of Truth*; J. Whiting, *Penny for a Song*, *Saint's Day*	J. Bridie d.	Vilar founds Théâtre National Populaire
J. Bridie, *The Baikie Charivari*; J. B. Priestley, *Dragon's Mouth*; T. Rattigan, *The Deep Blue Sea*		
T. S. Eliot, *The Confidential Clerk*; G. Greene, *The Living Room*; N. C. Hunter, *A Day in the Sun*; T. Rattigan, *The Sleeping Prince*; E. Williams, *Someone Waiting*		Anouilh, *L'Alouette*; Beckett, *En attendant Godot*; Miller, *The Crucible*; O'Neill d.
B. Behan, *The Quare Fellow* (in Dublin; in London 1956); C. Fry, *The Dark is Light Enough*; T. Rattigan, *Separate Tables*; J. Whiting, *Marching Song*		Brecht, *The Caucasian Chalk Circle*
Enid Bagnold, *The Chalk Garden*; S. Beckett, *Waiting for Godot* (English version)		Miller, *A View from the Bridge*

Date	Historical events	Theatrical events	Non-dramatic literary events
1956	Hungarian Revolt; Suez disaster	Berliner Ensemble at Palace Theatre; English Stage Company leases Royal Court Theatre; Peggy Ashcroft created DBE	Golding, *Pincher Martin*; Wilson, *Anglo-Saxon Attitudes*
1957		Dexter, Anderson, Tony Richardson, Gaskill and other new directors direct plays at Royal Court Theatre under Devine's management	Braine, *Room at the Top*; Durrell, *Justine*; Hoggart, *The Uses of Literacy*; Kerouac, *On the Road*; Pasternak, *Dr Zhivago*; Robbe-Grillet, *Jealousy*; White, *Voss*
1958		Belgrade Theatre, Coventry, built; Daubeny presents Moscow Art Theatre at Sadler's Wells Theatre; Artaud, *The Theatre and its Double* (translation), published	Achebe, *Things Fall Apart*; Durrell, *Balthazar, Mountolive*; di Lampedusa, *The Leopard*; D. Lessing, *A Ripple from the Storm*; I. Murdoch, *The Bell*; Sillitoe, *Saturday Night and Sunday Morning*; Wilson, *The Middle Age of Mrs Eliot*
1959		Playhouse, Nottingham, and Mermaid theatres built; Beckett, *Krapp's Last Tape* (broadcast)	Burroughs, *The Naked Lunch*; Golding, *Free Fall*; Grass, *The Tin Drum*; Waterhouse, *Billy Liar*

First performance of notable plays written in English (excluding American plays)	Births and deaths of notable playwrights	Theatrical events in Europe and the USA
S. O'Casey, *The Drums of Father Ned*; J. Osborne, *Look Back in Anger*; G. Savory, *A Likely Tale*; N. F. Simpson, *A Resounding Tinkle*; P. Ustinov, *Romanoff and Juliet*, *The Empty Chair*; J. Whiting, *The Gates of Summer*		Dürrenmatt, *The Visit*; Genet, *Le Balcon*; O'Neill, *Long Day's Journey into Night*; Brecht d.
J. Arden, *The Waters of Babylon*; R. Beynon, *The Shifting Heart*; R. Bolt, *Flowering Cherry*; D. Campton, *The Lunatic View*; G. Greene, *The Potting Shed*; R. Lawler, *Summer of the Seventeenth Doll*; J. Mortimer, *Dock Brief*; J. Osborne, *The Entertainer*; J. Osborne and A. Creighton, *Epitaph for George Dillon*	Dorothy L. Sayers d.	Beckett, *Fin de partie* (*Endgame*, 1958)
J. Arden, *Live Like Pigs*; S. Beckett, *Endgame*; B. Behan, *The Hostage*; Shelagh Delaney, *A Taste of Honey*; T. S. Eliot, *The Elder Statesman*; W. Hall, *The Long and the Short and the Tall*; N. C. Hunter, *A Touch of the Sun*; Ann Jellicoe, *The Sport of My Mad Mother*; J. Mortimer, *What Shall We Tell Caroline?*; H. Pinter, *The Birthday Party*; T. Rattigan, *Variation on a Theme*; G. Savory, *Come Rain, Come Shine*; P. Shaffer, *Five Finger Exercise*; A. Wesker, *Chicken Soup with Barley*, *The Kitchen*; E. Williams, *Beth*	H. Brighouse d.; L. Robinson d.	Brecht, *The Resistible Rise of Arturo Ui*; Genet, *Les Nègres*
J. Arden, *The Business of Good Government, Serjeant Musgrave's Dance*; G. Greene, *The Complaisant Lover*; J. Osborne, *The World of Paul Slickey*; A. Owen, *The Rough and Ready Lot, Progress to the Park*; H. Pinter, *The Room, A Slight Ache*; N. F. Simpson, *One Way Pendulum*; A. Wesker, *Roots*		Albee, *The Zoo Story*; Anouilh, *Becket*; Ionesco, *Rhinocéros*; Barrault director of Théâtre de France

Date	Historical events	Theatrical events	Non-dramatic literary events
1960		Hall appointed director of Royal Shakespeare Company (previously Shakespeare Memorial Theatre Company)	Amis, *Take a Girl Like You*; Barth, *The Sot-Weed Factor*; Durrell, *Clea*; Edna O'Brien, *The Country Girls*; Barstow, *A Kind of Loving*; Storey, *This Sporting Life*
1961	Major nuclear disarmament demonstration	RSC leases Aldwych Theatre; Barry Jackson d.; M. Esslin, *The Theatre of the Absurd*, published	Greene, *A Burnt-out Case*; Heller, *Catch-22*; Hughes, *The Fox in the Attic*; Naipaul, *A House for Mr Biswas*; M. Spark, *The Prime of Miss Jean Brodie*; Waugh, *Unconditional Surrender*; White, *Riders in the Chariot*; Wilson, *The Old Men at the Zoo*
1962		Chichester Festival Theatre built (Olivier appointed director); National Theatre Company formed at Old Vic (Olivier appointed director); Brook directs Scofield in *King Lear*, Aldwych Theatre; Victoria Theatre, Stoke-on-Trent, opens; Parliament consents to release of funds for the building of National Theatre	Burgess, *A Clockwork Orange*; D. Lessing, *The Golden Notebook*; Nabokov, *Pale Fire*; Solzhenitsyn, *One Day in the Life of Ivan Denisovich*
1963		*Wars of the Roses*, Stratford-on-Avon; Olivier and Redgrave in *Uncle Vanya*, Chichester and Old Vic; Joan Littlewood directs *Oh, What a Lovely War*; Lasdun appointed architect of National Theatre; Traverse Theatre, Edinburgh, opens	Pynchon, *V*; M. McCarthy, *The Group*; I. Murdoch, *The Unicorn*

First performance of notable plays written in English (excluding American plays)	Births and deaths of notable playwrights	Theatrical events in Europe and the USA
J. Arden, *The Happy Haven*; Enid Bagnold, *The Last Joke*; R. Bolt, *A Man for All Seasons*; D. Campton, *Four Minute Warning*; N. Coward, *Waiting in the Wings*; Shelagh Delaney, *The Lion in Love*; J. Mortimer, *The Wrong Side of the Park*; H. Pinter, *The Caretaker, The Dumb Waiter, The Dwarfs*; T. Rattigan, *Ross*; B. Reckord, *You in Your Small Corner*; A. Wesker, *I'm Talking About Jerusalem*		
S. Beckett, *Happy Days* (in New York); C. Fry, *Curtmantle* (in Holland); Ann Jellicoe, *The Knack*; H. Livings, *Stop It, Whoever You Are, Big Soft Nellie*; J. Osborne, *Luther*; H. Pinter, *The Collection*; J. Whiting, *The Devils*		Frisch, *Andorra*; Genet, *Les Paravents*
J. Arden, *Ironhand*; H. Livings, *Nil Carborundum*; J. Mortimer, *Two Stars for Comfort*; I. Murdoch and J. B. Priestley, *A Severed Head*; D. Rudkin, *Afore Night Come*; J. Saunders, *Next Time I'll Sing to You*; D. Turner, *Semi-Detached*; A. Wesker, *Chips With Everything*	Elizabeth Baker d.	Albee, *Who's Afraid of Virginia Woolf?*; Dürrenmatt, *The Physicists*
J. Arden, *The Workhouse Donkey*; Enid Bagnold, *The Chinese Prime Minister*; S. Beckett, *Play*; N. C. Hunter, *The Tulip Tree*; H. Livings, *Kelly's Eye*; A. Owen, *A Little Winter Love*; H. Pinter, *The Lover*; T. Rattigan, *Man and Boy*; B. Reckord, *Skyvers*; Theatre Workshop and Charles Chilton, *Oh, What a Lovely War!*; P. Ustinov, *Photo-Finish*; C. Wood, *Cockade*	J. Whiting d.	

Date	Historical events	Theatrical events	Non-dramatic literary events
1964		Olivier's Othello, Old Vic; Theatre of Cruelty, LAMDA Theatre; Brook directs *Marat/Sade*; Kott, *Shakespeare Our Contemporary*, published (in English translation); Daubeny's first World Theatre Season at Aldwych Theatre (to 1973)	Beckett, *How It Is*; Bellow, *Herzog*; Golding, *The Spire*; Wilson, *Late Call*
1965	Jenny Lee appointed Minister responsible for the Arts; Vietnam War	Barbican Theatre planned as future home for RSC	D. Lessing, *Landlocked*; Mailer, *The American Dream*; M. Spark, *The Mandelbaum Gate*
1966		Craig d.	Barth, *Giles Goatboy*; Capote, *In Cold Blood*; Fowles, *The Magus*; Greene, *The Comedians*
1967	Entertainment Tax abolished	Bolton Octagon Theatre built	Wilson, *No Laughing Matter*
1968	Student revolt in Paris	Stage censorship abolished; Brook directs Seneca's *Oedipus*, Old Vic; Theatre Upstairs and Open Space Theatre open; Grotowski, *Towards a Poor Theatre*, published; Wolfit d.	Solzhenitsyn, *Cancer Ward*, *The First Circle*; Updike, *Couples*

First performance of notable plays written in English (excluding American plays)	Births and deaths of notable playwrights	Theatrical events in Europe and the USA
J. Arden, *Armstrong's Last Goodnight*; G. Greene, *Carving a Statue*; H. Livings, *Eh?*; J. Orton, *Entertaining Mr Sloane*; J. Osborne, *Inadmissible Evidence*; J. Saunders, *A Scent of Flowers*; P. Shaffer, *The Royal Hunt of the Sun*	B. Behan d.; W. Browne d.; L. MacNeice d.; S. O'Casey d.	Hochhuth, *The Representative*
J. Arden, *Left-Handed Liberty*; S. Beckett, *Come and Go*; E. Bond, *Saved*; Ann Jellicoe, *Shelley*; F. Marcus, *The Killing of Sister George*; D. Mercer, *Ride a Cock Horse*; J. Osborne, *A Patriot for Me*; H. Pinter, *Tea Party*, *The Homecoming*; H. Porter, *The Professor*; P. Shaffer, *Black Comedy*; N. F. Simpson, *The Cresta Run*; A. Wesker, *The Four Seasons*	T. S. Eliot d.; W. S. Maugham d.	
G. Cooper, *Happy Family*; N. Coward, *A Song at Twilight*; D. Mercer, *Belcher's Luck*; J. Mortimer, *The Judge*; J. Orton, *Loot*; J. Osborne, *A Bond Honoured*; A. Wesker, *Their Very Own and Golden City*; C. Wood, *Fill the Stage with Happy Hours*	G. Cooper d.	
A. Ayckbourn, *Relatively Speaking*; T. Stoppard, *Rosencrantz and Guildenstern Are Dead*; P. Terson, *Zigger Zagger*; P. Ustinov, *Half Way Up the Tree*; C. Wood, *Dingo*	J. R. Ackerley d.; J. Orton d.	
J. Arden, *The Hero Rises Up*; Enid Bagnold, *Call Me Joey*; S. Beckett, *Breath*; E. Bond, *Early Morning*, *Narrow Road to the Deep North*; J. Orton, *What the Butler Saw*; J. Osborne, *Time Present*, *The Hotel in Amsterdam*; H. Pinter, *Landscape*; T. Stoppard, *Enter a Free Man*, *The Real Inspector Hound*; P. Terson, *The Apprentices*		

Date	Historical events	Theatrical events	Non-dramatic literary events
1969	'Bloody Sunday', violence in Northern Ireland begins in earnest	Olivier's Shylock in *The Merchant of Venice*, Old Vic; 69 Theatre opens at University Theatre, Manchester (to 1973)	D. Lessing, *The Four-Gated City*; Fowles, *The French Lieutenant's Woman*; Roth, *Portnoy's Complaint*
1970		Brook's *A Midsummer Night's Dream*, Aldwych Theatre; Young Vic Theatre opens; Olivier created Life Peer	
1971		Nunn succeeds Hall as director of RSC; Birmingham Repertory Theatre rebuilt; Crucible Theatre, Sheffield, built; Brook directs *Orghast* at Shiraz/Persepolis; the Living Theatre at the Roundhouse	
1972		Olivier's James Tyrone in *Long Day's Journey into Night*, Old Vic; Hall succeeds Olivier as director, National Theatre Company; *Jesus Christ Superstar* opens at Palace Theatre	
1973	Britain joins the Common Market	*Rocky Horror Show*, King's Road Theatre	
1974	Heath Government falls		
1975		Alan Howard's Henry V, Stratford-on-Avon	

First performance of notable plays written in English (excluding American plays)	Births and deaths of notable playwrights	Theatrical events in Europe and the USA
C. Exton, *Have You Any Dirty Washing, Mother Dear?*; J. Hopkins, *This Story of Yours*; Ann Jellicoe, *The Giveaway*; H. Livings, *Honour and Offer*; J. Osborne, *West of Suez*; H. Pinter, *Silence*; J. Saunders, *The Borage Pigeon Affair*; D. Storey, *In Celebration*		
R. Bolt, *Vivat, Vivat Regina*; C. Fry, *A Yard of Sun*; D. Hare, *Slag*; D. Mercer, *AfterHaggerty*; T. Rattigan, *Bequest to the Nation*; D. Storey, *The Contractor, Home*; A. Wesker, *The Friends*; H. Williams, *AC/DC*		
E. Bond, *Lear*; S. Gray, *Butley*; H. Pinter, *Old Times*	N. C. Hunter d.	
J. Osborne, *A Sense of Detachment*; D. Storey, *The Changing Room*; A. Wesker, *The Old Ones*; C. Wood, *Veterans*		
E. Bond, *The Sea*; J. Osborne, *A Place Calling Itself Rome*; P. Shaffer, *Equus*; T. Stoppard, *Jumpers*; D. Storey, *Cromwell*	N. Coward d.	
E. Bond, *Bingo*; T. Stoppard, *Travesties*		
A. Ayckbourn, *The Norman Conquests*; S. Gray, *Otherwise Engaged*; J. Osborne, *The End of Me Old Cigar*; H. Pinter, *No Man's Land*; D. Rudkin, *Ashes*		

Date	Historical events	Theatrical events	Non-dramatic literary events
1976	Economic crisis; the Social Contract	Bernard Levin becomes dramatic critic of *The Sunday Times*; Brook directs *The Ik*, Roundhouse; National Theatre opens; Royal Exchange Theatre, Manchester, opens; Sybil Thorndike d.; Edith Evans d.	
1977			

First performance of notable plays written in English (excluding American plays)	Births and deaths of notable playwrights	Theatrical events in Europe and the USA
	T. Rattigan d.	

I The social and literary context

Hugh Hunt

1 1880–1900

(i) Conservatism of British audiences

The period 1880–1900 marks the birth of the theatre of the twentieth century as a social and literary force. Between those years most of the seeds were sown that were later to blossom into the ideological ferment of Edwardian drama, and radical changes came about in the organization of the theatre as well as in the constitution and behaviour of its audiences. The theatre became fashionable, its artists respectable; the breach between stage and literature was healed; production and design took on an organized shape; and new acting styles were adopted.

It was an age of considerable material prosperity in which wealth was spreading among an increasingly large section of the population, but the solid Victorian virtues of diligence and thrift restrained the ostentation and worship of wealth that were to characterize Edwardian society. It was an age of scientific and technical progress in which education was available at primary level to the whole population. It was an age of humanitarianism and social welfare, expressed in the development of trade unions, in the championship of women's rights and in eagerness to embrace philanthropic causes.

Greater literacy, improvements in public amenities and a more even distribution of wealth resulted in larger audiences, finer theatres and greater rewards for actors, dramatists and managers. But the literary and social significance of the dramatic fare offered was poor in comparison with that of the Continent. Of the dramatists who established themselves during the last twenty years of the century, only Wilde, Pinero, Henry Arthur Jones and the librettist W. S. Gilbert could be claimed to have had any enduring importance. Although Shaw's reputation as a critic was established, only one of his plays had been seen by a public audience on the London stage by the end of the century,[1] and Barrie had hardly entered the lists as a serious dramatist.

In France and Germany André Antoine and Otto Brahm were winning influential audiences for the new social drama before J. T. Grein became 'the most abused man in London' for attempting to follow in their footsteps. In Moscow, Stanislavsky and Nemirovitch-Danchenko had founded the Art Theatre six years before Harley Granville Barker and J. E. Vedrenne presented a repertoire of new drama at the Court. Émile Augier, Henri Becque, Chekhov, Hauptmann, Maeterlinck, Strindberg and Tolstoy were hardly known to British audiences, while the greatest social dramatist of the century, Henrik Ibsen, was greeted with a chorus of detestation.

It is indicative of the general conservatism of the British stage, and of the audiences of the eighties and nineties, that Shaw chose to launch his campaign for the new drama in a journalistic and literary form rather than as a practising dramatist. From 1895 to 1898 he wielded his sword and dagger as dramatic critic of *The Saturday Review*, attacking the neo-Romantic tradition with the one and the fashionable drawing-room drama with the other. When he turned his talents to playwriting, it was as a published dramatist that he set about gaining a serious hearing for his plays.

Since neither the theatregoing public nor the profession itself showed any inclination for radical change, the only recourse for a dramatist who felt impelled to express the stirring beneath the surface of complacency was to appeal to a reading public. To attempt to change the taste of the theatregoing public through the published play rather than through the immediate impact of the live performance inevitably meant that the battle was to be long-drawn-out.

(ii) The structure of society

To understand the reluctance of the British theatregoer to accept a drama that expressed ideas relevant to the vital issues of social and political life, it is

[1] *Arms and the Man*, Avenue Theatre, 1894.

necessary to bear in mind the strength of the social structure and the ordered development of the country as a whole towards a progressive democracy under a predominantly liberal government.

The political doubts and upheavals that were reflected in the theatrical mirrors of France, Germany and Russia, and the frustrations of Scandinavian society, had little relevance to British society – a society that was sufficiently flexible to accommodate radical views without radically changing its structure. Only the South African war and the Irish question could seriously distract the Englishman's thoughts from an optimistic, insular and largely materialistic outlook. The benefits that British society enjoyed were surely due to Providence, and its stability and progress depended on the maintenance of the fundamental principles of order and degree. The flexibility of society's conception of these virtues was, for a time at least, a guarantee of its stability.

Degree was patterned to the principles of a complex class structure, the tone of which was set by a predominantly aristocratic order differing little in its structure from earlier years of the reign. Upper-class life was dominated by the Lady Bracknells with their town houses on the fashionable side of Belgrave Square, their visiting days and receptions, their country houses and weekend house parties. They employed butlers, footmen, ladies' maids, cooks and a host of lesser persons too low in the social scale to appear in the cast lists of theatrical entertainment. Their sons attended the public schools and completed their social education at Oxford or Cambridge; but 'fortunately, in England at any rate', as Lady Bracknell declared, 'education produces no effect whatsoever. If it did, it would prove a serious danger to the upper classes, and probably lead to acts of violence in Grosvenor Square.'[1]

The attitudes of high society, however, were no longer exclusively influenced by the aristocracy. Wealth was rapidly spreading over a far wider section of the population. Marriages of wealth and birth, the decline in the fortunes of the landowning class, the levelling influences of public schools and universities, were breaking down the frontiers between the sons of gentlemen and the sons of the merchants; and, while the merchant classes were anxious to share the privileges of the aristocracy, they introduced into high society many of the puritan virtues and prejudices that had previously kept them apart from the looser moral code of the London drawing rooms.

The new moral tone which regulated behaviour and conversation decently concealed the human weaknesses that lay beneath the surface of order and

[1] *The Importance of Being Earnest*, Act I.

degree. The duty of the upper classes – and this included the merchant as well as the aristocrat – was to set an example; and to present a façade of uniformity not only in the unquestioning acceptance of a moral code but in common attitudes to religion, patriotism, imperial supremacy, justice and humanity. If the stage was to qualify as a respectable pastime of organized society it must also set an example. It must not only reflect an idealized picture of social virtues, but must teach a wholesome lesson to fortify the converted and convert the uneducated.

The spread of wealth was by no means confined to the merchant princes. The development of joint-stock companies, in the place of family-controlled businesses, increased the number of middle-class shareholders. A shareholding public meant the extension of a leisured and retired class; and for many leisure provided an excuse for an evening out at the theatre – the respectability of which had been established by the patronage of the Queen herself. By 1880 some of the worst evils that urban and industrial development had brought to the poorer classes were being tackled, or were at least a matter of concern. The slums still existed, but settlements and model housing estates were evidence of the growth of a new humanitarian spirit. Wages had risen and free-trade policies were providing cheaper food and an abundance of household goods. The 1870 Education Act, which had made primary education universally available, was having its effect upon general literacy. The Workers' Educational Association and university extension lectures were offering opportunities to the underprivileged to extend their knowledge and improve their social status.

Thus the movement within the social order was an upward movement. The middle classes strove to ape the manners of their betters, and the lower orders dreamt of achieving the comfortable respectability of the middle classes. A society that is based on an accepted moral code, and which offers from within itself opportunities for the betterment of the individual, is not easily moved to violent change nor anxious to have the cracks and weaknesses of its structure exposed upon the stage. It was true that a handful of intellectuals were casting disturbing doubts on the validity of the existing principles of class, religion, morals and manners, including the well-worn conventions of the stage, yet society was sufficiently strongly structured to ward off, for the time being, the assaults of Fabian doctrines, the religious doubts arising from Darwin's evolutionary discoveries, and the powerful attacks of Shaw and Archer on the conventions and attitudes of the stage. Nevertheless, signs of a change in popular attitudes were evident, not only in drawing-room drama but also in the popular medium of melodrama. But there was to be no sudden revolution, rather a long and painful struggle before a new drama was accepted by more than a handful of the playgoing public.

(iii) The popularity of the theatre

The theatre was nevertheless an active force in the social life of the period. Writing of the London theatre in 1879, Henry James recorded this remarkable outburst of interest in the stage:

> It sometimes seems to an observer of English customs that this interest in histrionic matters almost reaches the proportions of a mania. It pervades society – it breaks down barriers. If you go to an evening party, nothing is more probable than that all of a sudden a young lady or gentleman will jump up and strike an attitude and begin to recite a poem or a speech. Every pretext for this sort of exhibition is ardently cultivated, and the London world is apparently filled with stage-struck young persons whose relatives are holding them back from a dramatic career by the skirt of their garments. Plays and actors are perpetually talked about, private theatricals are incessant, and members of the dramatic profession are 'received' without restriction. They appear in society, and the people of society appear on the stage; it is as if the great gate which formerly divided the theatre from the world had been lifted off its hinges.[1]

(iv) Social influences on the theatre

The extension of greater wealth and leisure to the middle classes brought about a change in the constitution and behaviour of the audiences as well as a revolutionary alteration in the organization of theatrical entertainment. Theatregoing became a social event to be indulged in with much the same ceremony as churchgoing. Dress was all-important. Normally evening dress was expected in the stalls and dress circle. Family parties and reunions were celebrated by a visit to the theatre. Refreshments were served in the intervals. The advance of the dinner hour in polite society to 7 o'clock necessitated the abandonment of the old multiple fare offered by the theatres. Instead of performances starting at 6.30 and continuing to midnight, offering a farce, a

[1] *The Scenic Art of Henry James, 1872–1901*, ed. Alan Wade (London, 1949), pp. 119–20.

tragedy or comedy and concluding with a pantomime or afterpiece, the new patrons came to the theatre at 8 o'clock and were content to see a single play, or at most a play and a curtain-raiser. Matinées too were introduced to cater for a more leisured audience.

To serve the needs of this refined and extended audience, new theatres were built and old theatres reconditioned. In London fourteen new theatres opened between 1880 and 1900. The new theatres, as well as the reconstructed older buildings, provided evidence of the demand for greater comfort and ceremony. Orchestra stalls, upholstered in velvet or plush, extended backwards to accommodate a public paying 10s. or 11s. for a seat. The pit, now accommodated in the rear of the stalls, acquired backs to its benches. New names were introduced to match the increasing wealth and grading of middle-class and lower-middle-class groupings. The new Her Majesty's Theatre, opened in 1897, was divided into orchestra stalls, pit stalls and pit. The first floor was devoted to dress circle and family circle; the second floor consisted of the upper circle, amphitheatre and gallery. Foyers, saloons, smoking rooms and buffets were added to the front of the house and lavishly decorated in various historical styles. Boxes were draped with hangings of red, blue or yellow plush. Proscenium arches were supported by groups of statuary or gilded pillars. Vases, medallions, frescoes and caryatids embellished the fronts of boxes and circles.

On the stage itself greater taste and verisimilitude complemented the refinement and material wellbeing of the audience. Real drawing rooms, furnished and upholstered by interior decorators, offered models for the ideal home. Women's dresses executed by leading couturiers, men's clothes tailored by Bond Street, provided fashion plates for the well-dressed citizen. Acting styles followed the new mode for the 'gentleman actor' popularized by the Bancrofts and Alexander. Meanwhile, the neo-Romantic staging of historical drama reached peaks of spectacular realism to match the popular academic style of Alma-Tadema. Alone and almost unnoticed by more than a handful of critics and actors, William Poel was sowing the seeds of a new approach to Shakespeare based on scholarly research.

(v) The dominance of London

Despite the growth and prosperity of the provincial cities and the multiplication of theatres throughout the country, London became, to a greater extent than in earlier years, the focus of social and theatrical life. Its predominance as the hub of the country was largely due to the extension of communications. The development of national newspapers and the perfection of the railway system destroyed much of the individual life of the provincial towns. More and more social events, including the theatre, tended to be focused on the London season. The seasonal visits by leading actors to the local stock companies ceased, thus depriving the stock companies of a source of their income and the towns themselves of a fashionable local event.

Local and national newspapers, fed by the electric telegraph and telephone and reinforced by magazines and periodicals emanating from London, brought the latest criticisms and theatrical gossip from the capital to the remotest parts of the country, creating a greater demand to see the London productions in all their glory. This demand could now be met by the greater facility for travel. As a result, two major changes were brought about in the organization of the theatre: the growth of the long-run system in the London theatres and the development of the touring system in the provinces.

Not only had the population of the metropolis increased vastly since the earlier years of the century, but the omnibus and improvements in street lighting made it possible for suburban dwellers to travel within the city in safety and comfort. The railways too made it easier for the provincial public to visit London theatres. The London theatres could therefore count on running their plays for extended periods with consequent opportunities for greater profits. The facilities that the railways offered for carrying bulky scenic equipment made possible subsequent tours of the provinces. To house the elaborate requirements of the tours, new theatres arose in the provinces. By 1880 the provincial stock companies were in the process of dissolution, and with their disappearance the stage lost an invaluable training ground for its actors.

(vi) The status and rewards of the actor and the dramatist

In London the social status of the actor was improving along with the respectability and popularity of the stage. Irving's knighthood in 1895, followed by that of Bancroft in 1897, set the seal upon the struggle of the actor-managers for the recognition of their status as leading members of society – a struggle that had occupied the energies of the leaders of the stage since Garrick. Not only was the social status of the actor rising but so was his pay.

In 1873 Irving, as a leading actor in Bateman's company at the Lyceum, was receiving £30 a week. When he assumed management himself, he paid Ellen Terry £40 a week plus half a clear benefit; by the early eighties, however, she was receiving £200 a week. The type of actor who entered the profession was also changing. The bohemian was giving way to the educated actor. In an address delivered at Edinburgh in 1881, Irving declared:

> The old days when good-for-nothings passed into the profession are at an end; and the old Bohemian habits, so far as they were evil and disreputable, have also disappeared. The ranks of the art are being continually recruited by deeply interested and earnest young men of good education and belongings.[1]

The dramatist too was changing his skin. The hack writer who shamelessly plundered the popular French theatre without acknowledgement or payment was giving way to the dramatic author. This change in the dramatist was partly due to the greater financial rewards – even fortunes – that were to be won from the British and American market; partly to the greater critical attention that was paid to the quality of the play; partly to the encouragement to dramatists to publish their plays brought about by the change in the copyright laws. In mid-century a dramatist either sold his play outright to a management or received a performance fee, but by the eighties the practice of paying royalties for original plays was becoming common practice. After his success with *The Silver King* in 1882, H. A. Jones was able to demand 10–15 per cent of the house receipts and, whereas his earnings for the year 1881 amounted to £527. 15s., his receipts from royalties in the year 1882–3 were £3398.

Increased rewards did not of themselves result in plays of better quality, but the chance of a fortune was instrumental in persuading the serious writer to turn from novels to the stage. Greater critical interest in the art of the dramatist was also a powerful incentive.

(vii) The copyright laws and the published play

Probably the most powerful influence in sowing the seeds of a new literary drama was the change in the copyright laws, which not only brought about a decrease in the practice of plagiarizing French plays but prevented the un-

[1] *The Drama Addresses of Henry Irving* (London, 1893), p. 12.

authorized performance of British plays on the American stage. The publication of plays was a dangerous practice for the established dramatist until
the latter years of the century. The Dramatic Copyright Act of 1833, as
amended by the Copyright Act of 1842, was incomplete and obscure. As a
result it was generally believed that publication before a performance was no
protection against unauthorized performance. Actors had therefore to be
hired to give a performance or reading of the play in order to preserve the
dramatist's rights. Whether this cumbersome procedure was legally necessary or not, publication either before or after a performance was no insurance
against unauthorized performance in America, where substantial rewards
were to be won. As a result dramatists seldom published their plays and the
reading public ceased to regard drama as a serious form of literature.

In 1887 an international copyright agreement was signed which covered
most of the European countries including France. Adaptation from the
French was no longer a cheap way of obtaining plays, and this led not only to
the reduction in the number of French adaptations but to a greater readiness
on the part of the actor-managers to accept the plays of British dramatists.

In 1891 the American copyright bill was passed, and the road was opened
to publication. Henry Arthur Jones, who had campaigned strenuously for
copyright protection and ardently believed that the failure to publish was one
of the main reasons for the decline in quality of dramatic literature, was the
first to place a successful contemporary play at the disposal of a reading
public, pleading strongly to his fellow dramatists in his preface to *Saints and
Sinners* (1891) to follow his example.

From now onwards the published play addressed to a reading public, as
distinct from the acting edition, became increasingly literary in its form.
Lengthy stage directions, often of little dramatic use, took the place of
theatrical abbreviations. While stage directions did nothing to improve the
dramatic value of the play, publication did much to enhance style and finish.

(viii) The conservatism of the theatre

Although greater rewards and opportunities provided new incentives to the
dramatist, the dramatists themselves were in no hurry to risk their new
chances of wealth by following too closely the 'slice of life' drama of the
Continent, nor did the theatregoing public show any great desire to patronize
such attempts as were made to present the more progressive Continental

drama. It is true that by 1890 the influence of Ibsen was making itself felt on the dramatists themselves. The aside and the soliloquy virtually disappeared, and subjects that would never have been contemplated in the seventies and eighties were creeping into the plays of H. A. Jones and Pinero as well as of lesser writers. Nevertheless, the theatre preserved the pose of respectability that society wished to see reflected in the mirror of its arts. The stage might present some at least of the problems of society, but the situations to which they gave rise must be solved in accordance with the Englishman's belief in justice in this world as well as in the next. The playgoer must go home satisfied that the recognition of respectability which he had accorded to the theatre was in no way tinged by the dangerous doctrine of the left-wing intellectuals, nor by the decadent aestheticism of the 'Yellow Book' set.

As a guardian of decency stood the Lord Chamberlain, against whose autocratic powers of censorship Shaw and Archer laboured in vain. But too much emphasis should not be placed on the influence of censorship, which did little more than express the attitudes of the majority of the public and of the profession itself. Behind the Lord Chamberlain stood Clement Scott, the most influential critic of the period, whose integrity and deep sympathy for the theatre as a national art made him a redoubtable antagonist to those with whose views he disagreed. The growth of national newspapers with circulations undreamt of in earlier years had made critics like Scott the leaders of public taste, and it was Scott's influence that held back any attempt to imitate too closely the social realities of Ibsen's plays.

Within the profession itself was the all-powerful influence of Irving, steadfastly determined to preserve the respectability of the theatre, and uninterested in encouraging the type of play that was neither suitable for his own style of acting nor likely to draw a public to the Lyceum. Above all it was the respectability of the theatre that occupied the minds of the actor-managers, for upon this depended the goodwill of their wealthier customers. It was not only the press and public who reacted with hysterical horror to the Oscar Wilde scandal, it was the actor-manager Alexander who had Wilde's name obliterated from the posters of *The Importance of Being Earnest*.

(ix) The renaissance

If the advanced Continental drama made little impact on the public, British drama of the nineties was showing distinct signs of its own type of renaissance. As yet the indications were timid, but the renaissance, when it came, was not brought about solely through the influence of Ibsen and the dramatists of Le Théâtre Libre. The native wit of Gilbert's Savoy operettas and the immortal epigrams of Wilde's comedies of manners were born of a tradition stemming back to Etherege, Congreve and Sheridan – a tradition that was palely reflected in the work of Pinero and H. A. Jones but eagerly seized upon and developed by Shaw. It was above all by infusing the traditions of the comedy of manners into the social problem play that British drama emerged from the turgid and stale conventions of Romanticism. It was in this genre that the dramatists found a way to introduce a new stage language as well as social comment and criticism which did not disturb the complacency of the public.

But wit alone was insufficient to make the treatment of important social problems acceptable to the Victorian public – to it must be added sentiment. The Englishman, though by no means lacking in a sense of humour, distrusts wit. It is a weapon against which he feels unprotected, and as such it appears to go beyond his sporting instinct of fair play. If his conventional ideas are to be attacked, he demands some concession to his fundamental sentimentality. The combination of sentiment and wit as ingredients of realistic social drama was harder to achieve than the stark pessimism of Continental naturalism, but nevertheless it was this combination that resulted in the popularity of Gilbert, Wilde, Pinero and Jones, and it was lack of sentiment that made Shaw's path to popular recognition the harder – if more honest – approach.

(x) Social and philosophic influences

Outside the influences that arose within dramatic literature itself there were other powerful influences leading to a reorientation of dramatic subject matter. Crime had always played a large part in the material of drama, and it would be almost impossible to be precise about its specific influence during the latter years of the nineteenth century. The melodrama had always favoured the deeds of villains, and as in *Maria Marten* and *Sweeney Todd* these were often based on actual crimes. The increase in the size and circulation of newspapers undoubtedly gave rise to the popularity of dramas concerned with court scenes and scandals. The Parnell divorce case and the Dilke scandal, the Osborn Pearl Case and the Tichborne Claimant Case were either directly or indirectly influential in supplying topics for social drama. H. A. Jones's *Mrs Dane's Defence* was based on the Osborn Pearl Case. Irving appeared in one of the many plays based on the Tichborne Case. Charles Young's *Jim the Penman* was based on the career of James Townsend, the forger. The scandals involving eminent politicians probably provided Wilde with the subject of *An Ideal Husband*. The morality or immorality of the 'wild women' of the emancipation movement was to supply the subject for more dramatists than Shaw, and the temptations and crimes of the clergy were strong meat for the playgoer when served up by H. A. Jones. In all these the influence of the national newspapers can be traced, more especially in the themes of upper-class scandal and divorce.

In the generally conservative atmosphere of the theatre it would be premature to expect any direct reflection of the theories of the more advanced philosophers, scientists and novelists, but there were stirrings in the air which suggested that the popular dramatists were not wholly unaffected by the changing outlook of the times. A greater depth of psychological observation, doubts about the efficacy of repentance and a questioning of religious dogma, stemming from the passions aroused by post-Darwinian controversy and the Oxford Movement, are noticeable in many of the plays of the last ten years of the century. The errors and sins of society were seriously treated, and, whereas in the earlier melodrama and domestic plays the wicked and misguided were usually converted or reconciled in the final hasty dénouement, during the latter years of the century there was no happy solution for those who stepped outside the bounds of social propriety. Strip away the sentiment from most late Victorian dramas and an Ibsen drama is revealed; but it was sentiment that the public wanted, and it was sentiment that provided the theatre's strength as a major social force. It must be remembered that there is a vast difference between reading a novel by Zola, Hardy, Henry James or D. H. Lawrence, and seeing and hearing the same incident and language in a public theatre. In any case, the readers of Hardy's novels and the followers of Darwin's evolutionary theories were not the average middle-class theatregoers, the majority of whom probably confined their reading matter to the popular novels of Mudie's circulating library. Thus the theatre constituted a reactionary resistance to the new literature, and the dramatists of the late nineteenth-century renaissance were obliged to introduce socially relevant subject matter into their plays by a skilful compromise between reality and artificiality. But compromise between these two rarely results in a work of art. Only when wit, fantasy or poetry are organically allied to the artificial does that 'noble artifice' of which Plato spoke result. Poetry was absent from late Victorian drama, but wit and artifice created the masterpiece of *The Importance of Being Earnest* and the lasting brilliance of Shaw; and wit joined hands with fantasy in the music and lyrics of the ever-popular operettas of Gilbert and Sullivan.

2 1901–1914

(i) The social scene

In 1901 Queen Victoria died. The prosperity that had marked the last years of Victorian England now turned to ostentation. London society, taking its tone from Edward VII and his flamboyant friends, indulged in extravagance and display. The aristocracy sought to rival the Marlborough House set; the middle classes were bent on keeping up with the Joneses. The 'shopocracy', hitherto considered unacceptable for presentation at court, bought their way into the highest circles. The sword of knighthood fell monotonously on the shoulders of the actors, and the actresses moved gracefully through society's drawing rooms – sometimes into the bedrooms of the highest in the land.

Now more than ever the middle classes felt themselves released from the puritanism of the past. Manners were more relaxed, morals less rigid, language less literary, women more emancipated, their fashions more revealing, their children more indulged. *The Wind in the Willows* and the tales of Beatrix Potter took the place of the awe-inspiring *Struwwelpeter*, and at Christmas there was *Peter Pan*.

But community and family life were disintegrating. Throughout society religion was under severe attack from rationalists, scientists and philosophers. Bible reading and family prayers were rapidly declining. The established church was rent by faction; the nonconformists were losing their appeal to the working class. Loss of faith and the decline in the influence of church and chapel resulted in a general loosening of morals and the bonds that held society together. But the decline of organized religion was not the sole cause of the decay of the family unit. Increased mobility in the form of the motor car and the bicycle were providing opportunities of escape from rigid family life. The ties that held the working–class families together were loosened by factory work. Separate earnings for each member of the family led to greater independence for the young, and secondary education offered them the chance to rise above the social position of their parents. In all classes of society parental authority was being questioned. The young men were in revolt against the family lore that required them to follow the professions of their fathers. The young women were forcing their way into more responsible professions. Between 1901 and 1911 the census showed that female authors had increased by 40 per cent. In 1903 Emmeline Pankhurst founded the Women's Social and Political Union. Disintegration of the family was speeded by the encouragement given by the stage and literature to the exercise of unlimited independent judgement. The gospel according to Ibsen, as translated by Archer, was penetrating beyond the intellectual minority. Intellectually and artistically England was like a showground in which a host of showmen barked their wares at a public avid for new doctrines. Sidney and Beatrice Webb, H. G. Wells, Bertrand Russell, Hilaire Belloc, G. K. Chesterton, D. H. Lawrence, Rudyard Kipling and the Bloomsbury Circle offered conflicting and entertaining substitutes for the established beliefs, morals and social attitudes. As if these were not enough to entertain the new society, a jester arrived to beat his tabor and sound his beguiling pipe in the form of George Bernard Shaw, making his true appearance in the costume of a playwright before the general public. In the world of artistic criticism – the frontiers of which are questionable and confusing – the showground displayed a variety of advertisements for naturalism, symbolism, impressionism, Romanticism and a dozen other creeds to choose from.

Today we look back on Edwardian England as the utopia of a prosperous, leisured civilization for a fairly wide section of society, but though materially prosperous the country's economy was rooted in sand. Its leisurely pursuits were little more than an escape from unpleasant realities. Its social progress was achieved at the expense of uncertainty and a sense of impermanence. Unemployment was rising – so too was the cost of living. Wages responded unevenly, producing fierce discontent among workers and culminating in the strikes of 1911 and 1912. Employers, having achieved wealth and social status for themselves, were resistant to improvement in the economic and social positions of their employees. Philanthropists and liberal politicians, having brought about a measure of social welfare and reform, were content to rest on their achievements. The decline in the family business, the growth of industrial monopolies and ruthless commercialism led to the development of militant trade-unionism. In 1892 Keir Hardie was elected as the first Labour Member of Parliament, and during the first ten years of the new century the Labour party became a powerful political force.

It was an age of increasing violence. Militant suffragettes destroyed property and endangered lives. Lords and Commons clashed in a political crisis that threatened the monarchy. Irish nationalists, weary of the ineffectual political manœuvres to achieve home rule, planned rebellion; while Ulster Unionists prepared armed resistance. Throughout Britain capital and labour were approaching a state of open confrontation, and by 1914 the period of 'the great unrest' had reached a stage when civil war may only have been averted by a greater war which, of necessity, brought some of the reforms that peace and prosperity had failed to achieve.

No historian would assert that in modern times the death of a monarch could of itself bring about definitive changes in social structure or literary subject matter, yet Lord Esher was surely justified in marking the death of his sovereign by the following entry in his journal:

> What a series of changes political and social this event will produce. It is like beginning to live again in a new world.[1]

(ii) The decline of the actor-manager

In 1905 Henry Irving died. Flags flew at half-mast, cab drivers tied black bows on their whips, and the pillars of his old theatre were draped in black. His death, like that of his sovereign, may be said to mark the end of an era. The age of the independent actor-manager was drawing to a close; the age of the commercial manager had begun. Yet such was Irving's influence that for a time at any rate most of the West End theatres were under the control of the actor-managers. Though Irving died penniless, his followers still strove to mount the heavily decorated productions that had made the Lyceum under Irving the foremost theatre in England. Perhaps the nearest approach to Irving's style of management was that of Herbert Beerbohm Tree at Her

[1] *Journals and Letters of Reginald, Viscount Esher* (London, 1933), I, p. 275.

(later His) Majesty's – a management that continued successfully until 1914. But whereas Irving was essentially Victorian in his passionate integrity and professionalism, Tree's flamboyance and carefree amateurism were typically Edwardian. Mounted on a white horse in *The Merry Wives of Windsor*, commissioning Sir Laurence Alma-Tadema to reproduce the Roman forum for *Julius Caesar*, or introducing live rabbits in *A Midsummer Night's Dream*, Tree appeared like a witty and genial host entertaining his guests at a lavish social function. For Tree the theatre was fun; for Irving it was dedication.

The last of the actor-managers continued to produce the same sort of plays that had drawn mass audiences to the Victorian theatre. But popular and often moving as many of the actors were, they lacked the power that Irving had to transform indifferent dramatic material into a work of histrionic art. Increasingly the leading actors were degenerating into matinée idols, more famous for their looks than their histrionic powers. Increasingly they had to rely on commercial exploitation to draw their audiences. The press extolled the sexual attractions of the actresses or devoted its columns to the trivialities of their home lives and social engagements. They appeared coyly clutching bunches of violets on picture postcards, or advertising beauty preparations in magazines. Increasingly the intellectual public turned away from the spectacular theatre and the dramatic author came into his own.

(iii) Social influences and the dramatist

If commercialism was becoming increasingly powerful on the one hand, the dramatic author was regaining his position as a significant partner in the theatrical hierarchy on the other. Publication of plays and critical interest in dramatic authorship were bringing dramatists' names and their works before a wider public. Ibsen, though hardly popular, was no longer taboo, and the new Continental drama was exciting the curiosity of a small section of the public. The ferment of ideas and creeds that inspired and divided Edwardian society was reflected in the work of the new dramatists. Whereas the Victorian theatre sought to idealize life – presenting a model of behaviour and ethics that bore little resemblance to realities – the Edwardian theatre, belonging to an age that questioned and doubted the values of orthodox beliefs and behaviour and was no longer afraid to say so, showed life as it was and achieved its popular appeal by introducing arguments and treating subjects that had hitherto been considered unsuitable for theatrical presentation. The virtuous were not necessarily victorious, the criminal was not necessarily condemned. In *Raffles* (1906) E. W. Hornung upset all traditional values by portraying a burglar not only as a gentleman but also as a hero. The infallibility of the law was questioned by H. A. Jones in *Mrs Dane's Defence* (1900) and by John Galsworthy in *Justice* (1910). Social conventions were treated critically by St John Hankin in *The Cassilis Engagement* (1907). The narrow life of the middle classes was the subject of *Chains* (1909) by Elizabeth Baker. Galsworthy dealt with the suffragette movement in *The Fugitive* (1913) and with industrial unrest in *Strife* (1909), Stanley Houghton with the revolt of the young in *The Younger Generation* (1900). The falseness of class barriers was satirized by Barrie in *The Admirable Crichton* (1902). Githa Sowerby portrayed the ruthlessness of industrial attitudes in *Rutherford and Son* (1912). Harley Granville Barker's plays – *The Voysey Inheritance* (1909), *The Marrying of Anne Leete* (1901) and *The Madras House* (1910) – attacked hypocrisy, social conformity and prejudices. In *Waste* (1907) he introduced the subject of abortion. But this was too much for the Lord Chamberlain to swallow, though a Joint Committee of the Lords and Commons in 1909 succeeded in bringing about a greater degree of liberalism in the application of his censorship.

These few examples of the range and permissiveness of the new drama omit the greatest debunker of social conventions of the age. Shaw's plays tilted at every folly and vice of society, sparing neither religion nor patriotism, marriage nor romantic love, medicine nor politics. Thus the drama, which had hitherto largely remained aloof from actual involvement in the burning questions of contemporary society, or had heavily sugared the pill with sentiment, now boldly took the lead as the mirror of the time – and not only on the boards themselves but in the libraries and bookstalls. The new dramatists were gaining reputations that threatened to rival the popularity of actors as box-office attractions. As a result their social status was raised and the texts of their plays were treated with greater respect by the actor-managers.

(iv) Escape from reality

Not all the new plays followed the pattern of verisimilitude and social criticism. Stephen Phillips, John Masefield, Gordon Bottomley and Gilbert Murray (in his translations of Greek tragedy) attempted to reintroduce poetic drama, a genre fundamentally at variance with the materialistic and socially aware English society. Other escapes from reality were to be found in the fantasies of Barrie, in romantic dramas and in the popular forms of variety and musical comedy. However, Vesta Tilley, Marie Lloyd, Albert Chevalier, Harry Tate, Little Tich and George Robey not only catered for the greater permissiveness of Edwardian society but provided a form of social criticism no less stringent than the social drama.

For those who sought spectacle there was the London Hippodrome with its circus ring and aquatic shows, ballet at the Empire and the Alhambra, and towards the end of the period the visits of Diaghilev's Russian Ballet and the spectacles of Max Reinhardt.

Musical comedy, which may be said to have been born with the production of *In Town* in 1892, now flourished with such stars as Gertie Millar, George Grossmith and George Edwardes. *Floradora*, *Our Miss Gibbs*, *The Duchess of Dantzig*, *Miss Hook of Holland*, *The Merry Widow*, *The Dollar Princess* and *The Chocolate Soldier* offered a night-out in the company of pretty chorus girls with shapely legs.

(v) Social and literary influences in Ireland

However, if poetic drama had little in common with the taste of the material-istic British society, it was to serve a more potent cause in Ireland. In 1899 W. B. Yeats, together with Lady Gregory and Edward Martyn, founded the Irish Literary Theatre. The first play by Yeats to be per-formed by this literary organization, *The Countess Cathleen*, was to herald an astonishing development of poetic plays which, if they were not all written in verse, made full use of the rich cadences of the Anglo-Irish language and drew largely on Celtic epic poetry and mythology. Yeats's theatre was in-tended as a poet's theatre: as such it was doomed to remain a theatre for a tiny minority, but many of the plays by the new Irish dramatists not only revealed the untapped wealth of the life of the country but touched so pertinently on religious and political questions that the Irish theatre quickly attracted popular attention – it also became a centre of controversy. Already *The Countess Cathleen* had aroused a degree of religious and nationalist cri-ticism that focused the limelight on the new movement; from now on the Irish dramatists were to become increasingly entangled – often to their dis-comfort – with political and religious sensitivity. In 1901 the Literary Theatre merged with a group of enthusiastic Irish amateurs under the guid-ance of W. G. Fay and his brother Frank, and this led to the foundation of the Irish National Theatre Society. A brief visit to London in 1903 established the reputation of the Irish players and as a result an English patroness appeared in the person of Annie Horniman. It was through Miss Horniman's patronage that the company was able in 1904 to acquire its own premises – the Abbey Theatre – and to transform itself into a professional repertory company. In 1924 the Abbey was given an annual grant by the Government of the Irish Free State. Thus it was not only the first theatre in the British Isles that could claim to be regarded as a national theatre, but was also the first company to be administered not by actor-managers or impresarios but by poets and dramatists.

(vi) The influence of the Court Theatre

But the Abbey was not the only theatre to seize power from the hands of the actor-managers. In the same year as the Irish National Theatre acquired its new home, Harley Granville Barker joined forces with J. E. Vedrenne to present a series of matinée performances at the Royal Court Theatre in Sloane Square. The Barker–Vedrenne management proved so successful that in 1905 a lease of the theatre was taken and a full repertory policy adopted. Between 1904 and 1907 the Court Theatre became the leading avant-garde theatre of London, offering a repertoire of the work of the new Continental and British dramatists, including the plays of Barker himself. But it was above all Shaw's plays that formed the backbone of the repertoire and proved, as Shaw so ingenuously said, 'a windfall unprecedented in the commercial history of the stage'. But the success of the Court was not due to Shaw and Barker alone; it was the culmination of the efforts made by dramatists, actors, critics and stage societies over twenty years or so to interest the theatregoing public in a more meaningful form of theatre. C. B. Purdom in his biography of Barker has stated that 'no theatrical enterprise of this century has left a deeper mark upon the theatrical history of London than the Vedrenne–Barker management at the Royal Court Theatre in the first decade of the century'.[1] Its importance as a theatrical landmark not only concerns the establishment of Shaw's reputation as the major dramatist of the time but also marks the public's final recognition of the importance of the dramatist as a box-office attraction. There were, however, other important and far-reaching influences that emanated from the Court seasons. First, it provided one

[1] *Harley Granville Barker* (London, 1955), p. 26.

of the earliest examples of the work of a new functionary in the stage hierarchy – the independent producer or director – a functionary who was to
replace the actor-manager as the normal leader of the theatrical team. Second,
it provided a rallying point for those who sought to establish a national
theatre. Third, it was a model of a new form of theatrical organization – the
repertory theatre. The example offered by the Court was to be followed in a
number of provincial cities and to bring new life to the theatre outside
London.

(vii) The influence of the director

The separation of the director from the actor was not consistently practised
in this country during the early years of the century. Many of the early
directors continued to take part in the performances they directed, though no
longer in the virtuoso manner of the actor-managers; even Barker during his
Court seasons appeared in many of the plays produced under his guidance. It
was largely due to the influence of literary and scholarly works on the art of
the theatre that the full implications of the director's contribution as an independent artist were realized. Edward Gordon Craig's *The Art of the
Theatre*, published in 1905, became a rallying point not only for the new
British directors but for the conception of the theatre as an art as opposed to
an entertainment. From now on the word 'art' was increasingly used in connection with the stage, and the division between the commercial theatre and
the art theatre became more apparent. Although Craig's dream of a master-
mind controlling every aspect of the stage and replacing the dramatist, the
scenic designer, the composer and even the actor has never been totally
realized, nor is likely to be, his influence as a propagandist for the art of a new
stagecraft contributed to the decline of the actor-manager.

(viii) The propaganda for a national theatre

The impetus provided by the Abbey Theatre and the Vedrenne–Barker
management at the Court gave new life to the somewhat desultory attempts
to found a national theatre. The demand for a national theatre, subsidized by
the state and housing a permanent company of artists, had been voiced from

time to time in lectures and newspapers throughout the nineteenth century, but it was the enthusiasm of William Archer and Barker that gave practical shape to the rather vague ideas of Bulwer Lytton, Henry Irving, H. A. Jones and others. In 1904 Archer and Barker issued a privately printed volume, *Scheme and Estimates for a National Theatre*, which suggested how the national theatre should be organized and financed. The 'Blue Book', as it was called, showed that £350,000 was needed (later the sum was considerably increased); but, despite the strenuous efforts of the National Theatre Committee, not a penny was raised for the project from the public. In 1908 the committee merged with the Shakespeare Memorial Committee which had been formed to commemorate the tercentenary of Shakespeare's death, and an appeal for funds was made supported by an impressive array of names from the social, literary and theatre world. A major contribution of £70,000 was made by a single donor (Sir Carl Meyer), but the fund made little headway, and the appeal was finally suspended by the outbreak of war. Barker's disillusionment with the public's response to the idea of a national theatre contributed to his decision to abandon the theatre and retire to a self-imposed exile. The foundations of the movement had been considerably strengthened by his work, but the movement lacked grass roots. The British public, accustomed throughout the nineteenth century to regard the theatre as an industry rather than an art, had yet to adjust itself to the idea of the theatre as a national institution. One of the most important factors in providing the grass roots for a national theatre was the growth of the repertory theatres outside London.

(ix) The influence of the repertory-theatre movement

The example set by J. T. Grein's Independent Theatre, the subsequent work of the Stage Society, the foundation of the Abbey Theatre and the Court seasons provided the impetus for the development of a number of repertory theatres in the provinces. Miss Horniman, having helped to establish the Irish theatre, turned her attention to Manchester, and in 1908 established the first repertory theatre in England at the Gaiety. In common with the Abbey, the Gaiety became for a time a focal point for local drama, presenting plays by Allan Monkhouse, Stanley Houghton and Harold Brighouse, as well as an impressive range of the new Continental and British dramatists. From Manchester the repertory idea spread rapidly to Glasgow, Liverpool and Birmingham. The Glasgow Repertory Theatre, which began its seasons in 1909, also included among its principal aims 'to encourage the initiation and development of a purely Scottish Drama', but in this it was less successful than the Abbey and the Gaiety. The Liverpool Repertory Theatre, established at the old Star Theatre (renamed the Playhouse) in Williamson Square in 1911, distinguished itself from the other repertory enterprises by the fact that it was founded and run by a group of local citizens as opposed to being dependent on patronage. Perhaps the greatest patron of the theatre outside London was Barry Jackson, who in 1913 founded the Birmingham Repertory. Once again the emphasis was on the play rather than the actor, and on the development of the aesthetics of production under an independent director. Personal patronage also provided for the Shakespeare festivals at Stratford, where C. E. Flower had paid the greater part of the cost of building the theatre. It would be difficult to overestimate the importance of the repertory movement in expressing the new attitude of provincial society towards the theatre. The movement arose out of a deeply felt need in the provinces to possess a creative theatre of their own, and to be free from dependence on the London-based tours. But it was more than a mere expression of provincial pride or a rich man's toy. It was an important manifestation of public dissatisfaction with the outworn conventions of the actor-manager's theatre on the one hand, and the trivialities of commercial theatre on the other. More positively it demonstrated a national interest in the new dramatists – an interest that had been brought about by the publication of plays and the increased critical attention paid to authorship by the national newspapers and magazines. If the repertory idea represented a new social attitude – albeit a minority one – it also expressed a small but influential actors' attitude: the attitude of the younger actors towards their profession.

(x) The actor as a member of organized society

As already noted, the status of the professional actor had risen considerably during the latter years of the nineteenth century. From the Edwardian age onwards knighthoods were showered on leading actors and managers, and there was a general tendency for members of what might be loosely called the educated classes to enter the profession. University men, like Arthur Bouchier, Frank Benson and H. B. Irving, were graduating from university dramatic societies into the professional theatre.

The profession itself was becoming organized. The Actors' Association, the Society of West End Managers, the Touring Managers' Association and the Theatrical Managers' Association provided a degree of coordination and standard practice; while the Actors' Benevolent Fund, the Actors' Orphanage Fund, the Theatrical Ladies' Guild, the Actors' Church Union and other charitable organizations bore evidence of the integration of the profession into the fabric of organized society. But perhaps the most important development within the profession was the provision made for training the actor through schools of acting.

The disappearance of the provincial stock companies and the laws governing apprenticeship and children's employment had brought to an end the old forms of training. During the last twenty years of the nineteenth century the need for a training school had been recognized. Various private classes were provided, but it was not until Tree founded the Royal Academy of Dramatic Art in 1904 that a properly constituted school was established. This was followed by the Central School of Speech and Drama founded by Elsie Fogerty in 1906.

The new attitude of the actor towards his profession, both as an art and as an organization, was reflected in a greater sense of pride and purpose among the supporting players. The days of Crummles's actors were over. The younger and better-educated actors were no longer content to be supporters of the virtuoso performance by the star; they had their own ideas on how to play their parts and a desire to make a personal contribution to the interpretation of the text. This new conception of the actor as an artist – no matter how small his part might be – was largely influenced by the rise of the director as a coordinating functionary. It was strengthened by the new importance of the dramatist and by the opportunities offered by the repertory-theatre movement.

(xi) The influence of theatre research

The repertory movement did not solely concern itself with the new drama; it also provided scope for a new interpretation of the great plays of the past, in particular the plays of Shakespeare. To some extent the new look at the production of Shakespeare's plays was the result of lack of financial resources. The repertory theatres could not afford to mount the spectacular productions offered by the actor-managers and were forced to search for a form of simplified staging. The search for simplification brought the stage into contact with new movements in the visual arts on the one hand, and with scholarly research on the other. Clearly the independent director and the educated actor were key factors in bringing about the alliance between the stage and the scholar, nor must the influence of informed criticism by Shaw and others be overlooked. It would be impossible to record here the advances made in theatrical research or to list the scholars who were contributing to the knowledge of Shakespearian stagecraft. A glance at the list of authorities quoted by Sir Edmund Chambers in his monumental works on the medieval and Elizabethan stages[1] provides an indication of the vast amount of literature which, during the latter years of the nineteenth century and the early years of the twentieth, was radically altering conceptions of Shakespeare's stagecraft and increasing an interest in the revival of neglected plays of the past. Foremost among the pioneers of this interest was William Poel, who in 1887 had startled some critics and enlightened others by presenting a performance of the first quarto version of *Hamlet* in its entirety on the curtained stage of St George's Hall, London. Influenced by De Witt's sketch of the original Swan Theatre and working on the dimensions of the Fortune Theatre, Poel reconstructed his conception of an Elizabethan stage in a portable form which he set down within the proscenium arch of the theatres in which he worked. Poel's demonstrations of the advantages of the open stage were to be one of the influences which led to Barker's productions of Shakespeare's plays at the Savoy Theatre between 1912 and 1914. The war interrupted the progress of the new staging of Shakespeare, but Poel's experiments, as developed and modified by the repertory theatres and reinforced by Barker's *Prefaces to Shakespeare*,[2] were to bring about a revolution in Shakespearian production.

Lack of financial resources, nicely balanced by aesthetic considerations, provided the basis of the Shakespeare productions mounted under Lilian Baylis's management at the Old Vic. Between 1914 and 1923 the Old Vic presented the complete repertoire of Shakespeare's plays, and established itself as the seed from which the present national theatre, as well as the national opera and ballet companies, was to grow. Besides live performances, the Old Vic housed during its early years the new and most powerful rival the stage had encountered during the whole history of the entertainment industry – the film.

[1] *The Mediaeval Stage*, 2 vols (Oxford, 1903); *The Elizabethan Stage*, 4 vols (Oxford, 1923).
[2] London, 1927, 1930, 1937, 1945, 1947.

(xii) The influence of the cinema

During the 1880s Edison had invented the means of recording moving pictures on celluloid; but it was the invention of the projector that made it possible to present moving pictures to a theatre audience. From 1896 onwards short motion pictures began to be shown as a part of vaudeville programmes. These novelties were at first mostly documentary in character – Queen Victoria's Jubilee and funeral, the Derby and the coronation of Edward VII. In 1899 the first story film, *The Jewel Thieves Outwitted*, was made, and from then on what had started as a mere addition to vaudeville entertainment became a popular entertainment in its own right, housed in picture palaces that sprang up in all the large towns in the country. The pre-war cinema was essentially a popular recreation. Its patrons were mostly drawn from the masses, and its subject matter, based on crude comedy, farce and melodrama, provided a serious threat to the popularity of live theatre. The opportunities that the new medium offered for massive spectacle, as first demonstrated by *Quo Vadis* in 1912, were to prove the final death blow to the actor-managers' spectacular productions. Through the succeeding years the theatres were gradually robbed of their mass audiences. The commercial theatre responded to the threat to its box office by turning to musical comedies and revues on the one hand, and to drama based on safe formulae of success on the other. It was left to the art theatres with their insecure financial position to maintain under severe difficulties of taxation and public apathy the cause of serious drama. The cleavage between the art theatres and the commercial stage became complete, and for a time at any rate the great renaissance heralded by the new century came to an abrupt end when the shots rang out at Sarajevo.

3 1914–1918

The old world did not die when the lights went out in Europe. It took many years, lasting long beyond the end of hostilities, before society accepted the full implications of the changes that war had wrought on its structure.

Fighting men and civilians alike dreamt that victory would bring back the old world purified by the sword and united by sacrifice. At first England seemed to welcome the war as a salve to its conscience. After the long years of conflicting creeds a purpose had been found and a common cause provided. Industrial strife was stilled, political parties united. The suffragettes diverted their energies to the factory benches and the hospitals. Families were drawn together by partings and reunions. Class warfare was forgotten as the daughters of the privileged and underprivileged laboured in the munition factories and their brothers fought side by side in the Flanders mud. The war would be short. Victory was certain. The cause was just.

As the years passed and the rolls of honour lengthened; as the wounded and shell-shocked poured back from the front; as the Zeppelin raids caused the bright lights in the cities to be extinguished, and the places of amusement closed their doors at an early hour; as submarine warfare cut off supplies and food was rationed, the certainty of victory grew more remote. The glamour of patriotism wore thin, allies began to fall apart, generals quarrelled and politicians manœuvred. Then did men long for peace and dream of a new world – 'a world fit for heroes'. But morale had to be strengthened, money had to be raised for War Bonds, the hatred of the enemy had to be stepped up in order to divert men's minds from war-weariness and disillusionment. In all phases of the war the stage played its part, from flag-waving to Hun-hating. It raised some millions for war funds. It stimulated patriotism and strengthened the faint-hearted. It cheered the armed forces on leave and the soldiers at the front. Above all, it kept the public in good spirits – a public upon whose morale the whole war effort depended. Despite its value in maintaining morale on the home front, the wartime theatre received no help or recognition from the government. Unlike other war industries, it was not made a certified occupation, nor was it assisted by grant or subsidy. A faint sign of official interest was shown, however, in 1916 when the armed forces set up an Entertainments Department under the auspices of the Navy and Army Canteen Board to provide facilities for theatrical companies to perform in camps and depots.

The problems that the public theatre faced were considerable. Paper restrictions prohibited poster advertisement. Travel restrictions, rationing and shortage of accommodation crippled the touring of plays in the provinces. There were restrictions on the sale of refreshments. There was a shortage of materials and labour. Prices rose – so too did the rent of theatres. Trade was subject to violent fluctuations as the fortunes of war rose and fell. An Order in Council during the first months of the war required theatres in certain cities, including London, to close at 9.30 pm. This time limit was later raised to 10.30 pm, but reduction of train, taxi and bus services made it necessary for some theatres to restrict performances to matinées. There was a shortage of plays to meet the requirements of a public predominantly requiring relaxation and escape from reality.

At first the theatre was obliged to rely on productions of pre-war vintage – musical comedies, revues with inserted patriotic numbers (like 'By Jingo if We Do'), farces and light comedies, with the occasional patriotic Shakespearian play. Then came the plays with a war theme – jingoistic in tone and suitably distant from disturbing reality. A few titles speak for themselves: *Der Tag* (Barrie), *The Man Who Stayed Behind* (Lechmere Worrall and Harold Terry), *The Invisible Foe* (Walter Hackett), *Home on Leave* (Edward Knoblock), *The Pacifists* and *Loyalty* (H. A. Jones), *Monica's Blue Boy* (Pinero).

E. A. Baugham writing in the *Stage Year Book* in 1915 joyfully asserted that one effect of the war would be to 'sweep the boards of finicking problem plays'. It was not only problem plays that were swept off the boards, but nearly all plays of quality. The dramatists who had provided the new drama of the early twentieth century could neither ignore the war nor deal with it adequately. The great forward movement of British drama was halted, and the stage suffered a blow almost as severe as the closing of the theatres in 1642. The art theatres closed down; many of the repertory theatres disappeared; the national-theatre movement was halted; Craig and Granville Barker withdrew from the theatre; the actor-managers were driven out of business; and the London theatres lost their distinctive characteristics. Tree died in 1916, Alexander in 1917. The emphasis was on long runs, and *Chu-Chin-Chow* achieved the longest run in the history of the British stage, only to be overtaken in our own age by *The Mousetrap*. Nor was this to be a mere lull in the pattern of the theatre to be succeeded by a great forward movement when peace was proclaimed, as some critics hoped. The West End theatres were taken over by a handful of multiple managements, and commercialism dug its roots into real estate so deeply that it was not to be shaken off when hostilities ceased. Above all the theatre was stripped of its young manhood. By 1915 Tree estimated that 1500 actors had joined the forces, and by 1918 nearly every able-bodied young actor and many hundreds of young actresses had been conscripted or directed into war work. When they returned to the stage they were to find that it belonged not to the actors nor to the dramatists; the new show-businessmen had taken it over.

4 1918–1930

(i) 'A land fit for heroes'

The Armistice brought a patchwork peace – a peace made by old men, while the young (or those who were left) plunged into the hectic whirl of the twenties. The Bright Young Things danced the tango, the foxtrot, the Charleston, the blues and the black bottom. The 'flappers' discarded their corsets, Eton-cropped their hair and affected the 'schoolboy' shape. They smoked cigarettes in long holders, drank cocktails and took advantage of the advice tendered by Dr Marie Stopes. Their boyfriends wore 'Oxford bags' and 'plus fours', drove fast sports cars and gatecrashed parties. But the change on the surface of society was more apparent than real. Women won the vote, but Parliament remained stubbornly male. A Labour government achieved power in 1923, but Baldwin led the country back to 'normality' in 1924. Secondary schools increased and grants were provided for students to attend the universities, but only a minute percentage of elementary school children climbed up the educational ladder to the universities. The public schools and the universities ensured that the professions, the business world, the commissioned ranks in the armed forces and the civil service were reserved for the privileged classes. The gap between the younger and older generations widened; so too did the gap between the classes. The old order of high society was gone, high taxes and death duties were redistributing wealth, but a new privileged society was forming. The nouveau riche war profiteers drove their Rolls Royce cars to the hunt meets and were pictured with the aristocracy in the glossy magazines. The new technology and improved means of communication – express trains, the development of air services, motor buses, the family car, above all the rapid spread of broadcasting – seemed to offer opportunities of a richer life for a wider section of society, but the prosperity of the manufacturers was achieved at the expense of the workers. After the boom year of 1919 prices began to rise and wages to fall. Throughout the twenties the number of unemployed never fell below a million. In 1920 the first of the many marches of unemployed wormed its way to London. In 1921 the 'dole' was introduced. In 1926 the life of the country was halted by a general strike. Class issues that had remained dormant during the war were revived more virulently than before. Bolshevism spread outwards from Russia, percolating into cells on the Clyde and into intellectual circles in London. In every sphere of social life there was a need for reassessment and reform to meet the new world that emerged from the war, but the privileged society of the twenties was divided between those who sought to turn the clock back to 1914 and those who spun round in the hectic whirlpool of the present.

(ii) Theatre for the privileged

J. C. Trewin has shown a sharp distinction between *The Gay Twenties*[1] and *The Turbulent Thirties*.[2] Certainly it may be said that the prevailing mood of the theatre, as well as of literature and art, during the former decade reflected the gaiety, cynicism and escapism that characterized the attitude of the younger and more privileged members of society and paid little heed to the dark shadows of poverty and unemployment that were rapidly spreading across the land. The bookstall trade boomed with the new craze for detective fiction and the side-splitting adventures of Bertie Wooster – the former epitomized by Edgar Wallace's dramatized 'thrillers', the latter reflected in the Aldwych farces.

Escapism found its predominant expression on the musical stage in the fantasies of *Rose Marie* and *The Desert Song*, in the revues of André Charlot

[1] London, 1958.
[2] London, 1960.

and C. B. Cochran. Their catchy songs were sung and swung from the stages of the Palace, the London Palladium, the Gaiety, the Vaudeville, the Winter Garden, the Adelphi and Drury Lane. If there was one tune that expressed the spirit of the twenties, it was, as J. C. Trewin has pointed out, 'I want to be happy'. This restless search for happiness, this gay abandonment of the taboos of sex was satirized in the novels and plays of Somerset Maugham, in the plays of Frederick Lonsdale and above all by Noël Coward.

Serious literature was largely concerned with criticism of this brittle world of the twenties. Aldous Huxley's *Chrome Yellow* (1921) and *Antic Hay* (1923) found a dramatic echo in *The Vortex* (1924), Noël Coward's scathing satire on the hypocrisy of middle-class morals. But dramatic subject matter was confined to the habits of the privileged classes. No hint of the life of the masses was permitted to soil the elegant flats and country houses. The poverty and pride of D. H. Lawrence's Nottinghamshire miners moved the readers of his novels, but his plays found no outlet on the stage.

It was in Ireland that the first plays by a proletarian playwright were produced. Sean O'Casey's portrayal of life in the Dublin slums – *The Shadow of a Gunman* (1922), *Juno and the Paycock* (1924) and *The Plough and the Stars* (1926) – were the only major expression of the humour and poverty of working-class people and their antiheroic attitude to war. By the end of the decade war had indeed lost its glamour, patriotism had become unfashionable, but in Europe the clouds of war were gathering again as territorial ambitions challenged the provisions of the Treaty of Versailles and political ideologies clashed. At home, class antagonisms bred of the General Strike and unprecedented unemployment threatened national collapse. The jazz age was drawing to a close, and a younger generation, more politically aware than the Bright Young Things of the early twenties, looked back at the follies and horror of the war-to-end-war. The novels of Richard Aldington and Ernest Hemingway – *Death of a Hero* and *A Farewell to Arms* (1929) – were reflected on the stage by R. C. Sherriff's *Journey's End* and O'Casey's *The Silver Tassie* (1928). Sherriff's play with its public school officers, though at first rejected by West End managers, ran for two years, while O'Casey's condemnation of war's inhumanity with its war-weary 'tommies' and its caricatured staff officer was rejected by the Abbey and proved a prestige failure in London. But it was undoubtedly the introduction of expressionist techniques into a naturalistic drama that most puzzled theatre audiences. Expressionism, surrealism and constructivist scenery, which were introducing new forms in the theatre of Russia and Germany, found little response on the commercially dominated British stage whose spotlights were focused on the country-house drawing rooms and hotel bedrooms of a theatre that equated society with the moneyed classes.

(iii) The influence of commercialism

But money was not easily made in the post-war theatre. Expenses rose sharply. Putting on a play without considerable capital became increasingly risky. Audiences, no longer based on a broad section of popular support, proved more fickle than the captive public of the war years. Above all there was the competition of the cinema and broadcasting. The war profiteers who had purchased theatres as a capital investment, and valued them no higher than the rest of their real estate, sought protection from loss by leases and subleases, creating a complex network of landlords and sublandlords all seeking a protection for their money. Theatres changed hands with alarming rapidity. Rents rose steeply and to them was added the crippling tax on entertainments. No management could afford to gamble for long on a single play or in running a single theatre. Theatre combines and multiple managements stretched out into the provinces, resulting in a situation very close to monopoly. The actors, variety artists and stage workers, seeking to protect themselves from the threat to their freedom, formed their own trade unions. The confrontation of capital and labour that threatened the prosperity of industry was echoed in the theatre. The patriarchal rule of the actor-managers was replaced by the far less happy relationship between businessmen on the one side and theatre artists on the other. The unity of the stage was split, and creative work suffered. Managements looked for the stereotype play, preferably with a small cast and a single setting: inevitably the dramatists were forced to supply their needs. The box office relied more and more on the drawing power of the star, and security could be bolstered by employing established actors and conventional directors. The West End stage was becoming a closed shop; the provinces were used for exploitation and 'try-outs'. It was in revolt against the deadening hand of commercialism, threatening the life-force of the theatre, that the little-theatre movement was born.

(iv) The little-theatre movement – theatre for the minority

The impetus of the repertory movement was largely halted by the war. Of the major companies only the Liverpool Playhouse and the Birmingham Repertory under the patronage of Barry Jackson, who more than any other manager kept the West End supplied with experimental productions, managed to survive the economic pressures and the competition of the cinema. The post-war repertories were mostly seasonal or weekly 'reps' inadequately reproducing the 'hits' of the London stage. Two notable seasonal theatres arose in the provinces during the twenties: J. B. Fagan's Oxford Repertory Company, which lasted from 1923 to 1929 and brought *The Cherry Orchard* to London in 1925, and Terence Gray's highly experimental Cambridge Festival Theatre, founded (also in 1923) to make war on what he described as 'the old game of illusion and glamour and all the rest of the nineteenth century hocus pocus and bamboozle'.[1]

Of the West End theatres that offered opportunities for young actors to prove their worth and for new methods of production to be developed, the following were important examples: the Lyric Theatre, Hammersmith, under the management of Nigel Playfair, the Gate Theatre Studio founded by Peter Godfrey, and the brief but brilliant productions of Theodore Komisarjevsky at the Barnes Theatre. These and other little theatres, whose lives were often pitifully short, supplemented by the Memorial Theatre at Stratford (under the direction of W. Bridges Adams) and by the Old Vic (shortly to blossom forth as a major London theatre under Tyrone Guthrie), fed the appetite of a small but influential section of society – a society that was no longer content to regard the theatre as a purely post-prandial entertainment.

But the popular audience had deserted the theatre. New forms of mass entertainment – the films and the radio – had lured them away.

(v) The cinema – theatre for the majority

The war effectively destroyed any hopes that existed in Britain of taking a major part in the new cinema industry. By 1919 Hollywood had established a firm hold on the production and marketing of what was to prove for a time

[1] Quoted by Norman Marshall, *The Other Theatre* (London, 1947), p. 53.

the most popular and lucrative entertainment industry. By astute business methods, the American film companies controlled the distribution of films in most British cinemas. By a no less astute use of advertising, backed by a far larger capital than the theatre could command, the Hollywood producers created a star system that had little relation to acting merit.

The cinema became a form of cheap dope – a relief from the boredom of unemployment. In 1921 52 per cent of unemployed youths in Cardiff were visiting the cinema once a week and 25 per cent twice a week. In the same year, two million tickets were being sold in cinema box offices throughout the country. Cinemas sprang up in remote villages and in every district of the cities. In 1911 there were 94 cinemas in London; in 1921 the number had increased to 266. In Liverpool the number of cinemas was doubled between 1913 and 1932, and the number of theatres was halved. The cheaper prices and greater accessibility of the cinemas spirited away the gallery and pit audiences from the London theatres, and all but killed the provincial theatre.

But not all cinemagoers were anaesthetized by Hollywood. Just as the theatre of the twenties developed its own minority audience for 'the other theatre', so a small but enthusiastic number of cinema perfectionists supported the avant-garde films of Germany, France and Soviet Russia. The films of Ernst Lubitsch, Fritz Lang, René Clair, Jacques Feyder, S. M. Eisenstein and V. I. Pudovkin proved that the film had a language of its own, and was an art form totally different from the theatre. The enthusiasts who supported the film societies believed that in time the European directors of the art cinema would prevail against the pedlars of Hollywood dope. So long as the silent film provided an international language, their hopes seemed capable of realization, but at the end of the decade a bitter blow was delivered not only to the dreams of the *cinéastes* but also to the theatre – Hollywood introduced the 'talkie'.

(vi) The influence of broadcasting

The talking film was adopted – not without reluctance – by Hollywood as a protection against the competition of the radio. In 1920 the Marconi Company made its first experimental broadcasts in Britain, and in 1922 the British Broadcasting Company was licensed by the Postmaster-General. The first plays broadcast by the Company were little more than dramatic readings, but soon the particular qualities demanded by radio drama began to emerge

and in 1924 *Danger* by Richard Hughes – the first play written for the radio –
was produced. In 1926 the Company was incorporated under Royal Charter as
the British Broadcasting Corporation (BBC) and became, under the high moral
direction of Sir John Reith, the accepted mouthpiece of Britain. Between
1922 and 1927 the number of receiving licences rocketed from 10,000 to $2\frac{1}{2}$
million. Theatre managers panicked. Clauses were inserted in artists' contracts debarring them from broadcasting. Live broadcasts from theatres were
prohibited. But the decline in theatre audiences during the thirties, more
especially in the provinces, was more certainly due to the economic crisis and
to the popularity of the cinema than to the competition of the radio. If the
radio kept some playgoers away from the theatre, it introduced many more to
the great works of dramatic literature, and it built up over the years a solid
defence for the English language against the Americanization threatened by
the Hollywood film.

5 1930–1939

(i) The depression and the leftist movement

By the end of the twenties the gaiety had grown sour; the cult of unrestricted freedom was no longer exciting; the mood became grim. Society looked inwards and beheld the frightening spectacle of a nation that was predominantly ill fed, ill housed and on the verge of financial ruin. The factor that brought this home most forcibly was the Wall Street crash of 1929. Markets were affected the world over. Unemployment in Britain mounted to $2\frac{1}{2}$ million by the end of 1931, and the years of the great depression began which were to affect all aspects of social life, not least the theatre. If, however, life on the 'dole' was to have a demoralizing effect on a great part of the country's youth and leave traces of bitterness and decay in the afflicted areas that have never been eradicated, it was also to bring about an important change in writers' attitude to social questions. A new spirit of compassion for the underprivileged, a new social consciousness, a compulsion to express new ideas for the reformation of the social structure characterized an increasing proportion of literature and drama. To some extent this was a leftist movement, but not exclusively. Much was written about the condition of England in social surveys as well as in fiction and documentary literature.

Among many other publications, the following were influential: A. Hutt's

Condition of the Working Class in Britain; Ellen Wilkinson's *Town that was Murdered*; *Men without Work: a Report Made to the Pilgrim Trust*; J. B. Priestley's *English Journey*; George Orwell's *Road to Wigan Pier*; and Walter Greenwood's *Love on the Dole*, dramatized by the author in collaboration with Ronald Gow in 1935. Interest in the Russian experiment spread through the universities and was generally considered more respectable than in the twenties. The Webbs published *Soviet Communism: A New Civilisation?*, Shaw wrote *An Intelligent Woman's Guide to Socialism*, O'Casey became a member of the Communist Party. Russia was visited and written about by such people as Lord Lothian and Lady Astor. The Soviet theatre, too, became an object of interest: directors like André Van Gyseghem in *Miracle at Verdun* (1932) and dramatists like O'Casey and Shaw in *Within the Gates* (1934) and *Too True to be Good* (1932) adopted some of its techniques. The leftist movement was furthered by political reviews and magazines such as *The New Statesman*, *The Left Review* and *New Writing* and by new publishing ventures such as the Left Book Club, founded in 1936 by Victor Gollancz. Publishers helped in the general movement for the enlightenment of society. In 1935 Penguin Books began to offer sixpenny paperbacks, and in 1937 Pelicans appeared. Some of these publications were concerned with social problems, others were reprints of fiction and literature. They were the publishers' attempt to counteract the competition of cinema and broadcasting. But hope of a brighter future was not lost, though eyes were often blinded to the tensions that were building up in Europe. In 1931 Noël Coward – the mouthpiece of the Bright Young Things of the twenties – proposed the toast to the future in *Cavalcade*: 'Let's drink to the hope that one day this country of ours, which we love so much, will find dignity and greatness and peace again.'

(ii) Towards war

It was an idle hope. The economic crisis was followed by a military crisis. In 1935 Mussolini invaded Abyssinia. In March 1936 German forces occupied the Rhineland. In July of the same year civil war broke out in Spain. In 1937 Japan pressed her undeclared war into the heart of China. In 1938 Austria became part of the Nazi Empire. In March 1939 it was the turn of Czechoslovakia. On 1 September Hitler's armies invaded Poland, and on 3 September Neville Chamberlain announced over the wireless that Britain was at war.

Throughout this crescendo of aggression and political manœuvring, society in Britain moved slowly from the famous resolution in the Oxford Union that 'this House will in no circumstances fight for its King and Country' to the TUC manifesto of 7 September 1938 – 'The time has come for a positive and unmistakable lead for collective defence against aggression . . .' More than any other international event – more even than Hitler's atrocities against the Jews, Stalin's purges or Mussolini's barbarities against the Abyssinians – it was the Spanish Civil War that awoke the international consciousness of writers. Many of them visited Spain or fought there, and such poets as W. H. Auden, Christopher Isherwood, Cecil Day Lewis and Stephen Spender expressed in their poems strong antifascist views and their opposition to the indifference and futility of bourgeois attitudes. The plays of Auden and Isherwood, *The Dog Beneath the Skin* (1935), *The Ascent of F6* (1936) and *On the Frontier* (1938), were expressions of this type of left-wing commitment.

But poetry had little power to influence theatre audiences and less to provide the needs of theatre box offices, now facing the full impact of the 'talkies'. One way in which the stage sought to meet the competition of the 'talkies' on the one hand, and of the economic slump on the other, was to turn to spectacle and theatricalism. Productions such as *Cavalcade, Elizabeth of England* (by Ferdinand Bruckner, adapted by Ashley Dukes), *White Horse Inn* and *Late Night Final* (an American importation by Louis Weitzencorn), all of which were mounted in the crucial year of 1931, made use of cinematic techniques in the form of hydraulic lifts, revolving and multiple stages and composite scenes. Managers continued to favour the stereotype play, treating similar themes or subjects as a formula of success. Thus in 1931 Austria was a favourite theme with *White Horse Inn, Waltzes from Vienna* and *Autumn Crocus*. The author of the latter play, C. L. Anthony – later known as Dodie Smith – became one of the leading exponents of the country-house plays of the thirties. Then, too, there was the ever-popular formula of the detective play, relentlessly pursued throughout the decade by Edgar Wallace and successfully developed by Anthony Armstrong in *Ten Minute Alibi* (1933) and Emlyn Williams in *Night Must Fall* (1935). There was the brilliant succession of sophisticated comedies by Coward. There was a nice mixture of comedy and sentiment in the plays of Terence Rattigan; both he and Coward knew precisely how much social satire they could add to their recipes without offending the taste of 'Aunt Edna'. There were the Ben Travers farces, the Cochran Revues and Ivor Novello's musicals. Formula drama of a different character was developed with the object of exploring a theme in depth in the time plays of J. B. Priestley – *Dangerous Corner* (1932), *Time and the Conways* and *I Have Been Here Before* (1937). Perhaps more than any other dramatist Priestley embodies the real England of the thirties. Starting with *The Good Companions*, adapted from his novel with the help of Edward Knoblock in 1931, he marches four-square through the decade, speaking in the accent of his native Yorkshire, as the voice of the lost generation of citizen soldiers. Here was the backbone of England of the thirties – an England that had no part in the cocktail-swilling London – an England that knew and suffered the pangs of its decaying Northern cities – an England that wanted change, but honoured its traditions – an England expressed in the suburban conservatism of *Laburnum Grove* (1933), but willing to explore new avenues in *Time and the Conways* and *Johnson over Jordan* (1939). It was hardly surprising that, in the dark years that were to come, it was Priestley's voice on the wireless as much as Churchill's that lifted up men's hearts and gave hope for the future.

(iii) Shakespeare, opera and ballet

Shakespeare production generally was entering a new phase. A new generation of leading actors was adding lustre to the productions. John Gielgud, Laurence Olivier, Ralph Richardson, Ion Swinley, Charles Laughton, Peggy Ashcroft, Edith Evans, Gwen Ffrangçon-Davies, Flora Robson and, above all, those mighty pioneers of all that was new and important in the theatre – Sybil Thorndike and Lewis Casson – were transforming the old tradition of the star actor into a new conception of the leading actor as an integral part of a team. In this movement towards the modern conception of an ensemble, H. K. Ayliff in Birmingham, W. Bridges Adams in Stratford and Tyrone Guthrie at the Old Vic were largely instrumental. The new simplicity of scenery, partly forced on the directors by economic necessity and partly inspired by scholarly research, was dragging the works of the national playwright out of the past into a form more allied to contemporary life. Shakespeare was no longer treated as an excuse for a spectacular orgy, nor as a dusty educational bore: his plays became vitally relevant to contemporary society. Barry Jackson's presentation of *Hamlet* in modern dress in 1925 was to lead to Henry Cass's production of *Julius Caesar* in 1939 as a direct comment on fascism; and Michael Macowan's production of *Troilus and Cressida* at the time of the Munich crisis had an almost frightening topicality in its condemnation of the futility of war.

In 1937 Lilian Baylis died, but not before she had added to the prestige of the Old Vic by establishing a permanent opera and ballet company at Sadlers Wells. The influence of Diaghilev's ballet seasons had led to a growing demand for a native ballet company. In 1930 the Camargo Society was formed with the object of encouraging British ballet. And from 1931 onwards the Sadlers Wells Ballet under the direction of Ninette de Valois was steadily increasing the audience for an art that had been almost exclusively confined to foreign importations. By restricting production costs to the minimum, the Sadlers Wells Opera Company was able to provide a continuous repertoire of opera for the people in place of the prestige seasons that had up to now been the sole manifestations of serious opera in London. The fact that the operas were presented in English widened the appeal of opera to a far greater public. For the more privileged members of society there were Sir Thomas Beecham's international seasons at Covent Garden and delightful summer evenings at John Christie's opera house at Glyndebourne. The popularity of opera was advanced by the perfection of the recording processes of the growing gramophone industry and by the musical education of the public through the wireless.

(iv) The influence of the talking film

The Wall Street crash and the ensuing years of economic crisis that wrought havoc at theatre box offices had the opposite effect on cinema audiences. The advent of the 'talkie' not only proved to be a popular novelty, but the cheapness of cinema prices offered entertainment to mass audiences who were no longer able to afford regular visits to the theatre. But the 'talkie' had other effects on the theatre and its audiences. First, the spoken film made demands for a different emphasis on the dramatic material that was suitable for the cinema. Inevitably the first producers of 'talkies' leaned heavily on the novel and the play for their film scripts. British dramatists could therefore hope for a new and highly lucrative market for their work. Barrie, Maugham and Lonsdale had already found this market; now notable films were made of such plays as *Laburnum Grove* (1936), *Pygmalion* (1938) and *Gaslight* (1940), while *The Good Companions* (1932), *Goodbye, Mr Chips* (1939) and *Love on the Dole* (1941) are examples of novels adapted for the screen. Second, the spoken film made different demands on film actors, and many of the actors of the silent screen proved unsuitable for the new medium. While Hollywood lured away a high percentage of leading players from the New York stage, there was also a demand for British stage actors in films with a British background. The considerably higher salaries offered by the film industry meant that some leading actors, such as Charles Laughton, were permanently lost to the British theatre, and many others began to make increasingly rare appearances on the stage, often at inflated salaries that caused an escalation of production costs.

But the main influence of the films was on the taste of a large section of the public. The British film was slow to develop a popular audience, and its progress as a marketable commodity was not helped by the tactics of American producers and distributors who were anxious to retain their hold on the lucrative British market. The sheer quantity of films provided by Hollywood, supplemented by massive advertising, acted as a brainwashing process. The Hollywood star was the only actor known to the masses who visited the cinema once or twice a week. Hollywood culture began to percolate the British way of life. Hollywood type of entertainment became the only type that was acceptable. Thus a divorce took place within society between cinemagoers and theatregoers from which the stage emerged poorer in the quantity of its audiences, though eventually richer in the quality of its products. Not until television robbed the films of their mass appeal was the cinema able to shake itself free from the domination of purely commercial interests and rediscover its individual art form.

6 1939–1946

(i) The social mood in wartime

To chronicle the social movement in the Second World War and its effect on
the theatre would be largely to repeat history – but not entirely so. Once
again theatres were closed and opened according to the fortunes of war. Once
again restrictions on travel, rationing and fuel shortages presented formidable
economic and administrative problems. Once again new plays of quality
almost ceased to be written. Once again the emphasis was on revivals and
light entertainment. Once again actors were called to the colours. But this
time the mood of the country was not jingoistic. Society was united in a
common cause, but society was now far more aware of what the real issues
were, and of the problems and needs of the nation. The day-to-day fortunes
of war were brought into the home; the leaders of the nation spoke directly
and frankly to the people; the workers explained their problems, and the
strategies of war were discussed. For this the BBC was largely responsible.
Victory was by no means certain, but the consequences and responsibilities
of victory, if it was achieved, were firmly faced. There could be no going back
to the past. Recovery would only be purchased at the price of hardship. A
new society would have to be built, and its foundations must be laid during
the war itself. It was a different war – a war of technology. Britain was no

longer a fortress secure within its moat while its troops fought amid the devastation of foreign lands. The Channel was no more than a ditch to be crossed by night and day by enemy air power, manned and unmanned. Britain was a battlefield in which civilians as well as the armed forces were in the front line. Devastation was spread through the length and breadth of the country. Aerial warfare and the threat of invasion entailed evacuation. Government departments, factories, women and children were dispersed from the cities into the country areas. Some theatres were destroyed, others commandeered for war purposes. Sadlers Wells was taken over. Drury Lane became the headquarters of the Entertainment National Service Association (ENSA), catering for the entertainment of the armed forces. The Old Vic was bombed, and its drama, opera and ballet companies were forced to find hospitality in Burnley, Lancashire. As in the First World War, civilian morale had to be maintained, but this could no longer be effectively done by the city theatres. There was a need for touring units, to bring not only theatre but also music and the other arts to remote evacuation centres and service camps. It was at this point of history, and only under the pressure of emergency, that the state acknowledged it had a role to play as patron of the theatre.

(ii) State patronage – CEMA

The principle of patronage for the arts, other than from private sources, had already been pioneered by the Pilgrim Trust and the Carnegie United Kingdom Trust. In 1939 the Council for the Encouragement of Music and the Arts (CEMA) was formed, whose aims were to fortify national morale, to spread the arts geographically and socially, and to provide employment for artists during wartime. Its finances were derived partly from the Pilgrim Trust and partly from the Board of Education; initially each contributed £25,000. In 1942 the Pilgrim Trust withdrew, and from then onwards provision for CEMA was the sole responsibility of the state. Tours were sent out either under its direct management or through the medium of existing managements – the Old Vic and Sadlers Wells being particularly active – to factories, service camps, hospitals, air-raid shelters, hostels and internment camps. Classical drama, ballet and opera were made familiar to a largely new audience. Grants increased rapidly as the service grew. At one time there were sixteen theatrical companies, including opera and ballet, circulating through the country. When the war came to an end, CEMA had clearly demonstrated that there was a continuing role to be fulfilled in making the theatre and the other arts more accessible to a wider section of the population; and in 1946 the Government decided to incorporate it under Royal Charter as the Arts Council of Great Britain, deriving its funds directly from the Treasury.

The cause of public subsidy for the theatre would have been arduous and protracted in peacetime. Not only would it have been difficult to persuade and reconcile the theatres themselves to a measure of centralized control, but there would have been strong opposition from commercial elements and considerable controversy in the press. The success of CEMA was mainly due to the fact that the theatre audience in the evacuation areas was largely a captive one; as a result a taste was created for the theatre – and especially for Shakespeare – that was to be the foundation of the future development of the provincial repertory movement, and the basis upon which the National Theatre was to be built. Had the live theatre not received government aid during the Second World War, which imposed far more severe conditions on the theatre and was more protracted than the First, it is likely that the greater part of the provincial theatre at least would have fallen victim to the competition of the cinema. It should not be forgotten, however, that there was another potent factor in forming the taste of the British public for the drama of the spoken word during the war: the radio.

(iii) The influence of radio drama

The influence exerted by radio drama on the public was largely due to the captive nature of the audience. To a public largely tied by the blackout to the home or the air-raid shelter, waiting anxiously for the news bulletin, the radio set was a necessity of life. Radio drama was able to reach millions who had never entered a live theatre. Once again the fact that the radio was a public service and not a commercial enterprise ensured the quality of its drama and the educational role it played in forming public taste. If the theatre suffered much from the effects of war, and was to feel those effects for many years afterwards, it might also be said that its survival and future pattern were largely due to the timely patronage it received from the new organs of public patronage: the state and the BBC.

7 1946–1956

(i) The aftermath of war

Victory brought with it neither an end to the restrictions of war nor a release from its anxieties. The economy of the country was dislocated, and there were shortages of food and materials. Victory had been purchased at the price of the horror of Hiroshima; and former allies confronted each other across the 'Iron Curtain', each armed with weapons of apocalyptic destruction. To many the immediate post-war years presented greater hardships and more acute tensions than the 'blood, sweat and tears' of the war itself.

But by the beginning of the fifties the country began to free itself from the after-effects of war. The Welfare State introduced a period of comparative affluence for the average citizen – if not for the wealthy. For a time the fundamental cracks in the social structure, created by the war, were papered over by a false sense of optimism, and a new reign conjured up visions of a second Elizabethan age. Under a Labour government unemployment was reduced to manageable proportions; slums were cleared; new universities, training colleges and polytechnics provided higher education for a vastly enlarged student population. The House of Lords opened its doors to life peers; while hereditary peers opened theirs to the public. Despite the 'cold' war – indeed partly because of it – a new spirit of internationalism arose.

Britain became aware that its future depended upon closer political and cultural relations with Europe. Higher wages enabled millions of Britons to travel abroad; while the country itself acquired a prosperous tourist trade. Sport, from football to table tennis, became a powerful medium of international exchange; jet planes and motorways brought more rapid communication between countries. The new spirit of internationalism was reflected in the theatre. Theatre companies travelled to the capitals of Europe, subsidized by the British Council; the Edinburgh Festival acted as a host to European opera, orchestras, ballet and, to a lesser extent, theatre companies. To his country-house opera theatre in Glyndebourne John Christie invited European conductors, directors and singers. Covent Garden Opera House, renamed the Royal Opera House, provided a permanent home for opera of international status as well as for the Sadlers Wells Ballet, now rechristened the Royal Ballet. Perhaps the most important international influence upon British theatre was the glittering array of international companies, including the influential Berliner Ensemble, brought to London from 1951 onwards by the private impresario Peter Daubeny. Daubeny's enterprise was to blossom into his World Theatre Seasons at the Aldwych Theatre in 1964.

As if to herald this new desire for international understanding, Britain opened its gates to the world in 1951 with the Festival of Britain. Centred in London, and celebrated in various provincial cities, the Festival was a symbol of Britain's cultural revival and of its new attitudes to the arts. In Liverpool colourful processions wound through the streets; in London architects, painters and sculptors indulged their fancies in gay pavilions, murals and fountains on the south bank of the Thames; in Battersea Park Cockneys and their visitors shed their inhibitions in a brightly coloured funfair; the Royal Festival Hall arose on the south bank of the Thames; and beside it, on 13 June 1951, Queen Elizabeth, deputizing for her husband King George VI, laid the foundation stone for the National Theatre.

(ii) Post-war theatre

The British theatre was slow to mirror the social changes brought about by the Welfare State. Commercial interests adopted a cautious approach to plays which departed radically from pre-war patterns. Between 1946 and 1956 British theatre was largely living on its past both in subject matter and in staging. Revivals were frequent: Shakespeare became increasingly popular;

the Old Vic's seasons at the New Theatre, enriched by the acting of Laurence Olivier and Ralph Richardson, drew packed audiences. The Stratford seasons, too, achieved national importance under the direction of Barry Jackson, Anthony Quayle and Glen Byam Shaw. But it was mainly to foreign drama that managers looked for new work. The period was characterized by a host of imports from the French and American stages. In 1955 there were fourteen American plays and musicals running in London. But it was not only the scarcity of British plays that haunted the dreams of theatre managers; two other phantoms arose – the competition of the subsidized theatre and television.

(iii) Problems of public patronage

At first the Arts Council, under Lord Keynes's chairmanship, pursued a dual policy. It endeavoured, on the one hand, to foster the repertory movement; on the other, to encourage the commercial managers to embark on plays of a 'partly educational' character. The definition was vague and led to increasing criticism. The main principle of the Council's support was based – as it still is – on non-profit-distributing organizations registered as public charities; but limited finances restricted direct subsidy to comparatively few enterprises. Subsidies were extended to such companies as the Old Vic and Sadlers Wells and a small number of provincial repertory theatres but were not provided for the commercial theatre. However, certain managements that were willing to form non-profit-distributing subsidiary companies were able, through a form of association with the Council, to gain exemption from entertainments tax. Exemption was in fact granted by the Board of Customs and Excise, but was, in practice, automatically extended to companies in association with the Council. This system led to a number of anomalies and to increasing hostility from those commercial managers who did not enjoy the privilege of association. It was felt, not without reason, that the Council favoured particular West End managements, and that not only was the label 'partly educational' open to question but the activities of the non-profit-distributing subsidiaries were indirectly benefiting the shareholders of the favoured companies. The matter came to a head in 1949 with the production by Tennent Productions Ltd of *A Streetcar Named Desire*. A Select Committee of the House of Commons investigated the position, and in 1950 the association between the Council and the commercial theatre ceased.

MR HENRY IRVING

1 Henry Irving as Mathias in *The Bells*

2 Beerbohm Tree in *Trilby*

3 Ellen Terry and Henry Irving in *King Lear*

4 Violet Vanbrugh and Beerbohm Tree in *Macbeth*

5 Ellen Terry as Lady Macbeth

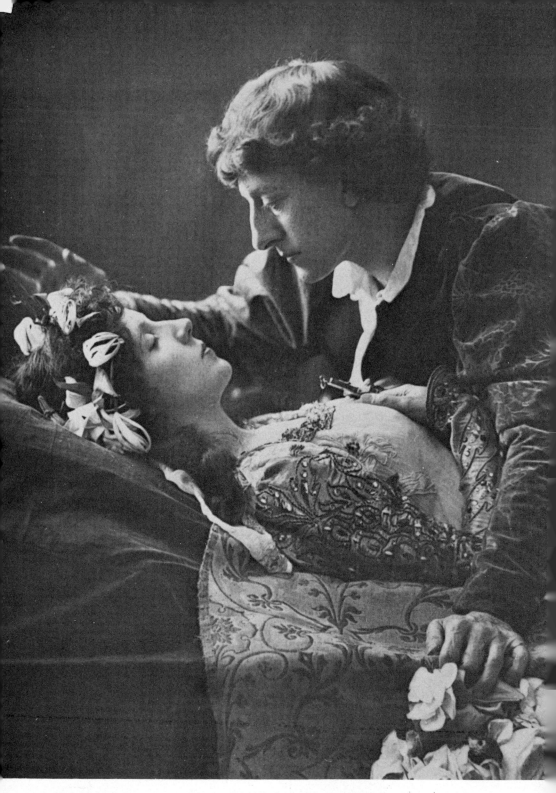

6 Mrs Patrick Campbell and Forbes Robertson as Romeo and Juliet

7 Mrs Patrick Campbell and George Alexander in
The Second Mrs Tanqueray

8 Wilson Barrett and Maud Jeffries in *The Sign of the
Cross*

9 The Haymarket Theatre, 1880, showing Bancroft's Picture Frame Stage

10 The Lyceum Theatre, mid-1890s

11 *Hindle Wakes* at the Gaiety, 1912

12 *Twelfth Night* at the Savoy, 1912

13 Dion Boucicault and Gerald du Maurier in *Raffles*

14 *The Beggar's Opera*, 1920

17 Paul Robeson and Peggy Ashcroft in *Othello*

18 John Gielgud in his first *Hamlet*

19 *Gammer Gurton's Needle*, 1933

20 *The Three Sisters*, Queen's Theatre, 1938

Meanwhile the popularity of the Old Vic seasons at the New Theatre revived hopes of establishing the National Theatre. A Joint Committee of the Old Vic and the Shakespeare Memorial National Theatre Committee was formed; and in 1949 Parliament agreed to contribute up to one million pounds towards the cost of a building on the South Bank of the Thames 'upon such terms and subject to such conditions as the Treasury think fit'.[1]

But the laying of the foundation stone in 1951 proved an idle gesture. It was clear that building costs would far exceed the Treasury contribution, and the annual subsidy required would be considerably more than Arts Council finances could provide. Pressing social needs, together with 'stop-and-go' economic policies, made any major increase in the funds available to the arts undesirable, and the Treasury had no desire to release the government contribution until the full costs of the building could be met. It was not until 1968 that the 'go ahead' was given for the building, by which time the costs had escalated enormously.

For a time commercial managers remained suspicious of what they regarded as unfair competition from the state. The Local Government Act (1948), which permitted local authorities to contribute up to 6*d*. (2½p) in the pound from the rates for the provision of entertainment, aroused suspicions of a state monopoly. If this provision had been fully implemented, local repertory theatres would have benefited by several million pounds; but since the provision was not mandatory its effect was minimal. By 1964 the average spending on the performing arts was about five per cent of what was authorized. In the provinces, too, it was feared – not without some justification – that the subsidization of repertory theatre would seriously affect the declining business of the touring theatres. Lack of adequate finance made it impossible for the Arts Council to assist the vast number of smaller repertory theatres which had sprung up since the war. Consequently its funds were concentrated on developing and strengthening those companies that were able to command a large enough public to run their plays for at least two weeks, thus permitting longer rehearsal periods and higher standards of performance. But a more potent competitor to the declining business of the commercial touring theatre was television.

[1] National Theatre Act, 1949.

8 1956–1968

(i) Television drama and its effect on the theatre

Television was introduced on the BBC services in 1936. Transmissions were closed down during the war and resumed in 1946. During its early years drama was largely borrowed from stage plays, presented with act intervals. It was not until Independent Television (ITV) began to spread its network in 1956 that television drama finally assumed its present form. With the advent of commercial television the number of licences rose steeply; by the end of the sixties 95 per cent of the population owned – or more frequently hire-purchased – a television set.

As the home-viewing public increased, so the theatregoing public declined. Weekly 'reps' began to disappear, and theatrical tours became increasingly uneconomic – with the result that, between 1956 and 1968, over eighty provincial touring theatres were forced to close down, and many others diversified their business to include films, Bingo and amateur theatre. The loss of the weekly theatregoing habit affected the social and economic aspects of the provincial theatre, though in many respects the results have been beneficial to its quality. Smaller audiences resulted in more discriminating theatregoers, better-quality plays and higher standards of presentation. While television cannot be credited with the improvement in the artistic quality of the provincial theatre, there are areas where its effect on the theatre in general has been directly beneficial – nowhere more so than in the stimulus it has given to playwrights.

Television and sound radio between them consume over 2000 dramatic items each year. Although this necessarily results in a percentage of indifferent material, John Arden, Samuel Beckett, David Mercer, John Mortimer, Harold Pinter, Tom Stoppard, Arnold Wesker and many others have found a new market and stimulus for their work. New writers of talent, who previously might have chosen to write novels, were encouraged by the opportunities and financial incentives of television to turn their attention to dramatic material. The journalistic nature of television has tended to result in plays based on current social problems; and the fact that many of the new writers have come from working-class backgrounds has opened the door to the presentation of genuine working-class drama. The regional constitution of ITV has made its companies particularly attentive to local speech and subject matter; thus it was largely under the auspices of the commercial network that the new television drama arose, in the form both of plays such as those presented between 1958 and 1962 by Armchair Theatre (ABC Television) and of serials, Granada's *Coronation Street* being the classic example.

While it would be difficult to prove that the new mechanical drama directly influenced stage plays, it certainly helped to condition theatre audiences more easily to accept changes in their social orientation. It could also be asserted that television has had its influence on theatrical production, if only because play directors, aware that the stage cannot compete with the visual realism of television, have been encouraged to use less illusionary methods of staging. Similar motives, too, have at least been partially responsible for closer relations between actor and audience in theatre architecture; though here the main factors have been changes in social attitudes. A society intent upon eliminating class distinctions, and with greater equality of wealth, no longer accepted the old divisions between gallery, pit, stalls, boxes, upper and dress circles.

Thus it can be said that while not solely, nor intentionally, responsible for the changes it has brought about, television has acted as a catalyst for the theatre: forcing it to find new ways of serving the public; providing a reservoir of new playwrights from which the theatre has been able to draw. If theatre audiences have been diminished by it, the small screen has provided drama to a vastly larger audience than ever patronized the theatre. Though quantity is not a measure of quality, it is a sobering thought that in 1960 many millions saw Harold Pinter's play *The Birthday Party* after its failure in the theatre; and it was a televised excerpt of *Look Back in Anger* that turned its failure into success, and rescued the Royal Court from an untimely demise.

(ii) Factors affecting the renaissance of British drama

It is frequently contended that the success of John Osborne's play, *Look Back in Anger*, at the Royal Court, opened the way for the rebirth of British drama. Without denying the considerable contribution of George Devine's inspired management of the Court, and the merits of Osborne's play, there were other factors – political, social, theatrical and (not least) financial – to make the year 1956 a turning point in British theatre.

Nineteen fifty-six was a crucial year for the growing feeling of social and political disenchantment among the new intellectuals of the under-thirties age group. The post-war Labour government had been overthrown without achieving the utopia of the Welfare State. Britain, shorn of its empire, was no longer a world power; yet it still strove to honour its world commitments, hanging on the coat-tails of the United States. The Hungarian revolt and the Suez disaster – both in 1956 – created a mood of disillusionment with the ideologies of the political Left on the one hand, and confirmed the bank-ruptcy of the Right on the other. The nation, and the individual, seemed to be no more than pawns in the hands of powers over which they had no con-trol. This breakdown in the confidence of the young in established political parties was matched by their revolt against the whole social structure. The sanctity of marriage, the taboos of sex, the values of family life, as well as the consolations of established religion, were more acutely questioned than ever before. For many of the new graduates of the universities the hopes of chang-ing society through democratic methods seemed futile. Educated to be more politically aware than their parents, their disenchantment took the form of cynicism and protest, to which expression was given in the novels of John Wain and Kingsley Amis. Osborne's play appeared at precisely the right moment of time to meet this mood of disillusioned youth. Its success – apart from its merits – was aided not only by television, to which allusion has already been made, but by its enthusiastic championship by Kenneth Tynan in *The Observer* and, as John Russell Taylor has pointed out,[1] by 'the whole publicity hullabaloo about angry young men' that ensued. Its importance to British playwriting in general was: first, that its success demonstrated to

[1] John Russell Taylor, *The Second Wave* (London, 1971), p. 9.

commercial and repertory managements that plays by unknown young play-wrights could be profitable 'show business'; and, second, that it focused attention on the Royal Court as a rallying point for a whole generation of young writers.

Social protest was, however, only one expression of the disillusioned young. There were some who, while sharing the cynicism of Kingsley Amis's Lucky Jim and Osborne's Jimmy Porter, saw no point in protest in a world where man's actions were senseless, absurd and useless. The production of Samuel Beckett's *Waiting for Godot* at the Arts Theatre in 1955, and its subsequent transfer to the West End – again enthusiastically championed by a theatre critic, Harold Hobson, in *The Sunday Times* – was to strike a responsive, if somewhat mystified, public mood.

In the same month and year (May 1956) that saw the opening of *Look Back in Anger* at the Royal Court, critical attention was focused on a second rally-ing point for the new generation of playgoers when Joan Littlewood's Theatre Workshop presented *The Quare Fellow* by the Irish dramatist, Brendan Behan, at the Theatre Royal, Stratford, E15. The successful transfer to the West End of Littlewood's productions of Behan's *The Hostage* (1958), Shelagh Delaney's *A Taste of Honey* (1958) and *Oh, What a Lovely War!* (1963) marked the final acceptance of the avant-garde drama by the estab-lished theatre – a typical example of British society's ability to absorb its revolutionary elements, and to profit by them.

Nineteen fifty-six was, also, the year in which the third revolutionary element invaded the British theatre. In August of that year the Berliner Ensemble paid its first visit to London. The influence of Brechtian techniques upon production, design and playwriting owed much to Kenneth Tynan's forcible and persistent advocacy in his articles and reviews. A major influence of Brechtian theatre, as publicized by Tynan, was that of a highly subsidized, large-scale ensemble company developing its own distinctive production style. The turning point for the formation of a major British ensemble came in 1961, when Peter Hall led the Royal Shakespeare Company to its second home at the Aldwych Theatre, thereby providing the opportunity for a com-pany to develop a production and acting style based on its 'house' dramatist – Shakespeare – in much the same way as the style of the Moscow Art Theatre was based on Chekhov, and that of the Berliner Ensemble on Brecht.

Journalism was not the only support of the new forms of drama; other literary influences played an increasingly vital part in public understanding of the changes that were taking place. Books about contemporary theatre be-came the stock-in-trade of many publishing houses: John Willett's *The*

Theatre of Bertold Brecht (1959), Martin Esslin's *The Theatre of the Absurd* (published in the USA in 1961 and in Britain in 1962), John Russell Taylor's *Anger and After* (1962), together with important contributions from the USA – Eric Bentley's *Theatre of Commitment* and Robert Brustein's *The Theatre of Revolt* (the former published in Britain in 1964; the latter in 1965). These are but a few examples of how closely literary analysis followed upon the new movements. New forms of theatre architecture, and relationships between actor and audience, were publicized in the books of Stephen Joseph and Richard Southern. Every aspect of theatre, both past and present, became a favourite thesis subject for university examination. An increasing number of theatre journals provided informed criticism of new plays and a forum for playwrights; while the paperback drama encouraged the performance of their plays throughout the professional and amateur theatre.

Theatre literature not only followed on the heels of performance; it also, in some cases, preceded it. This was true not only of the publication of plays but of analytical and critical literature. Peter Brook, in his preface to the English translation of Jan Kott's thought-provoking essays on Shakespeare,[1] acknowledged his debt to the author in formulating the ideas that led to his production of *King Lear*, with Paul Scofield, in 1962. The publication in 1958 of the English translation of Antonin Artaud's essays and letters, under the title of *The Theatre and its Double*, was to bear fruit in the same director's experiments in the shock techniques of Artaud's Theatre of Cruelty,[2] and of Brook's subsequent productions of *Marat/Sade* (1964) and *US* (1967). The latter production followed other precepts advocated by Artaud, including his call for improvisation and an anti-literary theatre.

Artaud's theories – shock techniques, assaults upon the complacency of the audience, the use of ritual and improvisation, together with his call for the abandonment of literary plays – were further developed by 'happenings'; a term first used by the American director, Allen Kaprow, in his publication *Something to Take Place: A Happening*. 'Happenings' were introduced with a flourish of publicity at an international theatre conference in Edinburgh in 1963; they were substantially a rebirth of the Dadaists' manifestations from the First World War. The visits of Jerzy Grotowski's Laboratory Theatre, with its emphasis on the physical training of the actor, and of Julian Beck's Living Theatre – the latter an example of an ensemble company dedicated to social and political revolution – drew wide publicity in the press and theatre journals.

[1] *Shakespeare our Contemporary* (London, 1964).
[2] 'Theatre of Cruelty' season, LAMDA Theatre, London, 1964.

Finally, a paramount factor stemming from the decline in the wealth of the private patron, together with the example of Continental subsidization of the arts, was the annual increase of government grants to the Arts Council. Between 1956 and 1968 theatre subsidies, excluding capital grants, rose from around £85,000 to £1,850,000. Increased subsidy meant greater opportunity for theatres to experiment – and, if necessary, to fail – with new plays. Special grants to theatres presenting new plays, bursaries to playwrights and financial provisions for dramatists attached to theatre companies provided concrete encouragement to writers to turn to the theatre for a livelihood.

(iii) Theatre as a social amenity

The flow of money into the arts brought about significant developments – many of them long overdue. In 1965 the appointment of a minister with special responsibility for the arts within the Department of Education and Science brought considerable benefits to the theatre. Ministerial pressure could now be exerted on local authorities to subsidize their local theatres, and to undertake responsibility for new buildings. The formation of regional arts associations has done much to complement, and give local impetus to, the work of the Arts Council. The study of drama in schools and universities, and its inclusion in the syllabus of teacher-training colleges – not merely in its literary but also in its physical form – has given greater impetus to theatre scholarship and provided a valuable educational addition to the curricula of primary and secondary schools. At the apex of this recognition of the theatre's role in society, and of its importance as a national asset, was the formation in 1962 of the National Theatre Company under the direction of Sir Laurence Olivier and temporarily housed in the Old Vic.

9 1968–1976

If 1956 can be held to be the turning point in British theatre, similar claims could be advanced for the year 1968. Two events in that year were to have far-reaching results: the abolition of the Lord Chamberlain's censorship of plays, and the student riots in Paris which gave rise to a new militancy among young people in Britain. In 1968, too, the Arts Council published its investigation into Theatre Today.

(i) The abolition of censorship

The sixties were years not only of violence but of changes in social attitudes to sexual expression: the removal of laws governing homosexuality; the descriptions of sex in books, newspapers and magazines; 'porno' shops, 'blue' films, strip clubs and 'the pill' had clearly made the censorship restrictions placed on the theatre untenable. Matters were brought to a head by the publicity surrounding the unsuccessful struggle of the Royal Court to reverse the Lord Chamberlain's ban on Edward Bond's play *Saved* in 1965. In 1967 a Joint Parliamentary Committee on Censorship advocated the abolition of the

Theatres Act (1843), which had placed responsibility for the licensing of theatres and plays in the hands of the Lord Chamberlain. In September of the following year effect was given to its recommendations by the Theatres Act (1968). From now on censorship of the stage was abolished; it was left to the normal process of law to provide the necessary protection of the public interest.

Inevitably there were fears that this would lead to a wholesale outbreak of obscenity, blasphemy and defamation of character. Theatre managers feared that leaving responsibility to the courts might well prove harsher than the recently more permissive attitude of the Lord Chamberlain's office. In fact, neither fear was justified. Certainly sexual deviations were openly expressed; the novelty of nudity – more especially male – was exploited to financial advantage in productions such as *Hair* (1968) and *Oh! Calcutta!* (1969). Exception could be taken to some of the more erotic productions, as well as to the tendency to introduce nudity into revivals irrespective of textual – or aesthetic – justification. But obscenity and pornography are not synonymous; the latter has always held a valid – if minor – place in the literary and visual arts; and any definition of obscenity is necessarily subjective and transitory. Defamation of character was considered to be adequately covered by the laws of libel; and the lifting of the ban on the presentation of the deity has perhaps done more to popularize religion than to offend religious scruples.

(ii) Political militancy in the theatre

The militancy that characterized the student demonstrations and 'sit-ins' from 1968 onwards extended to a wider section of young protestors than the left-wing revolutionaries of the universities movement. Its theatrical expression has taken the form of a whole series of left-wing, underground and 'fringe' theatre groups, holding a variety of political views. Political stimulus to this movement was given by the Vietnam war, which became a focal point for protest in Britain as well as in the USA. The removal of censorship also permitted greater licence in attacks on political personalities. Many of the groups adopted the methods of the proletcult and agitprop theatres of the Russian Revolution; while others followed in the footsteps of the Living Theatre in its assaults upon the audience. For some, the general tendency has been anti-professional and anti-literary – placing their emphasis on social, racial and political evils, rather than on technical accomplishment. But politics without technique can prove an inadequate cohesive force; and the life of those groups that relied solely on agitational methods has mostly been short. The groups, however, that have combined political and social commitment with genuine artistic and technical accomplishment, like the Freehold and 7.84 Companies, provide a relevant service to the community, and a valuable forum for the expression and clarification of public opinion.

All avant-garde theatre is eventually absorbed into the mainstream of theatre; but without its challenging and often aggressive criticism of social attitudes and political policies the theatre would stagnate. A live theatre is an expression of its age; and so long as violence and militancy continue to be part of social, industrial and political life they will be mirrored in 'the purpose of playing'.

While it would be foolhardy to prognosticate future events, the indications are that the upheavals of the fifties and sixties have accomplished their task of renewing, for the present at any rate, the life-blood of the British theatre: widening its means of expression to meet the challenge of the seventies; expanding its audiences beyond the middle-aged and middle-class; extending its activity beyond the confines of theatre buildings into the streets and pubs. Competition from the mechanical media has shorn the live theatre of its mass audience; but has strengthened, and will further strengthen, its social purpose. Its final recognition as a vital social amenity was expressed in the official opening of the National Theatre on 25 October 1976.

II (a) Actors and theatres 1880–1918

Kenneth Richards

1 Some theatrical trends

Reviewing the English theatrical scene about 1880, Henry James remarked that theatregoing in London had become all the fashion; it was to remain so until the outbreak of the First World War.[1] This was the great age of 'star' performers and, particularly, of the actor-managers: they consolidated the reawakened appeal of serious theatre to middle-class audiences, and some succeeded in bridging the gap between popular and select entertainment. In doing so they capitalized on a new demand for live theatre that was the outcome of complex social and economic factors: political stability and national self-assurance; the comparative prosperity of the numerically substantial middle and lower-middle classes; the changes that flowed from technological progress, like improved communications, better lighting and policing of the towns, and higher standards of safety and hygiene in streets and public buildings. Newspapers and journals gave performers and managements opportunities for national self-advertisement, and created and fed an appetite for information and gossip about theatre and theatre personalities. The very height of the theatre's prosperity coincided with the invention and development of cinematographic devices, and by the time of the First World War the

[1] Henry James, *The Scenic Art*, ed. Allan Wade (London, 1949), pp. 130 ff.

threat to theatre presented by moving pictures had become a real one.[1] But for most of the period large audiences eagerly sought diverse forms of live entertainment, and many performers and managements prospered, artistically and financially, in furnishing it.[2]

(i) Variety and musical stages

In brief space discussion here must be highly selective and will focus mainly on the London straight theatre and its actors. But the entertainment to which audiences flocked encompassed a wide range of theatrical genres. The most popular theatre of the period was almost certainly not provided by Irving or Tree, Wyndham or Alexander, but by the artists of the music halls and variety theatres, just as the most frequently attended type of drama, at least from the 1890s onwards, was probably musical comedy. Here we can do no more than indicate their important presence.

The turn of the century saw the apogee of music hall and the triumph of great popular entertainers like Dan Leno, Harry Champion, Vesta Tilley and Marie Lloyd. Throughout the period music hall can fairly be called the national theatre: London was its base but it had many and deep roots throughout the provinces, its great 'stars' toured and were household names, and perhaps more than any other form of entertainment music hall reflected the interests, attitudes and lifestyles of the majority. The popular arts of the music hall were of international scope and their heyday coincided with the ascendancy of realism and stage illusion in serious theatre, rather as the popular performance of the *commedia dell'arte*, 300 years before, had complemented that of the Cinquecento decorative, perspective stage. Close performer-and-spectator contact, and the combination in music-hall bills of diverse 'turns', not only drew a large working-class audience, as music hall proper evolved in mid-century from saloon entertainment, but from the 1880s gave some halls in the metropolis a bohemian appeal. This *fin de siècle* intellectual approval, part inspired by French cultural example, was quickly followed by the attempt of music-hall entrepreneurs to make variety fit for family audiences. The middle classes early accepted music-hall entertainers

[1] The 1870s and 1880s saw the invention of many devices for moving pictures, including the Praxinoscope, the Stroboscope, the Kinetoscope and the Bioscope. By the 1890s short films were being shown publicly.

[2] Though doubtless many in the lowest ranks of the profession benefited only marginally, whether in London or the provinces.

in winter pantomime, in London dominated by Drury Lane where Augustus Harris from 1879, and Arthur Collins from 1897, allowed spectacle and music-hall fare to supplant the old harlequinade. The trend to refinement in full variety entailed shedding the halls' reputation in the suburbs and provinces for overcrowding, vulgarity and dubious morals, and in London for being at best, like, for example, the Empire, the haunts of well-heeled, pleasure-seeking males. The Palace, first under Charles Morton, then Alfred Butt, from the mid-1890s became the paradigm of variety theatres; the Coliseum (1904) sported facilities including an elaborate revolve and a lift to the roof garden; the Palladium (1910) had a ladies' orchestra and a Palm Court tea room.[1] Of course, these were the fashionable and affluent extremes, and by comparison the majority of halls saw only modest change, though sufficient to bring complaint that respectability and higher entry charges were excluding traditional audiences. The final social accolade, a Royal Command Performance, was bestowed on variety at the Palace in 1912. But the fortunes of music hall began to decline with the challenge of cinema, gramophone and, later, radio, and its territory was increasingly usurped in the metropolis by a new theatrical kind, musical revue.

No single factor can account for the popularity of the lyric stage throughout this period, but in part it was a consequence of the success won by D'Oyly Carte opera. Established at the Savoy Theatre from 1881, Gilbert and Sullivan virtually cornered the market in *opera buffa* and gave a social standing to the light musical stage it had not enjoyed hitherto. Musical comedy as a distinct form was said to have been the 'happy inspiration' of George Edwardes at the Gaiety Theatre, who there and, later, at Daly's, in shows like *The Shop Girl* (1894), *The Geisha* (1896) and *A Country Girl* (1902), transformed burlesque with a recipe of colour, spectacle, dancers, showgirls and stylish dress.[2] Musical comedies and musical plays became staple fare at some theatres, and alternated with straight drama at others. Musical comedies assembled in London, toured the major provincial cities, and some impresarios, such as George Dance, made fortunes by travelling companies in the provinces. Musical comedy 'stars' – George Grossmith, Marie Studholme, Hayden Coffin, Gertie Millar, Seymour Hicks, and so on – became the cynosures of fashion, and the tunes of composers Sidney Jones, Paul Rubens and Frederick Norton were nationally familiar. Provision of 'books' became a highly sophisticated art as writers competed for winning novelties

[1] Raymond Mander and Joe Mitchenson, *The Theatres of London* (London, 1963), pp. 42–4, 128.
[2] John Hollingshead, '*Good Old Gaiety*' (1903), p. 72.

in plot, location and 'characterizations'. Exotic oriental settings were perennial favourites, from *The Geisha*, through *A Chinese Honeymoon* (Strand, 1901) and *Kismet* (Garrick, 1911), to the record-running *Chu Chin Chow* (His Majesty's, 1916). Musical revue, which emerged in the first decade of the century to rival music hall, was manifestly a hybrid form, taking elements from musical comedy and variety, and drawing on memories of burlesque, which had lingered at theatres like Toole's until the mid-1890s. By the outbreak of the First World War revue had displaced variety from theatres like the Alhambra, the Palace and the Empire. The war years brought a boom in escapist entertainment from which musical comedy and revue particularly profited.

The professional attitudes and concerns of actors and variety entertainers were generally distinct, and actors lagged behind variety entertainers in organizing themselves professionally: the Music Hall Artists' Association was formed in 1885 and the Variety Artists' Federation in 1906, and it was music-hall artists who called the first major strike in theatres.[1] But the growing popularity of musical comedy, musical spectacle and revue helped to blur boundaries never entirely clear. When the great home of burlesque and musical comedy, the Gaiety, was demolished in 1903, it was Irving who gave the farewell address. Players like Marie Tempest moved from lyric to straight theatre, and actors like Cyril Maude and Oscar Asche were accomplished in musical drama. Some entertainers crossed from the halls to musical comedy, like Little Tich for *Lord Tom Noddy* (1896), and of course revue absorbed variety talent. The theatre of the music halls and variety palaces in turn drew players from straight theatre: at first, as Albert Chevalier found, by providing more appropriate venues for their skills, later by offering 'star' actors powerful financial inducements to give playlets as part of variety bills. The economics of actors' and entertainers' theatre were to converge.

(ii) Changing theatres

With the decline of the old 'stock' company system, straight theatre was now dominated by the long run and two kinds of management: actor-management, and what the critic Clement Scott called lay management.[2] Scott's

---

[1] An Actors' Association was formed in 1891 and the Actors' Union in 1905, but neither was very effective: see A. Nicoll, *English Drama 1900–1930*, (Cambridge, 1973) for detailed discussion.

[2] Clement Scott, *The Drama of Yesterday and Today*, 2 vols (1899), Vol. II, pp. 406 ff.

preference tended to be for the latter which, its decisions determined by commercial rather than personal and artistic considerations, respected experience but was not loth to advance new talent. Certainly lay managers like Augustin Daly and Charles Frohman were more than mere profiteers; they had a knowledge of theatre and pride in the productions they mounted. But Scott wrote at a time when the actor-manager hegemony over serious theatre appeared unassailable, and its faults perhaps the more pronounced. The situation was to change. Musical theatre and music hall were very big business, and commercial managers and managements, controlling groups of London theatres and provincial networks, came increasingly to exert a powerful influence on, and control over, not only music hall and variety but straight theatre. The gradual decline of music hall encouraged syndicates to diversify. By the First World War 'show business' as a species of financial investment was firmly entrenched in many areas of theatrical entertainment. It was to bed itself in even deeper during the war years and by the early 1920s, with an influx of quick-profit speculators, had helped to force out the independent actor-manager and drive London theatre rents to a height which made production of untried drama a financial hazard.

At the beginning of the period this threat was already implicit in the formal changes being brought about in theatre, many of which emphasized opulence and comfort, and entailed ever greater monetary outlay. Important changes were initiated in 1880 when the Bancrofts took over the Haymarket, adjusted the proscenium to complete the full 'picture frame' stage, and (undeterred by a first-night demonstration) abolished the pit and introduced higher-priced stall seating. Although the pit remained a feature of theatres throughout the period, the new trend was towards orchestra and pit stalls. Electric lighting, first fully used at the Savoy in 1881, was not immediately welcomed by all: some actor-managers like Henry Irving retained the more mellow effect of gaslight, to the approval of those who found the harsh electric illumination destructive of stage illusion.[1] But the new lighting was gradually refined, and was later to contribute substantially to radical developments in the art of scenic design.[2] By the end of the century electricity was being used in most theatres. It improved heating, ventilation and front-of-house facilities, as it did the functioning of stage machinery, and as a means of lighting was not only cleaner but safer than gas, a prime consideration as

[1] Like Percy Fitzgerald, 'The True Principles of Stage Scenery', *The Playgoer*, ed. Dangerfield, II (April–September 1902), pp. 339–46.
[2] These and other changes are discussed in detail in A. Nicoll, *A History of Drama 1660–1900*, V (Cambridge, 1962) and George Rowell, *The Victorian Theatre* (Oxford, 1956).

safety regulations became increasingly stringent. The employment of fire curtains, adequate and carefully positioned water tanks and 'sprinklers', and the use of heat-resistant applications on woodwork, are measures of the increasing concern for safety, as is the attention given in new theatre design to the width and placing of gangways and ease of egress.

Many of these changes were furthered in the 1890s and Edwardian years by the construction of new and well-appointed theatres like Her Majesty's (1897), Wyndham's (1899), the New (1903), the Aldwych (1905) and the Queen's (1907). The cantilever system permitted projecting balconies unbuttressed by pillars, and the latest facilities for operation and convenience were incorporated. London theatres, one journal claimed, were 'temples of architectural art'. Not all agreed. Surveying British theatres of the last decades of the century, a contemporary authority, Edwin Sachs, thought they fell short of their Continental, and particularly their German, counterparts: British architects were notably superior only in the provision of drainage and lavatory facilities. Sachs's arguments were partisan: in his view the British theatre suffered from want of state subsidy and the domination of theatre building by commercial interests; a new theatre like Her Majesty's had to satisfy above all 'the requirements of the typical theatre speculator, who primarily demands the greatest accommodation in a limited space at as low a cost as possible'.[1] But in theatres designed by men like C. J. Phipps and W. R. G. Sprague, such constraints did not exclude taste and grandeur. Architectural styles in general tended to the eclectic, with a bias towards decoration that was internally and externally expressive of luxury and prestige. Professional adaptability was characteristic of many theatres, for they could expect to house different kinds of entertainment.

This proliferation of expensive new theatres, however, while a sign of the stage's prosperity, also helped to push up rents; and the need to renovate old theatres to compete with the taste for plush, as well as to satisfy safety regulations, made management increasingly costly. Although *The Theatre* in 1878 could still complain that pit and gallery audiences were crude, and included spectators who 'suck oranges and crack nuts and indulge in various habits not recognized in polite society', it was the deliberate policy of many managements to court sophisticated audiences and to give to theatregoing a sense of occasion.[2] Most new managers on assuming control reappointed the interiors of their theatres for elegance and refinement: Irving at the Lyceum had the interior painted 'sage green and turquoise blue' and introduced programmes

[1] *The Playgoer*, I (October 1901–March 1902), p. 78; Edwin O. Sachs, *Modern Opera Houses and Theatres*, 2nd ed., 3 vols (1897–8), Vol. I, p. 6, Vol. III, p. 122, p. 106, Vol. II, p. 35.
[2] *The Theatre*, NS, I (August 1878), p. 101.

printed in 'light chocolate ink' on buff paper; the Hare–Kendal management made the St James's, for their opening in 1879, 'the most tasteful [theatre] in the metropolis', the dress circle foyer hung with paintings by modern artists.[1] Provision of audience comforts took cognizance of class divisions: for Tree's new theatre, Her Majesty's, foyers and cloakrooms were designed to house five distinct social groups.[2] By the turn of the century *The Playgoer* could with some justice claim that London theatres were 'more numerous, more comfortable, and more elegant' than in any earlier period, and insist that 'there is nothing in the modern playhouse to which the most prudish person can take exception'.[3] The refinement of theatre was most noticeable in the inner London theatres like the St James's, the Garrick and Wyndham's, but this social movement at the centre necessarily made itself felt in suburban and provincial theatres. Perhaps little is more illustrative of the popularity theatre enjoyed than the great success of the matinée: some actor-managers like Charles Wyndham even took quick trains into the local provinces for afternoon stands. The matinée indicates, too, the extent to which women were becoming an important determinant of theatre policy, as, equally, do the attention devoted to theatre in women's magazines and the tendency for some theatre journals to provide women's pages devoted to cosmetics and fashion.[4]

By the end of the century serious theatre, at least in inner London and the major provincial towns, was socially respectable. In 1895 Irving became the first actor ever to be knighted, and in the following years knighthoods showered on actors and managers. But if this theatre had won social respectability, from some it had not won respect. To its critics royal approval of the lay and actor-manager systems seemed at best an endorsement of the worthy, the picturesque and the unchallenging. The hard-won social acceptance had proved a snare: established theatre had become merely Establishment theatre, and was too narrowly circumscribed by commercial imperatives. New practitioners and new audiences had emerged who demanded more of theatrical art than the systems seemed willing or able to give. A catalyst was the discovery in the 1880s and 1890s of the plays of Henrik Ibsen – noticed first in the writings of Edmund Gosse, then made available in William

[1] Austin Brereton, *The Life of Henry Irving*, 2 vols (London, 1908), Vol. I, p. 271; *Illustrated London News*, 11 October 1879.
[2] Richard Leacroft, *The Development of the English Playhouse* (London, 1973), discusses the theatre in detail.
[3] *The Playgoer*, I, p. 339, though it expressly excluded music halls. A House of Commons Select Committee Report in 1892 concluded that the character and tone of theatres and music halls in London was generally healthy.
[4] See *Queen* and *Playgoer and Society* as instances. Not all players welcomed the theatrical gossip of the journals: see Madge Kendal's lecture *The Drama* (1884), pp. 16–17.

Archer's translations, and finally given much-discussed theatre productions. Psychologically disturbing and socially challenging (Shaw lectured to the Fabians on 'Socialism in Ibsen'), although their symbolism bewildered, they clearly exposed the artificialities of fashionable quasi-naturalistic formula drama, and by so doing set new standards not only for dramatic writing but for realistic acting. Dissatisfaction with the theatrical status quo was further generated, albeit indirectly, by the visits of foreign acting companies like the Comédie-Française (1879), the Rotterdamers (1880), the Meiningen (1881), the Théâtre Libre (1889), Lugné-Poë's Théâtre de l'Œuvre (1895) and the Japanese troupe of Kawakami and Sada Yacco (1900).[1] Such visits encouraged the questioning of accepted British theatre values and furthered a mood of significant discovery: the Comédie-Française stimulated interest in disciplined training; the Meiningen productions influenced the mounting of crowd scenes; the Théâtre Libre prompted the growth in Britain of specialist minority theatres.[2]

Although the commercial theatre was not unresponsive to change, effectively for the first time in British theatre, as elsewhere in Europe, significant revolt against the mainstream came not from new forces at the centre but from practitioners, amateur and professional, working on, and making their impact from, the periphery. In the final decades of the century alternative theatre ventures were started, in London and the provinces, devoted in their various ways to experimenting in performance and staging, or to propagating classical and modern drama of intellectual quality and of supposedly limited audience appeal. They prepared the way for the development of the repertory movement in the early years of the new century, and pointed forward too to the formation across the length and breadth of the country of amateur acting clubs. It has rightly been urged that the work of these last should not be cavalierly dismissed; they helped shape a theatre-conscious public, and from them some young actors and actresses passed over to the professional stage.[3] Their growth, however, was perhaps not wholly rewarding, for they helped to increase the hold over theatre of 'naturalistic' acting.

[1] Perhaps equally important were visits like that of the French pantomime company which gave L'Enfant prodigue at the Prince of Wales's Theatre (1891) and impressed as an experiment in mime and movement. A. B. Walkley, Playhouse Impressions (1892), p. 220.
[2] See below, pp. 105 ff.
[3] Allardyce Nicoll, English Drama 1900–1930 (Cambridge, 1973), p. 80.

(iii) Acting

It is peculiarly difficult to generalize about acting in the period, for the art of acting was in a state of complete flux. In the 1880s a caustic critic of English acting, Henry James, set against it the schooled technique of the French, and complained that in England 'elocution and action, the interpretation of meanings, the representation of human feelings, have not been made the objects of serious study'.[1] The situation had not much altered more than twenty years later when Granville Barker virtually repeated James's strictures, and distinguished two root vices in English acting: that in which the actor exploited himself, and that in which he was exploited, to the detriment of his talent, by producer or dramatist in order to polish a play.[2] 'The art of acting,' complained Shaw, 'is half strangled by the professional tailor'; when free of the tailor, it was often at the mercy of the 'personality' performer.[3]

For much of the period acting was in a wide range of styles, more or less realistic. Some players, like Irving, Forbes-Robertson and Martin-Harvey, cultivated a poetic and heightened playing which, while it eschewed the extravagant flourishes of the grand style, none the less retained a bias to the rhetorical, and was at once familiar and elevated beyond the depiction of the everyday: measured, psychological, romantic acting. Yet this playing was fundamentally realistic, often striking for its careful and original accumulation of significant detail. So too was that of players as diverse as Beerbohm Tree, a versatile 'character' actor who relied heavily on the imaginative impulse of the moment, or Charles Wyndham, whose technical expertise accommodated as easily to drawing-room restraint as to the bravura demands of comic roles like Rover in O'Keeffe's *Wild Oats*. Other performers, such as John Hare, Madge Kendal, George Alexander and Charles Hawtrey, in their very individual ways, furthered the Bancroft manner of refined realism: a discreet and quasi-representational playing that was a meticulous reflection of bourgeois living. The acting of 'star' players inclined to the display of craft: exponents of heightened realism were overtly histrionic; practitioners of refined realism cultivated techniques which only part-concealed technique; ensemble playing in the *pièce bien faite* as much served the 'personality' performer as it served the play performed. More searchingly representational

[1] James, op. cit. p. 165.
[2] H. Granville Barker, 'Repertory Theatres', *New Quarterly*, II (1909), p. 498. Cf. Barker, *The Exemplary Theatre* (1922), p. 37.
[3] George Bernard Shaw, *Our Theatres in the Nineties*, 3 vols (London, 1931), Vol. II, p. 47. Cf. also Vol. III, p. 234.

was the 'strong' realism of the Ibsenites, who sought subtle psychological depth in character portrayal: approaches best seen in the work of actresses Janet Achurch and Elizabeth Robins. Champions of Ibsen and social drama, and pioneers of the repertory idea, fostered an ensemble playing that denied 'personality' dominance in acting in the name of a truer exploration of character and situation. For much of the period, in both practice and theory, there were complex frictions and yet tight interconnections between presentational and representational acting, between heightened, refined and 'strong' realism. But there was too a marked drift towards the exercise and approval of ever more 'naturalistic' acting. The term, of course, is incorrigibly relative, and in large measure plays determined styles. But 'naturalness' was the quality generally admired, whether in farce, melodrama, domestic comedy, costume drama or Shakespeare. By the turn of the century perhaps the dominant mode, though one with few major practitioners and eliciting little sympathy from the more discriminating critics, was what Granville Barker called 'crude, impersonative realism', thought by many to have jettisoned technique in its pursuit of the casual hesitancies of everyday speech and movement.[1] With the decline of melodrama under the impact of cinema, the new century brought the final demise of grand rhetorical acting and the virtual occupancy of the straight stage by an acting so 'naturalistic' that even the refined realism of many Bancroft-schooled players began to look artificial and dated.

Irving and Coquelin engaged in hot debate on the relationship between dramatic character and the emotional involvement of the actor; Dion Boucicault joined in, as did the Dutch actor, Louis Bouwmeester.[2] It fired William Archer to attempt a detailed investigation, which eventually led to his study *Masks or Faces?* (1888). But the debate itself was inconclusive. Some early acting handbooks retained respect for elocutionary skills and the formal classification of facial and bodily gestures according to 'fundamental rules'; other and later guides discountenanced elocution and attempts to formulate 'a technique of acting'.[3] Many schemes were piloted for acting schools, often

[1] *The Exemplary Theatre*, p. 155.

[2] For papers in the debate by Irving and Boucicault, see *Actors and Acting*, Publication of the Dramatic Museum of Columbia University (1926). There is an amusing discussion of the subject in *Dame Madge Kendal*, by herself (London, 1933), pp. 220 ff.

[3] G. Garcia, *The Actor's Art* (1888), p. 30; Louis Calvert, *Problems of the Actor* (n.d.), p. xvi. Percy Fitzgerald, *The Art of Acting* (1892), remarked the decline of 'formal *elocution*' and deplored 'the gross realism so popular in our day' (pp. 36, 73). J. A. Hammerton's *The Actor's Art* (1897) is a useful compendium of the views of leading players and reflects the wide variety of attitudes current on impersonation, presentation and representation.

in association with an equally much-aired issue, the desirability of establishing a national theatre.[1] The need for acting schools was felt to be a direct consequence of the old stock system's replacement by the long run. The virtues of both were fiercely defended. Some claimed that the decay of 'stock' had deprived young actors of a valuable provincial training ground, and had left them to the not obvious beneficence of the actor-managers. Others urged that the stock system had not schooled talent but rather wasted and exhausted it, for frequent changes of role encouraged casualness in preparation and performance, and bred overreliance on stage tricks and mannerisms.[2]

Early in the new century Granville Barker sought to discipline realistic acting, rejecting both the realism, heightened or refined, of the 'personality' performers, and the new 'impersonative realism'. Barker favoured a mode of playing that wedded acquired technique to a judicious calculation of the style and characterization of the particular play performed. Other reformers, like Gordon Craig and W. B. Yeats, radically questioned realism of any kind, and asserted the need for theatre (including acting) to be above all theatrical – intense, poetic, stylized – and to work by symbolic suggestion. The reaction against realism was in part furthered by the growth of photography and the cinema: filmed life had an apparent immediacy and fidelity to the real world with which theatre could not compete. But although the development of moving pictures spelt the end of some popular theatre genres, like spectacular sensation melodrama, it reinforced 'naturalism' in stage acting; for the cinema employed stage actors and fostered in audiences a preference for verisimilitude. The issue of appropriate acting styles in the theatre was not to be resolved but passed as a teasing legacy to later generations. What did not pass beyond the period, except in attenuated form, was that system of theatre organization which was the most characteristic feature of the late Victorian and Edwardian stage, actor-management.

[1] Tree founded the Academy of Dramatic Art (later RADA) in 1904; Benson and Elsie Fogerty began a school in 1906. Within a few years many schools were springing up in London and the provincial cities. See C. F. Armstrong, *The Actor's Companion* (1912).

[2] See, for example, W. Davenport Adams, ' "Stock" versus "Star" Companies', *The Theatre*, NS, I (1 November 1878). Another consequence of the decline of 'stock' was the growth of scenic factories supplying London and provincial theatres, and the gradual elimination of the old resident scenic artists: W. J. Lawrence, 'Scenery on Tour', *The Magazine of Art* (November 1895–October 1896), p. 478; and William Telbin, 'The Painting of Scenery', ibid. (November 1888–October 1889), p. 200.

2 The heyday of the actor-manager

According to Clement Scott, London in the late seventies 'began to rain actor-managers new and old', as many were enticed by the promise of artistic independence and financial success to form their own companies.[1] Yet 1880 must not be taken as an obvious *terminus a quo*. Earlier, Charles Kean with Shakespeare at the Princess's, and even more the Bancrofts with 'well-made' plays at the Prince of Wales's, had given signal direction to actor-management by meticulous attention to detail in production, and to quality, elegance and refinement in playhouse organization. They strengthened, too, the notion that an actor-manager working in his own theatre, by choice of play, kind of production and interpretation of lead role, should evolve a distinctive house style. Again, the earlier decline of stock, and the consequent re-organization of provincial theatre, made later touring an important factor in the economic stability of London-based, actor-managed companies. In acting and management there were many continuities. The Bancrofts, triumphant in the late sixties and seventies, achieved the summit of their reputation and prosperity at the Haymarket between 1880 and 1885. The structure of Irving's repertoire was basically fashioned in the seventies. Wyndham, Hare and the Kendals were secure in management before 1880. If the period under

[1] Clement Scott, *The Drama of Yesterday and Today*, Vol. II, p. 371.

review is in any way singular, it is for the sheer quantity and variety of actor-management undertaken.

An actor-manager started, said Bram Stoker, 'with one great attraction – his own reputation with the great public'.[1] He had to capture a following and hold it against his competitors, invariably carrying prime responsibility in his own performance for a production's success or failure. He was inescapably a 'star', and a prisoner of his box-office appeal. Running a company, mounting new plays and satisfying public taste for spectacle was costly and the risk of financial loss was great. Some actor-managers, like the Bancrofts, made substantial fortunes and retired early. Others, like Wyndham and Tree, built expensive theatres from their profits. But most had to keep a close season-by-season watch on returns. Irving continued playing against illness into old age; a predecessor of Alexander at the St James's, Rutland Barrington, went bankrupt in management; touring in the provinces Constance Benson met a melancholy 'super' who had once commanded companies.[2] Actor-management was an artistic temptation but a commercial gamble. Economics and public image perforce dictated repertoire. Hence the actor-manager's apparent predilection for classics, past successes and formula plays which reiterated his house style; and his understandable, if unfortunate, reluctance enthusiastically to champion untried, controversial or 'intellectual' drama – notoriously Ibsen, Strindberg or early Shaw. For some critics the system appeared to license egotism and to subordinate artistic concerns to the profit motive. Certainly during this period of his ascendancy the actor-manager was British theatre's epitome of nineteenth-century artistic individualism and *laissez-faire* economics.

(i) Henry Irving at the Lyceum

English theatre in the final decades of the nineteenth century was as much dominated by the personality of one actor, Henry Irving (1838–1905), as in the second and third decades it had been by the personality of Edmund Kean. Irving's achievement lay in effecting a subtle fusion of outstanding performance skills with meticulous attention to the multiple details that composed the moving stage pictures in which he appeared. His influence was extensive both as actor and as stage manager.

[1] Bram Stoker, 'Actor Managers', *The Nineteenth Century* (June 1890), p. 1045.
[2] Constance Benson, *Mainly Players* (London, 1926), pp. 38 ff.

Born Henry Brodribb, on joining a professional company at Sunderland in 1856 he assumed the stage name of Irving, and for the next ten years learned his craft in provincial theatres, a 'probation' he considered 'the potential cause of any later acting success'.[1] Boucicault's *The Two Lives of Mary Leigh*, retitled *Hunted Down*, carried him permanently to London, and by the late 1860s he had developed a strong line in callous but engaging villains, had acquired something of a reputation as 'a clever character actor', and was noted for his playing in light comedy roles, particularly Digby Grant in Albery's *Two Roses* (1870).[2] But it was only when he joined the company of the American manager H. L. Bateman at the Lyceum Theatre that his signal abilities became apparent. He persuaded the manager to let him put on, under his own stage management, Leopold Lewis's adaptation of a French play, *Le Juif polonais*. Entitled *The Bells*, it opened on 25 November 1871; his triumph in this play, like Kean's in *The Merchant of Venice*, has become part of theatrical history. Irving's portrayal of Mathias, the respectable burgomaster racked by guilty conscience for his murder in earlier and poorer days of a rich Jew, far surpassed anything he had done before; few 'were aware that he possessed so much undeveloped power, and would be capable in such a character, of succeeding so well'.[3] *The Bells* was predominantly an actor's vehicle, and the lead role gave Irving opportunity to blend certain lineaments of the villain type with his talent for acting rounded, deeply studied character parts. It made Irving the most discussed actor in London, and he confirmed his success the following year in W. G. Wills's *King Charles the First*. In 1873 he challenged comparison with Macready and Phelps in a Lyceum revival of *Richelieu*, and in 1874 essayed the definitive test, Hamlet.

His interpretation was unfamiliar. Opening in low key, at first it baffled, but gradually the first-night audience attuned itself to the actor's purpose: what Irving offered was a complete reconsideration of Hamlet as scholar, gentleman and artist, a man who 'thinks aloud'.[4] Although not all were persuaded, for the majority the performance confirmed Irving as the leading

[1] Article by H. J. W. Dam, based on conversations with Irving, in *The Playgoer*, I (October 1901–March 1902), p. 70.

[2] Austin Brereton, *The Life of Henry Irving*, Vol. I, p. 40; Clement Scott, *The Drama of Yesterday and Today*, Vol. II, p. 49.

[3] Clement Scott, *From 'The Bells' to 'King Arthur'* (1897), p. 5.

[4] Scott (ibid. p. 62), arguing that Irving's Hamlet was that pictured by Goethe, Hazlitt and Taine. The response of the first-night audience to Irving's Hamlet has been described in detail by many writers; see particularly Laurence Irving, *Henry Irving* (London, 1951), pp. 242–9, and Scott, *From 'The Bells'*, pp. 59–67.

actor of his generation: in its rejection of 'point'-making and traditional 'business', and in Irving's 'thoroughly colloquial manner of speaking', familiar delivery of the soliloquies, and emphasis on unity of conception from scene to scene, it was considered by some to be 'revolutionary'.[1] *Hamlet*, however, was followed by two productions which were by no means unqualified successes, *Macbeth* (1875) and *Othello* (1876). The former restored much of the original text and removed Locke's music, but Irving's emphasis on Macbeth's psychology 'enshrouded the character' in a 'poetic, metaphysical glamour' that alienated the older school of critics and audiences;[2] *Othello*, inevitably inviting comparison with that of Tommaso Salvini which had electrified London audiences less than a year before, was ultimately beyond Irving's physical and vocal means. But if these roles proved a slight check to his progress, they were amply countered by the enthusiastic reception accorded his Richard III in 1877. In the same year he expanded his popular repertoire by creating Dubosc and Lesurques in a revival of the melodrama *The Lyons Mail*, and added another of his staple plays in 1878, the Boucicault–Delavigne *Louis XI*: his portrait of the ageing and irascible French monarch was considered by many to contain much of his finest stage work.[3]

In 1878 Irving acquired the lease of the Lyceum from Bateman's widow and embarked on actor-management. The theatre was refurbished, with new seats in the stalls and backing provided for those in the pit and gallery; charges for the use of cloakrooms and for programmes were abolished; the auditorium was tastefully redecorated. Among new recruits to the company was Ellen Terry, who was to remain Irving's leading lady throughout his personal management. Under him the Lyceum became the centre of theatrical art in London. Part of his success there lay in his ability to bridge the gulf between popular and select audiences by supplying drama of distinction, spectacle and excitement. When Irving finally relinquished control at the end of the century J. T. Grein echoed the common view in lamenting the passing of a theatre that 'was the embodiment of all that is refined, sumptuous and noble in English histrionic art'.[4] The Lyceum achieved this with a repertoire that alternated quality melodrama, romantic verse plays providing opportunity for elegant scenic display, and carefully prepared revivals of Shakespeare. In effect Irving's repertoire was the repertoire of Frédéric Lemaître,

[1] *The Times*, 2 November 1874; *Illustrated London News*, 7 November 1874; *The Athenaeum*, 7 November 1874.
[2] *The Playgoer*, I, p. 73.
[3] One admirer was Henry James, *The Scenic Art*, p. 113.
[4] J. T. Grein, *Dramatic Criticism* (1899), p. 260.

transmitted through and augmented by that of Charles Kean, supplemented by a handful of carefully chosen contemporary plays suited to sumptuous mounting, and given distinctive stamp by his own histrionic personality and flair for stage management.[1] But it was also a programme that was to irritate the younger critics committed to new developments in contemporary drama, like A. B. Walkley and Bernard Shaw, just as it did critics such as Henry James who deplored a drama that was often thematically and verbally trivial; and it was to blind Irving himself to the theatrical and artistic potential and quality of much modern drama, particularly Ibsen. Yet as George Rowell has perceptively said, most of the 'new' drama 'would have afforded no scope whatever for [Irving's] particular gift of theatrical illusion'.[2] Again, by the time Ibsen's drama reached England, effectively in the late 1880s, the pattern of Irving's repertoire was too firmly settled to permit of drastic change. Attuned as he was to the Lyceum audience's taste and response, it is hard to fault his calculation that Ibsen was beyond the Lyceum meridian. Part of Irving's genius lay in his recognition of just what it was that he could do consummately well.

Here it is possible to make only passing mention of some of the finest Irving productions and roles during the period of his Lyceum management. The kinds of drama with which he had established his reputation in the 1870s recur: many of the plays in which he had performed under the Batemans became staples of the theatre under his own control, and some of them (like *The Bells* and *The Lyons Mail*) were his most popular and lucrative vehicles; of the eleven Shakespeare plays he presented during his management, four were revivals from the Bateman era.[3] Irving's roles were many and wide-ranging: they included later and more mature revivals of Mathias, Louis XI, Hamlet, Macbeth and Richard III; among the Shakespearian roles he added were highly original and inventive impersonations of Shylock (1879), Iago (1881), Benedick (1882) and Malvolio (1884), a dignified, austere Wolsey (1892), a Romeo (1882) rather too much the restrained gentleman, and a Lear (1892) magnificent in its conception and moving in many of its details but which he did not have quite the power to sustain;[4] other parts

---

[1] A. B. Walkley, *Playhouse Impressions*, characterized Irving as 'a flamboyant, a romantic in the grand style, drums beating and colours flying' (p. 257).

[2] George Rowell, *The Victorian Theatre* (Oxford, 1956), p. 101.

[3] *Hamlet, Macbeth, Othello* and *Richard III*, though all in new and richer productions. *Coriolanus* was done under the management of the Lyceum Ltd.

[4] Although Irving's Lear was by no means as inadequate as Henry Arthur Jones's description suggests – 'slow, laboured, mannered, uninspired, screechy, forcible-feeble': *The Shadow of Henry Irving* (1931; repr. New York, 1969), p. 54.

included the love-wan and revenge-bound dei Franchis in *The Corsican Brothers* (1880), the title-part comic villain of *Robert Macaire* (1883), Goethe's malicious, limping demon Mephistopheles in Wills's adaptation of *Faust* (1885), Tennyson's *Becket* (1893) and Comyns Carr's *King Arthur* (1895).[1] The repertoire stood Irving in good stead to the end of his life. But the expense of theatre and productions was ultimately defeating. In 1898 he was forced to sell out to a consortium, although he continued to act at the Lyceum. In 1902 the theatre was unable to meet the crippling cost of implementing LCC fire regulations, and Irving's long association with the Lyceum came to an end.

Irving's ascendancy as actor in the 1870s was controversial, and although few doubted in the final analysis that he was 'on a wholly different level from almost all his contemporaries' he remained a controversial figure throughout his career.[2] Early criticism was directed particularly at his innovatory style.[3] Later criticism was motivated by complex factors and was aimed as much at Irving the actor-manager as at Irving the player. Criticism of his acting attacked his stage movement and diction: an apparently awkward, jerky gait, with a tendency to stomp, and a pronunciation that drawled and distorted vowels. For William Poel, Irving's physical and vocal limitations made it impossible for him to do justice to many parts, a view rather shared by Henry Arthur Jones and William Archer. But for other commentators, both early and late, these idiosyncrasies were assets rather than defects. It was noted of his 1874 Hamlet that the interpretation was helped by 'little ineffaceable peculiarities which, while not inconsistent with the character, give the representation of it a stamp of personal individuality'; Gordon Craig, writing much later, thought Irving's mannerisms an integral part of his performing technique – 'measured, rhythmic, planned', his walk 'was a whole language', his movement and speech a calculated histrionic dance and song fundamental to his stage *persona*.[4]

Idiosyncrasies apart, throughout his career Irving's voice betrayed him in vocally taxing roles. In the storm scene in *King Lear* 'the explosion of his

[1] For details, see Laurence Irving, op. cit.
[2] *The Times*, 9 March 1882.
[3] 'Many are disposed to encourage him in the formation of a new style and the founding of a new school of acting,' dyspeptically complained the critic of *The Illustrated London News*, 7 November 1874. See also Edward R. Russell, *Irving as Hamlet* (1875), p. 44. Ellen Terry described his limitations at this period: 'He could not speak, he could not walk, he could not *look*,' *The Story of My Life* (London, 1908), p. 74.
[4] William Poel, *Monthly Letters* (London, 1929), p. 3; Edward R. Russell, op. cit. p. 4; Edward Gordon Craig, *Henry Irving* (London, 1930), pp. 78, 71.

wrath' was 'almost too great for his powers of enunciation'; when he acted Othello for a second time in 1881, attempting to avoid rant he fell into artificial 'drawling' and 'doled out his words with a sort of sepulchral monotony of effect'. A tendency to rant in powerful emotional passages marred parts of his 1879 Shylock, and one critic averred that no actor could 'tear a passion into such indistinguishable tatters as Mr Irving'.[1] But Irving's performing strengths far outweighed his weaknesses.[2] Most agreed he was outstanding in pantomimic roles. In *The Bells* his performance was an extraordinary *tour de force*. From the moment he made his brisk first entrance, flinging off 'a coat encumbered with snow', he riveted attention. Recalling a later performance, Craig graphically described the way Irving established an acute tension in this opening scene with the most casual actions: 'It was, in every gesture, every half move, in the play of his shoulders, legs, head, and arms, mesmeric in the highest degree.'[3] Irving's playing of Mathias was essentially physical, and exhibited the range and quality of his technique: his mastery of pause, gesture and facial expression; the way he could effect sudden transitions – from dreamy remoteness, to an outward display of ease that barely concealed inner turmoil, to sudden fierce outbursts of terror and despair. The most powerful scene was the third-act 'dream sequence', where the terrified Mathias defies his court accusers but finally, under mesmeric influence, confesses his guilt: it was played by Irving with such energy as to create a mood of horror 'painful' in its intensity.[4] Another masterpiece of physical playing was the way in which he acted out the description of the murder in *Eugene Aram* (1873), conjuring up so powerful a phantom to his mind's eye that in movement, gesture and facial expression he re-enacted the crime in all its violence and horror, and fell crouched over the imaginary corpse.[5]

Irving's genius for expressive facial play dominated a performance: 'no one on our stage can express the passions of the mind in the face with more striking effect'. His acute sense of the pictorially vivid enabled him instinctively to create memorable byplay and attitudes: his Iago nervously played with hair, dagger, moustache and ornaments on his girdle as he

[1] *The Times*, 11 November 1892; *The World*, 18 May 1881; *The Times*, 3 November 1879. Irving was 'hampered in the vehemence of passion', said Ellen Terry, op. cit. p. 160.
[2] See, for example, Edwin Drew, *Henry Irving, On and Off the Stage* (1889); W. H. Pollock, *Impressions Of Henry Irving* (1908), and other contemporary studies.
[3] *The Times*, 28 November 1871; Craig, op. cit. p. 58.
[4] *The Times*, 28 November 1871.
[5] Scott, *From 'The Bells'*, p. 32. Irving, like another master of melodrama, Charles Dickens, was fascinated by crime, and like the novelist attended the law courts to study the psychology and physiognomy of criminals.

manœuvred for ascendancy over Othello; the distraught bewilderment of his Lear was conveyed 'by a trick of dishevelling his hair with his hand'; the noble calmness of his preparation for martyrdom in *Becket*, 'so exquisitely tender, so absolutely beautiful', was brought to climax in a death scene 'grotesque' and 'terribly realistic'; the submission to defeat and death of his Richard III eschewed all customary melodramatic writhings and was conveyed in a single gesture – 'passionately tearing his gauntlet from his stiffening fingers, he flings it defiantly at the conqueror's feet'.[1] Numerous similar instances could be given of 'business', tableau and interpretation which made an indelible impression on his contemporaries. But these were not merely isolated moments or self-contained stage images; they were integral parts of a controlled interpretation. For what characterized Irving's acting was a concern for the organic unity of a role. We have noted this in his 1874 Hamlet; it was equally a feature of his Malvolio ten years later. Traditional buffooneries were abandoned. This Malvolio was a 'tragic comedian', 'grim and fantastic rather than humorous', 'an ascetic Puritan, sober and quaint in garb, and, moreover, aged in appearance', no butt for practical jokes. Malvolio's confinement was staged, and in a dark cell 'chained as a madman' Irving shed comedy and 'rose to tragic dignity and passion'. For many, however, the reading was too much *comédie noire*, a Malvolio who was second cousin to Shylock and brought 'the destructive inroad of reality on the world of romance'.[2]

Irving's fidelity to authorial conception was at times questioned. Shaw protested that he adapted characters to his own personality and plays to his own house style: his Shylock was 'not "the Jew that Shakespear drew", but the one he ought to have drawn if he had been up to the Lyceum mark'.[3] There was justification for such complaint, although critics were not always prepared to acknowledge how often Irving created drama from the inherently undramatic, as he did with most of the contemporary verse plays he staged.

Not only a great actor, Irving was also a master of *mise en scène*. Of course

---

[1] *The Times*, 3 November 1879; *The Athenaeum*, 7 May 1881; *The Times*, 11 November 1892; Scott, *From 'The Bells'*, p. 356; *The Times*, 7 February 1893; Grein, op. cit. p. 187.

[2] *Illustrated London News*, 12 July 1884; *The Times*, 9 July 1884; *The Athenaeum*, 12 July 1884; *The World*, 16 July 1884. A short account of Irving as actor will tend to focus on his serious roles, but should not conceal his brilliance in comedy. Jingle, in an adaptation from *Pickwick Papers*, was one of his most popular parts: *Playgoers' Magazine*, reviewing his career in 1888, particularly remarked his 'delightfully quaint and delicate sense of humour', I, 1, p. 4.

[3] Shaw, *Our Theatres in the Nineties*, Vol. I, p. 286. Of Irving's Philip II Ellen Terry said, 'Tennyson never suggested half what Henry Irving did.' Ellen Terry, op. cit. p. 123.

he was not a director in the modern sense of that word; he stage-managed with great patience, energy and care, and imposed upon his productions a distinct unity of tone, but he did so, as Craig remarked, 'for the sake of one actor, himself'.[1] This was understandable: he was the main Lyceum attraction. The 'personality' actor needed to be seen to the best advantage, hence the importance of presentational details. Ellen Terry has described Irving's working methods: he studied a play in depth for some three months, read it entire to the company, analysed individual parts and character relationships, and in rehearsal explored the most minute details of interpretation, grouping and performance. As the scene painter Harker noted, 'every gesture had to be just right; every word and every inflection perfect'.[2] Sets and costumes too had to be appropriate to the characters in colours, shapes and quality. Equally important were tonal and spatial relationships within the proscenium frame. The finest stage presentations at the Lyceum advanced a series of beautifully composed stage pictures to which spectacular décor and the movement and groupings of the actors all contributed: Irving stage-managed to achieve the consistently picturesque. Specially composed music and careful lighting completed the effects. Irving was the first stage-manager regularly to lower the house lights during performance, and the stage itself was often 'barely and vaguely lighted' to establish a mood that complemented the romantic and mysterious quality characteristic of Irving's personality and performance.[3]

In 1882 *The Athenaeum* complained that 'a Shakespeare revival has come to mean a pageant'. The occasion of the complaint was Irving's *Romeo and Juliet*. Irving himself demurred, defending the practice as being what Shakespeare would have done 'had his own opportunities been brought up to the level of our time'.[4] It is said that his conversion to spectacular production was gradual. Certainly economic exigencies at the Lyceum under the Batemans restricted show: *Hamlet* was reputedly mounted on a budget of £100. Yet from the outset of his personal management Irving moved quickly towards elaborate and expensive décor, and plays like *The Merchant of Venice* and *The Corsican Brothers* were richly set out. But perhaps the crucial turning point came with *The Cup*, sumptuous costumes and scenery helping to carry Tennyson's rather static tragedy. *Romeo and Juliet* established the approach

[1] Craig, op. cit. p. 87.
[2] Ellen Terry, op. cit. pp. 167 ff.; Joseph Harker, *Studio and Stage* (London, 1924), p. 125.
[3] Rowell, op. cit. p. 96; Jones op. cit. p. 81. Irving's scene painter William Telbin considered lighting 'the last and most important touch to the picture – its very life', 'The Painting of Scenery', *The Magazine of Art* (November 1888–October 1889), p. 200.
[4] *The Athenaeum*, 11 March 1882; *The Times*, 9 March 1882.

for Shakespeare: said to have cost more than £6000 and with 'a prodigal wealth about the whole arrangements', the 'almost unprecedentedly beautiful dioramic effects' evoked the rich, pulsating atmosphere of an Italian city. Seven months later in *Much Ado* the action was 'almost overweighted with [Italianate] upholstery and wardrobe'.[1] A production aesthetic was now confirmed, and it characterized the later Irving presentations, both new plays and major revivals. Many of the leading scene painters of the age, such as William Telbin, Hawes Craven and Joseph Harker, were employed at the Lyceum, and Irving recruited fashionable artists like Alma-Tadema and sought advice and contributions from architects and scholars.

Such an approach had undeniable audience appeal: 'the sensuous, plastic, pictorial side of Shakespeare had never been seen before he showed it'.[2] But by some it was hotly contested. Shaw brooded on what Irving would have to say in the other world when confronted by 'Shakespear whom he has mutilated, Goethe whom he has travestied'.[3] Irving's keen sense of what would appeal brought him both a fashionable and a popular following, but at times he allowed this too determinedly to condition his choice and approach: in his production of *Faust* he ruthlessly cut the 'philosophy' for fear that the audience would yawn and leave. He was justified in concluding that the 'new' drama was not his *métier*, but on occasions aggravated hostility by his apparent conservatism. He reportedly declared that Ibsen had had no 'permanent effect on the theatre', was disconcerted by Janet Achurch in *A Doll's House*, supported the censorship of the Lord Chamberlain's office and considered Bernard Shaw 'disrespectful to dignitaries'.[4] But for two decades, although his Shakespearian interpretations were much questioned, none could seriously dispute that he was the greatest English actor-manager.

Irving's early acting style was considered 'naturalistic'. One critic recalled his first London success, in *Hunted Down*, as presaging 'the early dawn of strong, natural acting in drama'.[5] But with Irving this slippery term 'naturalistic' is particularly elusive. 'Naturalism' was for Irving a reduction of the art

[1] Brereton, op. cit. Vol. I, p. 160; *Illustrated London News*, 18 March 1882; *The Times*, 12 October 1882. Archaeological accuracy was a feature of some Lyceum staging: thus Nuremberg was scoured for props to dress *Faust* (Terry, op. cit. p. 241), and 'authorities' were sought in the British and South Kensington Museums for the sets and costumes for *Macbeth*, M. H. Spielmann, 'A Shakespeare Revival: "Macbeth" ', *The Magazine of Art* (November 1888–October 1889), p. 98.
[2] Walkley, op. cit. p. 260.
[3] Shaw, op. cit. Vol. I, pp. 15, 288.
[4] Byron Shaffer, Jr, 'Henry Irving's Theories of Drama', *Ohio State University Theatre Collection Bulletin*, No. 15 (1968), pp. 23, 31; Laurence Irving, op. cit. pp. 535, 546, 607.
[5] Scott, *Drama of Yesterday*, Vol. II, p. 4.

of acting: he was 'essentially artificial in distinction to being merely natural'.[1] Nor can he adequately be called a transitional figure between the old and the new – the term is too confining. The composition of his staple non-Shakespearian repertoire is instructive: he had a predilection for the fine artificialities and theatrical extravagances of early and mid-nineteenth-century melodrama and romantic historical verse drama. Irving's achievement was to shape a new style for traditional material, and one peculiarly hard to define: a late romantic 'idealization' that evoked a mood of mystery and wonder, yet was imbued with a dense, realistic immediacy.[2] The style encompassed both his own performance and the total setting-out of a play, all those elements which made up the stage world in which he was the chief inhabitant.

Inhabitant with him was Ellen Terry (1847–1928), and her career is inextricably bound up with that of the Lyceum's actor-manager. Her playing almost uniformly exhibited a charm and spontaneity of which the age approved, yet for all that has been written about it her qualities remain curiously elusive. She had a particular talent for pathos, a feature of her Camma in Tennyson's *The Cup*; grace, delicacy and wit marked her playing of Olivia in the play of that name, adapted from *The Vicar of Wakefield* and one of her most popular pieces. She was at her best, said Bram Stoker, in plays 'abounding in life', unequalled in parts like Beatrice in *Much Ado*; certainly it was in Lyceum comedy that she came into her own.[3] Her Viola in *Twelfth Night* had 'the archness, the *espièglerie*, and the vivacity of a young girl'. Her Portia in *The Merchant of Venice* 'was full of the most delightful touches of womanly wit, grace and feeling'; a more mature interpretation than when she had first played the role in 1875 at the Prince of Wales's, and one which 'abolished for ever the priggish and unfeminine Portia from the theatre'.[4] In comedy she could give full rein to her talent for quick, light transitions of mood and sudden flashes of anger or stern decision, made picturesque by a pose or gesture: in *Much Ado* her 'Kill Claudio' was marked by 'her statuesque attitude, her vengeful countenance', and her Viola in *Twelfth Night* displayed sudden switches into 'delicate and unobtrusive

[1] Craig, op. cit. p. 74.
[2] Bertram Joseph, *The Tragic Actor* (London, 1959), p. 378, in a sensitive account of Irving's tragic acting, characterizes his style as 'romantic realism', and also uses the apposite word 'Gothic'. Cf. Giovanni Calendoli, *L'attore. Storia di un'arte* (Rome, 1959), p. 486.
[3] Clement Scott, *Ellen Terry* (New York, 1900), pp. 130 ff.; Bram Stoker, 'The Art of Ellen Terry', *The Playgoer*, p. 44.
[4] *Illustrated London News*, 12 July 1884; *The Times*, 3 November 1879; Charles Hiatt, *Ellen Terry and her Impersonations* (1898), p. 143.

pathos'.[1] But although she was fine as Cordelia and Desdemona, roles which enabled her to exploit her beauty of appearance, ease of delivery and talent to depict the pathetic, in more demanding tragedy she was perhaps less effective: Lady Macbeth and even Juliet taxed her powers. The latter role she regarded as her first important Lyceum part and she studied it deeply. Her comparative failure pointed a general limitation in her acting. In the scenes with the Nurse, and in conveying the fragile grace and beauty of Juliet in the balcony scene, she was excellent; but the later, tragic scenes were considered by some beyond her scope – she lacked 'the *physique* to deliver with sustained force a soliloquy of agonized terror'.[2]

Graceful in movement and posture, possessed of what James called a Burne-Jones face, Ellen Terry was a perfect complement to Irving, and although many complained that he confined her talent she admirably suited his preference for the pictorial in staging.[3] Irving was a great actor and a great *metteur en scène*. His 'personality' acting endorsed the 'star' system and licensed it among his younger contemporaries, just as his genius for stage-management 'brought his tableau methods into favour and they had many imitators'.[4] The most notable of the younger generation who followed in Irving's wake was Herbert Beerbohm Tree.

(ii) Herbert Beerbohm Tree at the Haymarket and Her Majesty's

After the death of Irving, Beerbohm Tree (1853–1917) at Her Majesty's Theatre was generally acknowledged to be head of the profession.[5] But Her Majesty's, as Desmond MacCarthy remarked, never held the place in London theatre and society that the Lyceum had enjoyed under Irving, nor was the personal achievement of its actor-manager of the same magnitude. Not only was Tree a more limited actor, but in certain respects the tone and composition of his repertoire, with its calculated appeal to a public taste for spectacle in classical and quality popular drama, was too similar to that of

[1] *Illustrated London News*, 21 October 1882; *The World*, 16 July 1884.
[2] *Illustrated London News*, 18 March 1882.
[3] James, *The Scenic Art*, p. 143. E. J. West, 'Ellen Terry – Histrionic Enigma', remarks 'their common interest in, and use of, the picturesque and the pictorial in pose and general technique', *Colorado College Publications* (April 1940), p. 47. Cf. also Edward Gordon Craig, *Ellen Terry and her Secret Self* (London, 1931).
[4] Poel, op. cit. p. 3.
[5] Strictly, Her Majesty's was now His Majesty's, but will be referred to throughout under the former title.

Irving to make any distinctively new impact. It is true that Tree, unlike Irving, was sympathetic to drawing-room comedy and Ibsenite drama, but there is some truth in Craig's remark that his best Shakespearian presentations were 'beautiful copies of Irving productions'.[1]

Tree entered the profession in 1878 after a period as an amateur actor, and first went into management in 1887 at the Haymarket where he 'succeeded in almost every venture' that he undertook.[2] Among the many popular pieces he mounted there were a Ned-Kelly-inspired melodrama, *Captain Swift* (1888), its bushranger villainy toned down to suit the *mores* of society *drame*, and Oscar Wilde's first epigrammatic 'sensation' play, *A Woman of No Importance* (1893). But his greatest Haymarket success was a theatrically powerful adaptation of a Du Maurier novel, *Trilby* (1895), the box-office takings from which enabled him in 1897 to build Her Majesty's, 'the handsomest theatre in London'. Tree capitalized on the quality of his new house by his flair for the theatrically and financially viable, and by skilful self-publicity (engineered, according to Clement Scott, by 'literary assistants, expert in the art of personal advertisement and conversant with the new journalistic world').[3] Like Irving's repertoire at the Lyceum, two staples of Tree's programme now were Shakespeare and sophisticated historical verse drama: between 1900 and 1910 he produced no less than four plays by the contemporary white hope of poetic drama, Stephen Phillips.

Tree's first really big success at Her Majesty's was *Julius Caesar* (1898). It inaugurated a series of Shakespearian productions that has become notorious for the extreme to which it carried nineteenth-century spectacular 'romantic realism' and the unabashed confidence with which Tree modified the texts, introduced wholly unwarranted stage additions and helped out Shakespeare with 'little strokes of genius': Richard II was provided with a politically sagacious dog who at crisis point, and to the final mortification of his master, switched sides to Bolingbroke; in *Henry VIII*, as Tree's Wolsey made a magnificent last exit, his robe was allowed to fall from his shoulders symbolizing loss of all worldly things, albeit in direct contradiction of some lines near the end of his last long speech. Such touches gave the more discriminat-

---

[1] Desmond MacCarthy, in Max Beerbohm (ed.), *Herbert Beerbohm Tree* (London, n.d.), p. 218; Edward Gordon Craig, *Index to the Story of My Days* (London, 1957), p. 234.

[2] Scott, *The Drama of Yesterday*, Vol. II, p. 379. Hesketh Pearson, *Beerbohm Tree* (London, 1956), p. 52, notes that Tree not only refurbished the theatre but cut prices in an attempt to cater for poorer audiences.

[3] Shaw, op. cit. Vol. III, p. 123; Scott, *The Drama of Yesterday*, Vol. II, p. 379. Tree's advertising at the Haymarket was equally impressive: see, for example, his publicity for *Hamlet* in *The Times* in January 1892.

ing critics pause, as did Tree's spectacle. Desmond MacCarthy caustically noted that in *Antony and Cleopatra* the Sphinx got louder applause than anything else in the play, 'which proves there was something wrong'.[1] But not for the bulk of Tree's audiences, and of the enormous appeal of his productions there can be no doubt.

Nor would it be just when discussing Tree's Shakespeare to dwell exclusively on the grosser distortions and scenic over-elaborations. The productions were supremely of their age and may be seen as classic examples of the art of dressing the plays with heavy sets and busy stage action. The crowd scenes and stage fights in Tree's *The Merchant of Venice* and *Julius Caesar* were organized with a meticulousness and ebullience that would have done credit to the Meiningen. His production of *Macbeth* provided some striking stage pictures, like the murder of Duncan and its sequel: in a pictorial scene 'beautiful in its pre-Raphaelite symmetry' twin flights of steps at centre rose to the door of Duncan's room, which became the tight, tense focus of attention as in the murky light Macbeth and (later) Lady Macbeth crept stealthily through it; the grouping of the roused household after the murder had 'the beauty of ordered disorder'. Admittedly, a liability was that the sheer beauty of the staging tended to nullify any mood of horror.[2] Exactly how Tree, or his stage-manager Cecil King, succeeded in mounting such delicately organized moments and patterned crowd scenes is something of an enigma, for Tree's approach to rehearsal was often casual, and in Shaw's view downright chaotic. Yet, for all that, Tree was an accomplished deviser of spectacular pageantry. Most impressive was his *Henry VIII* (1910), 'a model and masterpiece of its kind', in which he upstaged for show the earlier productions of Charles Kean and Irving. The first-act feasting and dancing at Wolsey's palace, and the coronation procession at the end, with 'music and the ringing of bells, and the shouts of the crowd', were generally agreed, even by hostile critics, to be 'two great scenes, which it is surely no exaggeration to describe as "masterpieces" of the pictorial art of the theatre'.[3]

Although a 'personality' actor, Tree did not in the main treat Shakespeare's plays merely as vehicles for his own performance. For example, he cut and

[1] William Archer in *The Nation*, 10 September 1910; the business of Richard II's dog was taken from Froissart via Benson: J. C. Trewin, *Shakespeare on the English Stage 1900–1964* (London, 1964), p. 29; Desmond MacCarthy, in Beerbohm (ed.), op. cit. p. 218. For the controversy prompted by his *The Tempest* and Tree's defence, see Mrs George Cran, *Herbert Beerbohm Tree* (1907), pp. 67 ff.

[2] *The Times*, 6 September 1911.

[3] *The Nation*, 10 September 1910; *The Times*, 2 September 1910; *Playgoer and Society*, II, p. 238.

reorganized *Julius Caesar* for general theatrical effect, not to focus attention on his own role, and played Antony with a genuine attempt to interest the audience in the character. Nor did he cast weakly in order to advance himself. Perhaps the two most distinctive qualities of Tree's acting were romantic finesse and spontaneity. 'His method on the stage was for "flashes",' said Mrs Patrick Campbell, and observed that 'his slightly foreign manner, distinction and elegance, and fantastic grace, gave an arresting charm to his work'.[1] He was something of an improviser and was inclined to scant acquisition of technical skills: as Shaw noted of his Antony, 'a good deal of the technical part of his work was botched and haphazard'; in the course of a run his performances could become casual and be highly variable.[2] A strong romantic vein in his acting fitted him for roles in which the note of pathos is prominent, as in Richard II and Wolsey. But in the more physically and vocally taxing Shakespearian parts, like Macbeth and Othello, where character development has to be conveyed through subtle, sustained performance, particular excellencies in his playing could not conceal his basic shortcomings. In such roles he lacked force. His Macbeth excited no terror: 'he gives you what he can, sweetness, perfect taste, romantic melancholy, a sense of beauty'. His Shylock was in direct descent from Irving's in its emphasis on the humanity of the Jew, but though 'full-blooded' it wanted the transitions of mood, the guile and strength of Irving's reading. His Antony was 'more picturesque than forcible, more striking than convincing, more excellent in elocution than great through eloquence'.[3] If his characterization was effected by 'flashes', his delivery had an inclination to dwell on the purple passage. In the lyrical verses on sleep in *Macbeth* 'he became almost the virtuoso, pausing to enjoy the poetry, to turn it over on his tongue – it was Macbeth as the exponent of *l'art pour l'art*', and the dignity and pathos of his Wolsey fell occasionally into vocal overstress: in the 'long farewell' the 'ebb and flow of his rhetoric' made it a lengthy farewell indeed.[4]

Tree's contemporaries regarded him as pre-eminently a character actor, but he insisted that all acting entailed interpretation of character.[5] Unquestionably his forte was in the slightly extravagant, the role in which play-

---

[1] Mrs Patrick Campbell, *My Life and Some Letters* (London, 1922), p. 239. Cf. Pearson, op. cit. p. 191.

[2] Shaw, op. cit. Vol. III, p. 316. Tree rationalized reliance on the mood of the moment by equating it with the working of the actor's imaginative faculty: lecture of 1893, *The Imaginative Faculty*.

[3] *The Times*, 6 September 1911; *The Nation*, 11 April 1908; Grein, op. cit. p. 37.

[4] *The Times*, 6 September 1911; *The Nation*, 10 September 1910.

[5] Tree, cited by J. A. Hammerton, *The Actor's Art*, p. 155.

ing could border on the caricatural without doing violence to the spirit of the play. Such was his Malvolio in *Twelfth Night*. He was unsurpassed in depicting characters of an evil and menacing disposition, like his Fagin in *Oliver Twist* and his Svengali in *Trilby*. Writing of his Svengali, Shaw noted what was a recurring tendency in Tree's acting – a habit of succumbing to his taste for immediate theatrical effect by going for broad strokes which undermined the disciplined development of a role. It began well, but as the play progressed there was 'a decline into the stagey, the malignant, the diabolic, the Wandering-Jewish', as Tree vainly tried 'to make our flesh creep'.[1] In certain roles Tree delighted to revel in his assumed *persona*. Yet Tree's Svengali was without doubt one of the great *tours de force* of high 'theatrical' acting in this period. Exploiting his genius for make-up, Tree presented a 'weird, spectral' figure; 'with his long, matted black hair and beard, his hooked nose, his unwholesome, sallow face, his piercing eye, and his long, octopus-like limbs [he was] positively demoniac', dominating the production and providing a graphic death scene, 'his body falling back over a table, with his pallid and distorted face hanging downwards in full view of the house'.[2]

It would be unjust to conclude that Tree was merely a great showman. Impresario he was, but he was also a pioneer. The Shakespeare Festivals he ran annually at Her Majesty's from 1905 to 1913 not only gave London what Benson was providing at Stratford but anticipated the work of the Old Vic and gave impetus to the national-theatre movement.[3] He championed new, serious drama – like Ibsen's *An Enemy of the People* – by running matinée performances supported by his reputation and financed by the profits of his evening repertoire. His ostentatiously upholstered productions of Shakespeare are what are most frequently remembered of Tree's work; it is a useful counterbalance of that view to recall Shaw's warm tribute to Herbert Beerbohm Tree's 'repeated and honorable attempts to cater for people with some brains'.[4]

[1] Shaw, op. cit. Vol. I, p. 253.
[2] *The Times*, 31 October 1895. Tree himself thought *Trilby* 'hogwash': Pearson, op. cit. p. 93. His ability with make-up is described by Cran, op. cit. pp. 40–1.
[3] They are discussed in detail by George Rowell, 'Tree's Shakespeare Festivals (1905–1913)', *Theatre Notebook*, XXIX, 2 (1975).
[4] Shaw, op. cit. Vol. I, p. 253. Shaw was writing in 1895 of Tree's occasional work at the Haymarket.

(iii) From the Bancrofts to Alexander

The theatre of Irving and Tree was one of spectacle and illusion. Equally so in its own kind was the theatre of actor-managers noted for their mounting of 'well-made' plays, drawing-room comedy and society drama. At its most sophisticated the fashionable 'naturalistic' stage was richly pictorial: interiors meticulously depicted the actual, trends were established for use of costly furnishings and for sartorially impeccable modern costuming, and imaginative stage-management provided eyecatching images of everyday, particularly bourgeois, living.[1] This stage was the immediate end product in English theatre of innovations made in the late sixties and seventies at the Prince of Wales's Theatre by the Bancrofts, Marie (1839–1921) and Squire (1841–1926), working in close collaboration with the dramatist Tom Robertson. Their work with 'cup and saucer' plays and refinement of Vestris-inspired verisimilar practicable settings and props, and their flair for organization and stage-management, set standards for house control, rehearsal and presentation which were widely influential. Between 1880 and 1885 they managed the Haymarket, where they polished their style of discreet realism in a repertoire that drew on earlier successes, like *Money* and *Society*.

Heir to their methods was a former member of the Prince of Wales's company, John Hare (1844–1921), who first ran the Court Theatre, then joined in management with William and Madge Kendal at the St James's for a decade from 1879, before taking over the Garrick from 1889 to 1895. It was the formidable combination of Hare and the Kendals at the St James's which partly prompted the Bancrofts to move from the small Prince of Wales's to the larger and more central Haymarket. Their work with Robertson was now complemented by Hare's with the young Pinero, whose stagecraft was schooled by collaborating with Hare at the St James's to shape tight ensemble performances of adaptations from the French and of his own plays like *The Squire* (1881). A master of make-up and of physical, pantomimic playing, Hare had a particular acting genius for sharply observed elderly types and for roles demanding a comic show of quaintness, tetchiness or eccentricity. Commenting on his Pontifex in *Mamma* (1891), Shaw praised his 'swift, crisp method, and his habit of picking up a cue as if it were a cricket-ball', and in

---

[1] Approving the sets for *The Second Mrs Tanqueray* at the St James's, William Archer argued that English realistic interiors had been brought to a perfection that surpassed the French: 'The Limitations of Scenery', *The Magazine of Art* (November 1895–October 1896), pp. 432–6.

some of the detail of his playing compared him favourably to the greatest comic actor of the age, Coquelin.[1] A brilliant technical actor, Hare, like the Kendals, brought disciplined 'naturalness' and immaculate timing and pacing to a repertoire of mainly transitory pieces – entertaining actors' vehicles sustained by their immediate appeal and by performer skills and personality. Often stage-managed by Hare was Madge Kendal (1848–1935), at her best in polite comedy and the emotionally strong roles of domestic drama, and outstanding in plays from Sardou or in the work of Pinero. Reviewing her Claire Derblay in Pinero's *The Iron Master* (1884), one critic noted the chief marks of her acting: 'her passion, her pathos, and her earnestness'. The professional expertise with which she reproduced the surface detail of life was much admired; 'she is the personification', wrote J. T. Grein, 'of a perfect school of stage-craft' – a highly disciplined playing whose movements and accents were precisely calculated for the drawing-room box set. If there was at times, as some felt, 'too much of self, a little too much consciousness, too much insistence of manner', her depiction of the everyday was rarely casual and self-indulgent, but stylized representational acting informed by a sense of craft: 'subtle changes of expression', small, significant gestures, 'delicate inflections of voice'.[2]

Influence of the Bancroft–Robertson methods was felt too in the later work of one of the most respected actor-managers of the period, Charles Wyndham (1837–1919), from 1876 in long and prosperous connection with the Criterion Theatre, the scene of his most varied work and the house which brought him a theatrical and financial success equalled by few of his contemporaries. Wyndham was the paradigm of the thoroughly professional actor-manager: he cast and drilled well, controlled backstage and front-of-house with intelligence, economy and a sure sense of audience taste. Aided by his actress partner and later wife, Mary Moore, his expansion in management was an example of speculation at its most constructive: by the turn of the century he had an interest in the Criterion, Wyndham's (1899) and the New (1903, now the Albery), was an indefatigable provincial and foreign tourer, and was justly called then 'the doyen of managers'.[3]

[1] Shaw, op. cit. Vol. I, p. 296.
[2] *Illustrated London News*, 26 April 1884; Grein, op. cit. p. 114; *The Times* commenting on her Kate Verity in Pinero's *The Squire*, 31 December 1881; T. Edgar Pemberton, *The Kendals* (London, 1900), p. 157; Irene Vanbrugh, *Dare to be Wise* (London, 1950), pp. 50–1, 86.
[3] Scott, *Drama of Yesterday*, Vol. II, p. 377. There is an excellent revaluation of Wyndham by George Rowell, 'Wyndham of Wyndham's', in Joseph W. Donohue, Jr (ed.), *The Theatrical Manager in England and America* (Princeton, NJ, 1971). See also T. Edgar Pemberton, *Sir Charles Wyndham* (London, 1904).

Wyndham's forte was from the beginning, and remained, elegant farce and light comedy. His natural, easy, 'airy method' won him a quick London success in *Brighton* (1874) and at the Criterion the almost stylized *brio* of his playing carried comedies like *Pink Dominoes*, *Bachelor of Arts* and his stock-piece *David Garrick*. By the mid-eighties he was judged to have inherited the mantle of the younger Mathews as the 'most mercurial and vivacious of light comedians'. Wyndham made peculiarly his own a line in breezy, frank, impudent comic heroes, whose insouciant romantic grace gave charm and plausibility to the most extravagant comic plot lines.[1] His ability in farce and comedy to shift into the serious presaged the development in the nineties of 'his later style as the shrewd middle-aged man of the world'. Exercised in plays like *The Case of Rebellious Susan* (1894), *The Physician* (1897) and *The Liars* (1897), it particularly distinguished his Justice Carteret in Jones's *Mrs Dane's Defence* (1900), to which he brought a combination of light comic emphasis, dignity and social aplomb, highlighted in the confrontation scene by an easy transition into authority and firmness of purpose.[2] He was accomplished too in 'powder' plays, though some disapproved the *fin de siècle* gloss he gave to Sheridan. Occasionally he extended his range in plays less characteristic of his repertoire. A *tour de force* was his Sir Jasper Thorndyke in *Rosemary* (1896): for three acts he played in his most urbane, witty manner this role of a forty-year-old squire in love with a younger woman; then in the final act held the stage as Thorndyke in old age, closed in the decaying house of the girl convention had forced him to give up, brooding in monologue on friends and days long gone and the beloved he can barely recall. It was a more demanding role than he had attempted hitherto: for Shaw his performance was so impressive in a play of such little consequence that it amounted to a display of 'acting in the abstract'; others acknowledged the new range and the expertise but declared preference for the more familiar Wyndham of light comedy.[3] A not dissimilar response was evoked by his most ambitious undertaking, *Cyrano de Bergerac* (1900).[4] Wilde's choice to mount *The Importance of Being Earnest*, he was tied up in the long run of *Rebellious Susan* and passed the play to George Alexander (1858–1918).

Wyndham's achievements as actor and manager have been rather overshadowed by the success of Alexander at the St James's Theatre, the most

---

[1] *The Times*, 3 April 1877; *Illustrated London News*, 19 April 1884 (see this same number for an artist's impressions of the interior of the refurbished Criterion Theatre).
[2] *The Times*, 26 March 1897; ibid. 10 October 1900.
[3] Shaw, op. cit. Vol. II, p. 144; *The Times*, 18 May 1896; *The Athenaeum*, 23 May 1896.
[4] Discussed by Rowell, 'Wyndham of Wyndham's', op. cit., and Pemberton, *Sir Charles Wyndham*, op. cit.

fashionable playhouse in London devoted to a mainly non-classical repertory from the early 1890s to the First World War. Although Alexander never worked with the Bancrofts, he was in respects their most notable successor in shaping a distinctive house style and working fruitfully with an important dramatist, Pinero, as they had worked with Robertson. He began in the provinces, joined Irving's company in 1881 for a revival of Albery's *Two Roses*, was at the St James's in 1883 with Hare and the Kendals, and later returned to the Lyceum playing among other roles Faust to Irving's Mephistopheles, his performance inevitably marred by the vocal and technical inadequacies of inexperience. Yet within five years, in 1890, Alexander had set up in independent management, first briefly at the Avenue Theatre, then, in the same year, at the St James's, which he made 'a theatre of high prestige and financial success' by deliberate appeal in his repertoire and house tone to a socially rather exclusive audience.[1] Smooth efficiency in backstage organization, and the elegance, refinement and taste that characterized auditorium comfort and front-of-house reception at the St James's, provided the requisite air of occasion for the *haut bourgeois* playgoer.[2]

In his administration of the St James's Alexander was polar opposite to Tree at Her Majesty's: his control over theatre finances was tight, his pre-rehearsal preparation of plays meticulous, and his rehearsals were conducted with a rigour economical of time and energy and conducive to securing for the end product the polish and finish he sought. His biographer A. E. W. Mason has described working at the St James's on his play *The Witness for the Defence* (1911): on a model stage, with draughtsmen used for characters, Alexander worked through the text with author and technicians, exploring character and dialogue and arranging preliminary blocking, before carrying the play into intensive three- or four-hour daily rehearsals over a period of three weeks.[3] The neat precision of Alexander's working methods was innate to the man, though perhaps it was reinforced by his close working relationship with Pinero, a stickler for rehearsing his own plays in detail. A balanced, well-paced, mannered 'naturalism' was Alexander's production ideal, and he cast and stage-managed carefully and unselfishly.

[1] A. E. W. Mason, *Sir George Alexander and the St James's Theatre* (London, 1935), p. 7. Joseph W. Donohue, Jr, gives a fascinating account of a St James's first night in 'The First Production of *The Importance of being Earnest*: A Proposal for a Reconstructive Study', in Kenneth Richards and Peter Thomson (eds), *Nineteenth Century British Theatre* (London, 1971).

[2] But Alexander was businessman enough to oppose compulsory evening dress in the stalls as it would adversely affect takings: Frank Harris, *Shaw* (London, 1931), p. 117.

[3] Mason, op. cit. pp. 22 ff.

'The established home of polite comedy,' said *The Playgoer and Society* of the St James's.[1] The staple of Alexander's repertoire was society drama, particularly sophisticated comedy and urbane 'sensation' *drame*: among his successes were *Lady Windermere's Fan* (1891), *The Second Mrs Tanqueray* (1893), *His House in Order* (1906) and, though perhaps only in its Edwardian revivals, *The Importance of Being Earnest* (1895). He was both astute and fortunate in tapping a rich new vein in English drama. But although the characteristic fare of the St James's was the play of polite social *mœurs*, Alexander varied his programme to encompass a range of dramatic genres. Expensively mounted romantic costume drama supplied him with major box-office successes. One such was *The Prisoner of Zenda* (1896), adapted from Anthony Hope's novel, in which the Winter Palace scene offered 'such a display of uniforms and Court costumes as . . . has never been surpassed on the stage'. Though Shaw thought the production 'curiously haphazard', and was critical of rough blockings and awkward groupings, its colour, pace and romantic story made it one of the St James's most rewarding pieces.[2] Another success, in more lush romantic vein, was Stephen Phillips's verse drama *Paolo and Francesca* (1902), its long run helping, along with Tree's production of *Herod* (1900), to launch that poet's 'bubble reputation'. More artistically adventurous, albeit a failure, was Henry James's *Guy Domville* (1895). Although Alexander tended to eschew classical drama he mounted two Shakespeare plays, *As You Like It* (1896) and *Much Ado About Nothing* (1898). The former was admired by Shaw and ranked by him above Irving's Shakespeare largely on the strength of Alexander's respect for the text. *Much Ado* had a *mise en scène* of 'the first rank': for the church scene William Telbin created a 'heavy incense-laden atmosphere' with a pillared altarpiece and decorated canopy that roofed the stage. But although a popular production, for some critics the playing was too riotous and bustling, a physical rather than a vocal performance.[3] Alexander never produced or appeared in a Shaw play: Higgins in *Pygmalion* was written with him in mind, but after earlier experience with *The Second Mrs Tanqueray* he was unwilling to act again with the temperamental Mrs Patrick Campbell; he was offered Marchbanks in *Candida* and accepted on condition that Marchbanks be made blind – Shaw was not prepared to oblige.[4]

It was as actor-manager of the St James's rather than as an actor that

[1] *The Playgoer and Society*, II, p. 196.
[2] *The Times*, 8 January 1896; Shaw, op. cit. Vol. II, p. 11.
[3] *The Times*, 17 February 1898; Shaw, op. cit. Vol. III, p. 337; Grein, op. cit. p. 45.
[4] St John Ervine, *Bernard Shaw* (London, 1956), p. 339.

Alexander excelled. Not a player of the first rank, he was a natural, romantic, light comedian, and was skilled in carrying roles of witty, self-assured upper-middle-class gentlemen: characteristic of these last was his Aubrey Tanqueray in *The Second Mrs Tanqueray*, which he played with 'sustained force and feeling', establishing a 'skilful compromise between passion and benevolence'. The grace and polish that marked his playing in drawing-room plays he easily extended to roles in romantic drama that called for breeding and panache; his heroic playing in *The Prisoner of Zenda* was said to have lifted the play 'from the plane of comic opera to that of serious drama'.[1] His Shakespearian characters, Orlando and Benedick, were able but not outstanding, sustained mainly by a bright buoyancy of playing. Shaw accused Wilde, Pinero and Henry Arthur Jones of treating Alexander as 'a tailor's dummy' and denying him opportunity to develop the skill and judgement he brought to his acting of Guy Domville.[2] But the choice was more Alexander's than any imposition by those dramatists whose work formed the base of his St James's repertoire, and whose male leads he interpreted, if not with outstanding flair and originality, undeniably with impeccable taste, assurance and ease.

Hare, the Kendals and Alexander extended the Bancroft–Robertson methods in house-management, staging and acting. But they were not mere imitators. They adapted the methods to their distinctive talents and repertoires and to changing dramatic styles and audience tastes. The 'naturalness' of their staging and acting was much admired, though notions of what constituted the 'natural' in acting, and how it was best achieved, shifted in the course of the period.[3] They spawned many followers who lacked their technical finesse and they were replaced, complained Shaw, by a younger generation who did not possess 'as much power of acting as there was in the tip of Mrs Kendal's little finger-nail'.[4] Shaw's preference for the grand style disposed him to exaggerate the decline in acting as an exercise of skill. But the work of Hare, the Kendals, Alexander and even Wyndham furthered a general trend to the 'natural' in acting that by the turn of the century was to make consciously histrionic, heightened romantic realism look at best overstudied, at worst crude and operatic, and left their refined realism itself

[1] *Illustrated London News*, 3 June 1893; *The Times*, 29 May 1893; ibid. 8 January 1896.
[2] Shaw, op. cit. Vol. I, p. 8.
[3] Where early commentators thought Irving a 'natural' actor, later critics like Arthur Symons admired the histrionic quality of his performance: 'He has observed life in order to make his own version of life, using the stage as his medium, and accepting the traditional aids and limitations of the stage,' *Plays, Acting, and Music* (London, 1903), p. 49.
[4] Shaw, op. cit. Vol. I, p. 293.

exposed. A wide range of styles continued to characterize acting through to the First World War and beyond, and many leading players were decidedly more 'theatrical' than 'natural'; but varieties of 'naturalism' were now largely triumphant, and there was a distinct tendency, as Granville Barker complained, for younger players to skimp the acquisition of technical skills. Some older actors, like Wyndham, adjusted their styles to change; others, like Hare, retired to the provinces, where their repertoires and styles, basically shaped in the seventies and eighties, still enjoyed a respect no longer fully accorded them in London.

(iv) Other actors, actresses and actor-managers

Theatre from the late Victorian years through to the First World War is perhaps most readily identified with idiosyncratic 'personality' acting in adapted and upholstered Shakespeare and with the refined realism and mannered 'naturalism' of the drawing-room modes. These were characteristic, but, pervasive as was the influence of Irving and Tree on Shakespearian production, approaches were various. Again, some players who excelled in drawing-room drama won equal success in other kinds: for much of the period too there were fruitful interconnections between the popular and the fashionable. A distinctive feature indeed was the range and variety of theatre offered. The diversity was such that it defeats brief survey, as it confounds generalizations about representative performance and production styles. Here only passing mention can be made of some achievements.

Chief carrier of disciplined, heroical acting through to the outbreak of the First World War was Johnston Forbes-Robertson (1853–1937). He won success in a number of transitory pieces, as with his Dick Helder in a Kipling adaptation, *The Light that Failed* (1903), or as the supernatural visitor in Jerome's *The Passing of the Third Floor Back* (1908), bringing to them his 'beautiful elocution, his happy air of intellectual aloofness, his easy dignity, his personal distinction'.[1] But these qualities were best displayed elsewhere, in plays like Shaw's *Caesar and Cleopatra* (1907), the leading part of which was written for him, and in certain Shakespearian roles in which he was pre-eminent. His Romeo (1895) modulated from passionate intensity in the balcony scene to depiction elsewhere of 'the self-involved, absent character of the lover' lost in the world of his imaginings; his 'attitudes and bearing were

[1] Desmond MacCarthy, *Shaw* (London, 1951), p. 93.

natural, apparently unstudied, and yet heroical'.[1] In *Othello* (1902) he emphasized the Moor's chivalry and soul-wrought despair, his formal reading eschewing the physical violence and animal dynamism made fashionable by Salvini. His Hamlet, first acted at the Lyceum in 1897 when Irving was on an American tour, was 'dignified, youthful and picturesque', if rather lacking 'the whirlwind of passion' – a 'true classical Hamlet', played 'on the line and to the line, with the utterance and acting simultaneous, inseparable and in fact identical'.[2] Grace, melancholy and 'intellectual discursiveness' were keynotes; controversially, he virtually abandoned Hamlet's 'antic disposition', playing the scenes more for irony than for madness.[3] By general consent it was his finest Shakespearian part, and one he refined over the years until his farewell at Drury Lane in 1913. Like Irving, Forbes-Robertson preferred gas to electric lighting, was hostile to non-naturalistic décor, and was suspicious of drawing-room 'naturalism' in acting.[4] Like his mentor, Phelps, he tended to avoid fashionable heavy scenery, but willingly stage-managed for tableau effects and the picturesque. His most signal attribute was his sonorous, resonant voice, which he trained as a musical instrument. Blending gesture and movement with a vocal precision that gave full worth to the sense of the spoken word, he was, said Shaw, 'completely aloof . . . from the world of the motor car and the Carlton Hotel'.[5]

Equally remote from that world was Frank Benson (1858–1939). Where Forbes-Robertson was a sensitive interpreter of a handful of Shakespearian roles, Benson was a peripatetic Shakespearian missionary. Early in his career, while acting in the provinces in 1883, he bought up the costumes and fittings of a bankrupt company, announced the formation of the Benson Shakespeare Company, and launched out on his long, often financially chequered, sometimes scathingly ridiculed, but always honourable and dedicated task of carrying the work of the greatest English dramatist to audiences beyond the reach of the London and major provincial theatres. Benson was more than a tourer – the provinces were his theatre. Views of his acting in major parts conflict: Ellen Terry admired his Lear, Yeats his Henry V and Richard II; his Hamlet was dismissed by Beerbohm as 'dry, wooden, insipid'.[6] But he always showed a more responsible approach to characterization than is

[1] *The Times*, 23 September 1895; *The Athenaeum*, 28 September 1895.
[2] *Illustrated London News*, 18 September 1897; *The Athenaeum*, 18 September 1897; Shaw, op. cit. Vol. III, pp. 213, 216.
[3] *The World*, 15 September 1897; *The Times*, 13 September 1897.
[4] Johnston Forbes-Robertson, *A Player under Three Reigns* (London, 1925), pp. 225–6.
[5] Ibid. p. 45; Shaw, *Play Pictorial*, 10 October 1907.
[6] Ellen Terry, op. cit. p. 223; Max Beerbohm, *Around Theatres* (London, 1953), p. 72.

allowed for in Gordon Craig's terse dismissal, 'Benson's idea of Caliban was to come on the stage with a fish between his teeth.' What irritated Craig in much of Benson's work was the air of welfare bardolatry: 'the Benson–Baylis type seems to me to belong to the Salvation Army.'[1] Certainly the Company productions could not always stand comparison with the more expensively mounted Shakespeare of the London theatres, and Benson's notorious, if endearing, enthusiasm for sport provided at least one metropolitan critic with irresistible copy around which to write his reviews.[2] Like Phelps before him, Benson presented some of the less frequently revived plays in the canon, introduced 'business' and staging which were taken up by others, and provided in his Company an invaluable training ground for many young players. Whatever London thought, the Company's acting and mounting were ideally appropriate for touring: the adaptation of the texts was purposeful, devised to provide rapid, lively pace and continuous flow from scene to scene, and in choice of costumes and props one commentator on provincial touring noted that 'the Benson *mise-en-scène* moulds itself admirably to the particular play under performance'.[3] Benson's athletic Shakespeare helped prepare the ground in the provinces for the development, in the first two decades of the century, of the repertory movement, and his annual Shakespeare Festivals at Stratford from the 1890s through to 1919 laid the base there for a permanent Shakespeare company.

The one English actress of the period who might have approached the quality of the great Continental actresses like Ristori, Bernhardt and Duse was Mrs Patrick Campbell (1865–1940), who won overnight success as Laura in Pinero's *The Second Mrs Tanqueray* (1893), the 'realistic fidelity' and 'variety of emotion' she brought to the role carrying the play, in the opinion of some critics.[4] Temperamental, occasionally difficult to work with, she was considered by some undisciplined and too dependent on innate ability. Clement Scott's praise of her Agnes in Pinero's *The Notorious Mrs Ebbsmith* (1895) is revealing: 'she was distinct, she was audible, she did not slur her words, or indulge in monotonous "sing-song", she did not scamp her work.'[5] In Shakespeare she had little success. Her Juliet, Ophelia and Lady Macbeth

---

[1] Craig, *Index to the Story of My Days*, p. 221. For an excellent and detailed study of Benson, see J. C. Trewin's *Benson and the Bensonians* (London, 1960).
[2] Namely, Beerbohm: his review of the Benson *Henry V*, reprinted in *Around Theatres*, pp. 61–3.
[3] James Hawley, 'Touring with Benson', *O.S.U. Theatre Collection Bulletin*, No. 6 (1959); W. J. Lawrence, 'Scenery on Tour', in *The Magazine of Art* (November 1895–October 1896), p. 479.
[4] *The Times*, 29 May 1893; *Illustrated London News*, 3 June 1893.
[5] Clement Scott, *Drama of Yesterday*, Vol. II, p. 340.

– all under Forbes-Robertson's first ventures into actor-management – although they contained local excellencies and were graced by her singular, dark-eyed beauty, betrayed an inability to master the techniques of verse delivery. Playing Lady Macbeth, she lamented, 'you can't say such words *naturally*'. Of her Juliet one critic complained she 'has never learnt the grammar of her art. She plays with the aid of her temperament merely.'[1] Yet in roles that fired her imagination she was outstanding. Grein noted a 'Yellow-Book' modernity about her talent, an ability to exhibit by turns the fury and langour of 'the modern *névrose*', but her talent was more substantial than that allows.[2] In formal modern tragedy and brisk, ironic modern comedy she was unsurpassed, ranging from Maeterlinck's Melisande (1898) and Yeats's Deirdre (1907) to Shaw's Eliza Doolittle in *Pygmalion* (1914). She had a dynamism and directness in performance, a physical self-assurance and an ability to shift rapidly through emotional registers, beyond the capabilities of the majority of her English contemporaries. In matinées at the Court Theatre under Granville Barker she was a powerful Hedda Gabler (1907), dominating the stage with her intense but controlled playing and inventive use of business. Her performances in Ibsen were highly variable, as Shaw noted of her Rita in *Little Eyolf*, but under firm stage-management and in a more adventurous theatrical climate she might have developed into an even greater Ibsen interpretess. For critics like Shaw, who recognized her skill and potential, Mrs Patrick Campbell was brilliant and erratic, bewitching and exasperating. She remained a chameleon product of the 'star' system, spending much of her great talent on minor stage vehicles.

What Mrs Patrick Campbell lacked, lamented her biographer, was the application of Duse or Bernhardt.[3] If no English actress had quite the power, originality and electric presence of the Continentals, many possessed the application. It underpinned the searching, realistic performances, notably in Ibsen, of Janet Achurch (1864–1916) and Elizabeth Robins (1862–1952), the skill which enabled Marie Tempest (1864–1942) to switch from the musical stage to 'artificial' comedy, and the technically faultless playing which Irene Vanbrugh (1872–1949) matured in plays by Wilde and Pinero, Maugham and Barrie.[4] The trend among leading actresses was decidedly the 'naturalistic',

---

[1] Cited in Alan Dent, *Mrs Patrick Campbell* (London, 1961), p. 162; *The Times*, 23 September 1895.
[2] Grein, op. cit. p. 184, writing on her performance as Magda in Sudermann's *Heimat*.
[3] Dent, op. cit. p. 73.
[4] The effect of Janet Achurch in *A Doll's House* is interestingly discussed by Elizabeth Robins, *Both Sides of the Curtain* (London, 1940), pp. 195 ff. When Elizabeth Robins

though few scorned the acquisition of craft, and some, like Lillah McCarthy (1875–1960) who schooled for six years in the provinces with Wilson Barrett, retained sufficient of the expansiveness in gesture and delivery of the grand style to win the respect of Shaw and make them admirable Shavian players. Many actresses went into management themselves. Some were unashamedly 'star' heads, like Mrs Patrick Campbell at the Royalty and elsewhere, or Ellen Terry, late in her career, at the Imperial, Westminster. Sarah Thorne ran an important training stock company in the eighties at the Theatre Royal, Margate; Janet Achurch at the Novelty in 1889 anticipated Tree by mounting matinée performances of uncommercial intellectual drama; Florence Farr at the Avenue, 1893–4, with plays by Yeats and Shaw presaged the growth of the repertory idea; that idea was furthered later by Lena Ashwell, in management at the Kingsway in 1907, and by Lillah McCarthy's several ventures in partnership with her husband, Granville Barker. The contribution of actresses to new movements in theatre was notable.

Notable too throughout much of the period was the vitality of popular forms, and the extent to which links were maintained between the popular and the fashionable. The craft of Hare and Wyndham embraced traditional methods and materials. Master of broad comedy and burlesque, and influential in shaping the styles of many comic players, was the most admired low comedian of the eighties and early nineties, J. L. Toole (1830–1906), who at his own theatre, Toole's, with skills long exercised in the provinces, worked a large repertoire of mainly familiar pieces, but also took up new plays, like Barrie's farce *Walker, London* (1892), and made a characteristic contribution to the Grein-sparked Ibsen debate by impersonating the dramatist in *Ibsen's Ghost* (1891).[1] Burlesque proved vulnerable in the nineties to the development of variety, but the enthusiasm for stage melodrama continued to the Edwardian period. Building on Irving's achievement in the seventies, a concerted attempt was made to elevate the form. Wilson Barrett (1846–1904) in a curtain speech on the hundredth performance of *The Silver King* (1882) declared his intention to raise melodrama 'into the region of literature, poetry, and natural tragedy'.[2] With a skill in stage-management matched only by that in advertising, if he failed to persuade all that plays like *The Sign of the Cross* (1896) and *Quo Vadis* (1900) had literary merit, few could gainsay

herself played Hedda Gabler there was a rumour that Ibsen was to visit London, attracted by reports of the quality of the English acting: *The Athenaeum*, 16 May 1891.
[1] *The Athenaeum*, 5 March 1892; Joseph Hatton, *Reminiscences of J. L. Toole*, 2 vols (1889), especially Vol. I, pp. 160 ff.
[2] *The Times*, 19 March 1883.

their quality as theatrical spectacle and their box-office appeal.[1] Equally assertive of the rights of melodrama was Irving-trained William Terriss (1847–97). Under the management of the Gattis at the Adelphi he turned what was dubbed his distinctively English style of playing, 'strong, powerful, virile', to the service of fullblooded thrill and spectacle, and urged the artistic merits of his great popular successes like *The Harbour Lights* (1885).[2] Their efforts, together with the reputations of Irving and Tree, gave melodrama a social standing, and in its various kinds it was a staple in the repertoire of many players, bringing to some both comfortable returns and national reputations. Two of the younger generation who capitalized were John Martin-Harvey (1863–1944), 'all for dreamy and ethereal and contemplative romanticism', qualities he turned to gainful account in one of the most celebrated displays of high romantic acting in the period, his Sidney Carton in the Dickens adaptation *The Only Way* (1899), and Lewis Waller (1860–1915), who enjoyed a strident matinée following, particularly in plays offering bravura roles, like *The Three Musketeers* (1900) and *Monsieur Beaucaire* (1902).[3]

Like Irving and Tree, many actors who excelled in melodrama were leading Shakespearian players, and like them their approaches to Shakespeare were rooted in the spirit and strategies of popular theatre. If they invariably worked in the received tradition, sustained and endorsed at the Lyceum and Her Majesty's, of Shakespeare adapted to expensive costumes and heavy sets, they did so in part for the colour, spectacle and strong effects such staging admitted. Overdecorative it may have been, but theirs was essentially a theatrical, not a literary theatre. As such it suffered a setback with the gradual decline of stage melodrama before the competition of cinema.[4] Change was particularly felt in acting styles, and within a few years of the turn of the century, in London at least, such vestiges as remained of the old, grand style that verged on the rhetorical seemed to belong to a world long gone. In some measure, however, with the decline of melodrama, strong playing, big theatrical effects and exciting spectacle were displaced, and appropriately (given the importance of music in melodrama), to the musical stage. Musical comedy rather than melodrama now became the form most likely to provide rich box-office profit if a piece took with the public. Straight theatre

[1] See Clement Scott on *The Sign of the Cross*, *Illustrated London News*, 11 January 1896.
[2] Cited in Arthur J. Smythe, *The Life of William Terriss* (1898), p. 148.
[3] Beerbohm, *Around Theatres*, p. 257.
[4] The relations between the two are best discussed in A. N. Vardac, *Stage to Screen* (Cambridge, Mass., 1949), but merit further study.

had increasing intercourse with lyric. Thus a number of later actor-managers, like Seymour Hicks (1871–1949) and Cyril Maude (1862–1951), moved easily between comedy, costume drama and musical plays, and the forceful, ebullient Oscar Asche (1871–1936), a former Bensonian and a fine Falstaff and Othello, wrote and performed the title role in the record musical success *Chu Chin Chow* (1916), and carried new staging techniques – including an apron over the orchestra pit and action on the forestage sustained by mime and music – into the musical spectacle *Kismet* (1911).[1]

This orientation of some talent towards the lyric stage shows again the versatility of the 'stars' and actor-managers, as it is witness to their adaptability, but it left straight theatre and actor-management the more vulnerable when the war years brought increased demand for light, escapist entertainment and an invasion of speculators willing to provide it. The actor-manager system was at its strongest when it operated across a wide spectrum of dramatic kinds; high costs, the competition of the syndicates, the influx of American money, and a contraction in the range of theatrical fare supported by audiences, combined to weaken irreparably a system long subject to attack.

(v) The heyday in retrospect

Actor-managers particularly, and some 'stars' in lay management productions, were the object of much criticism: accused of blocking selfishly, stifling young acting talent, skimping on actors' salaries to pay for spectacle, usurping the role of the dramatist at rehearsals, and stunting the growth of new drama. Some of the criticism was warranted, although the conduct of most leading players was as diverse as their repertoires. Some young actors were no doubt held back, as Martin-Harvey felt he was by Irving at the Lyceum, but others switched between managements, maturing their talents and augmenting their salaries.[2] Many later were proud of their former engagements with Irving or Tree, Alexander or Wyndham.

The paternalism of the actor-manager system can be exaggerated, for there were frequent changes in company personnel. Indeed, it was through this mobility that actor-managers could exercise great power – the theatrical community was relatively small, and recommendation by letter or word of mouth could be decisive. But young actors were certainly encouraged: not

[1] *Oscar Asche: His Life, by Himself* (London, 1929), p. 137.
[2] Cf. Ellen Terry, op. cit. p. 25.

only provincial and touring companies, like those of Sarah Thorne and Frank Benson, were training grounds; working with the great London companies was a stage education.[1] Not all actor-managers cast selfishly or dominated rehearsals; most worked closely with actors and dramatists. Not all ignored the work of contemporary playwrights: Pinero, Jones, Wilde, Phillips and Galsworthy were among new dramatists they introduced. Even Irving, castigated by Shaw because his 'new acting was not applied to a new author', mounted a number of contemporary plays. Unfortunately, W. G. Wills, Lord Tennyson and Comyns Carr did not fall within Shaw's definition of the 'new'.[2]

Straight theatre won social recognition during the period, but that brought with it the liability to conform to consensus notions of the approved and respectable. Artistic caution was in part dictated by professional and commercial necessity. Maintaining without benefit of state subsidy an economically viable company in a competitive climate was taxing, and the more so as costs rose. It is noticeable that, whereas the older generation of actor-managers like Irving, Hare, Wyndham and Tree, who entered management in the seventies and eighties, were able to entrench themselves in particular theatres for long periods and even to build their own playhouses, most of the younger generation had no such fortune. In personal management short-term tenure was the rule, and the names of Forbes-Robertson, Martin-Harvey or Mrs Patrick Campbell are not indelibly associated with particular theatres. Their comparative rootlessness is an indication of changing conditions.

The 'star' system was to prevail, but the retirement in 1913 of Forbes-Robertson, and the deaths during the war years of Waller, Tree, Alexander and Wyndham, mark the passing of the great age of the actor-managers. Its decline had begun earlier. No single factor accounts for it: pressures for change were many. Perhaps Irving's success at the Lyceum in wedding public popularity, professional respect and high seriousness in matters theatrical had taken the actor-oriented, 'star'-focused artistic and economic individualism of the actor-manager system as far as it could go. It survived to the First World War, and intermittently beyond, but theatre was to take new directions. Faults the system undoubtedly had, but ultimately theatre was the *raison d'être* of the actor-manager. As much could not always be said of his post-war commercial successor, speculative management rampant. Nor was

[1] The fascinating *Autobiography of Sir John Martin-Harvey* (London, 1933) gives ample evidence of the lessons to be learned from working with Irving at the Lyceum.
[2] Shaw, *Our Theatres in the Nineties*, Vol. I, p. 287.

the rich diversity of actor-manager theatre, with its many taproots in traditional forms and strategies, always sustained by the alternative theatres which, however unwittingly on the part of reformers and innovators, often furthered a disjunction of the popular and the serious.

3 Some alternative theatres

The 1880s saw the beginning of activities which in their multiple amateur and professional dimensions were to contribute substantially, if gradually, to changes in theatre nationally. In the following decades societies, clubs, repertory theatres and individual projects were launched, in London and the provinces, whose artistic purposes ran firmly counter to many of the assumptions of the commercial and 'star' systems. Often they had little but these general purposes in common. In diverse ways they were expressions in British theatre of a 'modernism' whose spirit was elusive and its manifestations generated by various, often contradictory impulses. Some activities, by far the majority, tended to approve realism, and under domestic and Continental influence often sought a theatre consciously educative and socially reformist; some few others strove to subvert realism, rejecting the aesthetics of positivism for a sharper penetration of life accorded by a theatre that trafficked in the abstract, the symbolic, the impressionistic. Alternative developments in pre-war theatre, wrote John Drinkwater, sparked an excitement that was largely dissipated by the 1920s.[1] In fact the promise was more substantial than the achievement, and there was little in British theatre in the nineties or in the years up to and including the war comparable to the artistic

[1] John Drinkwater, *The Gentle Art of Theatre-Going* (London, 1929), pp. 41 ff.

ferment and radical re-exploration of theatre's basics to be found in Russian, French and German theatre of the period.[1] Yet it was partly through these activities that controversial new drama and new staging methods from abroad, new approaches to mounting the classical repertory, new ideas in lighting and design, and new plays by native dramatists were slowly filtered into the British professional theatre. Experimentation furthered the emergence of the play director, fostered new conceptions of ensemble playing, questioned the authority of the 'long run', and undermined the hegemony of the proscenium-arch stage and of heavy, representational stage sets. It brought change; and in the change there was both gain and loss.

(i) Two innovators: J. T. Grein and William Poel

In 1891 a young Dutchman, J. T. Grein (1862–1935), inspired by Antoine's revolutionary Théâtre Libre, initiated what Bernard Shaw called 'the second revolution that England owes to a Dutchman': the Independent Theatre Society.[2] The name of the Society was intended to proclaim its intentions: free of commercial considerations and official censorship, it was to stimulate the growth in Britain of a new drama comparable to that of France and Scandinavia. If Antoine was the practical model, Ibsen, at least initially, was the literary one, and it was with a production of *Ghosts* that the Society was launched at the Royalty Theatre, to the accompaniment of a critical furore that shaped the tone of Ibsen debate in England for some years. In retrospect it seems unfortunate that the Independent Theatre did not produce more Ibsen and make of him a 'house dramatist' as Shaw was to be for Granville Barker at the Court Theatre a decade later; such regular production might have given sharper definition to the Society's work. But of the twenty-eight plays it gave before its dissolution in 1898 only three were by Ibsen – *Ghosts*, *The Wild Duck* (1894) and a revival of *A Doll's House* (1897).[3]

Grein's declared intention was to promote new plays. After the performance of *Ghosts* he came before the curtain to champion 'a more literary and

[1] To say nothing of the Falk–Strindberg work at the Intima Teatern in Stockholm, or the theatre experiments of the Italian *Futuristi*.

[2] *Shaw on Theatre*, ed. E. J. West (New York, 1958), p. 137.

[3] *Ghosts* was repeated in 1893. Curiously, the Society mounted an Ibsen parody, Mrs Hugh Bell's *Jerry Builder Solness*, 1893. The critical response to *Ghosts* is discussed in Michael Orme, *J. T. Grein* (London, 1936), pp. 87–8. Edward Pigott, giving evidence before the House of Commons Select Committee in 1892, considered Ibsen's plays 'too absurd to be injurious to the public morals' (p. 553).

less artificial style of drama', and invited young dramatists to work with him.[1] To the Society's credit it did discover one important new dramatist, Bernard Shaw, whose *Widowers' Houses* was produced, again at the Royalty Theatre, in 1892. Unfortunately, either a streak of Victorian prudishness in Grein or an excess of caution prompted by the critical virulence (notably that of the conservative Clement Scott) which greeted *Ghosts* confined the Society's repertoire: Strindberg's *The Father* and Shaw's *The Philanderer* and *Mrs Warren's Profession* were among plays considered but not taken up.[2] In fact, after *Ghosts* the programme was not particularly challenging, and even some of the Society's more celebrated pieces, like Zola's *Thérèse Raquin*, were plays London managements would have had few qualms about putting on.[3] Nearly half the repertory consisted of foreign plays, particularly French and Dutch. Most were decidedly non-commercial; few have survived on the stage. Nor was the Society pioneering, as the Théâtre Libre had been, in its staging methods: stage décor, for example, was often more makeshift than purposefully economic, and the plays were for the most part acted by amateurs, competent but not always experienced. Although the very nature of amateur performance tended to undercut 'star' assumptions, there is little justification for the claim sometimes made that the Independent Theatre launched ensemble playing in England.[4]

What Grein and his colleagues pioneered was a dramatic rather than a theatrical revolution. In this as in other respects their work was distinct from the apparently more antiquarian concerns of William Poel (1852–1934) and the Elizabethan Stage Society he founded in 1894. Poel's experiments in the rediscovery of Elizabethan staging methods ran counter to much the professional theatre took for granted in production of Shakespeare: the adequacy of the proscenium-arch stage; the value of 'picture' staging, as a delight in itself and to provide convincing depiction of place; and the need to cut and adapt the texts to accommodate scenery and focus attention on 'star' performers.[5] In the course of a long career to 1932 he produced many plays by

---

[1] *The Times*, 14 March 1891.

[2] According to Grein's wife, Shaw himself decided that *The Philanderer* was not suitable for the Independent Theatre (Orme, op. cit.). *The Athenaeum* acutely predicted that the controversy excited by *Ghosts* would restrict the Society's future work (21 March 1891).

[3] *The Times*, 10 October 1891; N. Schoonderwoerd, *J. T. Grein, Ambassador of the Theatre* (Assen, 1963), p. 121; Jan McDonald, 'Continental Plays produced by the Independent Theatre Society, 1891–8', *Theatre Research International*, I, 1 (1975).

[4] Cf. Anna Irene Miller, *The Independent Theatre in Europe* (New York, 1931), p. 176.

[5] An interesting earlier attempt at quasi-Elizabethan staging is discussed by Jan McDonald, '*The Taming of the Shrew* at the Haymarket Theatre, 1884 and 1847', in Kenneth Richards and Peter Thomson (eds), *Nineteenth Century British Theatre* (London, 1971).

Shakespeare and other Elizabethans, as well as Milton's *Samson Agonistes*, Euripides' *Bacchae*, the first English performance of Molière's *Dom Juan*, and what many considered his finest production, the medieval *Everyman*.[1]

In 1893 Poel took over the Royalty Theatre in London for four performances of *Measure for Measure*, in which he himself played the part of Angelo. It was his first full attempt at Elizabethan staging and can conveniently illustrate his approach.[2] The Royalty's proscenium-arch stage was partially adapted on the model of the seventeenth-century Fortune. Behind the arch a second small proscenium was erected with a raised balcony or second stage, and 'two transverse curtains' were used to mark changes of scene and permit the fluid continuity of action characteristic of Elizabethan staging. Scenic accessories were reduced to a minimum, and stage decoration was supplied by a wide variety of colourful Elizabethan costumes. The bareness of the stage before the inner proscenium was partly broken by having 'supers' in costumes sitting on stools at the side, or occupying boxes specially stripped of their nineteenth-century upholstery. During the single ten-minute interval these actor-spectators smoked pipes. Some critics were irritated by the attention to minor detail 'while striking anachronisms obtruded themselves unchecked', such as use of footlights, gas lighting and actresses. Nor were Poel's players adequate to the sharp focus the staging put on performance.[3]

Occasionally when he worked in theatres Poel was able to break out of the proscenium frame and introduce an apron stage: thus a forestage covered the orchestra pit of His Majesty's for *The Two Gentlemen of Verona* he produced at Tree's 1910 Shakespeare Festival. In the more flexible Holborn Empire a full-scale Fortune-like platform was used for Rowley's *When You See Me You Know Me* (1927). He was not averse to using solid decoration and props when these were warranted: sketches in *The Daily Graphic* of furnishings for his production of *The Duchess of Malfi* (1892), a collaboration with Grein's Independent Theatre, show use of a canopied bed, chair and dressing mirror.[4] In his productions of Shakespeare and Elizabethan drama Poel gave chief place to the speaking of the text, and much of his early rehearsal time was

[1] All are discussed in detail in the standard work on Poel: Robert Speaight, *William Poel and the Elizabethan Revival*, Society for Theatre Research (London, 1954).

[2] Arthur Colby Sprague, *Shakespeare and William Poel* (Toronto, 1947), discusses in detail Poel's first venture, a reading of the 1603 'bad' Quarto of *Hamlet* in 1881. As J. Isaacs notes in *William Poel's Prompt-Book of Fratricide Punished*, Society for Theatre Research, Pamphlet 5 (1956), Poel was not concerned in this reading with creating an approximation to the Elizabethan stage.

[3] *The Times*, 10 November 1893; *The Athenaeum*, 18 November 1893.

[4] Cited in *Notes on Some of William Poel's Stage Productions* (London, 1933).

spent around a table practising the right delivery of blank verse according to what he called 'tuned tones': each speech was seen to possess a musical structure to which the actor had to be alert if his delivery was to capture the appropriate pace, variety and emphasis.[1] Unfortunately he often worked with amateurs of limited vocal skill, and the result in performance was at times an awkwardness and artificiality of delivery which, when allied, as occasionally it was, to under-rehearsed movements which failed to exploit the choreographic potential of the 'open' stage, reinforced in the minds of hostile critics and traditionalists the impression that he was a mere antiquarian eccentric. At times he undermined his own case by trimming his principles. Quick to criticize the actor-managers' mutilation of Shakespeare with cuts and substitutions, he was not above the practice himself, and his Victorian temper led him to censor or alter the scenic and verbal directness of some plays he produced.[2]

Both Grein and Poel were important pioneers of a 'new' drama and theatre. The Independent Theatre Society is of account less for its practical achievement than for the example it set. It helped to crystallize the need for repertory theatres free of commercial imperatives, willing to put on serious drama, and alert to new developments in England and abroad. Its policy of hiring a hall or theatre for occasional publicized performances set a precedent for groups like the New Century Theatre (1897) and the Stage Society (1899), as it did for Poel's Elizabethan Stage Society. The emphasis Poel placed on the basics of performance and his advocacy of a simple, permanent set helped to point staging in new directions. His work on medieval, Elizabethan, antique and even oriental drama advanced the cause of non-naturalistic theatre and encouraged the modern rediscovery of the neglected repertory of the past. He helped to bridge the gulf between academic study and professional practice, and was the forerunner of several distinguished scholar-practitioners who have united both disciplines.[3] Poel was not, as he rightly claimed, merely an archaeologist and antiquarian, but was in many respects a modernist and, as Peter Brook has said, 'a great innovator'.[4] Yet there was some alloy to these achievements: about both societies there was a

---

[1] Discussed in detail by Speaight, op. cit. pp. 61–9; W. Bridges Adams, *The Lost Leader* (London, 1954), p. 7.

[2] See particularly Speaight's discussion of the cuts made in *Measure for Measure*, op. cit. pp. 98–101.

[3] Including, fittingly, Poel's biographer, Robert Speaight.

[4] Peter Brook, *The Empty Space* (London, 1968), p. 80. One may note Poel's enthusiasm for Reinhardt's use of the 'open' stage in his London productions of *Oedipus*: William Poel, *Monthly Letters* (London, 1929).

certain élitist intellectual austerity. Their reaction against the professional status quo was a rejection not only of commercial and fashionable but in part of 'popular' theatre – the received tradition of farce, melodrama and spectacle.[1] The consequent divorce of 'mass' and 'minority' theatre was not all to the good, and is felt in the repertory movement which in some measure evolved from their example.

(ii) The repertory movement

The evolution of the repertory movement after the turn of the century was complex. It drew inspiration, and sometimes direct support, from a variety of sources: the work of Grein, Poel and Benson; the achievement of Continental repertory companies; the example of embryo repertories piloted in the eighties and nineties like those of Janet Achurch and Florence Farr; the writings of critics and dramatists like Archer, McCarthy and Shaw; the enthusiasm of wealthy activists like Miss Annie Horniman and Barry Jackson; and the enlightened support of lay managers like Charles Frohman. The repertory idea, however variously fostered, was set against the governing principles of the commercial status quo: it was an attempt to counter the domination of the 'long run', the 'star' system, and the rotational occupancy of provincial theatres by London-based touring companies. In so far as aims were shared, repertory theatres aspired to frequent changes of bill, and had a conception of ensemble performance that organized individual excellence in acting to the needs of the play rather than to the aggrandizement of 'personality' leads. Most wished to encourage new British drama and to mount plays of all ages and nations. While hostility to the structure of established theatre was implicit in their aims, they saw themselves more as alternatives than as competitors.[2] Their aims were only partially achieved. What developed was not repertory proper, on the Continental model of several plays performed in a single week, but rather repertory of short runs. There had to be compromise with an apparently ineradicable audience taste for the long run, and with the sense of occasion that had come to be associated with theatregoing. Adjustment was necessary, too, to professional realities: habits of rapid study characteristic of 'stock' acting had been lost, and very frequent changes of bill were not economically viable.

[1] Poel was disparaging of variety and music hall: see William Poel, op. cit. p. 99, and *What is Wrong with the Stage* (London, 1920), p. 9.
[2] See P. P. Howe, *The Repertory Theatre* (London, 1910).

In London repertory companies were decidedly 'minority' theatres, attracting educated audiences interested in new drama, rarely performed foreign plays, or new developments in stagecraft. Such were the Barker–Vedrenne seasons at the Court Theatre, Lena Ashwell's work at the Kingsway, Charles Frohman's repertory at the Duke of York's (1910) or Gertrude Kingston's at the Little (1910). More specialist, but potentially of broader appeal, was an offshoot of the repertory movement, the Old Vic. In 1912 the redoubtable Lilian Baylis inherited management of this small theatre in the Waterloo Road and two years later, almost by accident, established there a permanent London base for Shakespeare when she began alternating plays with her first love, opera. Battling against economic exigencies and primitive house conditions, and often working with makeshift costumes and props, the Old Vic managed to reverse a general drift in the war years towards the trivial in entertainment. It consolidated its position under the artistic direction of Ben Greet and later of Robert Atkins. Its prodigious achievements are best evaluated in the context of theatre between the wars, as too are those of Barry Jackson and the Birmingham Repertory Theatre he started, from amateur beginnings, in 1913.

Most repertory theatres in major provincial towns had specific local purposes – to provide regular quality drama alternatives for towns mainly provisioned by touring companies, and to give provincial communities a sense of cultural identity. Alfred Wareing's shortlived Glasgow Repertory (1909) was a determined attempt to break with dependence on London offerings; the Liverpool Repertory, started in 1911 by a group of amateur enthusiasts on a shareholder basis, aspired for its foyer to be 'the centre of the artistic and intellectual life' of the city.[1] Yet provincial repertories were, in the main, although not 'experimental' or 'art' houses, no less 'minority' theatres than those of London. If they provided quality theatre at popular prices, quality was invariably conceived in literary and intellectual terms, and they were initiated and largely supported by the educated middle classes. Intellectual élitism allied with theatre's new-won social respectability to strengthen the middle-class hold on straight theatre.[2] Nor was adventurousness a marked feature of their programmes. In its early seasons Liverpool's choice of plays was eclectic, but if it won a certain reputation for mounting romantic drama,

[1] Cited by Grace W. Goldie, *The Liverpool Repertory Theatre 1911–1935* (Liverpool and London, 1935), p. 64.

[2] This is not to detract from the achievement of the repertory theatres, but merely to state a case. At first nights 'distinguished' and 'influential' local figures were prominent in audiences. The opening of the Liverpool Repertory Theatre, Goldie notes, was celebrated by Lord Derby presiding over a 'turbot and pheasant' supper for 200 shareholders (p. 67).

like Wilde's *A Florentine Tragedy*, only with James Sexton's *The Riot Act* (1914) did it advance a play based on Liverpool life. In finding local dramatic talent the Gaiety Theatre, Manchester, was more fortunate. This repertory company, started by Miss Horniman in 1907 at the small Midland Hotel Theatre as 'purely a dramatic artistic venture on honestly commercial lines', was richly stocked with players who had acted formerly with Poel, Benson and Granville Barker.[1] When it moved to the Gaiety in 1908 Poel supervised the opening production, *Measure for Measure*. Alone among the early English provincial repertories it nurtured a vigorous local drama. Its discovery of the Lancashire dramatists, Houghton, Brighouse and Monkhouse, together with Iden Payne's Barker-inspired direction of 'naturalistic' plays, quickly gave it a reputation for disciplined, sincere realism, which the company carried to London in successful short seasons at the Coronet Theatre. But with London success and American tours the Gaiety's hold on its Manchester audience began to wane. Indeed during the war the repertory movement rather lay dormant as public interest was diverted from theatre: in 1917 the Gaiety ceased to operate as a permanent repertory company, and after 1914 the Liverpool theatre was kept going only by the staff forming a small-salaried cooperative, The Commonwealth. In Birmingham Barry Jackson was more fortunate: his repertory survived the war and proved an inspiration to others. In various guises and with some subsidy, the repertory idea returned in the post-war years.

One repertory early supported by private and later by state subsidy was one of the most important: the Irish National Theatre. Its tangled early history has often been told. Conceived as the Irish Literary Theatre in 1898 by W. B. Yeats (1865–1939), Lady Gregory and Edward Martyn, in 1902 it merged with the National Dramatic Society of W. G. and Frank Fay to form the Irish National Theatre Society. This acquired a permanent theatre of its own when Miss Horniman, impressed with the Society's work and the genius and ambitions of Yeats, after consulting 'Tarot cards and charts' for reassurance, leased the Mechanics' Institute, spent some £6000 on modifications, and offered it to the Society together with a small annual grant.[2] Renamed the Abbey Theatre, and complete with official patent, it opened on a repertory basis at the end of December 1904 with Yeats's *Cathleen Ni Houlihan*. The early years were difficult: audiences were at first sparse; the Players were dubbed 'amateurish'; champions of Gaelic drama looked

---

[1] Rex Pogson, *Miss Horniman and The Gaiety Theatre, Manchester* (London, 1952), p. 23.

[2] James W. Flannery, *Miss Annie F. Horniman and the Abbey Theatre* (Dublin, 1970), p. 8.

askance at the Abbey's work; there were internal dissensions. In 1908 the Fay brothers left after the Abbey Directors had apparently refused W. G. Fay the right to select actors and to determine performance policy.[1] In 1909 Miss Horniman broke away and discontinued her subsidy. Yeats, ever the moving spirit, was now indisputably the key figure, and his influence was to remain dominant at the Abbey for decades.

From the outset Yeats's dedication to a repertory of high artistic standards was sure, though tempered by recognition of the limits within which the new and small company had to work: thus he rejected Shaw's *John Bull's Other Island* in 1904 as beyond the scope of the Abbey players and the taste of their Dublin audience.[2] His policy of cultivating new Irish drama was rewarded in the work of Padraic Colum, George Fitzmaurice and Lady Gregory, and notably in the plays of the most important and original dramatist discovered by the movement, John Millington Synge. Yeats himself, of course, wrote many of his plays for Abbey performance. The characteristic Abbey fare was a far cry from the sub-Boucicault melodrama that had dominated the Irish stage at the turn of the century. Nor did it have much in common with the contemporary intellectual drama of social engagement. Significantly, the only Shaw performed at the Abbey was *The Shewing-Up of Blanco Posnet*, and no play by Ibsen was produced there until *A Doll's House* in 1923. Yet the repertoire was not exclusively Irish. Indeed, an aim of the Abbey from its inception, and one championed particularly by Miss Horniman, was to mount an international programme, which included in the first decade plays by Maeterlinck, Molière, Goldoni and Strindberg. This aspect of the Abbey's early work has been rather obscured by understandable interest in the theatre's involvement with Irish drama and the nationalist movement.[3]

Yeats was an original theorist and an uncompromising reformer who sought radical change on the modern stage in plays, speaking, acting and scenery. His theory was strongly felt in Abbey stage practice. No advocate of a bare stage, he was alert to new developments in scenic design, as is

[1] For discussion of the controversy, see Lennox Robinson, *Ireland's Abbey Theatre* (London, 1951), p. 56, and Gerard Fay, *The Abbey Theatre* (London, 1958), pp. 101 ff.

[2] Robinson, op. cit. p. 59. Alternatively, St John Ervine has said that *John Bull* was not performed because Yeats 'could not make head or tail of the play when he read it', *Bernard Shaw* (London, 1956), p. 372.

[3] The growth of the Irish National Theatre movement was in some respects akin to the emergence of a distinctively Norwegian theatre at Bergen in the 1860s. See Frank J. Fay, *Towards a National Theatre, Dramatic Criticism*, ed. with introduction by Robert Hogan (Dublin, 1970), pp. 56–8. For a comparison between the ideals of the Irish movement and those of the Moscow Art Theatre, see Micheal O'hAodha, *Theatre in Ireland* (Oxford, 1974), pp. 31 ff.

witnessed by his interest in the work of Gordon Craig, Charles Ricketts and the designers of the Diaghilev company. Scenery in the Society and Abbey productions was perforce economical, but the economy was as much deliberate as imposed, a conscious decision to employ the modest and functional. Fundamental to Yeats's theory and practice was an attempt to re-explore the core of performance – speech and movement. Greek drama was his precedent for affirming the primacy of speech wedded to restrained yet expressive gesture, and he was hostile to stage 'business' and big physical playing: 'the actors must move, for the most part, slowly and quietly, and not very much, and there should be something in their movements decorative and rhythmical as if they were paintings on a frieze.'[1]

Yet the effect in performance was something different. There was from the beginning a contradiction in the National Theatre's artistic aims and methods: in drama, between stylized verse plays and plays of poetic prose realism; in performance between the hieratic and the representational. The contradiction was evident in early work: trained by Yeats for performance in his own verse dramas, when the Irish actors gave Synge's *Riders to the Sea* in London in 1904, their approach tended to 'impede the right effect of the play'.[2] The performance styles Yeats advocated were supremely suited to his own verse plays, less apposite for the work of others. But the contradiction provided a fruitful creative tension: working towards Yeats's ideal of disciplined, economical performance helped the Abbey Company to retain the ease and simplicity that had characterized the first productions of the National Theatre Society. At the same time the native dramatic materials and the natural vigour and independence of the actors preserved spontaneity and prevented their work from falling into quaint and precious ways of playing that Yeats's theory unrestrained might have encouraged. The Abbey players, said Shaw, settled down ruthlessly to the principle of 'making the audience believe that such things were happening to real people'.[3] But theirs was no mere reproduction of the actual. George Moore's claim that Yeats unwittingly founded a 'naturalistic' theatre was an overstatement. The Abbey players fashioned a very individual style of poetic realism and, together with Harley Granville Barker's actors at the Court Theatre, became an example to English-speaking theatre of controlled and fluent ensemble playing.

[1] *Samhain* (1904).
[2] Max Beerbohm, *Around Theatres*, p. 316.
[3] *Shaw on Theatre*, p. 155. Cf. Walkley in *The Times*, 8 May 1903.

(iii) The repertories of Harley Granville Barker

The role of the director in the theatre evolved gradually from the demands of stage-management, and was essentially the end product of the increasing need in late nineteenth-century theatre to harmonize the multiple details of a production. Traditionally, mounting a play had been in the hands of a leading actor or dramatist, closely assisted by a stage-manager. In British theatre the director effectively emerged as an autonomous figure when the triple qualities of actor, dramatist and stage-manager came together in the work of Harley Granville Barker (1877–1946), aptly described by Shaw as 'altogether the most distinguished and incomparably the most cultivated person whom circumstances had driven into the theatre at that time'.[1]

Shaw's plays formed the basis of Barker's first important venture, the repertory company he co-managed with John Vedrenne at the Court Theatre between 1904 and 1907: eleven were given during the two and a half years of the management. But if Shaw provided Barker with a wealth of plays, Barker in turn, by virtue of his acting talent, artistic sense and organizing ability, helped to launch Shaw's national reputation. He created many Shavian roles; his Jack Tanner in *Man and Superman* (1905), in which he was made up with red beard to look like Shaw himself, was particularly admired: 'never was playwright more lucky in finding a born interpreter of his talent'.[2] Shaw directed his own plays, but Barker worked closely with him and was fully responsible for the other Court productions. His actors 'either underacted, or were afraid to act at all lest they should be accused of ranting or being "hams" ', complained Shaw.[3] But this was not the general view. Rather, the carefully studied, almost stylized 'naturalism' of his staging of plays like Galsworthy's *The Silver Box* (1906) and his own *The Voysey Inheritance* (1905) was widely admired, and the productions approved for their 'qualities of proportion and completeness' and for 'the smooth illusion of life' they created.[4] Nor was Barker's direction confined to 'naturalistic' plays: he did

---

[1] *Shaw on Theatre*, p. 260. Perhaps equally important in establishing the idea of the director in the English theatre were the productions of *Sumurūn* and *The Miracle* (1911) and *Oedipus* (1912) by the visiting Max Reinhardt, for he was neither major actor nor major dramatist but a director *sui generis*.

[2] Desmond MacCarthy, *Shaw* (London, 1961), p. 32; A. B. Walkley, *Drama and Life* (London, 1907), p. 232.

[3] *Shaw on Theatre*, p. 267.

[4] MacCarthy, op. cit. p. 61; Beerbohm, *Around Theatres*, p. 481. Perhaps the most consummate of Barker's 'naturalistic' productions was Galsworthy's *Justice* (1910). The seasons are discussed at length in Desmond MacCarthy, *The Court Theatre* (London,

imaginative stagings of plays by Maeterlinck, Yeats and Euripides, and brought to these the same concern for meticulous preparations and tight ensemble playing.

Barker's aims at the Court were ambitious, and were inspired by his enthusiasm for the repertory idea and his concern to develop a National Theatre. He was committed to the principle of 'short runs': the most successful Court plays, like Shaw's *You Never Can Tell*, were not given for more than five or six weeks; even Mrs Patrick Campbell's brilliant Hedda Gabler received only seven matinées.[1] Barker's policy of cultivating new and foreign plays was close in spirit to that of Grein's Independent Theatre, but it extended Grein's policy by including rarely performed classical drama. Unlike Grein, Barker sought to reform staging, in particular to curb the spread of what he called 'crude, impersonative realism' in acting, a promiscuous and desultory 'naturalness' that scorned acquisition of performer skills in the name of the spontaneous and lifelike. If Barker suited styles to plays, the bias of his reform was towards a disciplined, premeditated realism. Yet although the repertory seasons were favourably noticed and attracted a regular clientele, the policy of new and quality plays presented in matinées and short runs could not 'bear the burden of London rents and London rates'.[2] Much the same fate was to overtake Barker's later repertory ventures. In the autumn of 1907, again with Vedrenne, he presented a season of Shaw, Galsworthy and Greek tragedy at the Savoy Theatre, in what was a deliberate but unsuccessful attempt to carry the principles of the Court closer to the heartland of London theatre. His work with the American manager, Charles Frohman, in 1910 at the Duke of York's, included productions of Galsworthy's *Justice* and his own *The Madras House*. He co-managed several repertories with his wife, Lillah McCarthy, one at the Little Theatre in 1911, and another at the St James's in 1913. All these were important if shortlived endeavours to advance predominantly modern drama in a repertory context that put a premium on intellectual and artistic high seriousness. Among critics and audiences they generated enthusiasm and hostility in equal measure, ran some danger of becoming the coterie taste of a progressive

1907), and C. B. Purdom, *Harley Granville Barker* (London, 1955). See also Anthony Jackson, 'Harley Granville Barker as Director at the Court Theatre 1904–7', *Theatre Research/Recherches théâtrales*, XII, 2 (1972); *Bernard Shaw's Letters to Granville Barker*, ed. C. B. Purdom (London, 1956).

[1] Dent, *Mrs Patrick Campbell*, p. 214. Barker's attitude to the repertory ideal and the theatre of his day is seen in his 'Repertory Theatres', *New Quarterly*, II (1909), and 'The Theatre: the Next Phase', *English Review*, V (1910).

[2] *Shaw on Theatre*, p. 262.

intelligentsia, and failed to demonstrate the financial viability of the short run. But they affirmed principles in organization and production which were to inspire many later repertory companies in London, and even more in the provinces. So too did three productions of plays by Shakespeare which Barker presented at the Savoy Theatre, *The Winter's Tale* and *Twelfth Night* in 1912, and *A Midsummer Night's Dream* in 1914.

Barker's Shakespeare productions were consciously reformist. They demonstrated, as the productions of William Poel had done earlier, that Shakespeare could be staged effectively without recourse to expensive and often irrelevant scenic decoration, and that the speed and continuity of Elizabethan staging could be achieved without resort to wholesale cutting of the text and transposition and modification of scenes. But Barker was acutely aware of the immediate needs of the professional theatre and recognized that the rediscovery of Elizabethan staging methods should serve as a guide to the modern director and not be regarded as an end in itself: he was in no sense an Elizabethan 'revivalist'.[1] At the Savoy he adapted the proscenium – arch stage by introducing a forestage over the orchestra pit and proscenium doors for exits and entrances when the proscenium curtains were closed and only the forestage was in use. This basic division into two performance areas was economical, for it permitted use of only two scenes in each production: one on the inner stage consisted (in all the productions) of a few carefully chosen and blended rostra and scenic units, like Perdita's cottage fronted by a green hedge in *A Winter's Tale*, or the formal garden and canopied dais in *Twelfth Night*; the other, before colourful and patterned proscenium curtains, was dressed only with one or two basic props, such as a throne or chair.[2] Scenes were varied by adjusting the backing drapes and rearranging the set furnishings. These settings provided a background that would 'reflect light and suggest space', and permitted 'many changes of scene and action, without pause, and without cutting down the text'.[3] Costumes, like sets, were colourful but essentially of no period, although in all the productions there was a remote and oriental quality about them suggesting that Barker's designers may have been influenced by the dazzlingly original and revolutionary décor of Alexandre Benois and the Diaghilev company which had performed in

[1] 'We shall not save our souls by being Elizabethan', *Play Pictorial*, XXI, 26 (1912), p. iv.
[2] M. St Clare Byrne, 'Fifty Years of Shakespearian Production', in *Shakespeare Survey* (Cambridge, 1949); Norman Marshall, *The Producer and the Play* (London, 1957); Hugh Hunt, 'Granville Barker's Savoy Shakespeare Productions', *Theatre Research/Recherches théâtrales*, X, 1 (1969), pp. 44–9; W. Bridges Adams, *The Lost Leader*, op. cit.
[3] Albert Rutherston, 'Decoration in the Art of the Theatre', lecture given at the University of Leeds, printed in *The Monthly Chapbook*, I, 2 (1919), p. 19.

London in 1911.[1] Writing himself of the 'confoundedly-puzzling' scenic elements, Barker observed, 'to invent a new hieroglyphic language of scenery, that, in a phrase, is the problem'.[2]

It is the scenic innovations which are most frequently remarked, but perhaps more important for Barker were his attempts with actors to continue the work he had begun at the Court – to explore methods of ensemble playing and fashion a disciplined and craft-conscious realistic acting. Both were allied at the Savoy with a search for right modes of delivering Shakespearian verse, and examining the new potentialities for blending speech, gesture and movement invited by a partially 'open' stage. This focus on acting and actor interpretation is felt in Barker's *Prefaces to Shakespeare*, written after the war when he had largely abandoned practical theatre work. These were to be highly influential during the inter-war years, particularly at the Old Vic, and to some extent may have deflected attention then from many new staging developments on the Continent.[3]

Barker's Savoy Shakespeare productions were not only original scenic re-orchestrations of the plays, but were genuinely fresh intellectual readings which scrapped much of the traditional scenic approach and jettisoned received 'business' and characterization – notably, in the clowning antics.[4] But they were not as revolutionary as some contemporary critics tended to suggest. A little selfconsciously novel, rather mannered, decidedly decorative and eclectic (as Poel thought), they modified English staging approaches to Shakespeare rather than initiated anything radically new. Interestingly, one of Barker's Savoy designers, Albert Rutherston, identifying the one figure equipped to bring about significant change in the British theatre, cited not Barker but Edward Gordon Craig.[5]

(iv) The practice and theory of Edward Gordon Craig

By the time Barker mounted his Savoy Shakespeare productions some younger stage designers had come radically to question the assumptions and status of traditional scene painting. Changes in approach to stage decoration were in part a response to new movements in the fine arts, and represented a

[1] Hunt, op. cit.; Rutherston, op. cit. p. 24.
[2] *Play Pictorial*, XXI, 26 (1912), p. iv.
[3] From, in effect, the search for 'a new hieroglyphic language of scenery'.
[4] *The Times*, 16 November 1912.
[5] Albert Rutherston, op. cit.

reaction against heavy sets and both a literal and a literary theatre. In part, too, they were a consequence of the emergence of the director in the theatre: the more marked the emphasis on overall unity of tone in a production, the more the functions of director and scenic designer appeared to converge. In a lecture on stage decoration in 1915, Rutherston urged that the designer should control not only costumes and scenes, but 'the grouping of the figures, the lighting of them, and of the scene'.[1] This was a basic tenet of one of the most potent forces in early twentieth-century stage design, Edward Gordon Craig (1872–1966).

The son of Ellen Terry and the architect and designer E. W. Godwin, Craig spent eight years of his early manhood acting with Irving at the Lyceum. In the late 1890s, equipped with drawing and woodcut skills, and in collaboration with a musician and composer friend Martin Shaw, he turned to design and direction, mounting productions of *Dido and Aeneas* (1900; the Hampstead Conservatoire), *The Masque of Love* (1901; the Coronet Theatre) and Handel's *Acis and Galatea* (1902; the Great Queen Street Theatre).[2] All three were distinctive for their imaginative use of light and space and exploitation of simple but highly functional materials. Particularly original were the 'grey box set' for *The Masque of Love* and the use of a diaphanous gauze tent for 'the mystic, far off, dreamy and visionary scenes' of *Acis and Galatea*.[3] Other Craig work quickly followed: three scenes for Fred Terry's musical, *For Sword or Song*, and a production of Laurence Housman's *Bethlehem* in 1902; and the scenery and lighting for *The Vikings of Helgeland* and *Much Ado about Nothing* in 1903, for his mother's management at the Imperial Theatre, Westminster. The two interior and two exterior scenes for *The Vikings* were particularly novel and ambitious experiments with colour tones and the deployment of stage figures in stage space. Craig departed from the detail of Ibsen's stage directions and sought to realize the scenes in terms of the moods implicit in character and action. Thus the setting for the first act was a sloping grey rock on a grey coast with an arching dark blue backcloth for sea and sky, and the final exterior a small

[1] Rutherston, op. cit. p. 12.

[2] Two important shaping influences were Hubert von Herkomer, who experimented with direction and lighting and whose lectures Craig attended, and Craig's father, Godwin, who realized his idea of a director-designer controlling all elements of a production in private productions of *As You Like It* and *The Faithful Shepherdess*. Their work is discussed in John Stokes, *Resistible Theatres* (London, 1972); Dudley Harbron, *The Conscious Stone: The Life of Edward William Godwin* (1949); Edward Craig, 'Gordon Craig and Hubert von Herkomer', *Theatre Research/Recherches théâtrales*, X, 1 (1969).

[3] Edward Craig, *Gordon Craig* (London, 1968), p. 136; *The Playgoer*, II (April–September 1902), p. 33.

grey hill set against a background of deep shadow; the two interiors contrasted, one a circular, doorless banqueting hall, its walls in vertical lines of variegated greys, the other, more intimate and brooding, a scene with a low wall backed by purple curtains.[1]

Craig's disillusionment with the easy acceptances of English professional theatre, and the general indifference to his work, prompted him to accept an invitation from Otto Brahm to design Otway's *Venice Preserved* for the Lessing Theatre, Berlin. His departure for Germany began a lifelong, self-imposed exile; in its course most of his practical theatre plans were to be frustrated. Although he made some designs for the Otway production the project eventually fell through, as did possibilities in 1905 of working with Max Reinhardt, and of designing Hofmannsthal's *Elektra* for Eleanora Duse. At the end of that year he conceived a brilliantly atmospheric scene, using basic drawing-room furnishings within a non-realistic architectural setting, for Duse's *Rosmersholm* at the Teatro della Pergola in Florence. But other work contemplated for Duse, including another Ibsen, never materialized. Nor did the Tree production of *Macbeth* (1910) for which Craig prepared designs and models: Tree was persuaded by his regular designer, Joseph Harker, that aside from 'their obvious ugliness' the sets were wholly unpracticable.[2] More fortunate was the *Hamlet* he designed for the Moscow Art Theatre: initiated in 1908 on Stanislavsky's invitation and subject to many delays, it was finally produced in 1912. Craig designed for it settings based on adjustable screens, a system he had evolved from his readings in Serlio and Semper and from experiments on model stages. These screens, perhaps Craig's major contribution to scenic art, were themselves to be dramatically expressive, easily shifted into a variety of positions, their planes catching light or throwing shadow. Unfortunately, when transferred from model to stage proper the screens, not metal as Craig had wished but made of plain canvas on wooden frames, proved difficult to move with safety without lowering the curtain between changes.[3]

Craig was to undertake only one other major production, Ibsen's *The Pretenders* at the Royal Danish Theatre, Copenhagen, in 1926. Increasingly, after the disappointments of 1905, he turned to writing and exhibitions of his designs as alternative ways of propagating his work and ideas. His first im-

---

[1] These scenes are described and discussed in detail by Ferruccio Marotti in *Gordon Craig* (Bologna, 1961), pp. 52–8. See also E. Craig, *Gordon Craig*, pp. 171–5.

[2] Harker, *Studio and Stage* (London, 1924), p. 176.

[3] The production is described in detail by Marotti, op. cit., and discussed also in the same author's *Amleto o dell'oxymoron* (Rome, 1966), pp. 175 ff.

portant statement, *The Art of the Theatre*, was published in that year and was later revised and extended as *On the Art of the Theatre* (1911); *Towards a New Theatre* followed in 1912 and *The Theatre Advancing* in 1921; in 1908 he launched his journal *The Mask*, which for the next twenty-one years provided him with an outlet for his ideas. In part this resort to books, articles and exhibitions was a strategy forced upon him by professional indifference or hostility, but it came, too, to reflect an important shift in his thinking. In 1911 he wrote in his private Day-Book:

> I want time to study the Theatre. I do not want to waste time producing plays – for that is vanity – expensive – unsatisfying – *comic* . . . I seek to know. I do *not* seek a position or success.[1]

By this time Craig had been involved practically in theatre for more than twenty years as actor, director and designer; his theory was the product of an experienced practitioner, not a mere thoughtful dreamer. Theory was to follow practice, because practice had shown the need for fundamental re-thinking.

A basic postulate for Craig was that theatre had had its origin in expressive, poetic movement. A true art of the theatre entailed a perfect fusion of action, word, line, colour and rhythm.[2] In the want of that fusion theatre lacked artistic 'form'. Much of Craig's practical experimentation was directed towards the rediscovery of form for the modern theatre.[3] His Moscow *Hamlet* had been an attempt to realize his ideal of a moving set that would complement, in a unity of significant motion, the movement of light and of actors and the shifting moods of the dramatic action. Unfortunately, his imagination at times overreached the staging possibilities of the theatre of his day: metal screens could not be moved; wood and canvas screens had no stability. But the perception was valid. So too was that which underpinned his highly contentious theory of the *Über-marionette* who should replace the familiar stage actor. What Craig asked of actors was not that they become puppets, but that they create a new mode of acting, or rediscover a lost one, the mode of 'symbolical gesture'.[4] Craig, indeed, sought not to reform theatre but to revolutionize it by a return to certain first principles. But the

[1] From a longer note cited by E. Craig, *Gordon Craig*, p. 261.
[2] Edward Gordon Craig, *On the Art of the Theatre*, 5th ed. (London, 1957), p. 138. For a discussion of Craig's ideas about movement, see Arnold Rood, ' "After the Practice the Theory": Gordon Craig and Movement', *Theatre Research/Recherches théâtrales*, XI, 2 and 3 (1971).
[3] E. G. Craig, *On the Art of the Theatre*, p. 111.
[4] Ibid. p. 61.

traditions of centuries were not to be so easily discarded. In design his original handling of colour, line and spatial relationships, and his attempts to create psychologically appropriate moods rather than to picture the actual, bewildered and alienated the older school of designers.[1] Although major players, from Ellen Terry to Tree and Duse, were enthusiastic about his work, it necessarily left them uneasy: their artistic sense recognized its originality, but their professional experience warned that ultimately it demanded radical adjustments in performance.

Craig himself was aware of the need for a new and comprehensive training in basics, hence his long-contemplated plans for a theatre school, finally, though briefly, established in 1913 at the Arena Goldoni in Florence. In fact his work was all of a piece throughout: he practised, studied, speculated, taught. Theatre of the past and present – Greek and Oriental, masks and marionettes, jongleurs, acrobats and music-hall entertainers, Renaissance perspective stage and *commedia dell'arte* performance – all had lessons to teach. Particularly to the new artist of the future, the *homme du théâtre* capable of designing scenes, costumes, lighting and actors' movement: the artist whose work would dissolve the hybrid actors' and playwrights' theatre in an art of the theatre *sui generis*. Much in Craig's work and thought appears to be a strong reaction against what Irving had stood for in theatre, notably 'personality' acting and heavy sets, yet Irving remained throughout his first and greatest master. Certain Irving qualities were more shaping: Irving's singleminded dedication to theatre, his pictorial sense, his pantomimic genius, his elevation of the theatrical above the literary. As actor and *metteur en scène* Irving part-presaged Craig's ideal of the all-governing artist of the theatre. Brief account of a period long dominated by the presence of the one can fittingly end with the practice and theory of the other, for it was against the challenges of that practice and theory that the achievement of British theatre after the First World War stood to be measured.

[1] One of Irving's designers, William Telbin, made a blanket estimate of the whole modern movement: 'Bolshevism and Cubism are – psychologically – related'; cited in Harker, op. cit. p. 210. See also B. Hewitt, 'Gordon Craig and Post-Impressionism', *Quarterly Journal of Speech*, XXX (1944).

II (b) Actors and theatres 1918 to the present day

Hugh Hunt

I Theatrical trends in the twenties

(i) The West End – managers, musicals and matinée idols

Flying Colours, *Joy Bells*, *Oh, Joy!*, *Bubbly*, *Tails Up*, *Kissing Time* – if titles told the mood of the theatregoing public the playbills of London's West End suggested the exuberance of a victorious nation. But the exuberance, like the playbills, was paper-thin. After four years of war, nervous tension could not easily be relaxed; nor could the war-weary mind turn speedily to the problems of a world that would never be the same.

London was crowded with a restless, bewildered public craving for entertainment that entailed no mental effort. The age of commercial 'show-business' had come. Fortunes could be won by those who were prepared to exploit the public mood. From 1918 to 1924 theatre box offices experienced the greatest boom they had ever known. Theatres were bought and sold, leased and subleased, by managers who had little concern for what happened on the stage. The old-style actor-manager, ruling as undisputed monarch in his own theatre, was replaced by the non-acting manager controlling and manipulating a number of theatres which presented widely different types of entertainment. No longer could actors and actresses count on the security of a season's work with the 'Chief' or the 'Guv'. No longer could acting potential be stretched by a variety of parts. Typecasting and personality-acting took the place of character interpretation. Whatever may have been the faults of the old paternalistic system, it bred mutual interest and loyalty between employer and employed. Now there arose division between actor and manager. In the midst of plenty there were hard times for those not fortunate enough to be exploited as 'stars'. In the race for profits managers sought cheap labour by employing incompetent and untrained actors. Self-defence was necessary if the professional player was to survive. In 1919 the easygoing Actors' Association was re-formed on a trade-union basis. The stage was split between capital and labour, and the theatrical agent became a necessary middle-man between the two.

But the ranks of the managers were split between those whose interest was property ownership and those who presented plays. Among the latter were many who possessed a genuine love of theatre and who, within the limitations of the commercial system, were prepared to gamble their fortunes and those of their backers to provide entertainment of taste and integrity.

Throughout the twenties the major demand for entertainment was centred on the musical stage. Variety, vaudeville, revue, operetta and musical comedy dominated the West End theatres. As the decade entered its second half the great boom was over. Competition from the cinema made extravagant demands on the showmanship of theatre managers. Hollywood musicals had to be rivalled with importations from the American stage. As costs soared upwards, the risks grew greater. André Charlot and C. B. Cochran were no strangers to bankruptcy, though the former produced his revues on a shoe-string and to the latter the word parsimony was unknown. Between 1915 and 1935 Charlot staged no less than thirty-six revues, discovering in the process many of the matinée idols of the twenties and thirties, and providing Noël Coward with his first opening as a revue writer.[1] But it was to Cochran, the master showman, who staged everything from boxing matches to *The Miracle*, that credit was due for promoting Coward's genius as a writer of revue and musical comedy. From 1924 to 1931 the association of Cochran and Coward provided Britain's most sophisticated contribution to musical theatre. A Cochran show was a hallmark of quality; his name was billed as large as those of the 'stars'. Yet it was the matinée idols of the period who provided the sure recipe for success: Alice Delysia, Josie Collins, 'June', Gladys Cooper, Adele Astaire, Gertrude Lawrence, Jessie Matthews, gowned by the leading couturiers, led the fashion for the Bright Young Things. George Grossmith, Seymour Hicks, Fred Astaire, Owen Nares and Jack Buchanan, sartorially immaculate in top-hats and tails, provided a dream

[1] *London Calling* (1923).

world for the Gallery Girls. The personality-acting of the matinée idols reached beyond the twenties, merging with the idols of the cinema, and stretching onwards to the 'pop' singers of today. In a world bereft of heroes the public worships the heroes of make-believe.

(ii) Acting styles

Personality and sex appeal being commercial commodities, many of the idols found the necessary backing to join the managerial ranks. Of these the most eminent was Gerald du Maurier (1873–1933). Du Maurier was the last of the great actor-managers. As leader of the post-war acting profession he ruled unchallenged at Wyndham's Theatre from 1919 to 1925 in much the same way as Irving had done at the Lyceum and Herbert Beerbohm Tree at His Majesty's. As a manager he followed the paternalistic tradition, but as an actor he has been credited with introducing a new style of acting. The du Maurier style was in fact a development of that of Hawtrey and Alexander to whose mannered naturalism he added the apparent ease of non-acting – the 'throwaway' line, the witty understatement, the perfect timing of a pause or gesture. The du Maurier style owed nothing to the realism of Stanislavsky, of which he and his contemporaries were totally unaware, nor could it compass the rhetorical style of the Victorian Shakespearian actors. It was essentially of its time; essentially British in its suppression of emotion; essentially professional in its apparent ease. Du Maurier was a powerful influence on the future of British acting.

The rhetorical or late romantic style lingered on, but its exponents were more likely to earn a living in the provinces than in the fashionable West End where Shakespeare spelt death. It was the melodramas – *The Wandering Jew*, *The Only Way* and *The Scarlet Pimpernel* – that provided the 'stand-bys' of Matheson Lang, Fred Terry and John Martin-Harvey. At the Little Theatre Sybil Thorndike and Lewis Casson made brave attempts to revive Greek tragedy for matinée performances, supported by Grand Guignol in the evenings. Alone among the Shakespearians Frank Benson, Charles Doran, Henry Baynton and Ben Greet soldiered on in the provinces, preserving for diminishing audiences the tattered remnants of heroic acting, while on Shaftesbury Avenue the modern-dress play held sway, dictating its particular style of the natural manner.

A more astringent form of the natural manner epitomized the acting of the younger generation of the mid-twenties with Noël Coward, Gertrude Lawrence, Beatrice Lillie and Tallulah Bankhead. 'The younger generation are knocking at the door of the dustbin,' wrote du Maurier in 1924, referring to Noël Coward's controversial play, *The Vortex*, with its exposure of the vices of high society. By the middle of the decade disenchantment, hidden with a bitter-sweet smile and a dancing toe, had introduced a note of satirical sophistication into the world of 'show-business'.

(iii) Production styles

The theatres that were built, or rebuilt, in the twenties[1] tended to conform to the architectural style of the new cinemas: straight lines and angles replaced the curved auditorium; stage boxes were abandoned; simplified decoration took the place of red plush and gilded enrichments. With one or two exceptions (mentioned later) there was, however, no change in the relationship between stage and auditorium. The picture-frame arch still continued to impose its form on the picture framed behind it, but now the picture had to appear more solid than before. After the giddy years of the early twenties the mood of society became increasingly materialistic. West End audiences favoured modern-dress plays presented, more often than not, in interior settings. The scenic designer was required to be an interior decorator rather than an artist. The more real the scenery, the closer to reality had to be its component parts: furniture, 'props', lighting and stage 'effects' had to match the solidly built interiors with their real doors, windows, staircases and ceilings.

For a time the stage was able to compete with the early realism of the silent cinema, but since reality in the performing arts, more particularly in the theatre, remains an illusion, the greater the illusion the greater is the need for artifice; so the stage picture had now to be controlled from outside the proscenium arch and the actor became increasingly dependent on the non-acting director.

Basil Dean, one of the foremost non-acting directors of the West End stage, was a master of theatrical verisimilitude. Meticulous in his stage directions, an expert in the use of the new lighting techniques, he insisted on

[1] West End theatres built in the twenties included the Carlton (1927), the Fortune and the Piccadilly (1928), the Dominion and the new Savoy (1929). The Carlton and the Dominion were to become cinemas in 1929 and 1931.

a highly autocratic form of production in which the actor's movements and 'business', the settings and stage management were strictly controlled by the director.

Since plays in the twenties were a safer commercial proposition when confined to modern dress, opportunities for more artistic design were limited – more likely to be found in the fantasy and spectacle of revue, ballet, operetta and musical comedy. Léon Bakst's designs for *The Sleeping Princess* (1921) burst forth in baroque splendour; the designers of André Charlot's revues and Nikita Balief's *La Chauve Souris* explored simple decorative devices and toy-like miniature scenes; C. B. Cochran employed Oliver Messel, Christian Bérard, Rex Whistler and Doris Zinkeisen for his lavish musical productions. It was, however, outside the inner circle of the fashionable theatre that the scenic designer came to be accepted as the artistic partner of the director in the production of the straight play.

(iv) The outer circle – Hammersmith and King's Cross

In December 1918 Nigel Playfair and Arnold Bennett took a lease of the Lyric Theatre, Hammersmith, known locally as 'The Blood and Flea Pit'. Playfair's production of Pergolesi's one-act operetta, *La Serva Padrona*, designed with simple elegance by Claude Lovat Fraser, persuaded him 'that it was as necessary for a theatre to have its sets designed by an artist of genius as to have its plays written by a good writer'.[1] Lovat Fraser's designs for *The Beggar's Opera* in 1920 set the seal on what became known as the Lyric style. The designs of William Nicholson, George Sheringham, Doris Zinkeisen and Charles Ricketts challenged the outworn tradition of stock scenery and costumes for period plays – a tradition that had already been broken by Granville Barker in his pre-war Savoy productions of Shakespeare. The clean lines of the Lyric's semi-permanent sets combined with costumes dyed in primary colours created a sense of period as seen through the eyes of contemporary artists.

Side by side with Playfair another manager backed his taste against the prevailing waste-land of the West End. In 1922 Barry Jackson transferred his production of Rutland Boughton's opera, *The Immortal Hour*, from the Birmingham Repertory Theatre to a converted cinema in King's Cross renamed the Regent Theatre. The misty blue-greens of Paul Shelving's 'lonely

[1] Nigel Playfair, *The Story of the Lyric, Hammersmith* (London, 1925), p. 32.

wood' offered a welcome relief from the usual tree borders and imitation grass. Shelving was to remain as resident designer at the Birmingham Repertory as well as serving Jackson's productions in London and Malvern for forty years – a tribute to the loyalty that Jackson inspired in those who worked for him.

At first both *The Beggar's Opera* and *The Immortal Hour* were slow to draw audiences to the unfashionable playhouses outside the West End, but both productions eventually confounded the commercial theorists. *The Beggar's Opera* ran for three and a half years, and *The Immortal Hour* was revived in 1923 and 1924. Jackson enjoyed his triumphs, as he suffered his failures, with superb disregard for his private purse, bestriding the British theatre from 1913 to his death in 1961 as its most enlightened patron. His repertory theatre in Birmingham's Station Street presented a repertoire of international drama that challenged comparison with the highly subsidized theatres of Europe. From 1929 to 1933 his Malvern Festival offered actors and actresses unique opportunities of acting in plays of such widely different styles as *Gammer Gurton's Needle*, Sheridan's *A Trip to Scarborough*, Bulwer Lytton's *Money*, and the latest play by James Bridie or Shaw. It was Barry Jackson who gave John Gielgud his first leading Shakespearian part in *Romeo and Juliet*, and under his management Edith Evans, Robert Donat, Cedric Hardwicke, Gwen Ffrangçon-Davies, Laurence Olivier, Ralph Richardson, Paul Scofield and Peter Brook were nurtured.

(v) The Old Vic

On the south bank of the Thames a third force was moving into the assault on the citadel of show-business, though no such backing as the ready purse of a wealthy patron and the three and a half years' run of *The Beggar's Opera* smoothed the Old Vic's path. Nor can it be claimed that Lilian Baylis possessed the artistic taste of Jackson and Playfair. With a dogged determination to provide 'wholesome entertainment' for her 'dear audience', and aided and abetted – as she used to claim – by the Almighty, Lilian Baylis founded a theatre whose success was due above all to the loyalty of its audience. This is not to deny the contribution of those who worked for her, many of whom were to become leading artists in opera and ballet as well as in the straight theatre. Miss Baylis insisted that nothing but the best was good enough for her audience; but, whatever it was, she was determined to get it cheap – including her actors. Under her guidance the Old Vic offered golden opportunities for talented young actors to scale the heights of their profession, though the gold was noticeably absent.

Between 1920 and 1925 Robert Atkins, a disciple of William Poel, staged every play in the Folio, except *Cymbeline*, with a robust gusto that made little allowance for subtleties of characterization. Using a semi-permanent set with curtains for front scenes and a small apron stage, he provided the continuity of action that Poel had demanded as a prerequisite of Elizabethan staging. The simplicity of his scenic arrangements – as much due to financial stringency as to Poel's influence – and his belief in Shakespeare as a stage craftsman enabled Atkins to demonstrate that Shakespeare's plays can only yield their full dramatic power when spared the cuts, transpositions and scenic waits of nineteenth-century staging.

Under Robert Atkins and his successor, Andrew Leigh, the Old Vic began to emerge as something more than a suburban playhouse. In 1924 Cochran engaged the company for a month's season at the New Oxford Theatre in the West End, but the fashionable public was not yet ready to support Shakespeare without 'stars'. It was, as Cochran has recorded, 'Shakespeare or nothing, and Shakespeare lost, much to my disappointment.' The Old Vic audience created its own stars uninfluenced by the ballyhoo of West End publicity. Sybil Thorndike and her brother Russell, Dorothy Green, Baliol Holloway, Ernest Milton and Ion Swinley were among its early favourites. Edith Evans, fresh from her triumph as Millamant in Playfair's production of *The Way of the World* – 'the finest reproduction of eighteenth-century manners the twentieth century has seen'[1] – laid aside the chances of a 'star' career in the West End to play the great Shakespearian women including an exquisite Rosalind in *As You Like It*. Miss Baylis's achievement was the creation not only of a home for Shakespeare and opera in English, but – more important – of an audience for both. To her must be given the credit for laying the foundations of the National Theatre, the English National Opera Company and the Royal Ballet. It was her dominant personality, her direct and homely manner – so unlike the popular image of a theatre impresario – that provided a family feeling in her theatre, both within the company itself and between the company and her audience.

The Old Vic of the twenties, however, was no Moscow Art Theatre. Its performance style was rough and ready, born of the need to mount the plays in restricted rehearsal time and with limited finance. Inevitably this led to a form of acting, perhaps not unlike the style of Burbage's players, in which

[1] James Agate, *More First Nights* (London, 1936), p. 333.

reliance on the words themselves, stamina and teamwork, rather than psychology and scenic decoration, brought the plays to life.

When Harcourt Williams took over the direction of the plays in 1929 the performance style assumed greater refinement. As a disciple of Granville Barker he substituted lightness and speed for the mannered speech of the actor-managers' tradition. Histrionic gesture and traditional 'business' were laid aside, and his productions without being lavish had great visual beauty. His production of *A Midsummer Night's Dream* in 1929 bore many resemblances to Granville Barker's production of the play in 1912. Mendelssohn's music was replaced by Cecil Sharp's folk tunes; fairies – no longer suspended on wires – had green faces and seaweed costumes; the wood was suggested by bunched curtains against a silver sky. But it was the casting of John Gielgud as Oberon that won the applause of the Old Vic 'fans'. This was followed by Gielgud's triumph in *Richard II*, a part peculiarly suited to the tenseness and highly emotional quality of his acting. Except for a brief immature performance of Romeo under Barry Jackson's management, Gielgud, like many young actors of the time, had had little opportunity of widening his experience outside the modern-dress naturalism of the West End. As Trofimov in Komisarjevsky's production of *The Cherry Orchard* he had learned something of the Stanislavsky approach to the creation of character; as Lewis Dodd in *The Constant Nymph* – a part he had taken over from Noël Coward – he had experienced the problems of sustaining a leading part for a long run. Now at the Old Vic he was to make use of his fine, lyrical voice in the leading Shakespearian roles. In his second season he was acclaimed as the rising star of the classical theatre by the London critics when Harcourt Williams's production of *Hamlet* was transferred for a brief run to the Queen's Theatre. At the age of twenty-five Gielgud was the youngest Hamlet in living memory. He was to repeat the part in 1934, 1936 and 1939, each time bringing to it the growing mastery of his art, enhanced by his experience in a wide variety of Shakespearian parts.

(vi) Stratford-upon-Avon

Meanwhile at Stratford's Memorial Theatre a new sense of style was sweeping away the worn-out scenery and shabby costumes, the mannered speech and traditional 'business' of the Bensonians. Already in 1918 Nigel Playfair's production of *As You Like It* had set the Avon on fire by discarding the stuffed stag that from time immemorial had been paraded across the stage, and insult had been added to injury by Claude Lovat Fraser's orange and vermilion costumes and 'futuristic' settings which, in fact, were based on medieval illuminated manuscripts. In 1919 Bridges Adams was appointed director of the annual festival. Although an admirer of William Poel, Bridges Adams did not share Poel's passion for neo-Elizabethan staging. Like Harcourt Williams, he followed in the footsteps of Granville Barker. He desired 'The virtues of the Elizabethan theatre without its vices, and its freedom without its fetters: scenic splendour where helpful, but . . . the play to be given as written: the text unmutilated whether in the interests of the stage carpenter or the leading man.'[1] Above all he held to the principle that the director should not act – a principle that Benson had been unable to accept. Working within the limitations of minimal rehearsal time, and a poorly equipped Victorian playhouse, Adams designed settings suggestive of period and locality but devoid of the overdecoration of the Victorian tradition.

In 1926 the old playhouse was burnt to the ground (to the jubilation of George Bernard Shaw, who dashed off a telegram of congratulations). Within less than a month Adams provided the local Picture House with a stage larger than that of the Memorial Theatre. In this new setting he staged some of his finest productions. Meanwhile the new theatre was arising beside the Avon, to be opened in 1932.

(vii) The little theatre

From 1920 to 1926 Norman MacDermot presented a programme of new plays and revivals at the Everyman Theatre, Hampstead, a playhouse that he converted from a whist palace. Imaginative use was made of black velvet curtains and Gordon Craig's screens. The Everyman, with its distinguished repertoire of revivals and new plays (including Noël Coward's *The Vortex*, later transferred to the West End), was in many ways comparable to the Court Theatre under the Vedrenne–Barker management. It was at the Everyman that Theodor Komisarjevsky, recently arrived from Russia, was given his first opportunity to direct a full-length play in Britain.

Komisarjevsky's productions of Chekhov, Gogol and Andreyev at the Barnes Theatre, under Philip Ridgeway's management, in 1925 and 1926

[1] Note appended to a letter to J. C. Trewin, quoted by Robert Speaight in *A Bridges Adams Letter Book* (London, 1971), p. 32.

introduced to Britain something of Stanislavsky's style without its photographic realism. John Gielgud has pointed out that it was from Komisarjevsky that he learned 'not to act from outside, seizing on obvious effects and histrionics; to avoid the temptations of showing off; to work from within to present a character, and to absorb the atmosphere and general background of a play'.[1]

At the Gate Theatre, under Peter Godfrey's management, more recent Continental styles were introduced. In 1925 Godfrey produced Kaiser's *From Morn to Midnight*, the first expressionist play to be seen in Britain. The Gate was the first of the club theatres; as such it was able to produce plays that did not come under the Lord Chamberlain's jurisdiction. Experimental and avant-garde plays from France, Germany and the United States offered British actors opportunities to experiment with Continental techniques that hitherto had made little impact on the British theatre. The intimacy of the Gate, both in its first home in Covent Garden and later in Villiers Street, demanded absolute sincerity of performance. Norman Marshall, later to become manager of the theatre, has pointed out that 'the Gate combined most of the advantages of the theatre with those of the radio and the cinema. . . . Without the no-man's-land of the orchestra pit or the barrier of a row of footlights, [the actor's] contact with his audience was constant and direct.'[2] Under Norman Marshall's directorship the Gate became one of the earliest pioneers of intimate revue, bringing a new sophistication to the musical theatre of the thirties.

(viii) The Cambridge Festival Theatre

This conception of intimacy and contact between actor and audience was also pioneered by Terence Gray at the Festival Theatre, Cambridge. Gray, in partnership with Harold Ridge, remodelled the stage of a disused Regency playhouse, removing the proscenium arch and extending the forestage in descending levels till it was at the feet of the front row of spectators, thus eliminating the barrier between stage and auditorium. Many of the features of the open stage which were to be exploited later by theatre architects were present in Gray's theatre. It was here that Guthrie, under Amner Hall's tenancy, cut his teeth as a director in 1929. Gray's productions owed much to

[1] John Gielgud, *Early Stages* (London, 1939), p. 3.
[2] Norman Marshall, *The Other Theatre* (London, 1947), p. 46.

the radical techniques of Meyerhold and the Soviet directors of the twenties. Costumes were stylized regardless of period; scenery was abolished in favour of levels and steps set against a bare cyclorama; no attempt was made to conceal stage lighting; texts were adapted to suit the director's whims. But Gray lacked a social or political purpose: he was essentially an amateur, indulging his taste for theatre as he did his taste for wines. Eccentricity was often cultivated for its own sake. Yet his productions, for all their whimsicality, were a sign of the growing discontent of theatre artists with the conservatism and insularity of the West End stage.

Looking back on the theatre of the twenties we can see that, while commercial interests acted as a barrier to the radical changes that were taking place on the Continent, most of the developments in the performance styles of the next two decades had begun to appear in the little theatres and progressive repertory theatres of the provinces. British theatre was growing from its grass roots, but in order to make a lasting impact on the commercial stage the new developments in direction and design required a more professional leadership.

British theatre owes a lasting debt to the pioneering spirit of Barry Jackson, to the taste and elegance of Nigel Playfair's productions and to the experimental work of Terence Gray, but the charge of amateurism that has sometimes been levelled against them is not entirely unfounded. Their motivation was tinged with a love of the theatre as a personal hobby. They lacked the competitive drive that enabled the Cartel des Quatre[1] to provide a professional rival to the commercialism of the Parisian *boulevard* theatres. The Old Vic and Stratford were as yet parochial in their outlook, and the little theatres lacked the means to support the livelihood of those who worked for them.

[1] A managerial association founded in 1926 by Charles Dullin, Louis Jouvet, Georges Pitoëff and Gaston Baty. Among its objectives were the promotion of theatrical art against the commercialization and crude naturalism of the Parisian stage.

2 Theatrical trends in the thirties

It was in the thirties that West End managers began to move out of the rut of pure commercialism, though financial pressures from the radio and 'talkies' were increasing their financial risks. *The Stage Yearbook* for 1930 calculated that out of 100 plays (exclusive of musicals) produced in London seventy-five lost money for their backers. To attract the dwindling audiences musicals had to be more glamorous, spectacle more spectacular. *Cavalcade* and *White Horse Inn* stretched the technical resources of Drury Lane and the Coliseum to the limit. Matinée idols were in even greater demand; Ivor Novello reigned supreme at Drury Lane in a series of splendidly staged musical romances from 1936 onwards. Musical farce flourished with Jack Hulbert, Cecily Courtneidge, Bobby Howes, Sydney Howard, Jack Buchanan and Leslie Henson. At the Aldwych Ralph Lynn and Tom Walls led their inimitable team of *farceurs*. There were thrillers by Edgar Wallace, Emlyn Williams and Agatha Christie, and marital complications by Dodie Smith. But there was much serious drama too. J. B. Priestley, T. S. Eliot, St John Ervine, Charles Morgan, Somerset Maugham, John Van Druten, Shaw, the American dramatists – Eugene O'Neill, Elmer Rice and Clifford Odets – and productions of Chekhov's plays were making greater demands on depth of characterization. Above all the return to favour of Shakespeare in the West End, as well as of classical comedy, introduced the new developments in acting and production that had been nurtured outside the fashionable theatre.

(i) The classical revival

In the year 1930 there were four productions of *Hamlet* in the West End: Gielgud's performance at the Queen's, Esmé Percy's at the Court, Henry Ainley's at the Haymarket and the Viennese actor Alexander Moissi's at the Globe. In the same year Paul Robeson appeared as Othello with Peggy Ashcroft as Desdemona, a performance that established her as a leading actress. Baliol Holloway gave a notable performance in *Richard III*; there were revivals of *The School for Scandal* and *The Beaux' Stratagem*. Between 1931 and 1934 Shakespeare productions could be seen at the Haymarket, the Fortune, the Arts, the Duchess, the St James's, the Winter Garden, the Phoenix, the Alhambra and His Majesty's, where George Robey appeared as Falstaff complete with raised eyebrows and red nose. At the Open Air Theatre in Regent's Park Robert Atkins began his annual seasons of Shakespeare in 1933. From 1938 to 1939 John Gielgud, in partnership with the leading West End commercial management of H. M. Tennent Ltd, presented a season of classical plays at the Queen's. The Old Vic and Stratford, shedding their parochial status, were enticing the leading players, directors and designers from the West End. Once again it was recognized that to play leading roles in the plays of Shakespeare was the measure of an actor's claim to 'stardom'. As the actor's career became increasingly dependent upon his ability to span both classical and contemporary acting, so the frontiers between the two styles of acting were eroded: Shakespearian acting became more realistic; modern-dress acting became less dependent on casting to type. A further influence on the extension of acting techniques was provided by the development of training in the schools of acting.

The decline of the touring companies and the stricter demands of British Actors' Equity put an end to the system by which an actor learnt his trade as an unpaid or paying apprentice. At the same time an increasing number of recruits from comparatively well-to-do families, who were able to afford the training offered by the acting schools, were entering the profession. While it would be wrong to suggest that acting schools provided a substitute for the experience of playing to an audience, the new generation of actors, trained in the acting schools, brought with them a more technical approach to their craft, as well as a greater appreciation of the values of teamwork in which each part, however small, contributes to the total interpretation of the play.

(ii) The influence of the director

If the new style of acting was influenced both by the greater demands of the written text on the one hand, and by the acting schools on the other, it was also influenced by the overall control of the play director. The twenties had seen the growing importance of the director, more especially in the classical and little theatres. In the thirties his control of the interpretation of West End plays became fully established. Even when the leading actor directed the play himself it was his interpretation of the play as a whole, as well as his personal performance in it, that was a necessary concomitant to critical acclaim. It was largely through the acceptance of the director's function as the interpreter of the play that emphasis was placed on the team rather than on the virtuoso performance of the leading player.

From 1933 onwards the spotlight focused on the growing maturity of John Gielgud both as a leading actor and as a play director.

Gielgud began his career as a director in 1932 with a production of *Romeo and Juliet* for the Oxford University Dramatic Society (OUDS) in which Edith Evans and Peggy Ashcroft made their first appearances as the Nurse and Juliet, while among the undergraduate performers George Devine played Mercutio, William Devlin played Tybalt, Christopher Hassall played Romeo, and Terence Rattigan appeared briefly as a musician. The production was designed by the Motleys with the elegance and taste that marked their subsequent cooperation with Gielgud. In the same year Gielgud launched into West End production with Gordon Daviot's *Richard of Bordeaux* at the New Theatre. His performance in the leading part together with the elegance of his production established his popularity with London audiences and critics alike. In 1934 he made his second assault on *Hamlet* at the same theatre, directing the play himself. The production ran for 155 performances, a record second only to Irving's Lyceum production. Using a cyclorama and elaborately draped curtains, the play moved with the freedom and pace that Granville Barker demanded in his *Prefaces to Shakespeare*. In many ways it was a landmark in West End productions of Shakespeare of the time, combining faithfulness to the text with a carefully matched team of actors. Teamwork, too, characterized his 1938–9 season at the Queen's in which he brought together a superb group of players including Peggy Ashcroft, Angela Baddeley, George Devine, Alec Guinness, Leon Quartermaine, Anthony Quayle, Michael Redgrave, Glen Byam Shaw and Harcourt Williams in a repertoire consisting of *The School for Scandal*, *Richard II*, *The Three Sisters* and *The Merchant of Venice*, an ensemble company and a repertoire of plays that the subsidized theatres today would be hard set to equal. As a director John Gielgud's sense of style has shown itself at its best in classical comedy; in 1939 he set the seal on his reputation both as an actor and director in *The Importance of Being Earnest* at the Globe in which his performance as John Worthing was matched by Edith Evans's definitive performance as Lady Bracknell.

The thirties saw the rise to prominence of two other directors of very different tastes – Michel Saint-Denis and Tyrone Guthrie.

In 1931 Saint-Denis visited London with his Compagnie des Quinze in a repertoire of plays by André Obey. The impact of this highly disciplined ensemble with its precise choreography and effective use of mime led to an invitation to Saint-Denis to direct *Noah*, an English translation of Obey's *Noë*, with Gielgud in the leading part at the New Theatre in 1933. Saint-Denis subsequently worked extensively in London. As a nephew and close associate of Jacques Copeau he introduced to the British theatre many of the ideals that had inspired Le Vieux Colombier. In particular he sought to establish a company of actors dedicated to the mental and physical training that under Copeau's inspired direction had brought about a fusion between the powerful classical tradition of the French stage with the new realism of character interpretation. His work was seen at its best in his production of *The Three Sisters* for Gielgud's season at the Queen's.

As a personality he elicited from those who fell under his spell unquestioning obedience and loyalty. 'You either believed in the man or you didn't, but something told you instinctively that you had better do so if you were to get any good out of him,' wrote Laurence Olivier in his introduction to *The Rediscovery of Style*.[1] His influence on British theatre was most keenly felt by those who, like Gielgud, Olivier, Michael Redgrave, George Devine, Peggy Ashcroft and Glen Byam Shaw, were already sufficiently established to follow his demanding leadership without loss of self-confidence.

Tyrone Guthrie was a director of a very different temperament. Instinctive and provocative in his approach to Shakespeare's texts – a process that he chose to call 'grappling with the Bard' – he was no believer in Saint-Denis's analytical approach to production. Possessed of a superb flair for improvising

[1] Michel Saint-Denis, *The Rediscovery of Style* (London, 1960), p. 9.

in rehearsal, a master of crowd scenes, he was ever at his best in tilting at traditional preconceptions – unearthing an Oedipus complex in *Hamlet* or a homosexual relationship between Iago and Othello. His productions, however wayward and capricious, seldom failed to be intensely theatrical.

Guthrie's appointment as director of the Old Vic in 1933 inaugurated a drastic change in policy. Sadler's Wells Theatre had been rebuilt in 1931 as a second home for the drama and opera companies, but was soon found to be unsuitable for drama, and was therefore devoted to opera and ballet, leaving the Old Vic as the permanent base of the drama company. Guthrie was no believer in a poor theatre. 'After many years in theatrical affairs,' he was to write later, 'during most of which I have had some responsibility for other people's money, I have learned, often painfully, that cheese-paring just is no good. If you want to make money, you must be ready to spend it like water. This does not mean wastefully; it must be spent with care and discrimination, but handsomely.'[1]

Opportunity to spend money 'like water' was scarcely possible under Lilian Baylis's management, but Guthrie was determined that Shakespeare and the classics should no longer be treated as poor relations of Miss Baylis's opera and ballet companies. Costumes and settings were to be as handsome as the company's budget would allow – and sometimes more so. The Old Vic was no longer to be a suburban theatre creating its local 'stars'; the West End 'stars' must come to the Old Vic. Charles Laughton, fresh from success as a film actor, was engaged as his leading actor supported by Flora Robson and a strong acting company. The audience were no longer to be wooed with 'safe' productions, but shocked by Guthrie's original, and often highly controversial, 'comments' on Shakespeare.

Guthrie's *brio* and showmanship as a director placed the Old Vic on the road to national importance, not without causing some misgivings among Miss Baylis's loyal audience. He left at the end of his first season, feeling that the time was not ripe for the changes he sought to bring about. It says much for Lilian Baylis's managerial sense that, despite her personal feelings, she invited him to return in 1936, recognizing that her people's theatre now called for the more professional leadership which it was beyond her power to provide.

[1] Tyrone Guthrie, *A Life in the Theatre* (London, 1960), p. 48.

(iii) Gielgud and Olivier

Guthrie's 1936–7 season included Alec Clunes, Alec Guinness, Ernest Milton, Michael Redgrave and Edith Evans (a delightful Rosalind in *As You Like It*), but its highlight was a new rising 'star' who was to rival Gielgud as the leading classical actor, and to become the first common player to be raised to the peerage.

Laurence Olivier had already made a name for himself in films and on the West End stage. In 1935 he had alternated with Gielgud in the parts of Romeo and Mercutio in the latter's New Theatre production of *Romeo and Juliet* – a production largely based on Gielgud's earlier production for the OUDS. The contrast between Gielgud and Olivier could be said to epitomize the two styles of contemporary acting – the new classical style and the new realism. Olivier has said, in an interview with Kenneth Tynan, that he has always seen Gielgud and himself as 'reverses of the same coin':

> . . . as if you had a coin, the top half John, all spiritual, all spirituality, all beauty, all abstract things; and myself as all earth, blood, humanity; if you like, the baser part of humanity without that beauty.[1]

Both actors were in fact in tune with their time – Gielgud the Apollonian and Olivier the Dionysian actor, as Richard Hayman has described them.

Gielgud possesses the Terry charm and an ability to speak verse without resorting to the old sweep of rhetoric, relying on the architecture of a speech to reveal its meaning; more at home in costume than in modern dress, he is aristocratic in appearance, but bodily inexpressive, and somewhat lacking in the power of impersonation. His natural temperament made him a superb Mercutio, though less successful as Romeo. In 1935 Olivier's experience had been largely confined to modern plays. He played Romeo as 'a tousled Italian boy in a fever of adolescent love, groping for words, choked with emotion'.[2] To some his performance in both parts seemed over-realistic.

> I was trying to sell realism in Shakespeare. I believed in it with my whole soul and I believed that Johnny was not doing that enough . . .[3]

In 1937 under Guthrie's direction he was to challenge Gielgud once again in a full-length performance of Hamlet. Critics still judged him short of lyrical

[1] Hal Burton (ed.), *Great Acting* (London, 1967), p. 17.
[2] Richard Findlater, *The Player Kings* (London, 1957, 1975), p. 211.
[3] Burton (ed.), *Great Acting*, p. 17.

quality, but praised his virility and mercurial virtuosity. Unlike Gielgud's sensitive and graceful prince, Olivier presented an urgent, athletic Hamlet, one who had (in Ivor Brown's phrase) 'more of thistle and sword-grass than of sensitive plant in his composition'. Guthrie's production of *Hamlet* subsequently visited Elsinore. It was the first time an English company had played there since 1585. Torrential rain on the opening night prevented the company from playing in the open courtyard of Kronborg Castle, forcing Guthrie to transfer the play to the ballroom of the local hotel. Here, without staging or stage lighting, surrounded on three sides by a crowded audience, the play assumed a new dimension that Guthrie was to declare 'strengthened me in a conviction, which had been growing with each production . . . that for Shakespeare the proscenium stage is unsatisfactory',[1] a conviction that was later to lead him to his championship of the open stages of the Edinburgh Assembly Hall, of Stratford, Ontario, and of the Tyrone Guthrie Theatre, Minneapolis.

Meanwhile in the Waterloo Road Olivier appeared as Macbeth, making elaborate use of make-up of which he was to become a master, whether it was the long reptilian nose of his Richard of Gloucester, the sunken cheeks of his toothless Justice Shallow, the red wig of his stammering Hotspur or the negroid features of his Othello. Michel Saint-Denis's production of *Macbeth* was dogged by the ill luck that traditionally accompanies the play; not only did the director's analytical approach fail to uncover the dark mystery of the play's magic, but Lilian Baylis died on the day before the opening performance. The season ended with Olivier's Coriolanus in which he displayed in his breathtaking death-fall the acrobatic prowess that has proved an exciting accompaniment to his acting. His performances at the Old Vic were to prove the first stage of his climb to greatness as a Shakespearian actor. James Agate described him as 'the nearest thing we have today in the heroic tradition', and added, 'The only thing to be settled is whether he is going to have the genius, which includes a feeling for poetry.'

That question remained unanswered for six years. Other events intervened. Olivier and Richardson who had partnered him were to don different costumes, and the Old Vic lay empty and charred while London glowed red in the night sky.

[1] Tyrone Guthrie, *A Life in the Theatre* (London, 1960), p. 172.

3 The Second World War and after

The birth of CEMA and its eventual transformation into the Arts Council of Great Britain has been recorded elsewhere.[1] In no area was the infusion of state aid into the theatre more significant than in the provinces, where it gave the impetus to the post-war development of the regional theatres with their high standards of acting and directing. During the war itself the need to provide entertainment for the armed forces, as well as for the evacuated civilian workers, led to the formation of touring companies under the aegis of CEMA. During the First World War the emphasis had been placed almost exclusively on light entertainment; in contrast, the companies supported by CEMA provided a high standard of theatrical fare. The Old Vic and Sadler's Wells organizations were established in the aptly named Victoria Theatre in Burnley, Lancashire, from whence, under Guthrie's driving direction, plays such as *King John*, *The Merchant of Venice*, *Macbeth*, *Twelfth Night*, *Medea* and *The Cherry Orchard* toured the North and Midlands and the mining villages of Wales with occasional forays into London, led by prominent players of the London stage.

In London theatres opened and shut spasmodically, struggling against the odds of blacked-out streets and the wail of the air-raid sirens. Only the

[1] See Section I, p. 46.

Windmill Theatre could boast that it never closed. But classical theatre was not lacking in the metropolis, though many theatres fell victim to the bombs, including the Queen's, the Shaftesbury, the Royalty, the Gate and the Little.

In 1940, the year before the Old Vic was bombed, Lewis Casson and John Gielgud invited Harley Granville Barker to assist in the production of *King Lear* in the Waterloo Road playhouse. Here, for the first time since his self-imposed exile, the man who had laid the foundations of the new school of directing Shakespeare returned to take ten historic rehearsals in which he was to prove once again his brilliant mastery of style. Gielgud, who owed much to his helpful criticism, was to write:

> Tempo, atmosphere, diction, balance, character – no detail could escape his unerring dramatic instinct and his superb sense of classic shapeliness of line.[1]

Above all it was Barker's power of drawing a performance out of the actor's own personality, rather than imposing the director's conception upon him, that was to become increasingly recognized as the ideal contribution of the director to the actor.

In the same year Donald Wolfit, an actor-manager whose methods displayed little sympathy with the new school of production, launched a season of Shakespeare's plays at the Kingsway which he repeated at annual intervals interspersed with tours of the provinces. Gifted with an outsize personality besides considerable physical stamina and vocal power, Wolfit believed unashamedly in the absolute predominance of the leading actor. His productions, often criticized for the poor quality of his supporting company, nevertheless introduced Shakespeare and other classical plays to new audiences throughout the country. For all his egotism – and perhaps because of it – there were parts in which no actor of his time could rival him. His Lear, acclaimed by Agate as the greatest tragic performance since the death of Irving, had the moral grandeur of Blake and a voice to still the thunder. It was only matched by the barbaric splendour of his Tamburlaine in Guthrie's spectacular production of Marlowe's play at the Old Vic in 1951; but Wolfit was a lone wolf, and his association with the new institutional theatre was doomed to disaster.

[1] John Gielgud, *Stage Directions* (London, 1963), p. 53.

(i) Institutional theatre – the battle for the National Theatre

By 1944 air attacks on London were sufficiently contained to warrant the return of the Old Vic organization from its provincial exile. The loss of its stage in the Waterloo Road gave Guthrie the opportunity to establish the company in the centre of the theatrical metropolis, backed by the financial support of CEMA. Olivier and Richardson were released from the forces to join a distinguished company at the New Theatre which was to be the home of the Old Vic Company for the next five years. After launching the new company in their first season with a production of *Peer Gynt* in which Richardson played the leading part and Olivier made a modest appearance as the Button Moulder, Guthrie handed over control to Olivier, Richardson and John Burrell, the latter an administrator and director whose contribution to the success of the historic seasons at the New Theatre has been underestimated by theatre critics. It is no easy task for an artistic director of a subsidized company – as future experience was to prove – to strike a balance between the highly specialized problems of theatrical organization and the theories of a board of directors often lacking in knowledge of theatrical affairs.

During the early years of the subsidized theatres in London and the provinces the relationship between the boards of management and the artistic direction of the theatres was a constant source of friction. The problems were not made easier by the ambivalent attitude of the Arts Council to the whole question of subsidization. Constant uncertainty as to the amount, and the recurrence, of financial support added to the difficulties confronting those upon whose shoulders rested the responsibility for artistic policy. It was Burrell's modest and unassuming guidance, no less than the brilliance of his 'star-studded' team, that led to the success of the 1944 to 1948 seasons. Burrell's production of *Richard III* proved to be the triumph of the 1944 season, providing Olivier with the opportunity to display the audacity, sardonic humour and acrobatic prowess that have rightly earned him the title of 'the bravest actor of our time'. Burrell, too, was responsible for the production of the two parts of *Henry IV* in 1945 in which Richardson's Falstaff was claimed to be the finest within living memory. The 1945–6 season also saw Olivier's superb virtuosity displayed in a double bill of *Oedipus Rex*, in which 'his two great cries of anguish shook the rafters of the theatre', and *The Critic*, Sheridan's lampoon of heroic drama, in which he appeared some twenty minutes later as the ridiculous Mr Puff.

So long as the Old Vic Company basked in the sunshine of popular acclaim its critics remained silent, but when its two great actors were absent during the 1948-9 season – Richardson in Hollywood and Olivier leading a second Old Vic Company in Australia – box-office receipts began to fall and the Arts Council pressed the directors of the Old Vic Trust to reorganize their administration. Burrell became the obvious target of the attack; and the directors, with their eyes on transforming the organization into the future National Theatre, felt that a company run by two powerful actors might prejudice their future expectations. All three artists were informed that their contracts would not be renewed and with a singular lack of tact a telegram to this effect was dispatched to Olivier whose Australian tour was earning new laurels for the Old Vic. Fate was to provide an ironic answer when in 1962 a new National Theatre Board was appointed and Olivier became the first director of the National Theatre Company.

Meanwhile Stratford made a powerful bid to rival the prestige of the Old Vic. In 1946 Barry Jackson was appointed as director of the Shakespeare Memorial Theatre, bringing with him the young Paul Scofield and the even younger Peter Brook. Jackson's brief period of management (1946-8) inaugurated a new era in the theatre's history. The annual festivals were now a showcase for leading actors, directors and designers. Peter Brook's production of *Love's Labour's Lost* in 1946 was hailed as the work of a young master-director, only equalled by his production of *Titus Andronicus* in 1955, a production that lifted the play above its immature text into a picture of universal human suffering. Memorable, too, were Michael Benthall's production of *Hamlet* in Victorian costume, John Gielgud's production of *Much Ado About Nothing*, designed by Mariano Andreu, and Tyrone Guthrie's production of *Henry VIII*, designed by Tanya Moiseiwitsch. Barry Jackson was succeeded first by Anthony Quayle, and then (in 1957) by Glen Byam Shaw. The casts included Peggy Ashcroft, Edith Evans, Vivien Leigh, Diana Wynyard, Harry Andrews, John Gielgud, Robert Helpmann, Laurence Olivier, Michael Redgrave, Ralph Richardson and Godfrey Tearle. Clearly Stratford was now in a position to outrun the Old Vic in the race for the National Theatre stakes.

In London jockeying for the starting position was intense. A Joint Council of the Shakespeare Memorial National Theatre Committee and the Old Vic was set up, and in 1950 the Old Vic Company returned to its restored playhouse in the Waterloo Road. A joint directorate was formed consisting of myself as artistic director and Llewellyn Rees as administrator of the Old Vic Company, together with the three directors of the Old Vic Centre. The latter was founded in 1946 under the general direction of Michel Saint-Denis. The

Centre embraced the Old Vic School of Acting under Glen Byam Shaw and the Young Vic administered by George Devine. Both in production and training the centre was orientated towards Saint-Denis's highly disciplined approach to style, strongly influenced by the ideology of Jacques Copeau. Doubts arose as to how far this somewhat exclusive approach – admirable for an ensemble company, such as the Young Vic – would be acceptable to a broadly based National Theatre Company. Moreover, the financial needs of the school, which rightly made talent rather than fee paying a condition of entry, were proving a heavy burden to the Old Vic Company now shorn of the box-office attraction of the two major 'stars' of its New Theatre seasons. The situation was handled with the tactlessness that had marked the termination of the contracts of Olivier and Richardson. The Centre directors resigned, and the school and Young Vic were abandoned.

Subsequent attempts to marry the Stratford and Old Vic companies under the National Theatre umbrella proved abortive, and in 1962 a National Theatre Board was set up independent of both companies.

(ii) Arts Council support in London

The subsidization of the Old Vic and of the non-commercial theatres by the Arts Council, together with their exemption from entertainment tax, was a matter of concern to other managements. Hugh Beaumont of H. M. Tennent Ltd was quick to realize that, if leading actors were to be lured away from the attractions of the Old Vic and Stratford, it was necessary for the commercial theatre to offer parts of equal prestige. This could only be achieved by relieving the non-subsidized theatre of entertainment tax. By spreading their activities to embrace non-profit-distributing companies, commercial managements were able, under the 1916 Finance Act, to claim exemption from this crippling tax. The formation of these subsidiary companies resulted in a number of prestige productions in the West End and at the Lyric Theatre, Hammersmith. At the latter theatre Tennent Productions Ltd embarked on an ambitious policy of classical drama and plays of specialist appeal presented in repertory and employing such actors as John Gielgud and Paul Scofield. In the West End non-profit-distributing companies presented an impressive number of finely mounted plays between 1946 and 1951 – notably Edith Evans and Godfrey Tearle in *Antony and Cleopatra* at the Piccadilly, Robert Helpmann and Margaret Rawlings in *The White Devil* at the Duchess, *The*

Relapse with Cyril Richard, *The Beaux' Stratagem* with John Clements and Kay Hammond, and Christopher Fry's first full-length play, *The Lady's Not for Burning*, with John Gielgud and Pamela Brown, designed by Oliver Messel. At the little Mercury Theatre in Notting Hill Ashley Dukes presented a programme of poetic plays, including those of Auden and Isherwood, Ronald Duncan and T. S. Eliot. At the Arts Theatre Club, Alec Clunes offered a succession of festivals of International Comedy and Tragedy.

For actors and directors whose reputation could command an audience it was a time of almost unlimited choice of play. Managements, anxious to benefit from tax exemption, were eager to accept any revival of a classic, providing it was equipped with a leading actor or director. The system was, however, open to abuse. In 1951 the Arts Council, upon whose support tax exemption depended, withdrew its association with commercial managements.

(iii) The provincial renaissance

If the newly formed Arts Council was divided over its role in relation to the London theatres, its policy in the provinces was no less equivocal.

The weekly repertories that had sprung up like mushrooms during the war perished almost as quickly when the cessation of hostilities led to the return of the evacuated population to London and other war-scarred cities. Recognizing the need to fill the provincial vacuum, the Council expanded the policy adopted by CEMA of subsidizing touring companies under its own management. The question of subsidizing the 'reps', however, raised dissensions within the Council, which was not wholly free from the pressures of commercial managements. There were powerful influences, including the chairman of the Council – Lord Keynes – who saw the Council's role as that of a theatrical entrepreneur developing its own policies and controlling its own companies. In 1942 CEMA had acquired a twenty-one-year lease of the Theatre Royal, Bristol – the oldest working theatre in the country – with the object of providing a 'date' for its touring activities as well as preserving the building for the benefit of the citizens of Bristol. The decline in audiences for touring companies that followed the end of hostilities and the unwillingness of leading actors to continue tramping the provinces enabled Charles Landstone, the Assistant Drama Director of the Arts Council and a strong supporter of the repertory movement, to persuade Lord Keynes to agree to a temporary scheme for the establishment of a repertory company under the aegis of the Old Vic in the Theatre Royal. A joint committee of management was set up by the Old Vic and the Arts Council – the Old Vic being responsible for the company, the Council for the theatre. Thus the Bristol Old Vic became the first state-subsidized repertory company in the provinces to be established in its own home theatre.

This was the beginning of a network of regional companies which, together with the established repertories in Birmingham, Liverpool, Glasgow and Sheffield, were able – with the Council's financial support – to provide the power-houses for the renaissance of the provincial theatre.

(iv) The Royal Court and Stratford East

In the 1950s rumbles of discontent were circulating among a younger generation to whom the prestige productions of the West End and the rivalry of Stratford and the Waterloo Road were of little relevance.

The new styles of playwriting, direction and acting in Paris and East Berlin were avidly studied. The plays of Beckett, Ionesco and Genet, the theories of Artaud's 'Theatre of Cruelty', the production techniques of Brecht's Berliner Ensemble, were a powerful influence on writing and interpretation. In 1956 Ronald Duncan, Oscar Lewenstein and others took a lease of the Royal Court Theatre in Sloane Square, and formed the English Stage Company with George Devine as its artistic director. After a shaky start John Osborne's *Look Back in Anger* provided the explosion that released a flood of writers whose plays were generally expressive of the frustrations and ideals of the generation who came of age in the fifties. The significance of the English Stage Company was not restricted to its new playwrights. There arose a new breed of directors (Lindsay Anderson, John Dexter, William Gaskill, Anthony Page, Tony Richardson) and of young actors (Colin Blakely, Albert Finney, Kenneth Haigh, Nicol Williamson) whose attitudes were akin to the climate of protest and social change that was sweeping through the 'red brick' universities. It is, however, impossible to label the English Stage Company with any particular style or political philosophy beyond the fact that the playwrights whose plays have found a home at the Royal Court have tended to be left-wing orientated, and its productions have shown Brechtian influences. The intention of its founders was to provide a theatre for writers; as such it has been subject to the financial pressure of having to exploit successful plays by transferring them to the West End. Consequently it has been subjected to constant changes in its acting team which, as well as financial restrictions, have prevented the formation of an ensemble company.

A determined attempt to achieve this ideal was made by Theatre Workshop with equally disappointing results. Beginning as a mobile company in 1943 based in Manchester, Theatre Workshop found a permanent home in the Theatre Royal, Stratford East, in 1953. Under Joan Littlewood's direction a recognizable style of acting and staging emerged, based on improvisation methods of rehearsal and making free use of music-hall techniques. The players, largely recruited from outside the acting schools, were refreshingly free from preconceived theories of acting. Plays were selected for their topicality and social comment; where necessary they were freely adapted to achieve this aim. Brendan Behan's *The Hostage* (1958) and Joan Littlewood's greatest triumph *Oh, What a Lovely War!* (1963) were largely developed through the collaboration of director and actors. Unlike the English Stage Company, Theatre Workshop has made no attempt to serve an intellectual public; its aim has been to provide entertainment for proletarian audiences in pursuit of Joan Littlewood's dream of a 'fun palace' for the people. It is, however, unfortunate that for the great majority of the working class the theatre remains a middle-class pursuit. The company's failure to secure a loyal audience in the East End, and the inadequacy of the support it received during its early years from the Arts Council, forced the management to rely on transfers to the commercial theatre with the consequent loss of its acting personnel.

(v) Theatre architecture in the sixties

Pressing need for houses, factories, schools and universities, together with shortages of materials, prevented the building of new theatres during the ten or more years that followed the war. Many of the new repertory companies were forced to perform in converted cinemas and halls that made little appeal to a wide public. Local authorities, reflecting ingrained puritan attitudes to the theatre, were slow to recognize its value to the community. A major breakthrough, however, was made in 1958 when the Corporation of Coventry built the Belgrade Theatre. In the following year new theatres arose in Leicester (the Phoenix) and Nottingham (the Playhouse), and the pattern of rehousing the repertory theatres continued its momentum as provincial audiences brought increasing pressure to bear on their reluctant city fathers. Many of the new theatres made a radical break with traditional theatre architecture. In 1959 Bernard Miles and his architect, Elidir Davies, constructed in the City of London a theatre – the Mermaid – which, having neither proscenium arch nor front curtain, offered a new challenge to scenic design and a more open relationship between actor and audience.

The society born of the Welfare State no longer required the wealth divisions represented by dress circles, stalls, upper circles, pits and galleries. There were, too, other factors at work. The documentary play on television together with cinema *réalité* were breaking down the barriers between theatrical art and life, while the new drama made no concessions to those who sought the illusionary world revealed by the rising of the curtain. The particular magic that the live theatre had hitherto provided had now to be achieved by other means and within new architectural forms.

To meet the need for a stage stripped of illusion, theatre architects sought inspiration in past architectural forms. In 1948 Guthrie presented a sixteenth-century play – the *Satire of the Three Estates* – on an open platform in the Edinburgh Assembly Hall. Exits and entrances through the auditorium brought actors and audience into closer relationship. In 1953, in collaboration with Tanya Moiseiwitsch, he designed a theatre in Stratford, Ontario, which combined the principles of the Greek auditorium with an Elizabethan stage. This in turn inspired the Chichester Festival Theatre, the first major theatre with an open stage to be built in England (though it is only fair to state that Nugent Monck in Norwich had constructed the Maddermarket Theatre on Elizabethan lines for his amateur players in 1921). A more radical relationship between actor and audience, based on the medieval Cornish rounds, was pioneered by Stephen Joseph who in 1962 converted a cinema in Stoke-on-Trent into the first permanent theatre-in-the-round. Variations on the three basic forms represented by the open end-stage of the Mermaid, the open or platform stage of Chichester and the central stage of the Victoria Theatre, Stoke-on-Trent, have been incorporated in subsequent theatre buildings, adding a new dimension to staging and bringing actors and audiences into closer relationship.

(vi) The National and Royal Shakespeare companies

In 1962 Parliamentary consent was finally given to the release of funds for the building of the National Theatre. A newly constituted National Theatre Board appointed Laurence Olivier as director of the acting company which, after a preliminary season at Chichester, moved into its temporary home in the Old Vic in 1963. Impetus was given to the decision to form a National Theatre Company by the acquisition of the Aldwych Theatre as a temporary London base for the Stratford company, pending the building of the Barbican Theatre in the City of London. Peter Hall together with Michel Saint-Denis and Peter Brook took over the direction of the Stratford company, renamed the Royal Shakespeare Company, in 1960. The new directorate set out to evolve a distinctive company style with an ensemble of actors engaged on long-term contracts. The effectiveness of an ensemble is dependent on a stable and united directorial team – a principle that Saint-Denis had consistently advocated. The example of Brecht's Berliner Ensemble and its visit to London in 1956 had inspired many actors and directors, but such a company could be created at Stratford only if actors were no longer engaged solely on seasonal contracts. If, however, actors were to be engaged on longer contracts an undiluted diet of Shakespeare's plays would be neither beneficial nor attractive to young players anxious to extend their acting experience and develop their techniques. A second base was therefore required in order to retain the company throughout the year and to introduce other forms of drama which would help to explore new approaches to Shakespeare's plays.

The effectiveness of this policy was demonstrated in the epic cycle of Shakespeare's history plays in 1963 and 1964. Thematic and visual unity was maintained by a directorial team of Peter Hall, John Barton and Clifford Williams, with John Bury as designer. This antiheroic interpretation of Shakespeare's history plays, stretching from *Richard II* to *Richard III* and incorporating John Barton's adaptation of the three parts of *Henry VI* under the title of *The Wars of the Roses*, owed much to Jan Kott's theories of Shakespeare's political views, as well as to Brechtian staging. Kott's influence was also present in the staging and interpretation of Peter Brook's production of *King Lear* in 1962 in which Paul Scofield's earthy and petulant monarch deliberately robbed the character of much of its grandeur.

In their initial stages the policies of the Royal Shakespeare and the National Theatre companies seemed similar. Both followed a similar pattern of repertoire, and both tended to recruit a strong element of players whose experience had been gained in contemporary rather than classical plays. The appointment of Kenneth Tynan (who, as a critic, had been a strong advocate of Brecht's ideals) as literary director of the National Theatre Company, together with the engagement of William Gaskill and John Dexter as associate directors (both of whom came from the English Stage Company, bringing with them a basic team of actors who had worked with them) suggested that the National, too, was intent on creating an ensemble company. But a major difference soon became apparent, due in part to the different personalities of Hall and Olivier and also to the primary roles of the two companies. The primary duty of the Royal Shakespeare Theatre is the production of plays by its 'house' dramatist. For this a specialized style of acting and performance is justified, entailing a close association of directorial attitudes to interpretation and design and a stable acting ensemble. Olivier, who was equally anxious to build up a strong basic company, considered that a national theatre should provide an opportunity for a variety of leading artists, directors and designers to participate in its work. The company's guest players included most of the leading performers of the British stage, while its directors and designers were chosen from a wide variety of national and international artists. Under Olivier's leadership the emphasis was not unnaturally placed on actors rather than on a specific directorial style. The engagement of directors and designers on a play-to-play basis differentiated the policy of the National Theatre from that of the Royal Shakespeare Company; the National's policy of engaging guest 'stars', however, did not prevent the development of many of the younger players. Joan Plowright, Maggie Smith, Colin Blakely, Frank Finlay, Derek Jacobi, Ronald Pickup, Robert Stephens and Denis Quilley were among those who established their reputations with the company.

Much of the National's work during Olivier's directorship was inevitably focused on his own performances – Astrov in his 1963 production of *Uncle Vanya* (in which he shared the honours with Michael Redgrave), a splendidly virtuoso Tattle in *Love for Love* and Brazen in *The Recruiting Officer*, his negroid Othello, Solness in *The Master Builder*, Edgar in *The Dance of Death*, an Edwardian Shylock, James Tyrone in *Long Day's Journey into Night*, a Glaswegian Trotskyite in Trevor Griffith's play *The Party*, provided a portrait gallery that challenged comparison with the finest achievements of British actors from Betterton to Irving. Even in an antiheroic age the 'star' actor still commands the respect of the public; and the appointment of a great actor to the leadership of the National Theatre brought a prestige to its initial years without which it might well have been still-born.

Olivier's replacement by Peter Hall in 1972 was the inevitable recognition that the complexities of administering the new theatre building made demands that were too heavy for an actor to fulfil.

If the National Theatre had so far shown no desire to adopt a closed shop for its actors and directors, the Royal Shakespeare Company too failed to retain its actors for longer than two or three years at a time.

An ensemble company depends upon dedication to a common ideal, be it political, social or artistic, as well as upon considerable financial resources. Television today is the main source of income for most of our actors; and it is doubtful if established actors, with their tendency to migrate from one medium to another and with the opportunities of an international market, would willingly commit themselves exclusively to the dedicated ensemble work that characterizes the politically orientated work of the Berliner Ensemble or the artistic ideals of Grotowski's Laboratory Theatre. Yet if theatre in Britain is to open up new ways of allying its work to the revolutionary changes in art and society, some form of commitment to experiment and discovery is necessary.

(vii) Peter Brook

In the forefront of the search for a team of players dedicated to discovering new forms is Britain's most internationally renowned director, Peter Brook. Brook's career has been marked by a constant progression of exploration pursued in opera, film and musical comedy, as well as in new and classical drama. Style for Brook is not something that is fixed, but something that must be questioned each time theatre occurs. 'I have tried desperately in Shakespeare to avoid style simply because style is the way to anticipate the performance,' he declared in 1966. Theatre is distinguished from all other arts by its impermanence, and the search for new forms is a journey that has no end. For Brook its special value as an art form is its immediate effect on the community. That effect must not be to lull its audiences into an easy acceptance of the values it has to offer, but awaken and disturb them. 'The theatre has one precise social function – to disturb the spectator' (1967).

In 1964, in collaboration with Charles Marowitz, he gave expression to the shock techniques advocated by Antonin Artaud in a season of 'Theatre of Cruelty', presented at the LAMDA Theatre. These experiments were further developed in his Aldwych Theatre productions of Peter Weiss's *Marat/Sade*[1] and the largely improvised *US* (1966). In 1970 he confounded all previous preconceptions of *A Midsummer Night's Dream* by setting the play in a white-walled gymnasium, suspending Oberon and Puck on trapezes, dressing the characters in costumes based on those of Chinese acrobats and substituting conjuring tricks for Shakespeare's fairy magic.

The pressures that surround actors in the British theatre have led Brook to pursue his experiments with a group of actors of different nationalities and backgrounds based in Paris. His belief that theatre today should no longer be confined to a conventional building, but redefine itself each time it occurs, owes much to Jerzy Grotowski's Laboratory Theatre, as does his demand for rigorous physical and vocal discipline in his actors. These principles were demonstrated in the first public performance of his international ensemble presented in the ancient tombs of Persepolis for the Shiraz/Persepolis Festival of the Arts in 1971. For this production the author, Ted Hughes, invented a new language, Orghast, which was also the name of the two-part drama, based on the myth of Prometheus' theft of fire. The actors spent many months mastering the languages used which included Avesta (the ancient Zoroastrian ritual language), Latin and Greek, as well as the musical intonations on which Hughes's invented language was based. Physical and vocal exercises included body and breath control based on Yoga and Chinese disciplines of body control.

In 1976 British audiences were introduced to the experimental work of Brook's ensemble through his production of *The Ik*, a factual account of the devastating effects of Western civilization on the nomadic culture of an African tribe. Here again the actors demonstrated their intensive training in their mastery of the tribe's language and behaviour, as well as their study of its attitudes and beliefs. The production, presented in the full glare of the house lights, and set against the bare walls of London's Roundhouse with actors devoid of make-up and theatrical costumes, was a relentless confrontation with a reality that made no concessions to the enjoyment of the audience. 'On the stage,' wrote J. M. Synge, 'one must have reality and one must have joy.'[2] For many young audiences today the make-believe of the stage is no more than a conjuring trick; and joy has no place for those who believe themselves to be victims of a system they see no reason to celebrate.

---

[1] *The Persecution and Assassination of Marat as Performed by the Inmates of the Asylum of Charenton under the Direction of the Marquis de Sade*, presented by the Royal Shakespeare Company, Aldwych Theatre, 1964.

[2] Preface to *The Playboy of the Western World*.

(viii) The fringe

Ensemble work and the pursuit of theatre with a social purpose is equally the aim of many of the so-called fringe theatre groups, variously known as avant-garde, underground or alternative theatre. It is impossible to categorize this movement. Its manifestations spread from the second-rate amateur to the professional attitudes of the Pip Simmons Theatre Group and the Ken Campbell Road Show; from theatre with a political purpose to the enjoyment of theatre as fun. The movement has been largely fostered by massive un-employment in the acting profession, as well as by its recruitment of uni-versity and school leavers to whom the theatre offers a way of life and an opportunity to express their desires to improve or change society, or merely to escape from its pressures. The development of drama departments in uni-versities, polytechnics and teacher-training colleges, the extension of drama as an educational medium in schools, have contributed to this theatrical explosion outside, and often antagonistic to, the established theatre.

In its early manifestations the movement was predominantly orientated towards left-wing militancy. Plays and 'happenings', designed to shock, offered naïve solutions to problems of international complexity; polished acting was regarded as bourgeois; caricature was substituted for character; social conventions and proprieties were flouted. The abolition of stage censorship in 1968, the permissive attitudes of contemporary society, and the absorption of new techniques of acting and production into the established theatre, have robbed the underground movement of much of its shock effect. Today the fringe has emerged from the underground to become a valuable alternative to the established theatre; it has shed much of its aggressive attitude and widened its horizons to serve a variety of social and educational aims. These extend from lunchtime entertainment, often of a purely conven-tional kind, to improvisations tailored from the transitory events of real life. While it would be a mistake to overrate the importance of some of its mani-festations, the 'alternative' theatre can play a demanding and vital role in the maintaining of live theatre. Actors cannot exist without a public; and a young public, nourished on the 'telly', 'blue movies', 'pop' stars and 'pot', will never return again to the formalities and conventions of Irving's Lyceum.

(ix) Social change and economic conditions

The tendency to break away from past formalities and conventions is seen not only in the fringe companies, but also in the work of young people's companies, such as the Young Vic, the Contact Theatre Company in Manchester and the Royal Shakespeare Company's Theatre-Go-Round, as well as in much of the work of the RSC itself. Entering the theatre before the commencement of the 1975 production of *Henry V* at the Royal Shakespeare Theatre, the audience found Alan Howard and his fellow players already on the stage 'limbering up' physically and vocally, setting up scenic elements, donning their costumes, relaxing, or exchanging pleasantries with the front rows of the stalls. This breaking down of the barriers between actors and audience is part of the process – already noted – of 'democratizing' the theatre, manifested in the architectural form of recent theatre buildings and the abandonment of 'star' billing. Theatre in the seventies can no longer rely on privileged audiences; its future welfare depends on its ability to adapt to the lifestyle and attitudes of a changing society. Its welfare, too, has always been more immediately sensitive to the financial climate than other industries.

The economic crisis of 1976 has presented theatre managements with a serious problem. To some extent the cushioning effect of state and municipal grants has prevented the decline in the standards of the subsidized companies, though salary increases and cutbacks in public expenditure have involved a reduction in output and in the employment of artists. The commercial theatre, however, faces a serious threat to its existence as a creative force. The Theatre Investment Fund, founded in 1975, by which commercial managements can draw upon funds for approved productions from a banking system not unlike the National Film Corporation, may offer future relief. In the meantime London managements have increasingly to rely on transfers from the subsidized theatres, or to pander to the tastes of a public seeking erotic entertainment.

(x) The National Theatre

Amid the uncertainties of the financial crisis the year 1976 ushered in two historic events.

In the City of Manchester, which since the demise of Miss Horniman's

Gaiety Theatre had lost much of its theatrical impetus, new life arose. The Royal Exchange Company (previously the 69 Theatre Company) opened a theatre, constructed in the round, within the imposing hall of Manchester's Royal Exchange. With generous help from the local authorities and the Arts Council the Company, directed by Michael Elliott, Braham Murray and Caspar Wrede and supported by such artists as Wendy Hiller, Tom Courtenay, Albert Finney and Alec Guinness, embarked on a repertoire of new and classical plays that bids fair to rival that of the National Theatre itself.

After 125 years of hopes, speculations and frustrated dreams, and seemingly endless delays in construction, the National Theatre opened its doors on 16 March 1976. The building, however, was not fully completed until October when it was officially inaugurated by Her Majesty the Queen.

One of the first decisions of the architect, Denys Lasdun, when he began to plan the theatre in 1963, was the rejection of the original idea of a single auditorium. The new and the old drama demand radically different staging, and the three theatres housed within the building – the Lyttleton, the Olivier and the Cottesloe – represent the three main forms of theatre architecture: the proscenium stage, the open stage and the laboratory studio.

The riverside site, presented by the London County Council, offered a unique opportunity to fulfil Granville Barker's demand for a building that would be 'its own advertisement'. Barker also declared that a national theatre must be 'visibly and unmistakably a popular institution'. It was this need that dictated the decision to provide a building that would be open to the public whether or not they were going to the plays. Open terraces and spacious foyers are, in the architect's words, 'available to the public just to mill around in. . . . So the building is not a temple with a door which says "Knock, come in" – it's already open.'

For the actors, designers, directors and technicians the National Theatre offers better working conditions, more modern equipment, more workshop space and rehearsal facilities than any other European theatre. Whether Lasdun's open theatre will encourage a wider public for the theatre as a whole, and whether those who control this vast complex can inspire the dedication of those who work within it, upon which the creative art of the theatre depends, remains to be seen.

III Dramatists and plays since 1880

John Russell Taylor

1 The heyday of the well-made play

The year 1880 was remarkable for nothing in English dramatic history, except that Henry Irving started it off in January by complaining to *The Times* about the 'unquestionable dearth of good dramatists', and virtually nobody saw fit to argue with him. Even that, all things considered, was not particularly remarkable. People had been starting and ending years with the same sort of complaint right back to the 1820s. Not always, of course, quite reasonably. The career of T. W. Robertson, from *Society* in 1865 to *M.P.* in 1870, had given some room for hope that a revival of some sort was under way for English drama; perhaps, even, a revolution. But though Robertson did succeed in bringing about a minor revolution in English staging, the marriage of neat French methods of dramatic construction with a rosy bourgeois realism did not seem to have any very obvious effect on dramatists of the next decade. James Albery produced one play, *Two Roses* (1870), almost as good as Robertson's best, and very much in Robertson's style, but then lapsed into conventional farce with plays such as his remarkably successful *Pink Dominoes* (1877). H. J. Byron wrote one self-proclaimed 'serious' play, *Cyril's Success*, in 1868, directly under Robertson's influence, but then he also went back to farce with *Our Boys* (1875). And so on almost universally: within a couple of years of Robertson's death in 1871 he might as well have never been for all the apparent difference it made to the work of surviving dramatists, and the Bancrofts, his enthusiastic collaborators in bringing about the hoped-for realist revolution in English drama, found themselves reduced to endless revivals of Robertson's own six major plays.

So the complaints continued. Almost the only bright spot in 1880 large enough for anyone to see was certainly not, however entertaining, to be taken seriously according to the criteria Irving had in mind. Irving sought serious drama in the works of Tennyson, and Tennyson, in *Queen Mary* (1875), *Harold* (1877) and *Becket* (1879), did his literary best to oblige with solid historical dramas written in supple if not very lively or speakable blank verse; but though *Becket* – when finally produced, suitably cut and rearranged, by Irving in 1893 – did achieve a measure of success, it was certainly not in such hopeful Shakespearian pastiche that the future of vital English drama lay. Anyone looking for life in English drama in the 1870s would have been best advised to look instead towards the most triumphant light entertainers of their day, Gilbert and Sullivan, whose long string of immensely popular comic operas began with *Trial by Jury* in 1875 and ended, effectively, with *The Gondoliers* in 1889.

William Schwenk Gilbert (1836–1911), though little of his writing independent of Sullivan, apart from his *Bab Ballads*, is remembered today, was already an established figure in the London theatre when he first collaborated with Sullivan on a comic opera, and the world in which the Gilbert and Sullivan operas exist is very much his own imaginative world, sketched in numerous earlier plays. Though Gilbert had written basic British farces in the manner common at the time, almost from the start of his dramatic career (*Dulcamara*, 1866) he had created his own type of play, the so-called 'fairy' or fantastic comedy, and, more important, his own characteristic tone and atmosphere, which are to be found even in works that are outwardly consonant with the accepted conventional genres of his period. The basis of Gilbert's humour is a simple process by which familiar characters, events and institutions are turned upside down or inside out. In *The Palace of Truth* (1870), a blank-verse comedy, for example, he presupposes a setting in which all the characters normally acting roles or assuming attitudes dictated by convention are, unexpectedly and unconsciously, constrained to tell nothing but the truth. Thus the scheming coquette is made to discuss and expose her wiles quite frankly even as she spins them, while the chilly and correct princess reveals her true passionate nature, the effusive prince his underlying *ennui*. Natural and supernatural characters mingle quite happily and unaffectedly, and the whole thing is bathed in a hearty humour tinged with a deep, underlying melancholy which will be at once familiar to any devotee of the Savoy operas. The melancholy comes nearer the surface in *Pygmalion and Galatea* (1871) and is uppermost in *Broken Hearts* (1875), a rather charming sentimental fantasy about a group of mournful young women alone on an island with a 'deformed ill-favoured dwarf'. But these plays are somewhat exceptional; as a rule the humour is evidently predominant, and of course, though the melancholy undertones remain, it is primarily as a humorist that Gilbert is appreciated in his collaborations with Sullivan.

The Savoy operas, as they are generically known, though the Savoy Theatre was not opened to house them until 1881, are a thing apart, in their own day and since. Traces of their influence crop up in some very unlikely places – early Marx Brothers films like *Animal Crackers* and *Duck Soup*, for which Kalmar and Ruby provided elaborate concerted numbers very much in the Gilbert and Sullivan manner, or the 1930s satirical musicals of the Gershwins and Rodgers and Hart – but all attempts to imitate them failed, even the efforts of Gilbert and Sullivan themselves to repeat their former successes in *Utopia Limited* (1893) and *The Grand Duke* (1896). Argument has been constant, and sometimes heated, from the first performances of the Savoy operas down to our own day, on the subject of which partner is more important in their continuing appeal. Book or music? The question is impossible to answer, and pointless anyway. Little of either partner's work outside the collaboration still has much life in it (an overture and a few songs of Sullivan, Gilbert's ballads), but the combination is unbeatable, each bringing out the best in the other.

And at least Gilbert, even if influences can be traced in his work – notably from the pantomime extravaganzas of Planché – is in final effect quite unlike anyone else writing at the time. He has even been called, by Allardyce Nicoll,[1] 'by far the greatest writer whom the English stage had attracted throughout the entire course of the nineteenth century'. His singularity is not so much one of style as one of vision. The peculiar form his fantasy takes is very personal, in that its broadest comic effects are nearly always based on cruelty and have about them an underlying melancholy, while his 'satire', like most Victorian attempts at the genre, stops short in a fairly amicable type of burlesque which even the ostensible victims can enjoy. It is not for nothing that *The Yeomen of the Guard* (1888) turns on an execution and skirts tragedy in its handling of the jester Jack Point's ill-fated love, or that *The Mikado* (1885) is full of references to execution, torture and such, or that *HMS*

[1] *A History of Late Nineteenth Century Drama* (Cambridge, 1946), Vol. I, p. 147.

Pinafore (1878) fantasizes the harsh facts of brutal naval discipline, or that *Ruddigore* (1887) abounds in family curses, vengeful ghosts, mad maidens and all the grimmer trappings of gothic melodrama. True, Gilbert (importantly aided by Sullivan) turns them all into good, fairly clean fun, but a slight yet perceptible sado-masochistic tang persists to complicate our reactions and to make the Savoy operas a good deal more complex in their effect on us than at first glance they may appear.

It is hardly surprising, though, that only a few commentators at the time, guided in their own view by the most serious interests of drama as an art, should have seen the Savoy operas as anything more than pleasing and expert light relief. And elsewhere, at the beginning of the 1880s, the picture was fairly black. Yet relief of some sort was already in the offing: a new movement in the drama, to be recognized resoundingly in 1882 by a new critic, William Archer, in his first, very influential book, *English Dramatists of Today*. The most remarkable thing about the book is the date of its appearance, for though Archer's predictions proved to be correct, it would with the best will in the world be very difficult to find any solid evidence for them at the time he was writing. He managed to get together a catalogue of sixteen 'dramatists of today', including, to be sure, Gilbert, Albery, H. J. Byron and Tennyson, as well as Sydney Grundy (1848–1914), indefatigable adaptor 'from the French' and indifferent original dramatist. But none of these, Gilbert apart, could be seriously regarded as an earnest of important new drama on the way. Nor could most of the other eleven. But among them, significantly, are two (in 1882) very unfamiliar names: Henry Arthur Jones and Arthur Wing Pinero.

Neither of them, at that stage, seems to be included on anything stronger than lucky guesswork or peculiarly acute instinct. Jones had written a handful of one-act plays, one of which, *A Clerical Error* (1879), had attracted favourable attention as an unusually effective light comedy. Pinero had written two quite successful full-length plays, a light comedy called *The Money-Spinner* (1880) and a 'strong' drama, *The Squire* (1881). Yet Archer was able, on this slender evidence, to divine in Jones 'a good deal of culture and a great deal of earnest aspiration', and in Pinero 'a thoughtful and conscientious writer with artistic aims, if not yet with full command of his artistic means'. And in both cases what was to come proved him surprisingly accurate. Almost at once, in 1882, Jones established himself as a leading figure in contemporary drama with his melodrama *The Silver King* (written in collaboration with H. A. Herman); Pinero began his series of great farces in 1885 with *The Magistrate*, and later on took up the promise of *The Squire* with social comedies such as *The Hobby Horse* (1886) and 'serious' dramas like *The Second Mrs Tanqueray* (1893).

To some extent, of course, Archer may have been calling on private knowledge of Jones and Pinero, and of the ambitions they had already expressed some time before they were able to realize them on stage. Henry Arthur Jones (1851–1929) in particular always regarded himself as a literary figure, and considered the drama as he found it in need, primarily, of elevation to a self-respecting field of literary endeavour again. He sent the texts of some of his early one-act plays to his literary idol, Matthew Arnold, and received kind comments in reply; Arnold wrote an influential review of *The Silver King*[1] in which he praised it because 'throughout the piece the diction and sentiments are natural, they have sobriety and propriety, they are literature'. Again, it is perhaps a reflection on the generally low standards of the time that *The Silver King*, an effective but quite unremarkable melodrama about the plight of a man who wrongly believes himself to be a murderer, should have caused such a stir. But from it Jones went on to write stronger, more distinctive and in general more interesting plays. The curious thing about his career, though, is that despite his literary aspirations, and indeed the measure of recognition he gained on this score, his all-out attempts to produce dramatic literature were among his least successful works, from any point of view, and his real reputation, as well as any lasting call he may have on our attention, came from his practical mastery of dramatic effect, his instinctive gifts as a man of the theatre.

From the first it is possible to see both his advantages and his limitations. His manner is based on the generally realistic conventions established for the treatment of contemporary subjects in the theatre by Robertson, but modified by a natural inclination towards melodrama. This means that even in his early plays he is never really content to stick at Robertson's chosen level of lightish social comedy: he seeks significant subjects, and introduces them mainly in terms of melodrama. *Saints and Sinners* (1884), for instance, aspires to deal with the place of religion in society, though in practice it is more about snobbery and hypocrisy masquerading as conscious Christian virtue; but the contrivance of the plot, with its mustachio-twisting villain, Captain Fanshawe (a vile seducer), and its moralistic speechifying, brings it unwittingly close to the basic melodrama of the time, and only its pretensions partially blinded critical opinion of the time to this fact. Much the same is true of *Wealth* and *The Middleman* (both 1889), but *Judah* (1890) marks a new maturity, and is, for Jones, unusually concentrated in its plotting and

[1] *Pall Mall Gazette*, 6 December 1882.

unadorned in its dialogue. In fact, it achieves for the first time what he seems to have been aiming at for some years, a workable modern problem play or, to put it another way, a fully fledged English well-made play, allying methodical construction learnt from the French with Robertsonian realism in the depiction of the English middle classes and a certain aspiration, not too heavily insisted on, towards valid comment on social problems of the day.

Again, the subject was religion, Jones's Achilles heel as a dramatist: a sincere cleric falls in love with a faith healer who proves to be a fraud, and at last brings her round to confession and a new start in life. Bolstered by the play's success, Jones went on to write his own two favourites among his plays, *The Tempter* (1893), a five-act verse tragedy about the Devil's intervention in a prince's love life during the Middle Ages, and *Michael and His Lost Angel* (1896), a battle of wills between a strongly religious man and the unhappily married free soul for whom he unfortunately conceives an overwhelming passion. In both of these, despite the respect they inspire for a writer willing to have a go at such subjects in such a style at such a time, Jones's skill and intelligence are no match for his material, and the results are relatively disastrous. Fortunately all his work at this time was not conceived on quite so lofty a plane. Descending to social comedy and freed for the moment from the shackles of his grander aspirations, he was able to produce wholly charming and effective plays such as *The Case of Rebellious Susan* (1894), which was considered agreeably risqué at the time because it showed a woman trying to turn the tables on men by breaking their monopoly on amatory dalliance, and *The Liars* (1897), a tangle of intrigues engaged in by the heroine and her friends to divert her husband's jealousy over what begins as a perfectly innocent escapade.

Mrs Dane's Defence (1900), probably Jones's best play, is something else again: though the subject matter – the right of a woman with a past to make a new start – is such as, earlier, Jones would have felt obliged to treat in terms of sentimental melodrama, he manages this time to steer almost entirely clear of sentimental or melodramatic cliché, and to treat his story with a clear-eyed appreciation of the way things really are, not forgetting the innumerable ambiguities and double standards which complicate decisions and finally make partial cynics of all sensible men. The play is harsh and ironical in its conclusions, and astonishingly free from any sort of comfortable compromise. But by the time *Mrs Dane's Defence* was produced, Jones was becoming something of a back number, and the unquestioned reign of the English well-made play he had done much to establish was nearing its end, under concentrated fire from George Bernard Shaw. Jones was able to modify his approach

according to the new spirit of the age (and, latterly, with some unacknowledged influence from the unmentionable Oscar Wilde) only so far, and
though he went on writing plays into the 1900s, they were given less and less
notice. He drifted off into political pamphleteering, writing enthusiastically
about patriotism in the modern world, the advisability of limiting education
for the masses, the uses of capital, and the political follies of H. G. Wells and
George Bernard Shaw. Only one of his later plays, *The Lie*, an old-fashioned
sentimental melodrama about two sisters and the illegitimate child borne by
one of them, achieved any kind of success on its belated London production
in 1923 (it had already played in New York nine years earlier). Nevertheless,
Jones remains a playwright of some intrinsic interest, and the most important
single precursor of the English well-made play's brief flowering in the 1890s.

The career of Archer's other discovery, Arthur Wing Pinero (1855–1934),
in many ways parallels that of Henry Arthur Jones, though his relative lack
of pretension brought him less serious attention at the time and makes him,
from the angle of today, a more consistently endearing figure. He was at all
times a much more various dramatist than Jones, turning his hand with equal
facility to farce, high comedy, sentimental drama, melodrama, the problem
play, satire, fantasy and even operetta. He seems to have shared none of
Jones's extra-dramatic preoccupations: social questions interested him only
in so far as they provided an effective motive for personal drama; he was
more interested in people than in ideas, and more interested in telling
theatrical entertainment than in either for its own sake.

Despite his beginning in serious (if, in the case of *The Money-Spinner*,
fairly lightweight) drama, he first really established himself in the public eye
as a writer of farces, beginning with *The Magistrate* in 1885, rapidly followed
by *The Schoolmistress* (1886), *Dandy Dick* (1887) and *The Cabinet Minister*
(1890). In these he may be said to have established virtually a new genre,
farce of character. Instead of building on two-dimensional stereotypes who
can be manœuvred from one embarrassing situation to another with the
maximum of elegant efficiency *à la* Feydeau, Pinero brings together a group
of extravagant, idiosyncratic but not finally altogether incredible characters
and lets the story develop from their wild and unpredictable interactions. In
this he is after his fashion harking back to the Jonsonian comedy of humours.
Mrs Posket in *The Magistrate* is singlemindedly dedicated to preserving the
deception whereby she has convinced her new magistrate husband of her
youthfulness by passing off her nineteen-year-old son as fourteen; Miss
Dyott, the schoolmistress, is determined to restore her husband's fortunes by
a short and deadly-secret interlude in *opéra bouffe*; all the misfortunes of the

Dean in *Dandy Dick* arise from his being innocently persuaded by his horsy sister to put £50 on a horse in aid of the cathedral restoration fund. Each story starts with one whacking improbability, but thereafter develops with complete consistency and perfect (if lunatic) logic according to the obsessions of the various characters involved. And the result is something as unmistakably durable as anything in nineteenth-century English drama, technically masterly and wholly personal.

But not, of course, 'serious'. It is highly doubtful whether Pinero made any necessary distinction in his own mind between his farces and his 'serious' plays – there were simply good subjects for plays and bad subjects – but his early critics made the distinction for him. Archer had praised him for his thoughtful and serious character and his artistic aims, and as the 1880s progressed Archer was not alone in thinking he should be doing something more substantial to justify the assessment. In 1884 he did, with *The Profligate*. It is hard to see now how this silly, badly constructed piece of melodramatic contrivance, full of naïvely rhetorical soliloquies, heavy asides and barefaced coincidences, could have made its author's name as a serious dramatist, but it did. No doubt partly because, whatever its technical deficiencies, at least it was a problem play: it concerned the marital history of a rake, and showed virtue triumphing, somewhat improbably, at the final curtain. It had a *succès de scandale*, and provoked earnest discussion as to whether Pinero's first thought, enshrined in the printed text, of having the libertine Renshaw take poison was right, or whether the acted ending, with a cobbled-up reconciliation between him and his wife, was preferable: all sublimely beside the real point – that both are totally unbelievable. And so Pinero was talked about, he was an advanced, even a shocking playwright, and great things might be expected of him.

In 1893 the first great thing appeared: his biggest success and even today his most famous play, *The Second Mrs Tanqueray*. Again, a problem play, about a misalliance between a man of the world and a woman with a past. Can it work? Should it work? Pinero's final answer is a conventional – indeed, much too conventional – no. But before Paula is manœuvred into a suicide which seems very much a sentimental gesture in favour of conventional right-thinking, rather than a believable expression of her practical, unsentimental character, we have three acts of highly satisfactory well-made play, beautifully constructed and written with an ease and economy quite extraordinary considering it is only four years later than the bombast of *The Profligate*. It is artificial, of course, as Shaw at once remarked and bitterly condemned it for being ('It is impossible to avoid the conclusion that what

most of our critics mean by mastery of stagecraft is recklessness in the sub-
stitution of dead machinery and lay figures for vital action and real characters').[1] But, Shaw notwithstanding, to call it artificial is only to say how it
works, not to question whether it does work; and Shaw, anyway, was being
more than a trifle disingenuous when he attacked it on these grounds, since
he himself, unless it suited his purpose, held no brief for the abandonment of
convention in favour of unvarnished naturalism. What he objected to really,
as he later explicitly admitted, was not the artifice of the well-made play,
which according to its own lights worked very well, but to its fundamental
unseriousness in its treatment of general social issues merely as an excuse for
personal drama rather than as matters worthy of discussion in their own
right.

Here Shaw was fundamentally opposed to Pinero in principle – and the
more bitterly in that Pinero was so accomplished at doing what he wanted to
do, and therefore inevitably the biggest single obstacle to the establishment
of the sort of drama Shaw wanted to see, and to write himself. For the while,
however, even Shaw had little effect on Pinero's popularity, and on the success of the plays in the manner of *The Second Mrs Tanqueray* which he wrote
in the next few years, notably *The Notorious Mrs Ebbsmith* (1895), *Iris* (1901)
and *His House in Order* (1906). But by the time the last of these appeared,
though it is in most ways the most satisfactory of Pinero's problem plays,
unspoilt for once by a facile, melodramatically contrived conclusion, Pinero
was already coming to be regarded as oldfashioned. Though like Henry
Arthur Jones he went on writing for some years more he never again had a
comparable success. One or two of his later plays, however, show curious
departures in style and subject matter, notably *The Freaks* (1918), a weird
symbolic fantasy about a collection of circus freaks willed to a conventional
suburban family who create havoc when the son and daughter of the house
fall for the human knot and the skeleton dude respectively, and *The Enchanted
Cottage* (1922), a vaguely Barrie-esque romantic fantasy about a couple who
are plain in the world but beautiful to each other in their cottage, where they
see with the eyes of love.

In the 1900s already Pinero's critical reputation was radically lowered, and
when revolution came it considerably modified the accepted picture of
Pinero's career and importance. Of those 'serious' dramas on which at the
time his reputation was thought to be most firmly based, probably only *His
House in Order* retains any real hold on our attention. On the other hand, his
farces are as fresh now as the day they were written, and many of the other

[1] *Our Theatres in the Nineties* (London, 1932), Vol. I, pp. 45–6.

plays, looked down on as flimsy and unserious at the time, wear remarkably well. Such lightly satirical pieces as *The Hobby Horse* (1886), about the dabblings of the rich in good works, *The Times* (1891), about the pretensions of a nouveau riche family, and *The Thunderbolt* (1908), about a genteel family showing their true natures over a disputed estate, are still lively and charming. *The Benefit of the Doubt* (1895), an elaborate comedy of intrigue, is breathtaking as a piece of sheer unflagging dramatic storytelling, without one slack patch. And *Trelawny of the 'Wells'* (1898) is that great rarity (especially in Victorian times), a comedy of sentiment which keeps its sentimentality within bounds, a delicate, nostalgic tribute to the theatre of Pinero's youth and to Tom Robertson, who appears in the play lightly disguised as Tom Wrench, the playwright whose new realistic drama is so difficult for the older actors to understand. A beautiful production of *Trelawny* by the National Theatre and many successful revivals of Pinero's farces have confirmed the judgement that, wherever his major dramas may stand in the opinion of posterity, here at least he has made a real and lasting contribution to dramatic literature.

2 Shaw and his influence

In following up the careers of Jones and Pinero we have had, perforce, to push ahead to the 1900s. But in doing so, it must be confessed, we have been ignoring remarkably little of any merit in the 1880s and early 1890s, until the advent of Shaw with *Widowers' Houses* (1892) and Wilde with *Lady Winder-mere's Fan* (1892). We have, however, bypassed some important background developments, because on the surface at least they seem to have little relevance to the development of drama in Britain. In particular, there is the emergence of Ibsen and his first tentative introduction to British audiences, often softened and bowdlerized in adaptation, and, especially when presented more or less as he wrote, regarded as the last word in uncompromising, outspoken modern realism. And true it is that though Ibsen began to appear on the London stage in the 1880s, he apparently had very little influence on the coming men of the time, Jones and Pinero, both of whom insisted that they saw no real connection between their practice and Ibsen's (even though one of Jones's early jobs was to adapt, in collaboration, *A Doll's House* as *Breaking a Butterfly*, 1884). It is conceivable that in their assessment of their own conscious mental processes they were right, but equally it is true, as Shaw acutely observed, that the example of Ibsen brought about a change in the expectations of the theatregoing public, and thus brought indirect pressure to bear on the popular British dramatists of the day to modify their subject matter and technique, as we can see if we compare the most success-ful plays of the 1880s with those of the 1890s:

> The change is evident at once. In short, a modern manager need not produce The Wild Duck, but he must be very careful not to produce a play which will seem insipid and old-fashioned to playgoers who have seen The Wild Duck, even though they may have hissed it.[1]

Shaw, understandably, was even less tolerant towards what he considered the hollow, disreputable, pseudo-problem plays of Pinero and his kind than towards the simpler, less knowing drama of the days before Ibsen had shown the right way to people who could only water down and vulgarize him. It was no doubt partly Wilde's complete innocence where Ibsenism in drama was concerned that disposed Shaw so sympathetically towards him. Wilde, in fact, was in a curious position, belonging decisively neither to the new drama nor to the old, but using elements of each to his own purposes. Before he embarked on his series of famous comedies he had already dabbled in drama twice, with *Vera, or the Nihilists* (1880, produced in New York in 1882), a historical piece set in Russia during the Napoleonic era, and *The Duchess of Padua* (1883, produced 1891) a harking-back to the Renaissance. Neither of these has found much critical support, though Professor Wilson Knight takes an indulgent view of *Vera*.[2] In 1892 he wrote in French an ornate, rather wil-fully perverse one-act poetic drama, *Salome* (translated into English by Lord Alfred Douglas). This had some *succès de scandale*, but much more as a text to be read than as a piece of practical theatre; indeed it really survives in per-formance only via Richard Strauss's operatic version of 1905.

But, in general, Wilde's reputation as a dramatist stands or falls on the four comedies, *Lady Windermere's Fan* (1892), *A Woman of No Importance* (1893), *An Ideal Husband* (1895) and *The Importance of Being Earnest* (1895). The first three use the same sort of material of social drama as Jones, Pinero and many lesser figures; their plot mechanism is creaky and even at times deliberately summary: one cannot believe that Wilde was not capable of covering up the improbabilities more convincingly and telling his tales in a much more natural-seeming way if he wanted to. But this is no doubt the point: he did not want to. He used the plot conventions of his time quite deliberately, cynically he might say, as excuses for his plays, relying on the built-in interest of unacknowledged parentage, women with pasts and men

[1] *Our Theatres in the Nineties*, Vol. I, p. 165.
[2] *The Golden Labyrinth* (London, 1962), pp. 305–6.

with guilty secrets to bring audiences into the theatre and keep them there, panting with anticipation, until all should be revealed. But what really interested Wilde in his plays was something quite different: the glittering superstructure of epigram with which these hoary old melodramatic plots could be decorated. Finally in *The Importance of Being Earnest* he had the courage, or the lucky inspiration, to dispense with the support altogether. Here the plot itself, though still turning on unacknowledged parentage, is reduced to an absurd geometrical formula, a piece of almost Gilbertian topsy-turveydom which is for once perfectly at one with the verbal wit in which it is dressed. To find anything like it in English comedy one must look back to Congreve, and even then the likeness is very superficial; it is an entirely personal creation, and not the least tragedy of Wilde's spectacular fall from grace is that afterwards he had neither the opportunity nor the heart to continue writing in the same vein.

At first glance it might seem paradoxical that Wilde, more barefacedly artificial than all his contemporaries in his use of stage contrivance, coincidence, soliloquy and aside, and all the supposedly outmoded paraphernalia of Victorian melodrama, should have been virtually the only British dramatist towards whom Shaw the critic was generally kindly.[1] But it is not after all quite so strange as it seems. Wilde's very brazenness in his use of these conventions is for Shaw his saving grace: he is not, like Pinero or Jones, trying to deceive his audiences by passing off superficial reworkings of stock characters and situations as the real thing, profound insights on life as it is really lived. Shaw's own natural inclination, in fact, was to look back past the currently fashionable well-made play to the now despised but to him more honest and valid British traditions of the melodrama and the farce, types of play which made no bones about their superficiality and artificiality.

If the new dramatists lacked the profundity, the social concern and the intellectual rigour of Ibsen, that was unfortunate, but not really their fault; but it was certainly culpable for them to try to pass off their shoddy entertainments as the genuine, serious article. Shaw attacked them not on the basis of their achievements, which he later admitted were, in their own terms, considerable, but at their weakest point – on their pretensions, or the pretensions which their more solemn, vocal supporters thrust upon them. Wilde had no pretensions, so he escaped Shaw's lash. Even Pinero, when he stuck to what he could do well – farce, *Trelawny of the 'Wells'* – could receive a few kind words from Shaw. But the higher a dramatist's aspirations, the less

[1] See his reviews of *An Ideal Husband* (*Our Theatres in the Nineties*, Vol. I, pp. 9–12) and *The Importance of Being Earnest* (ibid. pp. 41–4).

patience Shaw had with his failure to live up to them. He could be indulgent when he felt that a dramatic enterprise, even if not entirely well conceived, was actuated by true intelligence, as in the case of Henry James's *Guy Domville* (1895), and he would see the merits of basic unpretentious theatrical entertainment when it appeared, as in Brandon Thomas's perennial farce *Charley's Aunt* (1892). But in general his dramatic criticism in the 1890s was, as he acknowledged in the 'Author's Apology' to his first collection of dramatic criticism,[1] 'a siege laid to the theatre of the XIXth Century by an author who had to cut his own way into it at the point of a pen, and throw some of its defenders into the moat'. It is time now to consider what he did once he had penetrated the citadel.

To cover Shaw's whole career we shall have to range, of course, far beyond the 1890s. He was born in 1856, became a literary critic in the early 1880s, a music critic and, most influentially, the dramatic critic of *The Saturday Review* from 1895 to 1897. His first play, *Widowers' Houses*, was begun in 1885 and staged in 1892; his last produced work, *Far-Fetched Fables*, was first staged in the year of his death, 1950. The total tally of his plays is fifty-three, ranging in length from the marathon five-part *Back to Methuselah* (1918–21) to the ten-minute knockabout sketch for puppets *Shakes v. Shav* (1949). Though Shaw was, inevitably, to some extent a child of his time, he was much more, and more decisively perhaps than any other British dramatist of that time, his own master, creator of his own dramatic conventions, arbiter of his own destiny as a writer. Here and there an influence can be seen: *Widowers' Houses*, as one might expect, shows signs of Shaw's early enthusiasm for Ibsen; *Arms and the Man* (1894) is a fantastic variation on Ruritanian romantic melodrama; *You Never Can Tell* (1897, staged 1900) turns popular farcical conventions to Shavian ends; *Heartbreak House* (1916, staged 1920) suggests a sympathetic study of Chekhov; and if Shaw's ideas on staging owe little to Wagner's, Wagner probably contributed something to his conception of the superman, just as Mozart probably contributed Don Juan to *Man and Superman* (1903, staged 1905). But Shaw's drama remains essentially *sui generis*, taking little from anyone else and giving little back, in that Shaw as a direct influence on others has nearly always proved disastrous.

Partly this is because Shaw considered himself first and foremost a dramatist of ideas. In 1909, framing a statement to the Parliamentary Committee on Censorship, he offered a deliberately provocative but in general not inaccurate description of himself:

I am not an ordinary dramatist in general practice. I am a specialist in

[1] *Our Theatre in the Nineties*, Vol. I, p. v.

immoral and heretical plays. My reputation has been gained by my persistent struggle to force the public to reconsider its morals. In particular, I regard much current morality as to economic and sexual relations as disastrously wrong; and I regard certain doctrines of the Christian religion as understood in England today with abhorrence. I write plays with the deliberate object of converting the nation to my opinions in these matters.[1]

That, at any rate, is more or less how Shaw saw himself: as a propagandist and dramatic pamphleteer, for whom ideas were of prime importance, and who would use whatever techniques he found to hand which seemed most likely to be effective in making his point. There have been, at the time and since, enough commentators ready to take Shaw at his word, and consider his plays solemnly in terms of their 'ideas', of what philosophical point Shaw wanted to make in them. And yet this, whatever Shaw's conscious intentions, seems curiously beside the point. No dramatist, after all, survives on the strength of what he has to say, considered in the abstract: no amount of philosophical profundity or intellectual penetration can keep a play on the stage, but only its qualities as drama. Shaw's philosophy, or the ever-changing patterns of ideas which he took for his philosophy, would make a very shaky argument for his survival; all that counts now is the dramatic effectiveness with which he embodied his ideas.

And there, fortunately, his instinct took him much further than his conscious formulations of intention. Here the inevitable prefaces with which his plays were equipped in published form are both a clue and an obstacle to true understanding. A clue because the fact that he felt their necessity demonstrates that the full propagandist purpose of the plays is not realized on stage, and has to be elaborated or elucidated in argumentative prose. An obstacle in that it is often difficult for readers to dissociate the play as written and acted from Shaw's own commentary on it, which may in certain vital respects be quite misleading. It is wiser always to read Shaw's plays in a one-volume collection, shorn of their prefaces; the prefaces too are full of good writing, much wit, much provocation and some sense, but they are of a different kind from the plays, and to be read in a different spirit.

In any case, the plays should, whenever possible, be seen rather than read, for they are much more theatrical than literary. What gained Shaw his place in the London theatre of the 1890s, and kept him as a commanding figure in British drama at least until the mid-1920s, was not his ideas, but his comic gifts and his sure instinct for theatrical effect. Indeed, his plays are about as

[1] *Shaw on Theatre*, ed. E. J. West (New York, 1958), pp. 74–5.

completely theatrical as one can imagine, disdaining all literary assistance in the shape of psychologically rounded characterization and the detailed surface realism of the well-made-play school. Shaw's sympathy as a critic was with the most artificial theatrical genres – melodrama, farce, grand opera – and in his own plays he revitalizes their conventions and uses them to his own ends. His characters, as has often been observed, are seldom if ever rounded, independently believable human beings. Rather, they are ideas embodied. But this is as much a legitimate form of drama as any other, provided only that the author gives equally free play to the ideas as he would to his characters if they were independently conceived as human beings. And this Shaw certainly does. Whatever his protestations of social purpose for his plays, he is nearer the truth when he writes to Frank Harris: 'I am of the true Shakespearean type. I understand everybody and everything, and am nobody and nothing.'[1] His plays, therefore, may be intellectual in the sense that they are built on ideas, but they have, at their best, a warmth and humanity which comes from sheer disinterested delight in the interplay of ideas – which is, after all, an emotion like any other.

The spirit of comedy presides over Shaw's plays, right from the very first: however serious his intentions, he always appreciated the effectiveness of comedy as a means of expressing them, and in any case his temperament had a natural comic buoyancy which comes out even at the moments of deepest emotion. His great period as a dramatist runs from the earliest plays up to *Saint Joan* (1923), or arguably earlier, to (say) *Pygmalion* in 1912. Between *Widowers' Houses* and *Pygmalion* Shaw wrote eighteen full-length plays, all of which have continued to hold the stage, on and off, and most of which have entered the class of standard stage classics. It is a remarkable achievement; indeed in British drama, Shakespeare apart, it is unparalleled. Not all of the eighteen, admittedly, are what one would call major plays, but a series which includes *The Philanderer, Arms and the Man, Candida, You Never Can Tell, The Devil's Disciple, Man and Superman, John Bull's Other Island, Major Barbara, The Doctor's Dilemma, Misalliance, Androcles and the Lion* and *Pygmalion* can hardly be accused of lacking either substance or variety. And it is the lively play of ideas within them which keeps them alive: we probably feel little inclined to take seriously Shaw's ideas on war in *Arms and the Man*, his reflections on the life-force in *Man and Superman*, or his considerations of medical ethics in *The Doctor's Dilemma*, while the observations on the state of Ireland in *John Bull's Other Island* or poverty and capitalism in *Major Barbara* have been outdated by subsequent events. But the paradoxical wit

[1] Frank Harris, *Bernard Shaw* (London, 1931), p. 224.

with which the subjects are embodied remains fresh, the quality of the talk
gives the dramas a real theatrical *élan* of their own, even when, as in the case
of *Misalliance* (1910), they seem to consist of nothing but long static conversations occasionally punctuated by bouts of extravagant, farcical action.

Not that Shaw's plays, even at their most apparently static and conversational, are exactly lacking in plot. *Getting Married* (1908), for example, which
Shaw subtitles 'a disquieting play', has, when one stops to consider it, enough
plot for several plays, but it does not work by plot; the plot is the largely dis-
regarded backbone to one long, unbroken conversation about marriage seen
from various points of view, and it is the vitality of the talk that takes primacy
over the mere story. *Getting Married* is, even more than *Misalliance*, the
extreme example of Shaw's 'disquisitory' method, which moves towards its
apotheosis in *Heartbreak House*. And there is always another side to Shaw's
drama. He is equally capable of writing a play like *The Devil's Disciple*
(1897), in which what he wants to say is articulated by external plot and
action, or plays of personality-conflict like *Pygmalion* or *Candida*, in which
the quirky individuality of the characters largely if not entirely transcends the
abstract ideas which on one level they seem intended to embody. For in his
early years Shaw was, first and foremost, a practical, pragmatic dramatist,
putting the demands of drama first and the spreading of his ideas through
drama a long way after. He even admitted as much in the Preface to *Widowers' Houses*:

> You will please judge it not as a pamphlet in dialogue but as in intention
> a work of art as much as any comedy of Molière's is a work of art, and as
> pretending to be a better made play for actual use and long wear on the
> boards than anything that has yet been turned out by the patent con-
> structive machinery.

Of course, the admission was damaging to his alleged purposes as a phil-
osopher and propagandist in the theatre, and he soon forgot it, in theory if not
for a while in practice. Indeed, his long decline began only when he started to
follow his own ostensible programme too closely and seriously, when he
began actually to preach in his plays instead of letting the ideas in them sink
or swim according to their own inherent value to, and power over, audiences.
The turning point comes, really, in *Heartbreak House*, described in one of
Shaw's revealing subtitles as 'a fantasia in the Russian manner on English
themes'. This has always been the most controversial of Shaw's plays, if only
because it is the least superficially comic, and therefore because it is the play
that gives most ground to the supposition that with this key Shaw unlocked

his heart. Opinion has been fairly neatly divided between those who feel that, if he did, then the less Shaw he, and certainly the less effective dramatist; and those who see in the play a new seriousness and profundity which mark it as his best, as well as his most 'sincere', play. Certainly it appears to be a play over which no critical half measures are possible; though perhaps it is indicative that, with its curious shifts of mood, its dreamlike, semi-Chekhovian atmosphere and its violent unprepared conclusion (with bombs falling, though there has been no mention of war), it is one of those plays which, even for their most enthusiastic admirers, never seem in production quite to live up to their potential quality. Greater sincerity or not, it seems unarguable that here Shaw's grasp of theatrical effect, hitherto almost infallible, faltered a little: in *Heartbreak House* he seems to have written a play which defies completely satisfactory realization on the stage.

Thereafter, with the solitary exception of *Saint Joan*, Shaw's plays can be considered as, at best, half successes. The 'metabiological pentateuch' *Back to Methuselah* shows preaching assuming complete ascendancy over drama, and the bright spots in this endless chronicle of human folly are very few and far between. Even *Saint Joan*, though it survives firmly enough in the dramatic repertory, has about it a slightly manufactured air, and moments of terrible falsity when a note of true emotion is called for (as in Joan's evocation of the pleasures of country life which imprisonment would deny her for ever). *The Apple Cart* (1929), his next play after *Saint Joan*, is the latest of them to have enjoyed regular revival, and its satirical comedy about kingship in the modern world does have its good points, though the play suffers from Shaw's characteristic unevenness in a rather extreme form. All attempts at revaluing Shaw's later plays have failed, though *The Millionairess* (1936) has pleasing things in it and *In Good King Charles's Golden Days* (1939) more than a spark of the old power. But the overall impression is one of aridity, of the old dramatist going on writing, as he himself admitted, mainly because he did not know how to stop.

Shaw's place in living British drama remains as secure as anyone's, Shakespeare apart. His achievement in his best plays is the more remarkable in that he was more or less deliberately walking a tightrope, without any of the traditional aids in the form of 'human interest' in the characterization or elaborately articulated plots to hold attention. He could, as in *Candida*, or the first act of *Man and Superman*, construct tightly if he wanted to, but seemingly he rarely did: most of his plays are loosely organized, and depend for their continuing hold on the audience's attention entirely on the quality of the talk, the vitality of the conflict of ideas. Any flagging, and the audience is

21 Ralph Richardson, Joyce Redman and Sybil Thorndike in *Henry IV*

22 *Love's Labour's Lost*, New Theatre, 1949

23 Michael Redgrave in *Uncle Vanya*

24 Laurence Olivier's *Hamlet*, 1963

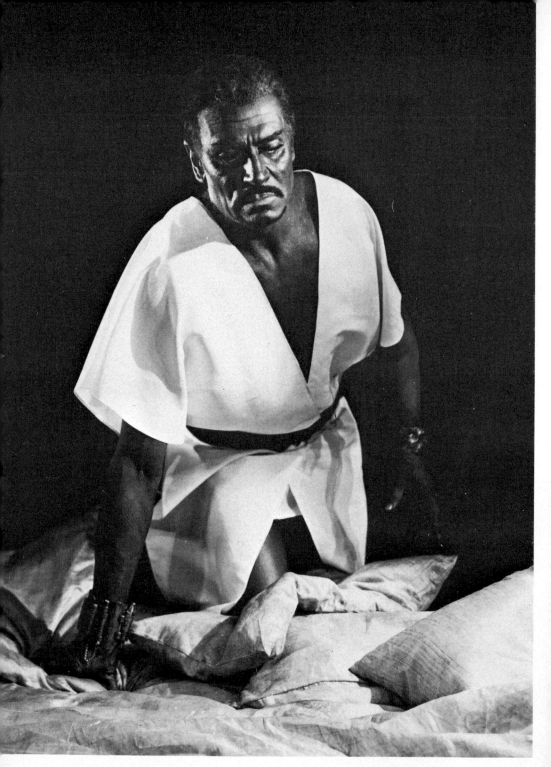

25 Laurence Olivier as Othello

26 Samuel Beckett's *Endgame*, 1964

27 Anthony Quayle and Keith Baxter in *Sleuth*, 1969

28 Sarah Kestelman and Davi
Waller in *A Midsummer Night'*
Dream, 1970

29 The National Theatre on London's South Bank

lost; any failure in logic or evident manipulation of the material is patent if it betokens, as it usually does, a momentary loss of confidence, for in a very important sense all Shaw's plays are confidence tricks, brilliant pieces of intellectual juggling in which the hand must always be quicker than the eye. For this if no other reason Shaw, having brought about a revolution in theatrical taste, proved absolutely impossible to follow directly, a figure on his own with no significant disciples and very few to manifest even a natural likeness of mind (perhaps Bridie comes closest). In destroying the credibility of the well-made play, he had created a vacuum which he could not fill all by himself, and provided hardly any guidance to help anyone else in its filling.

3 The reaction from realism

Understandably, when the smoke cleared after Shaw's successful attack on the citadel of the English dramatic establishment, the scene at the turn of the century was one of some confusion. The well-made problem play was dead, or anyway dying, but what, apart from the very special works of Mr Shaw, could be put in its place? There were all sorts of answers to that question, none of them quite compelling enough to carry the day all by itself. To begin with, foreigners were showing the way that a fundamentally realistic drama might be modified into something far more flexible than the formula problem play as generally conceived in Britain. During the 1890s productions of Ibsen in London were supplemented by the first appearances of Strindberg, Brieux, Hauptmann, Maeterlinck and many others, all of whom (Ibsen excepted) had started in a vaguely realistic tradition and developed it along highly personal lines to often quite unpredictable, virtually unrecognizable ends. Dissatisfaction with realism itself was rife, though the positive form this dissatisfaction might take remained problematic.

On the popular stage it took various forms, largely unconscious. There were during the 1890s many successful costume romances, mostly based on such popular books of the day as *The Prisoner of Zenda* or adaptations from Dumas, Dickens and others – the best-remembered is probably *The Only*

Way (1899), Freeman Wills's version of *A Tale of Two Cities* with a meaty part for Martin-Harvey as Sydney Carton ('It is a far, far better thing I do now . . .'). There was also something of a popular revival in verse drama, most notably in the fluent but ephemeral works of Stephen Phillips, which began their successful career with *Herod* (1901) and *Paolo and Francesca* (1902). Phillips wrote in a very passable imitation of Shakespearian blank verse, easy and not too archaic, and he did have a certain sense of theatrical effect, so that his plays worked better on the stage than in the study, where their thinness and derivativeness are all too obvious. Beerbohm Tree made a big thing out of *Herod*, and George Alexander's production of *Paolo and Francesca* satisfied audiences eager for a good romantic wallow, but none of his later plays had any comparable success with the public, and they were pretty evidently not built to outlive their first vogue. The only really notable figure to emerge in British drama during the 1890s, apart from Shaw himself, was J. M. Barrie (1860–1937). His work too, with its tendency towards whimsical fantasy, was in its way unique, making its own world, following its own laws and having little apparent influence on anyone else.

Barrie was already fairly well established as a novelist and essayist when he first tried his hand at drama with *Richard Savage* in 1891. His first play to catch on at all was *Walker, London* (1892); in 1894 he had a major success with *The Professor's Love Story*, and again in 1897 with his dramatization of his own novel *The Little Minister*. Both these latter showed Barrie's own individual vein of whimsical humour, but his real strength as a dramatist did not emerge until 1902, when two of his most famous plays were first produced, *The Admirable Crichton* and *Quality Street*. Neither of them is overtly supernatural, though the South Sea island on which the lord's household are shipwrecked in the first does have some of the qualities of enchanted ground where the true self can flourish, the lord becoming servant and the butler ruler in obedience to a natural order of things. (There is obviously also here an element of social satire, though it is not so insisted on as to antagonize Barrie's original audiences.) *Quality Street* is all lavender and lace, an evocation of an imaginary past straight out of *Cranford* in which old maids' dreams may flower into true love. Both plays belie their apparent slightness by showing extraordinary staying power, even surviving unscathed the ultimate tests of being filmed and turned into musicals. Of *Peter Pan*, which followed them in 1904, it is difficult to say anything: the play is so well established as an institution, an inalienable part of the English Christmas, that cool critical judgement of it is almost unthinkable, though the Freudian implications of its Never-Never-Land where children never grow up have excited a fair amount of irreverent comment.

Barrie's daintiest and most insubstantial fantasies were based, however, on a very strong and decided technical mastery. His comic drama showing the unobtrusive influence a wise woman can exert on her foolish menfolk, *What Every Woman Knows* (1908), has been cited by no less an authority than Noël Coward as a model of what the well-made play ought to be and very seldom is. The one-act puzzle piece *Shall We Join the Ladies?* (1922) was supposedly intended as the first act of a whodunit which was never written, and, whether the story is true or not, the play is certainly as impeccable a piece of dramatic construction as you could wish to find. This easily exercised power in the marshalling of material gives a firm substructure to such fantasies as *A Kiss for Cinderella* (1916), *Dear Brutus* (1917) and *Mary Rose* (1920), which otherwise might have been quite impossibly cloying in their sentimental toying with the wonderful world of might-have-been, their puckish manipulations of human destiny and fey, girlish *revenants* from worlds beyond time and space. There are also, though disguised, some hints of an underlying harshness in *Dear Brutus* and *Mary Rose*, where the heroine does not exactly benefit from her contracting-out of human society. Even so, many find them a bit hard to take. Barrie's last play, *The Boy David*, a biblical drama written for Elizabeth Bergner, dates from as late as 1936; but essentially he belongs to the 1890s and 1900s, and his success at that period provides a further demonstration that the London theatre public were tired of realism and ready for some sort of escape from it, if only a dramatist of recognizable power and individuality could be found to provide it.

Barrie was adept at doing this while staying sufficiently within the accepted conventions of drama not to worry his audiences. Others who tried to shift drama in the direction of fantasy, symbolism, new subjects and new styles in which to treat them were less canny. W. B. Yeats, for instance. Barrie's Scots whimsy was always couched in readily comprehensible terms. Yeats's attempts at Irish legendary poetic drama were generally too obscure, too undramatic, too remote from any accepted norm of the time, to reach more than a small and specialized minority audience. Though Yeats was first and foremost a poet, he wrote plays consistently throughout his career, few if any of them merely as closet dramas to be read rather than acted. His dramatic work is very much of a piece with his other writing, and the various phases his poetry passed through between the 1880s and the late 1930s are mirrored exactly in his drama. His earliest plays, *The Countess Cathleen* (begun 1889, produced 1899), the first version of *The Shadowy Waters* (begun 1885, produced 1904) and *The Land of Heart's Desire* (1894), all reflect the pale, aesthetic world of the Celtic Twilight, with legendary figures moving slowly and gracefully about a world of dreams. As Yeats the poet moved beyond this elementary Romanticism, so did his drama. Already in the mid-1900s he had come to take an altogether tougher line with his legendary material, and the sequence of five plays on the life of the hero Cuchulain, which began with *On Baile's Strand* (definitive version 1906), replaces the slight lyric grace of the earlier legendary plays with a tough practicality edged at times with irony.

Yeats continued with the Cuchulain cycle for most of his working life: the last of the plays, *The Death of Cuchulain*, was not completed until 1938. But during that time his work went through many changes of style and attitude, and his plays likewise. In particular, the material he wished to treat dramatic-ally became further and further removed from the possibility of dramatiza-tion along conventional lines, and at the same time he became increasingly interested in non-European stage conventions, especially those of the Japan-ese Noh play, for their own sake. The first-fruits of these interests were Yeats's 'plays for dancers', in which any approximation of realistic staging was totally abandoned; in two of the Cuchulain plays, *At the Hawk's Well* (1915–16) and *The Only Jealousy of Emer* (1916), and in *The Dreaming of the Bones* (1917) and *Calvary* (1920), he makes use of masks and conventionalized action accompanied by choric explanation or elaboration, as in the Japanese theatre, and these techniques leave their mark on his subsequent work.

In all, Yeats wrote some thirty plays, nearly all of them produced some time, somewhere (often at the Abbey Theatre, home of the Irish theatrical revival, of which Yeats was a director from its foundation in 1904), and though some of them, like the very earliest legendary dramas, have faded badly with the passage of time, while others, especially those like *Where There is Nothing* (1902) and *The Player Queen* (1908) into which he tried to cram as much as possible of his developing esoteric philosophy, remain almost impenetrably obscure, there are among his later works at least two, *The Words Upon the Window-Pane* (1930) and *Purgatory* (1938), which achieve complete mastery of the theatrical medium and a hard-won, entirely personal form of dramatic utterance. In *The Words Upon the Window-Pane* a group of spiritualists hold a seance in a house once occupied by Swift's Stella, and find themselves, somewhat to their resentment, witnessing a re-enactment of the crisis in the relationship between the Dean and his platonic love. In *Purgatory* a complex pattern of action and interaction is established between the living and the dead, with the guilt of repentant ghosts tem-porarily, but only temporarily, assuaged by a new crime in the present.

Yeats's drama has for some years now been undergoing a literary revaluation, reinforced by effective productions on radio and on gramophone records, but as yet the critics' new regard for it has been little tested in the theatre. When and if it is, these two later plays seem the most likely to survive.

Yeats, though after the 1900s he went very much his own way, was from the beginning of his career as a dramatist quite consciously and deliberately part of an 'Irish dramatic movement'. This movement, unlike most in the British theatre, had its theorists and a coherent programme, best outlined by Yeats in *The Irish Literary Theatre* (1901). Yeats, Edward Martyn and Lady Gregory set up the Irish Literary Theatre in 1898 and the Irish National Theatre Society in 1902, which in 1904 moved into the Abbey Theatre, where it became a specialized repertory group, partly amateur but mainly professional, dedicated to the advancement of a native Irish drama. This was all part of a general creative ferment in Ireland at the time, and in conse-quence during the 1900s the greater part of the most vital and original British drama was to be seen first of all not in London but in Dublin.

Apart from Yeats himself the most striking figure of the Irish dramatic revival was John Millington Synge (1871–1909). During his short life he completed five plays which brought Irish peasant drama to the point of per-fection, using the patterns of Irish folk-speech for their distinctive flavour and drawing their material from Irish country life, but filtering both lan-guage and material through a poet's imagination. His first play, *In the Shadow of the Glen* (1903), was a tragicomedy, and his second, *Riders to the Sea* (1904), a one-act tragedy. But then in *The Well of the Saints* (1905), *The Tinker's Wedding* and above all *The Playboy of the Western World* (1907) he turned to rich, slightly ribald comedy, far nearer to the true Celtic spirit than the misty Romanticism of the Celtic Twilight. *The Playboy of the Western World* takes place in a remote western Ireland untouched by the Industrial Revolution, in a world where fantasy and reality meet and mingle. But Synge's vital quality is the constant link he keeps with reality, even in his wildest flights of invention – a link maintained as much as anything by his strong, sinewy prose style and his slyly acute observation of human nature; the human nature that accepts Christy Mahon, the 'playboy', as a hero, when he is rumoured to have killed his father far away, but recoils in disgust when he (seemingly) kills his father on the spot. Of all the playwrights of the Irish literary renaissance, Synge was the only one to enforce belief in his peasants, the way they talk and the way they act; by comparison the peasant dramas of his contemporaries seem like faint literary abstractions.

At the end of his life Synge experimented with something rather different;

in his last, unfinished drama, *Deirdre*, he turned to the ancient legends of the Celts, so lovingly explored by Yeats. But even here his language has a tang of reality about it, his characterization is still toughly practical: he aims to bring his legendary characters within the sphere of our own knowledge rather than trying to transport us to another world of romance. It is hard to imagine what turn Synge's gifts would have taken had he lived, but as they stand his six plays constitute the most valuable legacy of the Irish literary theatre to world theatre at large.

By comparison the plays of Lady Gregory (1882–1932), though not without quality, seem thin and undistinguished. Though she began as a dramatist in collaboration with Yeats, her own independent works are closer in spirit to those of Synge: peasant comedies and dramas on the perennial Irish subject of the conflict between reality and fantasy, between things as they are and things as people choose to see them. Some of her one-act plays, such as *The Gaol Gate* (1906) and *The Rising of the Moon* (1907), continue to be performed, and of her longer plays the best are *Hyacinth Halvey* (1906), showing the battle of an ordinary young man to establish that he is not the paragon of virtue rumour has him to be, and *The Workhouse Ward* (1908), which concerns the struggle of a young woman to get her old uncle out of a workhouse where he wants to remain because there he can be always near his lifelong sparring partner, his longstanding quarrel with whom is his only reason for living. In a somewhat different vein, Lady Gregory also achieved an unexpected success with her translation of Molière into the Irish idiom (*The Kiltartan Molière*).

The talent of the third founder of the Abbey Theatre, Edward Martyn (1859–1923), was of a more sombre turn. Some of his plays, such as *Maeve* (1900) and *An Enchanted Sea* (1902), belong to the same world of dreams and visions as the early plays of Yeats, but in others, particularly *The Heather Field* (1899), he gives evidence of a closer study of Ibsen than any other of his Irish contemporaries; the social theme of one man's passionate determination to turn a heathered waste into fertile land, and its gradual thwarting, is worked out with a close and gloomy application reminiscent of Ibsen, and the use of symbolism, as in the final appearance of the hero's young son carrying a bunch of that heather he mistakenly believed he had banished for ever, is distinctly suggestive of Ibsen's practice.

By 1910 the powerful impetus of the Irish dramatic revival was already beginning to fade, though slightly younger figures, such as Lennox Robinson (1886–1958) and Padraic Colum (1881–1972), continued to appear. Robinson was a producer and manager at the Abbey on and off from 1909, and a director from 1923 until his death. His last play, *The Demon Lover*, was completed and staged as late as 1954, but his best plays date from his early years, starting with *The Clancy Name* in 1908, an effective if rather melodramatic study of crime, repentance and conflicting codes of honour. His most successful play is *The Whiteheaded Boy* (1916), a comedy somewhat in the style of Synge about a lovable rogue whose family are forced to pay for his peccadilloes while he always has the last laugh. *The Lost Leader* (1918) also has some lasting qualities, cunningly keeping its audience guessing about whether the old innkeeper Lucius Lenihan is or is not in fact Parnell, living on under an assumed name. Colum began in *The Broken Soil* (1903), revised as *The Fiddler's House* (1907), by writing rather Synge's sort of play in a pale approximation of Synge's style, but later his work became increasingly naturalistic and unremarkable.

Meanwhile, back in London the position was really not much clearer. It was difficult to decide whether Shaw's precepts and practice had had any positive result, though their negative result of discrediting Pinero, Jones and the well-made play as a medium of serious dramatic writing was clear enough. In the reaction against realism poets continued to write poetic dramas: better poets than Stephen Phillips wrote better plays which achieved nothing like the same instant success. John Davidson (1857–1909) wrote several grim symbolic dramas of a transcendental nature which Professor Wilson Knight, that great espouser of dramatic lost causes, has praised highly,[1] especially the last two, *The Triumph of Mammon* (1907) and *Mammon and his Message* (1908), parts of an unfinished trilogy which was to embody Davidson's mature thoughts on God, the Devil, money, power and other grand, hazy concepts. Other poets of the period, such as Gordon Bottomley (1874–1948), Lascelles Abercrombie (1881–1938) and Laurence Binyon (1869–1943) all worked consistently at the drama. It is altogether possible that the neglect into which the plays of Bottomley (*The Crier by Night*, 1902; *King Lear's Wife*, 1915; *Gruach*, 1921) have fallen will not continue indefinitely; in particular his adaptation of Japanese Noh techniques, suggested by Yeats, is often more practical and dramatically effective than any use Yeats himself managed to make of them. Abercrombie wrote several one-act plays and a full-length verse drama, *Phoenix* (1923), all concerned with violent sexual relations and considered in their time rather daring, though they seem tame enough now. Binyon wrote in two manners, a straightforward, slightly Stephen Phillipsish historical verse drama, and a sub-Noh drama in line with the contemporary work of Yeats and Bottomley (*Three Short Plays*,

[1] *The Golden Labyrinth* (London, 1962), pp. 312–17.

1928–9); he also, later, wrote *The Young King* (1934), about Henry II, for production in Canterbury Cathedral chapter house (the year before *Murder in the Cathedral*). But this activity was all very much on the fringes of the everyday theatre, and of the poets' plays perhaps only John Masefield's *The Tragedy of Nan* (1908), an isolated essay in grim realism, and James Elroy Flecker's *Hassan* (staged 1923), a belated expression of luxuriant ninetyish exoticism owing much to a spectacular production and Delius's incidental music, made any real impression on the commercial theatre and reached ordinary, non-specialist theatregoers.

4 The Edwardian era

Apart from Barrie, whose success was as obvious and as commercial as anybody's, all this activity took place very much on the margins of the theatre as the ordinary West End theatregoer normally saw it. And yet, meanwhile, the commercial theatre was flourishing in Edwardian London as seldom before. Who and what, Shaw apart, were the dramatists whose work helped to bring this about? To answer that question, we must first look back to the grounds for the London playgoers' reaction against the well-made play. Shaw had effectively ridiculed the artifices of the successful purveyors of well-made plays, and this, allied with Shaw's own theatrical practice and the illuminating cross-section of the best world theatre had to offer presented by the Barker–Vedrenne company during its tenancy of the Royal Court Theatre (1904–7), had brought it about that Pinero and Jones seemed not so much wrong, positively harmful in their ways of handling serious subjects in the theatre, as – much worse – oldfashioned, bypassed by the latest and most exciting developments in the theatre, and prisoners of a convention which, even at its best, prevented those who adopted it from ever rising above the second rate.

So, one might reasonably imagine, the well-made play was a thing of the past, something which might perhaps appeal to the less demanding theatregoer for a while, but which could certainly not give rise to lasting drama in the enlightened twentieth century. In London, at any rate, the age of Pinero was over and the age of Shaw just begun: from being our most influential dramatic critic he had leapt spectacularly in the last decade to being our most successful dramatist. But things are seldom quite so simple and clearcut. For who should be the next major dramatist to emerge on the London scene but a man who exemplified in his work all the concern for craftsmanship and construction, in a word for well-madeness, which Shaw despised and had apparently taught the rest of the thinking world to despise too? William Somerset Maugham (1874–1965), who in 1908, after some years as a mildly successful novelist and quite unsuccessful dramatist, took the London theatre by storm with no fewer than four plays running simultaneously.

This curious turn of events can be explained in one way only. Maugham hit below the belt: he wrote comedies. True, Shaw wrote comedies too, and everything he said about ideas in drama, intelligence in drama, applied quite as much to comedy as to anything else – more, in effect, since Shaw appreciated better than anyone that the best way to sugar the pill of ideas for an unwilling and suspicious British public was to present them as amusingly as possible. But critics and everyone else persisted in applying different standards to comedy and to 'serious' drama. Ibsen might provide the model for high seriousness in the theatre, but when it came to comedy there were still enough left who thought it a sufficient aim for the dramatist just to keep people amused. And on the whole, the more neatly and 'theatrically' he did it, the better they would be pleased. This Maugham did – superlatively; and by his practice he managed to win back a certain area – very roughly what we would call comedy of manners – for the despised and rejected well-made play.

Maugham's success was not immediate. He had been writing plays at least since 1897, and even his first big success, *Lady Frederick*, was written in 1902 but not finally produced until 1907; the two other major successes of that season, *Mrs Dot* and *Jack Straw*, had been awaiting production since 1904 and 1905 respectively. They were all unmistakably lightweight, and none had any pretensions to be anything else: Maugham opted at once for intellectual disreputability, and built most of his subsequent career as a dramatist on his reputation for frivolity and cynicism, even if, closely examined, some of his later plays belied this reputation. His plots were deliberately artificial, depending on patterns and correspondences too blatant and unashamed to be called coincidence. It might be a coincidence, for instance (and a fairly far-fetched one), that Lady Frederick, the perennial charmer, should happen to have at hand some compromising letters with which she can counter the emotional blackmail exerted on her by her current young suitor's uncle; but when the suitor's mother is able to hit back with a compromising letter from Lady Frederick it goes beyond coincidence to become the sort of formal, artificial device which we can accept only because it never pretends to be anything else. Equally, when Lady Frederick receives no fewer than four proposals of marriage, one after the other, in the same morning, the pattern-making is so patent that it seems merely naïve to object to it as unbelievable: after all, who ever asked us to *believe* in it? Certainly not the author.

Obviously Maugham had hit upon an ingenious formula for getting round the prejudices of the more seriousminded critics of his time. Significantly, J. T. Grein, founder of the Independent Theatre and first English producer of *Ghosts*, wrote of *Lady Frederick* on its first appearance:

> It is not quite a lifelike comedy, nor is it free from the artifice and cal-culation which was customary in the days of the 'well-made play'. There is something mechanical in the humour and the characters which would have prompted me if I had read the manuscript to change the time of the action. To me these delightful, well-spoken, gracefully conversational people are not of today. I see them in the formal surroundings and clothes of the late sixties; I see them even more forcibly in the pic-turesque raiment of powder and wig. Indeed, if light verse were substi-tuted for prose, Mr Maugham would have found in his story exquisite material for a poetic comedy. But I take the work as it is presented, and undoubtedly, despite its cossetted form and somewhat antiquated devices, it has drawn . . .[1]

Grein is clearly dubious about any suggestion of a return to the discredited well-made-play formula. But, equally clearly, he enjoys the play for what it is and offers a number of ways of acceptance. If the play were period it would be all right (though why it is difficult to see – presumably life was just as real in 1867 as in 1907). If it were in verse it would be entirely acceptable (with verse we expect obvious artifice; prose is real and prose is earnest). But any-way it is a comedy, only a comedy, and if it amuses, why should we be too captious? And if that was the judgement of Mr Grein, the famous Ibsenite, Maugham had unmistakably done the trick.

And having once pulled it off, he continued to do so with regular success until the end of the First World War. The best of the comedies he wrote in this period are probably *Our Betters* (1915), which chronicles the progressive

[1] *Sunday Times and Special*, 17 October 1907.

disillusionment of an impressionable American innocent with the way life is lived in Europe, and *Home and Beauty* (1919), a witty variation on the 'Enoch Arden' story which provides one wife with two husbands. Both plays seem, on the face of it, so slight that they could only survive a season's scrutiny, but they have proved well able to sustain repeated revival and come up as lively and undated as ever. Maugham himself, in explaining what he wanted to do with them,[1] evoked the 'artificial comedy' of the Restoration and Sheridan, and with that comparison there seems little reason to argue. At the same time, Maugham did intermittently dabble in 'serious' drama, but with no great success, and, it seems, no very profound ambition until 1918, when he wrote *Caesar's Wife*, a contemporary reworking of the theme of Mme de Lafayette's classic *conte*, *La Princesse de Clèves*, about a love triangle in which everybody knows everything and everyone behaves entirely well and honourably. What the play is, in fact, is an unmistakable example of our old friend the well-made problem play; and surprisingly successful too – the most successful Maugham wrote, since his later attempts, such as *The Letter* (1926) and *The Sacred Flame* (1928), do not escape superficiality and melodrama, and do not seem (despite Maugham's protestations of sincerity in the latter case[2]) to try very seriously to do so.

Maugham's masterpieces in drama date from the post-war period, when he wrote his three finest and, though he might baulk at the term, his most serious comedies: *The Circle* (1919), *The Constant Wife* (1926) and *The Bread-winner* (1930). These use the formal devices of the earlier comedies, but with a new freedom and a new depth in the ideas so lightly and playfully touched upon. *The Circle* is about how far, if at all, the experience and advice of the old can help the young not to make the same mistakes all over again. *The Constant Wife* considers a marriage in which both partners have been lucky enough to fall out of love with each other at the same time, and shows how the wife successfully claims just as complete freedom of action in the circumstances as the husband would naturally assume to be his. *The Breadwinner* turns upside down the assumptions of a not too likeable family about their 'right' to be supported by the long-suffering breadwinner, when he announces that he is no longer able or, more important, willing to do so.

In these plays Maugham reaches, though from the other end of the scale of dramatic effect, a sort of comedy of ideas comparable with Shaw's – though probably neither would be very pleased with the comparison. He also brought his own type of classically elegant, precise comic writing to a point

[1] Maugham, *The Summing Up* (London, 1938), p. 119.
[2] Ibid. p. 162.

where he may have felt that there was little he could then do except repeat himself. At any rate, after the production of *The Constant Wife* he resolved to take his farewell of the theatre, writing only four more plays which he felt would pester him until they were written, and about the success of which presumably he did not feel too confident. In the event, two of them, *The Sacred Flame* and *The Breadwinner*, were successful and seemed little outside his usual range. But the other two, *For Services Rendered* (1932) and *Sheppey* (1933), were strange, uncharacteristic and finally, it must be admitted, not very distinguished attempts to break out of the straitjacket of his own style. *For Services Rendered* tries to be a hard, true, bitter play about post-war neurosis, but its endless accumulation of suffering in one family becomes at last a trifle absurd, and not far from melodrama. *Sheppey*, even more oddly, is an attempt to write the sort of impalpable, symbolic drama Barrie wrote with the greatest ease, about a simple man with a vision of the good Christian life who acquires the money to live it out literally, is taken by the world to be mad, and is in the end led away by a personified Death, still feeling that his work is undone. But Maugham's technique, with its sharp outlines, its clarity and precision, was absolutely the last to make such a conception work in the theatre.

Maugham accepted what his instinct told him: 'I grew conscious that I was no longer in touch with the public that patronizes the theatre. This happens in the end to most dramatists and they are wise to accept the warning. It is high time for them to retire.'[1] And that is precisely what he did; though he lived for another thirty-two years he wrote no more plays. But by his success, both commercial and artistic, he had reopened and kept open a case, that of the well-made play, which at the turn of the century many, perhaps most, intelligent people connected with the British theatre imagined to be closed for ever. And, what is more important today, he had written at least half a dozen comedies which stand with the best the English stage has to offer.

Maugham's type of artificial comedy offered one way out of the dilemma into which Shaw had put British dramatists at large. But there were others. As Shaw himself was one of the earliest to observe, in the well-made play the dramatic conventions depended very much for their effectiveness on the acceptance of a corresponding set of social conventions. Obviously if, say, illegitimate birth were no longer considered shameful, then it would not be possible to build a play on the premiss that keeping it secret was as important as life itself. The genre depended on unquestioning acceptance of the assumption that God was in his heaven and all was, if not necessarily right

[1] *Collected Plays* (London, 1952), Vol. III, p. xvii.

with the world, at least ordered by certain immutable moral laws and social regulations. The plot in *Mrs Dane's Defence*, for instance, turns entirely on the young hero's willingness to agree without question or hesitation that if Mrs Dane is, as rumour has her to be, a woman with a past, of course he will give up all idea of marrying her and have nothing more to do with her. If he for one moment considered what to us would seem a more realistic line of reasoning – 'I love her, and I intend to marry her whatever she may or may not have done in the past' – then the whole plot would at once collapse. But, of course, this was not at the time a glaring dramatic artificiality: the assumption the hero makes is one upon which much of the stability of society was based. Shaw understood that what he was attacking in the well-made play was not so much a dramatic convention as a set of social conventions it reflected and supported. And once those began to crumble, or even be seriously questioned, the well-made play as it was then understood was bound to totter too.

But might it not be possible to use the given machinery of the well-made play as a means of autocriticism, to see just how far it was possible to question the basic social assumptions of the well-made play without tearing its structure apart? This experiment, whether arrived at consciously or quite by chance and instinct, was what a number of thinking dramatists embarked upon in the 1900s. Among the most interesting of them was St John Hankin (1869–1909), who did not begin writing plays until 1903. The cream of his work is to be found in the collection he rather defiantly entitled *Three Plays With Happy Endings*. In these he uses the well-made play form as understood by Pinero, but they are written from an entirely cynical point of view, which gives them a curious and individual flavour of their own. Their criticism of society and social convention is by implication only: the dramatist assumes that these supposedly immutable laws of society have no ultimate validity at all, but are purely arbitrary impositions, and as such can be played both ways, the winner in the social game being the one who can manipulate them with most skill to suit his or her possibly quite unconventional ends.

In the first of the plays, *The Return of the Prodigal* (1905), the winner is the prodigal, a self-confessed waster who comes back from Australia, having squandered the money with which he was sent there to make a new start, and casually blackmails his family into buying him off by threatening to disgrace them. They do not have to support him, of course, but if they do not he will have to go to the workhouse, and what good will that do their carefully nurtured social pretensions? They may be upright, hardworking and respectable, but he comes out on top because he refuses to hide what ought to be hidden, to feel shame over what any decent person should feel a fit subject for shame. *The Charity That Began at Home* (1906) shows how rational self-interest, in the person of Verreker, a freethinker, and high-principled un-selfishness, as represented by the beautiful young do-gooder Margery Denison, can arrive at the same conclusion: that it is best to ignore each other and go their own ways. *The Cassilis Engagement* (1907) goes a step further still, by showing the conventions of society as a liability that those not bound by them at birth would do everything possible to avoid: a loving mother prevents her son from making a misalliance not by opposing the match but by welcoming it with open arms, giving her son every chance to see the vulgar object of his affections for what she is; but in the event it is the girl's realization of just how boring and limited life in society can be which puts paid to the engagement. That was really turning the code of Jones and Pinero upside down by using their own weapons against them.

Harley Granville Barker (1877–1946) is that strange enigma, a practical man of the theatre who seems to have had little instinct as a dramatist. He was one of the most influential directors in the English theatre from the early 1900s until his second marriage in 1918, after which he virtually retired from the theatre; as a director he always put the greatest weight on careful attention to the dramatist's intentions, acting teamwork and character analysis, thereby confirming the natural tendency of English theatre at this time towards psychological realism. His own plays were curiously marginal to all this. His first unaided work, *The Marrying of Anne Leete* (1901), is a rather extravagant symbolic drama about the life-force rampant, with more than one anticipatory hint of D. H. Lawrence: a young woman of gentle birth throws over all conventions and proposes to a gardener who has already been turned down by a local farmer's daughter in favour of the heroine's brother. The consequences of this action are played out in a bold mixture of broad comedy and highly charged emotional drama, leading to a conclusion in which the oddly matched couple tot up the risks they run in their search for happiness and decide that on balance the game is worth the candle. To read, the play has considerable vitality, and it would be interesting to see it acted. The three plays by which he is best remembered, however, *The Voysey Inheritance* (1905), *Waste* (1907) and *The Madras House* (1910), are all at least super-ficially realistic drawing-room dramas, observing most of the conventions of the 1890s as though Barker's friend and associate Shaw had never existed.

In construction, to be sure, they can hardly qualify as well-made. *The Voysey Inheritance* is broken-backed, split between its second and third act by the death of the unscrupulous old Voysey: everyone in it talks too much, and far too many ideas about life, social morality, money, business practice and such are crammed in regardless of the play's groaning structure. The material is really that of a Shavian talk-piece, but apparently Granville-Barker could not see this or, if he did, did not feel himself capable of matching Shaw on his own ground. *Waste* is more concentrated and controlled, though it still suffers from over-verbalization, and Barker's later revisions, in 1926, did little or nothing to improve matters.[1] The waste concerned is that of three lives: that of a young woman in love, as she thinks, with a rising politician, that of the child she tries to dispose of by abortion and that of the politician, who kills himself when his career is ruined by the scandal. *The Madras House* returns to the overloaded manner of *The Voysey Inheritance*, and after a very skilful piece of exposition clarifying for us the complicated relationships within the Huxtable household on Denmark Hill it rapidly gets bogged down in endless explanation of action and emotion, as though Barker, for all his background in the practical theatre, could not bring himself to trust actors and director to make anything clear which was not spelt out in so many words. After his retirement from the theatre he wrote two more plays, *The Secret Life* (1923) and *His Majesty* (1928), but seemingly with little thought of having them staged, so that he was free to write the sort of completely 'literary', untheatrical play towards which he had always, perhaps unconsciously, yearned. *The Secret Life* is full of reminiscences of later Ibsen, concerning as it does a politician turned writer who realizes that he is a failure and that the only things worth having belong to the inner life, which for him has been reflected principally in his remote, unsatisfactory relationship with one woman. *His Majesty* is a study of idealism, and of a kingly ideal at that; the central character, a deposed middle-European king, refuses restoration unless it can be on terms acceptable to his conscience; there is also a mystical passage concerning his thrown-down sword, which no commoner dare touch. Both plays are clearly designed to be read rather than staged.

Compared with Hankin and Granville Barker, John Galsworthy (1869–1933) is a pillar of dramatic conservatism. He had the great advantage of coming to the drama when already well established as a novelist and essayist. He did not, therefore, like Barker, feel constrained to pour everything and anything he might want to express into a vaguely dramatic mould: so long as he could write novels or political pamphlets in reasonable certainty that they would be taken note of, he need only practise drama when he had a subject

---

[1] The first version was published London 1909; the second, of which Barker notes in his introduction 'I doubt if one scrap of the old dialogue survives', London, 1927.

that seemed ideally suited to it, and was forced to make no concessions to popularity in the theatre which he did not want to make. He was able to continue functioning, therefore, in a thoroughly anachronistic fashion, writing solidly constructed, workmanlike problem plays with a carefully detailed realism of speech and action. The stage conventions of his young days were good enough for him: they were, after all, perfectly honourable, allowing a gentleman to address other gentlemen with every consideration extended on both sides and fair play throughout.

It may not sound like exactly the most exciting or challenging formula for drama, but in fact in Galsworthy's hands it produced a number of powerful and durable plays. As much as anything this is a tribute to his very considerable intelligence and more than adequate grasp of practical stagecraft. In his principal plays of the pre-war period, *The Silver Box* (1906), *Strife* (1909) and *Justice* (1910), the stories are well constructed, effectively told in dramatic terms, and full of acute human observation. In all of them the leading quality is Galsworthy's own exceptional fairmindedness. We may feel in little doubt where his sympathies lie, but he takes scrupulous care to see that they do not intrude into the drama to overbalance it. The irony of *The Silver Box*, where two parallel thefts, by a rich man and a working man, are respectively hushed up as a harmless prank and punished with a month's hard labour, may be powerful, but it is all allowed to arise naturally from a realistically observed situation. In *Strife* the two sides in a strike are shown as equally reasonable, equally unreasonable: in the conflict between an irresistible force (the strikers' leader Roberts) and an immovable object (the company chairman, Anthony) neither can win, neither is obviously in the right or the wrong, both are intransigent idealists and both, finally, are broken, since the compromise which, but for them, could have been reached at the beginning is finally concluded when both are effectively removed from the scene. In *Justice* the overall cruelty of the judicial system is exemplified even though none of its individual servants is shown as a monster and its victim is presented as unappealing, with no mitigating circumstances in his favour, and unarguably guilty of the crime of which he is accused; if, finally, we sympathize with him and condemn the system that condemns him, it is simply because Galsworthy presents him as a fallible human being and then persuades us to think that no human being, however fallible, should be treated like this.

Galsworthy's unwillingness to cheat his effects, to indulge in dramatic special pleading to achieve his ends, makes him a curiously sympathetic figure in the drama of his time, and gave his work a weight and solidity which made it remarkably independent of fashion. Even in the 1920s he continued to write as he had always done, and his major plays of those years, *The Skin Game* (1920) and *Loyalties* (1922), are curiously timeless, abstracted altogether from fashion. Again, they are both confrontations of two ways of life, two codes of behaviour, which both have things to be said for and against them. In *The Skin Game* it is the effete aristocracy and the pushy nouveaux riches, battling over ownership of the same piece of ground. Either could win, and neither is presented as the 'right' victor: indeed, so far are they driven to depart from their own declared codes of honour in the course of the struggle that both might be judged the wrong party to win. In *Loyalties* there is a conflict between an aristocratic army officer and a rich Jew when the Jew claims the officer has robbed him during a country-house weekend, the officer's friends and superiors refuse to believe that such a thing is possible, and the Jew, stung by their disbelief, which he interprets as a symptom of antisemitism, insists on bringing the conflict into the open, with results almost equally disastrous for all concerned.

Loyalties, produced in 1922, was an exact contemporary of Noël Coward's *The Young Idea*: it must have seemed then like some prehistoric monster, and yet so totally convinced is it, so freshly conceived within its own conventions, that it remained and remains a perfectly valid dramatic statement, irrespective of the strange theatrical surroundings in which it found itself. Subsequently Galsworthy seems to have lost conviction, writing fewer plays and in one of them, *Escape* (1926), even trying a free form of short scenes, cinematically linked. But his best plays are a lasting achievement, and an extraordinary testimony to the power of strong individual conviction to transcend the dictates of temporary fashion, however definitive and universal they may seem at the time.

5 The twenties

During all this period, from 1880 to the end of the 1914–18 war, we have confined ourselves almost entirely to the discussion of individual dramatists as separate and independent phenomena; we have had remarkably little to say about schools and movements – the Irish literary theatre apart. And this is with good reason. The development of the English theatre has always been extraordinarily pragmatic. Though, naturally, dramatists may admire each other's work, even be close friends or professional colleagues, they have always tended in Britain to steer clear of formal programmes, to keep their own counsel and go their own ways. Thus the dramatists of this period – dramatists of any stature and lasting importance, that is – have remained on the whole surprisingly self-contained, little influenced by what was going on in their immediate vicinity and influenced hardly at all by what was happening in the world at large. To look at the total picture of British drama in the 1900s one would never think that abroad there were active (and sometimes already produced in London) Strindberg, Maeterlinck, Hauptmann, Chekhov, d'Annunzio, Andreyev, Wedekind, Sudermann, Brieux, even Jarry. Ibsen is the most apparent influence, and he only intermittently, peripherally, as much by bringing about a change of atmosphere as by providing a direct inspiration for dramatists.

Shaw had already remarked in the mid-1890s on the important effect that the existence of Ibsen, and London theatre audiences' consciousness of him, was having on even the most conventional, established British drama of the time, simply by making a lot of the drama which had formerly been acceptable in Britain seem insipid and oldfashioned. And so even Pinero and Jones, who rejected any notion of direct influence from Ibsen on their writing (Jones very heatedly), found themselves gradually modifying their style and subject matter in accordance with the new climate of opinion Ibsen's works had established in the London theatre. Some dramatists of the next generation, Edward Martyn especially, give more obvious evidence of direct influence from Ibsen's dramatic method. Of more 'modern' influences than Ibsen there is virtually no sign, at any rate in the writing of British dramatists, though in the ideas of staging put about by Edward Gordon Craig there is much derived from the most advanced European models. One would be hard put, though, to find any dramatic writing in English at this time which suggested even a vague consciousness of what, say, Strindberg or Maeterlinck or Brieux or d'Annunzio was doing with the drama. Right up to the First World War Ibsen seems to have remained the last word in modernity for the British theatre at large.

Nor can British dramatists of the time be accused of, or credited with, any great signs of enterprise and originality on their own behalf. The only thing vaguely resembling experiment we have encountered so far is the flirtation of Yeats, Bottomley and one or two others with the techniques of the Japanese theatre, following Yeats's discovery of Noh around 1913–14 through the agency of Ezra Pound. But that move in the direction of avant-garde technique was eccentric, esoteric and little concerned with the everyday theatre in Britain or anywhere else. And for the rest, British drama remained almost defiantly conservative and parochial – excepting only the sprawling, unclassifiable genius of George Bernard Shaw.

Even the great external upheaval of the First World War did not bring about any radical change in this state of affairs. In Germany the drama might plunge into expressionism, in France modify itself according to the elegant artifices of Copeau and his company at the Vieux Colombier, or flirt with the wilder possibilities of surrealism, in Italy follow Pirandello in his riddling preoccupation with the nature of reality, his teasing interplays of reality and illusion. But in Britain the drama, even at its wildest, newest and most allegedly iconoclastic, stayed safely on the highroad of stage realism, challenging its audiences, if at all, by slight changes in what it was saying rather than by any sweeping changes in how it said it. In the context of world drama

it is strange, though in the context of British drama it is entirely characteristic, that the first three plays to signal the emergence of important new
dramatists after the war should all have been conceived and written unashamedly in terms of traditional, realistic stagecraft: Sean O'Casey's *Shadow
of a Gunman* (1922), Noël Coward's *The Vortex* (1923) and Frederick Lonsdale's *Aren't We All?* (1923).

Lonsdale's inclusion in this list might raise a few eyebrows. And in fact,
any question of his 'importance' apart, he was by no means an unknown
dramatist when *Aren't We All?* had its decisive success. He was at the time
forty-two, and had been a consistently successful writer for the stage for
fifteen years, though in a way which got him little attention all to himself, as a
concocter of books for operettas and musical comedies like *The King of
Cadonia* (1908), *The Maid of the Mountains* (1917) and *The Lady of the Rose*
(1922). Even *Aren't We All?*, in an earlier version called *The Best People*, had
been staged and gone unnoticed as far back as 1909. But its appearance in
definitive form established Lonsdale at once as one of the leading comic
writers of his age, and the natural successor to W. Somerset Maugham. Not,
either, so very different in style and content: the plot of *Aren't We All?*
could, except for its extreme slightness, be the plot of a Maugham comedy.
A wife arrives home from the Middle East unexpectedly to find her husband
in the arms of another woman. She is full of righteous indignation, until her
father-in-law manages to exert some emotional blackmail on her when he
finds out that she came back from Egypt in order to escape romantic complications of her own. She submits, but in revenge succeeds in trapping her
father-in-law into marriage with a woman he has been running from for
years.

That hardly sounds like the sort of stuff from which a brave new world of
drama may be built, and indeed it was not. Lonsdale remained true to the
glittering artificial social comedy of early Maugham and late Wilde, conceived his only serious job as that of keeping his audiences entertained, and
acknowledged that he was writing in the 1920s rather than the 1890s only by
the greater freedom of behaviour assumed by his characters in mildly risqué
situations. Even his cynicism is muted compared with Maugham's: his
characters' bark is far worse than their bite, and the chief delight to be
extracted from *Aren't We All?* is a gleeful recognition of the intricate grada-
tions of rudeness his apparently well-bred characters permit themselves, nay,
revel in, when dealing with each other. His comedy of rudeness is developed
even further in *The Last of Mrs Cheyney* (1925), in which the titular heroine
has not only a past, but a very active present as a jewel thief, and, moreover,

admits happily to her calling and successfully turns the tables on those who would condemn her – to such effect that in the end they are competing to buy her off. It is developed even further in the delectable *On Approval* (1925) in which two monsters of egotism find themselves trapped, servantless, on a remote Scots island along with the two relatively harmless bystanders with whom they have chosen to enter into a species of trial marriage. Predictably they rend all about them and finally, as their chosen victims make good their escape, are left to rend each other.

Lonsdale continued to write plays along the same lines, with some success, right up to his death in 1954; the best of them were *Canaries Sometimes Sing* (1929), another play about four ill-assorted characters, two married couples, isolated in a country house, and *The Way Things Go* (1950), about the determined efforts of a very rich young American woman to marry a very poor young Englishman who is equally determined to let her money come between them. He was unashamedly a light entertainer, with no delusions of importance, and no one ever took him for an 'important' dramatist. And yet time brings strange revenges. Important or not, Lonsdale has proved to be a lasting dramatist: his three most famous plays at least survive to entertain later generations, and are sustained by their elegance and style when many other, far more pretentious works of the time are as dead as the dodo. Lonsdale, in fact, is another example of that curiously British phenomenon, the dramatist divorced from time and place, creating his own world according to his own rules in an apparently total vacuum. Since, like Galsworthy's later dramas, his plays were never products of their age in the first place, they cannot become dated as their age does; they are out on their own, to please or bore later audiences entirely on their own inherent merits. And the judgement of posterity would seem in this case to be considerably more favourable than anyone at the time would have thought possible.

Noël Coward (1899–1973) is a more complicated case. When *The Vortex* appeared he had already had two real but modest successes with light comedies, *I'll Leave It to You* (1919) and *The Young Idea* (1922). But it was *The Vortex* which marked him out at once as the young revolutionary, the iconoclast, the most dangerous, exciting embodiment of the new spirit of the 1920s. It is not very easy for us now to see quite what all the fuss was about. In form and construction the play is neat, well-made, a realistically conceived drawing-room drama which, surely, Pinero and Jones would have recognized at once as their own sort of problem play. Admittedly it was twenty years on, and the problems had changed slightly, but that was only to be expected, and everything else was safely in its normal, accepted place. What was it, then, which got critics and public so worked up about the 'excessive modernity' of it all? Certainly not its advanced technique, so presumably its advanced subject matter. And that particular sort of excitement, so potent at the time, is notoriously the most difficult to recapture or reconstruct after its moment has passed. The son who takes drugs, the still beautiful mother who takes lovers, and all the smart slang of the day, though exotic and shocking enough in 1923, very rapidly came to seem quite tame and acceptable, especially since they come to such a neatly moral conclusion in the play, the son's decent fiancée being packed off in virtuous romance with the mother's dull young lover while mother and son vow eternal dedication to sorting out each other's problems and renunciation of their respective sins.

It is this ending, as it happens, which seems today most indicative of the play's strengths and of its weaknesses. It brings the play to a thumping conclusion with a good, strong curtain, but it does not ring true. In the first two acts we are given a picture, assembled with artifice to be sure, but essentially quite believable, of how some people at the time probably lived. But nobody, at any time, possibly behaved as the two principal characters do in the last act – or not unless we are meant to believe, as nothing in the play itself indicates, that their renunciations are merely the temporary result of being carried away by the drama of their own situation, and will in a day or two be forgotten as everything returns to the status quo.

The conclusion is a 'well-made' ending to a well-made play, a sure-fire theatrical effect, but its very hollowness in any other terms of consideration suggests that Coward found himself here with something of a failure of confidence on his hands. Was it really possible, in 1923, to write a serious well-made drawing-room drama, making a serious, even perhaps a profound, point about life as it was then lived? If you were an ingrained conservative like Galsworthy you might just about manage to do it, but a lively young man like Coward was almost certain to have second thoughts. He could not, finally, argue through his characters and story to a conclusion at once neat and true; Shaw had said, and apparently proved, that it was not possible to do so, and to try again could only seem like an ill-fated attempt to put the clock back, thereby putting oneself voluntarily outside the class of dramatic thinkers, intelligent dramatists with important things to say.

It is notable, anyway, that after *The Vortex* Coward made only one further attempt for more than forty years to write a serious, well-made play, and that, *Easy Virtue* (1924), was a quite conscious evocation of and farewell to Pinero's kind of drama, a play which demonstrated, to Coward's credit as a social observer if hardly to his good judgement as a dramatist, that a well-made play about a woman with a past was impossible in an era when 'women with pasts receive far more enthusiastic social recognition than women without pasts'. Thereafter, Coward's plays fall into two groups: the comedies, which are impeccably well-made, using the Maugham get-out clause to Shaw's restrictions (if it's only meant to be funny, then well-madeness may still be a good thing, or at any rate acceptable), and the serious dramas, which always try to say what they want to say in free forms.

Through the long years of success, Coward came, inevitably no doubt, to be cast as the grand old man of British drama, the ultimate in establishment figures. But his whole career belies this. Though he began within the conventions of the well-made play, and in most of his most successful plays, his comedies, continued to pay reasonable lip-service to the form, he was for all that a considerable technical innovator, the more effectively so in that he worked by reform, rather than by revolution. It might be said, rashly but not altogether untruly, that he found traditional British comedy as literature and left it as theatre. For without underestimating the considerable stagecraft of Maugham in particular, it still remains true that for him and his contemporaries (not excluding Shaw) theatre was primarily verbal: the dramatist conveyed his meaning by what his characters *said*.

Coward changed all that. Few of his early critics saw quite what he was up to. Again and again the complaint comes up that comedies like *Fallen Angels* (1923), *Hay Fever* (1924) and *Private Lives* (1929) are thin, insubstantial, lacking in wit. Oh yes, the quickness of the hand may deceive the eye, so long as we are in the theatre, but carry the texts off, mull over them in the study, and we can very soon see how little there is there. True enough, but this is a compliment rather than a condemnation. Coward has stripped his plays to the bone, because he is not so much interested in what his characters say to each other – the literature of the thing – as in how they feel while they are saying it, and what they mean as opposed to what they merely say. Harold Pinter has said, in reference to his own drama and to much of the modern theatre:

> So often, below the words spoken, is the thing known and unspoken. . . . There are two silences. One when no word is spoken. The other when perhaps a torrent of language is being employed. This speech is speaking of a language locked beneath it. That is its continual reference. The speech we hear is an indication of that we don't hear.[1]

This is a very precise description of Coward's method throughout his

[1] 'Pinter Between the Lines', *The Sunday Times*, 4 March 1962.

comedy: when Amanda and Elyot, now divorced and married again to other partners, chatter on in the famous balcony scene of *Private Lives* about the size of China and Japan, the whiteness of white elephants, and whether the Taj Mahal by moonlight really does look like a biscuit box, they do so, not only to amuse us, but also because they are constantly fighting the growing realization (and we know they are fighting it) that they are after all still deeply in love. The endless arguments about details of Paris topography in *Hay Fever* conceal nothing in particular, but they do tell us all we need to know about the obsessively contained, nursery world in which the whole family lives, and into which their various friends and lovers are admitted only dubiously, on sufferance, and with no real hope of truly belonging. *Design for Living* (1932), a curious work which comes in some ways closest to a clear statement on Coward's philosophy of life, plays continuously with the fantastic conversational patterns beneath which the balance of power constantly shifts in the three-cornered relationship of one woman and two men who can apparently live at all satisfactorily only when in some measure *à trois*.

It is not by chance that the image of the nursery comes up again and again in Coward's works. All his characters – all his comic characters, anyway – are best seen as children, overgrown, privileged children, able to re-enter their nursery more or less at will. Despite the outrageous modernity of *The Vortex*, and the topicality of such *pièces d'occasion* as *Cavalcade* (1931), *This Happy Breed* (1939) and *Peace in Our Time* (1946), he was always essentially an abstractionist creating his own private world in which his characters could act out their own emotional dramas undisturbed by the interruptions and irrelevancies of the everyday round of financial and social obligations. This gives his plays their curious timelessness, and enabled him to carry out his formal experiments without anyone's apparently noticing that that is what he was doing.

Nor did he cease to try new things, even when established beyond question as the senior statesman of British drama. In *Waiting in the Wings* (1960) he found for the first time complete success in a free form for serious (though not too solemn) drama, showing a few months in a home for retired actresses through four beautifully managed, interlinked but independent scenes. In *A Song at Twilight* he did something more remarkable, and even, in the context of 1966, quite experimental: he wrote a complete, fully fledged well-made play, but this time, unlike *The Vortex*, argued through unflinchingly to its necessary conclusion. He was able to do this, no doubt, largely because he chose as his subject one of the few remaining areas of human conduct governed, at least in principle as far as the average man is concerned, by a clear line between what is and what is not accepted behaviour: homosexuality. Even in our own day the homosexual past of an eminent public figure is likely to be a secret as carefully guarded, and as explosive if revealed, as the 'past' of any fallen woman of the nineties. The play is a triumph alike of sheer technique and of dramatic thought; clearly Noël Coward, *enfant terrible* of his day, was still determined as he neared seventy to keep us guessing about what on earth he might take it into his head to do next.

Coward worked always well within the bounds of the ordinary commercial theatre. When, in *Post Mortem* (1930), he wrote a boldly non-realistic play which shows a young man at the point of death during the First World War being flashed forward in time to see what those he knows and loves will make of the brave new world he is supposed to be dying for, and what it will make of them, Coward significantly considered it as a sort of indiscretion to be read rather than played, and withheld it from production. In his work practically designed for the theatre of his time he was always content to bring about his changes and reforms quietly: almost unnoticeably, by discreet fifth-column action. No one could accuse Sean O'Casey (1880–1964) of quietness and discretion. Quite the reverse. From the very beginning of his career he was the centre of controversy, and seemed to thrive on it. He emerged, fully armed and spoiling for a fight, in the home of the Irish Dramatic Revival, at its true centre, the Abbey Theatre, where his three most famous early plays, *The Shadow of a Gunman* (1922), *Juno and the Paycock* (1924) and *The Plough and the Stars* (1926) were staged in rapid succession. In these he showed himself the obvious successor of the first generation of Irish literary theatre: like Synge's plays, they were generally realistic in form and structure, though by no means naturalistic in the details of their style – even making full allowance for the special eloquence of the Irish, it is highly unlikely that one could hear in any Dublin tenement talk of anything like the extravagant splendour with which O'Casey's characters express themselves. Of course in this too he was following in Synge's footsteps, doing for the urban working-class Irish and their speech what Synge had done for the peasants – taking the raw materials and transmuting them through a poet's imagination to give back something completely unlifelike but in some essential way true to what life ought to be.

The three plays have in common their background, their style, and their unpredictable mingling of comedy and tragedy. In *The Shadow of a Gunman* the hero functions in rather the same way as the Playboy of the Western World, making the most of his quite undeserved reputation as an armed tearaway when in reality he is only a harmless poet; but the story turns to tragic drama when his girl has to die while he lives on, haunted by his own disgrace. *Juno and the Paycock* extracts a lot of lusty fun from the bragging of the 'paycock' Boyle and his relations with his crony-dependant Joxer Daly and his sympathetic wife Juno, but ends again in grim irony when the son of the household is shot for betraying a comrade in the Troubles. *The Plough and the Stars* has less clear plot: it is rather a tragicomic panorama of Dublin in 1915–16, rich – perhaps too rich – in extraordinary characters and extravagant Irish rhetoric. The play caused riots at its first performances, quelled at length by Yeats, who scornfully drew a comparison with the riots at the early performances of *The Playboy of the Western World* and suggested that the very fact of the riot guaranteed the fame of O'Casey just as, earlier, it had guaranteed the fame of Synge.[1]

Alas, when O'Casey's next play, *The Silver Tassie* (1928), was submitted to the Abbey, Yeats refused it, and O'Casey took himself into voluntary exile in England, refusing to let any of his plays be played in Ireland for some years afterwards. The cause of Yeats's doubts is not far to seek, though it is surprising that he of all people should have baulked at O'Casey's venture into boldly non-realistic expression in the second act. The play, in fact, proved to be a transition in O'Casey's work. The outer acts recount the triumphant departure of the footballer-hero to the war and his return as a broken, paralysed shadow of his former self; they are in very much the heightened realistic style we know from O'Casey's earlier plays. But the second act attempts to bring home the horrors of war by changing style entirely, perhaps under the influence of German expressionist drama, using a symbolic set, chanted choruses and a more elaborately formal style of writing to universalize its subject. Opinion has always been divided on whether this violent stylistic dislocation works in the theatre; but, whether it did or not, this section of the play pointed the way that O'Casey was to go in his later plays.

These are fairly numerous, and much more familiar as reading texts than as part of the live theatre. His next play, and first 'English' work, *Within the Gates* (1934), is set in Hyde Park, and all the characters are abstractions labelled Bishop, Whore, Poet Dreamer, and so on – though abstractions, to be sure, with a remarkably concrete turn of phrase when it suits the dramatist's purpose. Strict canons would indeed suggest that the main trouble with nearly all O'Casey's later plays is that he lets his gift for splendid, highly coloured talk run away with everything else, so that the plays become little more than casually assembled, ramshackle fantasies within which people are allowed to talk endlessly, splendidly, but to little purpose beyond the pleasure

[1] P. Kavanagh, *The Story of the Abbey Theatre* (New York, 1950), p. 197.

of hearing their own voices. Perhaps so; yet at times it does at least make a very joyful noise, as in *Purple Dust* (1945), a symbolic fantasy in which two English plutocrats seek the simple life in a mouldering Irish mansion, and *Red Roses for Me* (1943), a Dublin piece about a Catholic fatally in love with a Protestant that gradually edges over into radiant abstraction. *Cock a Doodle Dandy* (1949) and *The Drums of Father Ned* (1956) are even more capricious, but have their own kind of wild, uncontrollable life, embodying O'Casey's comments on the New Ireland in the form of obviously expressionistic parables veering sometimes towards the gruesome morality (as in the final vision of *Cock a Doodle Dandy*) and sometimes towards a fairly gentle fantasticated satire, as in *The Drums of Father Ned*, which reflects on the relation between clergy and laity in Ireland today.

It is tempting to speculate what O'Casey's career would have been if *The Silver Tassie* had not been rejected by the Abbey, and if he had stayed on in Ireland, as part of the Dublin theatrical scene, instead of deliberately isolating himself from it. Tempting, but not finally very profitable. In all likelihood his own development would not have been so different, though it might have been more controlled with the regular discipline of a regular company to write for. On the other hand the difference his presence might have made to Irish drama is profound: after his departure it fell back into dull conformism and self-repetition, with few new names to catch the imagination, and those that did – Denis Johnson (b. 1901) with *The Moon in the Yellow River* (1931), Micheal MacLiammoir (1899–1978) with *Ill Met by Moonlight* (1946) – did little to sustain their promise. Indeed, the Irish drama sank back into obscurity and parochialism virtually from the departure of O'Casey to the arrival of Brendan Behan – and then it was not in Dublin at all, but in the East End of London, that his talent was first able to make itself felt.

Meanwhile, the focus of attention shifted back to London. Except for the great days of Dublin in the 1900s, it had nearly always been there, despite a valiant attempt to create a truly indigenous theatre in the English provinces during Miss A. E. F. Horniman's period in charge of the Gaiety Theatre, Manchester, from 1907 to 1921 (it was not entirely coincidental that Miss Horniman had built and financed the Abbey in its early days, until she disagreed with Yeats and Lady Gregory on policy in 1910). During her rule at Manchester she staged more than 200 plays, more than half of which were new. Chief of the dramatists brought forward by her during this time were Harold Brighouse (1883–1958), whose sharp working-class comedy about a woman who knows what she wants and a man who is persuaded to fit in with her, *Hobson's Choice*, was curiously enough first played in New York in 1915 and has recently had a very successful revival at the National Theatre; Stanley Houghton (1881–1913), author of *Hindle Wakes* (1912), a toughly ironic tale of a 'ruined' working-class girl who refuses to marry her rich seducer; and Elizabeth Baker (1879–1962), whose most famous play, *Chains* (1909), is set not in the North, but in a grim London suburb, where a clerk with dreams has all hope of their realization shattered by his wife's announcement of her pregnancy.

Another dramatist of moderate note, St John Ervine (1883–1971), had his best-remembered play, *Jane Clegg*, first produced at the Gaiety (1913), but this was something of an oddity, since Ervine was in fact an Irishman from Ulster who, just to complicate matters further, had been at one time manager of the Abbey, where several of his earlier plays were originally produced. *Jane Clegg* has an English setting: it is about a long-suffering wife who at last finds herself in a position to leave her dallying, unscrupulous husband and calmly, confidently does so. Among Ervine's Irish plays the most interesting are *Mixed Marriage* (1911), a Catholic/Protestant *Romeo and Juliet* story set in Belfast, and *John Ferguson* (1915), a stark drama set among the Ulster small-farming community in the 1880s. Latterly, he wrote also a number of ephemeral West End successes, the best of them probably *Robert's Wife* (1937), about the right of a married woman to continue her own career.

6 The thirties

The burst of activity in Manchester under Miss Horniman did not last long, and, apart from Sean O'Casey, virtually everything that happened in the British theatre in the 1920s happened in London. Not that, once we have disposed of the leading figures already mentioned, there was so much going on, not at least until 1928, when two dramatists of whom great things were expected put in an appearance, R. C. Sherriff (1896–1975) with *Journey's End* and Emlyn Williams (b. 1905) with *Glamour*. They belong really, though, to the 1930s, and before we come on to them, and the new crop of 1931, there is one more characteristic figure of the 1920s we must look at, however briefly: Ben Travers (b. 1886), the king of the Aldwych farce.

The Aldwych farce was a genre on its own, a type of loose-jointed, anything-for-a-laugh extravaganza tailored specifically to the talents of a regular company of actors, headed by Ralph Lynn, Tom Walls and Robertson Hare. The first to hit the jackpot was *Cuckoo in the Nest* (1925), followed by *Rookery Nook* (1926) and *Thark* (1927). All of these, and most of Travers's other works, were the absolute antithesis of Lonsdale's well-made comedies: their plots ramble, picking up and dropping characters without explanation and ever ready to go haring off in some new direction in search of a gag, no matter how farfetched. And yet, for all that, Travers has always known exactly what he was doing: his autobiography, *Vale of Laughter* (1957), is full of acute observations about the art of making people laugh in the theatre, and his first three comedy successes at least have shown surprising powers of survival, even long after the deaths of most of the original actors for whom they were apparently uniquely designed and suited. *Thark*, for instance, with its gleeful and shameless re-creation of every hoary old gag about innocents in a haunted house, may not be exactly the most sophisticated entertainment going, but even at this distance of time it does entertain, and that, given its original intentions and steadfast refusal to hope for more for itself than that, is surely the most important thing.

So it was at the time, but the critics rather naturally did not think so. Or at least, whatever they might think of Ben Travers on his own ground, and for that matter Lonsdale and the comical Mr Coward on theirs, they were inclined to think that an exclusive diet of laughter in the theatre was a bit too much of a good thing. What they constantly looked for was a new serious playwright, a writer of dramas who could hold his head up in competition with the best any other country had to offer. J. R. Ackerley (1896–1967) seemed to promise something of the sort with his intelligent and sharply observed study of life in a POW camp, *The Prisoners of War* (1925), but did nothing comparable subsequently. So it was with a perhaps exaggerated feeling of excitement and relief that in 1928 critics and thinking theatregoers pounced on another play of the First World War, *Journey's End*. It is a detailed, compassionate, sufficiently fresh and realistic account of the effect some time in the trenches could have on the best of men; it is hardly Sherriff's fault that some of the ideas which were new and original when the play was written subsequently, because of its success, went on to become clichés. Like Ackerley, Sherriff did nothing comparable later; but unlike Ackerley he did go on to a long and generally successful career in the theatre, his best later plays being no doubt *Badger's Green* (1930), a gentle cricketing comedy, and *Home at Seven* (1950), a psychological drama with a showy part for its leading actor, as a suburban businessman who finds he has completely lost memory of one whole day.

Emlyn Williams, the other new dramatist to emerge in 1928 (we may omit John van Druten, whose adroit drama of schoolboy passion *Young Woodley* prefigured no more and no less than the reliable succession of commercial hits its author subsequently turned out), is a much more complicated case. It may be felt, certainly, that he has never quite fulfilled his promise, but it is much more difficult to explain precisely what that promise was, and precisely how he has fallen short of it. From the earliest days he established himself first of all as a master of immediate theatrical effect – very much the actor-dramatist. *Glamour*, his first play in London, lasted briefly, but in 1930 he had a big success with *A Murder Has Been Arranged*, a cunning bit of ghostly atmosphere and well-sustained suspense. Suspense was even more evident in *Night Must Fall* (1935), a brilliantly managed and not unintelligent melodrama about a charming baby-faced psychotic who carries round the head of his last victim in a hatbox. Those who hoped, on the strength of the talent shown in these plays, for something more substantial were rewarded in *The Corn is Green* (1938), a quiet, well-observed piece, autobiographical in its outline, about the influence a dedicated schoolmistress is able to bring to bear on a talented but wayward pupil.

This play, perhaps because of its subject matter, stands rather apart from the rest of Williams's work in the theatre, and subsequently he has attempted little more demanding than the supernatural melodrama of *Trespass* (1947), in which a fraudulent medium finds he is not such a fraud as he thinks, and the race-against-time suspense of *Someone Waiting* (1953). *The Wind of Heaven* (1945) did have higher ambitions: no less than a re-creation of the birth of Christ in a Welsh mountain village in the last century. The intention is worthy, but many of the play's purple patches ring hollow, as though the author is trying to work himself up to the level of great drama because he feels he ought, rather than because he has anything to say which can be said on no other level. Since *Beth* (1958) Williams has written no more for the theatre, concentrating instead on acting and on writing autobiography and reportage.

At least, even if London was the practical and emotional centre of British theatrical activity between the wars, Emlyn Williams represented some exotic colouring. So did the next two dramatists to emerge, James Bridie (1888–1951) and J. B. Priestley (b. 1894). If Williams, in his volubility and emotionalism, represented Welshness to the London theatregoer, Bridie, with his gallows humour and Calvinistic preoccupation with the role of the Devil in life, represented Scottishness, and Priestley stood for the stolid, no-nonsense good sense of the North Country, which kept breaking through even in those plays most overtly based on the esoteric time theories of Ouspensky and J. W. Dunne.

Both Bridie and Priestley came to the theatre relatively late. Bridie was a doctor by profession (his real name was Osborne Henry Mavor), and though eagerly interested in the theatre from his youth he did not have a play produced until he was forty, and did not have a notable success until *The Anatomist* in 1930. Frequently, in his own time and since, Bridie was characterized as a sort of Scots Shaw, and indeed the two men did have some characteristics in common: both were more interested, dramatically, in ideas than in people, and both took a somewhat cavalier view of dramatic construction; both in a sense were inspired improvisers, compelling as long as the inspiration lasted but with little to hold the attention once inspiration flagged. In Bridie, notoriously, inspiration usually flagged in the last act: his first acts were generally superb, but he seemed to baulk at the wearisome work involved in tying up the loose ends in the last act, drawing his dramatic argument together, and sending his audiences out of the theatre with a satisfying sense of completion. He was himself aware of this, and tried at various times to build a theory of drama on his own drawbacks. 'Only God can write last acts, and He seldom does. You should go out of the theatre with your head whirling with speculations. You should be lovingly selecting infinite possibilities for the characters you have seen on the stage. What further interest have they for you if they are neatly wrapped up and bedded and coffined?'[1]

Be that as it may, most of Bridie's plays seemed to leave their audiences feeling more frustrated than stimulated by the ragged and inconclusive endings. But Bridie is essentially a dramatist who has to be taken all as a piece, faults and virtues inextricably mixed, or not at all. Perhaps the best and most lasting of his plays are those which draw extensively on his Scottish background and dramatize the conflict between rigid Scottish puritanism and the world or the Devil – a figure in whom Bridie took a particular interest. His first success, *The Anatomist*, belongs to this series: it is a grim refashioning of the history of Dr Knox the surgeon and his relations with the grave-robbers and murderers Burke and Hare, and, though far from a comedy, is shot through every so often with Bridie's own personal brand of black humour. In 1933 came what was in many ways his most ambitious work, and, as he suggested himself, his only attempt to write a 'great' play, *A Sleeping Clergyman*. It is a somewhat Shavian argument about eugenics, showing good and evil struggling for supremacy in one family through three generations; it is best at its glummest, in the early scenes, but carries less conviction as the good in the family gets the upper hand, and its futuristic finale rings quite false. The best of Bridie's Scottish plays is probably *Mr Bolfry* (1943), in which the Devil invades a manse disguised in clerical black, and is finally driven away by the incumbent, after an eccentric and witty battle of wills and wiles. Two later Scottish plays, *Dr Angelus* (1947) and *Mr Gillie* (1950) are simpler and more ordinary: *Dr Angelus* is a Victorian murder story in modern dress,

[1] *One Way of Living* (London, 1939), p. 298.

richly ghoulish, and *Mr Gillie* a quiet study of a village schoolmaster's life, showing how his high hopes for his pupils come to nothing but suggesting that this somehow detracts nothing from his success as a man.

However, Bridie, once he started playwriting, was immensely prolific – some thirty-four full-length plays, not including several rewrites so complete as to constitute new plays, and numerous adaptations, one-act plays and scripts for film and radio during a mere twenty years. The group of markedly Scottish plays makes up only a small part of his total output. Some of his most characteristic pieces were reworkings of biblical stories in picturesque modern terms, full of pawky and irreverent humour, such as *Tobias and the Angel* (1930) and *Jonah and the Whale* (1930, rewritten 1942), which again suggest a Shavian comparison, with *Androcles and the Lion*. He also wrote broad modern comedies like *What Say They?* (1939) and *It Depends What You Mean* (1944), the latter lightly satirizing the current fashion for brains-trusts; ballad operas like *The Forrigan Reel* (1944); historical drama like *John Knox* (1947); and such unclassifiables as *Lancelot* (1945), a reworking of Arthurian material, *The Queen's Comedy* (1950), a characteristically perverse view of the Trojan war, and *The Baikie Charivari* (1952), which sets Punch and the Devil at each other's throats on Clydeside. Rather apart from the rest of his work stands *Daphne Laureola* (1949), a strange play which gave Edith Evans one of her best parts as the lonely, unhappy Lady Pitts, who drinks, talks and enchants a young Pole who, rather mystifyingly, sees himself as Apollo to her Daphne. Again, last-act trouble prevented the play from working entirely in the theatre, but the first act especially contained some of Bridie's most effective writing, in an overtly poetic vein usually foreign to him but very much in the tone of the times (for this was the heyday of Christopher Fry).

Whatever else might be said of Bridie, there was no denying that he very effectively broke the tyranny of realism in his plays; their characters and action were anything but everyday, and he seldom tried to convince his audiences that they were seeing a facsimile of life as it is really lived, here and now. On the contrary, he deliberately kept them conscious of theatrical artifice: his plays were intended to turn the theatre into a penny plain, tuppence-coloured escape from everyday life, though not necessarily an escape which required one to check in one's intelligence on entering.

Priestley also managed to break the tyranny of realism, though generally in a rather subtler, more elusive way. He too came to the theatre fairly late, and more or less by chance, when he happened to work with Edward Knoblock on an adaptation of his own best-selling novel *The Good Companions* (1931).

The first play of any importance he wrote on his own, *Dangerous Corner* (1932), illustrates rather well the way he was going to go as a dramatist. It seems to be a quite straightforward realistic sort of play, with carefully documented backgrounds, rounded characters and lifelike dialogue. Except that it turns out eventually to be based on an alternative-time theory: the 'dangerous corner' is a chance phrase in casual conversation which can have disastrous consequences; after demonstrating what those possible consequences are, Priestley starts again, and shows us an alternative version of the action in which the corner is safely passed, the abyss skirted without anyone's being fully conscious it is there. *Laburnum Grove* (1933) and *Eden End* (1934) were more straightforward, really as well as apparently: the first is an ingenious comedy of crime made the more bizarre by its quiet suburban setting, the second a somewhat nostalgic harking-back to 1912 which constantly invites its audience to appreciate a double standard of judgement – that by which the characters see their own time as troubled and the future as a hopeful solution to all their problems, and that by which dramatist and audience look back to the pre-war years as a haven of peace and contentment compared with their own troubled 1930s.

Priestley, like Bridie, proved to be immensely prolific once he had decided to turn his attention towards the theatre. Plays of all kinds poured from his pen, sometimes quite simple and traditional in their effect, like his North Country farce *When We Are Married* (1938), a sort of tribute to the old Manchester school of drama, sometimes deliberately eccentric, like *Bees on the Boatdeck* (1936), which essayed a political allegory in terms of artificial comedy verging at times on fantastic farce. The most significant group of his plays during this time, though, were the 'time plays' *Time and the Conways* (1937) and *I Have Been Here Before* (1937), with which may be coupled *Music at Night* (1938), *The Long Mirror* (1940) and *Desert Highway* (1943). All of these play in some way with the idea of time: parallel time, spiral time, escape from time, and so on. *Time and the Conways* demonstrates Dunne's theory of serial time by picturing a family, the Conways, at various stages of their history, seen simultaneously or coexisting outside the normal, conventional sequence of development in time. *I Have Been Here Before* turns instead to Ouspensky's notion of spiral time, containing in it the idea that we may be able to modify what has happened and seems to go on happening in endless recurrence if we are determined enough to do so. *Music at Night* shows escape from time; during a performance of a violin concerto a group of listeners are liberated to wander freely in their own subconscious. *The Long Mirror* makes play with telepathic communication, bringing together a composer and a strange young woman who has had supernatural knowledge of him and his destiny for years although they have never met. *Desert Highway* juxtaposes, to their mutual illumination, parallel actions in the desert during the last war and during the eighth century BC. Along with these may be mentioned *An Inspector Calls* (1945), in which an apparently secure, united family is shaken to its foundations by the inquiries of an inspector who proves eventually to be some sort of premonitory visitant from another world, or from another level of reality.

All of these time plays start from the premisses of everyday theatrical realism, and then modify them progressively; not, except in *Dangerous Corner* and *Time and the Conways*, by means of purely technical innovation, but rather by trying to persuade us, within the general conventions of realism, that more and stranger things are 'real' than we would ever choose to believe. The attack is sidelong: not a frontal offensive against our expectations of just how the theatre should work on us, but a sly whittling-away of our ingrained notions about reality itself, and what we can and cannot believe. Priestley has not always settled for this modified realism, though most of his more effective plays belong to this middle range. In particular with *Johnson over Jordan* (1939) and *They Came to a City* (1943) he launched out into fully fledged, undisguised allegory. Johnson, an ordinary businessman in a bowler, has died just before the play starts, and the action chronicles – somewhat capriciously, since Priestley's normal style is really not up to the weight of poetic significance it is here required to bear – his slow progress towards understanding and acceptance of his situation. *They Came to a City* is equally non-realistic: the city to which its assorted group of characters come is a sort of utopia where work is play and all conflicts are resolved; the characters are broadly representative of various social, political and religious groups, and according to their training and preconceptions find the city a heaven or a hell. Though the play is somewhat preachy (in a way that Shaw's similar adventures with ideas seldom are) it succeeded rather well at capturing the mood of its time, and was surprisingly popular, though it is hard to imagine it withstanding revival now.

In the post-war period Priestley was, if anything, even more prolific – no fewer than seventeen plays, an opera libretto, an original film script and four television plays in twelve years. Only one of the plays had a notable success, *The Linden Tree* (1947), a sober, realistic family play about a professor who is being forced to retire and his battle against it. Of the rest, perhaps the most interesting was *Dragon's Mouth* (1952), a formalized quartet for actors written in collaboration with his wife, Jacquetta Hawkes. Since 1958 Priestley has turned away from drama, except for a handful of television scripts, the most ambitious of which, *Anyone for Tennis?* (1968), was a new approach to the time question concerning a young suicide who constantly creates and re-creates his own hell by summoning up his own image of figures from his life in order to justify his death, until one of them intervenes from the living world to help him reassess his view of things; and a commercially very successful collaboration with Iris Murdoch on an adaptation of her novel *A Severed Head* (1962). He has perhaps had his say in the theatre, and a very varied, provocative say it has been. Like Bridie he has poured out plays, good, bad and indifferent, with a fine generosity of effect and little concern for economy of means, conservation of material and other nice finicky matters which agitate other dramatists. This volubility may be his greatest weakness, but it is also in many ways his greatest strength: if his methods are hit-and-miss, at any rate there are enough hits among his plays to satisfy several lesser men.

7 The poetic revival

While Bridie and Priestley were, accidentally or deliberately, competing for the first place among regular providers for the West End stage, things were stirring elsewhere. The idea of a poets' theatre still continued to attract, though since the 1900s little of its product had achieved professional presentation in London, and it had tended to confine itself to the printed page, either deliberately, like Thomas Hardy's cosmic epic *The Dynasts* (1903–8), or *faute de mieux*. One poet's play, John Drinkwater's *Abraham Lincoln* (1918) – written in prose, admittedly – had won through to wider renown, but for the most part poets' plays tended to be staged, if at all, by amateurs in church halls or by professionals only for limited, private performances. In 1933 something of a departure from this pattern, in intention at least, was marked by the production of W. H. Auden's play *The Dance of Death* by the Group Theatre. This, though it was organized as a club theatre, partly to evade theatrical censorship, was intended to cater not merely for a small, informed minority audience, but to bring neglected classics and more or less experimental new plays, generally with a powerfully left-wing viewpoint, to as large and varied an audience as possible, presenting its productions wherever it could find a convenient home. *The Dance of Death* is a lightweight verse satire with a lot of clowning, a choric commentary, and the underlying theme that bourgeois society is doomed by its own death wish. Despite its avowed aim of reaching the masses, the play still seems to be addressed, primarily, to an educated audience, already prepared to accept sophisticated techniques for putting over points in the theatre and capable of catching fairly esoteric illusions. The same is true – perhaps even more so – of the three plays Auden later wrote in collaboration with the novelist Christopher Isherwood, *The Dog Beneath the Skin* (1935), *The Ascent of F6* (1936) and *On the Frontier* (1938).

The most effective of these is probably the first, in which a man disguised as a dog accompanies a simple village lad in a quest which turns into a sort of satirical travelogue of contemporary Europe. A lot of it is good knockabout fun with some serious points sufficiently but not too heavy-handedly made. *The Ascent of F6* tries more plot, with less success: it turns on a projected expedition to climb an unconquered mountain which comes to be invested with a quite irrelevant and arbitrary political significance. *On the Frontier* suffers from indecisiveness about what it is trying to say, turning aside from the naïve dramatic logic which would have the impending conflict between fascism and democracy resolved by the revolutionary will of the people, but finding no satisfactory alternative solution. Though the plays were undoubtedly influential in their time, it is unlikely that they would still be even read if it were not for the eminence of their authors in other fields; and even such considerations have not managed to keep some inherently more interesting works of the same group (such as Stephen Spender's *Trial of a Judge* (1938) which dramatizes the dilemma of a liberal judge torn between the Left and the Right in Germany just before the Nazis came to power) in print, let alone in any sort of dramatic repertory. The only poet of this generation who had some continuing success in verse drama, Louis Mac-Neice (1907–64), achieved it not so much with his solitary stage play, *Out of the Picture* (1937), which is Auden-and-water, but with a series of radio plays he wrote in the 1940s and 1950s, starting with *The Dark Tower* in 1946, which showed a brilliant command of a medium which should be (but seldom has been) a poet-dramatist's dream.

Elsewhere, however, more lastingly successful attempts at poetic drama were being made – primarily in an extra-theatrical sphere where little sympathy could normally be expected for the drama: the church. Here the work of another, older poet holds the most important position: T. S. Eliot (1888–1965). Eliot had tried his hand at fragments of an 'Aristophanic melodrama', *Sweeney Agonistes*, back in 1928, but since he did not complete the play he perhaps had no real hope that it would be staged; in 1936 he wrote the book for a sort of religious pageant, *The Rock*, though here, he said, he was required to do little more than dress a detailed scenario by the producer, E. Martin Browne, in speakable words, and he never reprinted any of it except the choruses, which appear in his *Collected Poems* as independent poems. *Murder in the Cathedral* (1935) was something quite different: an original verse play on the martyrdom of Thomas à Becket, designed for the stage, if, in the first instance, a rather special stage in the chapter house of Canterbury Cathedral, in a festival for which the play was commissioned. The play rapidly broke out of the narrow confines of its first performances, and took to the theatre proper, though rather less effectively: its elaborate use of a chorus of the Women of Canterbury, and the long sermon by Becket in the middle, though admirably calculated for performance in a specifically religious, non-theatrical setting, do tend to hang rather heavy anywhere else. However, the play was an unmistakable success, the first in what was at that time hopefully labelled the 'revival of religious drama' to survive its original purpose and occasion. Other writers rapidly followed in Eliot's footsteps: Charles Williams (1886–1945) in *Thomas Cranmer of Canterbury* (1936) and *Judgment at Chelmsford* (1939), as well as other more obscure and highly personal plays on religious themes; Dorothy L. Sayers (1893–1957) with *The Zeal of Thy House* (1937) and *The Devil to Pay* (1939); Christopher Fry (b. 1907) with *The Boy with a Cart* (1938).

But Eliot himself rapidly moved on. Now that he had become practically involved in writing for actors, he determined to evolve for himself a type of poetic drama which would work (as *Murder in the Cathedral* was patently not designed to do) in the modern theatre. In *The Family Reunion* (1939), therefore, he tried to apply dramatic techniques vaguely suggested by classical drama (and specifically the *Oresteia*) to a subject drawn from recognizable everyday life: the return to his family fold of a wandering son racked by some mysterious and apparently unappeasable guilt. Eliot himself subsequently said that he was dissatisfied with the play's methods and solutions, feeling that the supernatural machinery – the Eumenides who torment his hero – was too obtrusive and that the use of other members of the family sometimes as individual characters and sometimes as a sort of Greek chorus was excessively selfconscious. But with the passage of time *The Family Reunion* seems on the whole Eliot's best play, creating its own world with great conviction and mirroring the cosmic unease of its characters in verse of vivid distinction which nevertheless holds its own as a working form of dramatic speech.

True to his dissatisfaction with *The Family Reunion*, Eliot carried further in his three later plays his experimenting with subjects and styles which would conceal his poetic techniques and his religious purposes from the average theatregoer. In *The Cocktail Party* (1949) we are given what seems to be a drawing-room comedy, though based, Eliot assures us, on the *Alcestis* of Euripides, in which eventually three apparently quite ordinary characters turn out to be the supernatural agents of God's designs. *The Confidential Clerk* (1953), based obscurely on the *Ion* of Euripides, appears to be an intricate farcical comedy in the manner of Lonsdale about disguised parentage; *The Elder Statesman* (1958), based equally obscurely on the *Oedipus at Colonus* of Sophocles, seems to be a dignified drawing-room drama in the realistic manner of Terence Rattigan about the latter days of a distinguished politician. All three are plays which are hardly ever appreciable by the unwarned ear as *verse* plays, and stand or fall primarily by their inherent interest as examples of their ostensible genres with something added.

In these terms *The Cocktail Party* is the most successful, for though most of the characters remain shadowy and much of the writing lacks tension, the play really does give a disturbing feeling that something lies beyond the scene, the lines the characters speak have an elusive undertone which colours our understanding of them, and quite simple-seeming words and actions have some sort of ritual significance which is all the more compelling because we do not quite understand it. *The Cocktail Party* has in fact successfully withstood revival in the late 1960s, and in the process demonstrated that it has that clear mark of theatrical vitality, the power to work equally well in a variety of quite different interpretations. Neither *The Confidential Clerk* nor *The Elder Statesman* has yet had its staying power similarly tested, but one would guess that neither comes quite in the same class: in *The Confidential Clerk* Eliot seems a little ill-at-ease with the surface trifling, while *The Elder Statesman* remains on the page what it seemed on the stage: solid, dignified and just a trifle dull. But all the same, T. S. Eliot, both by the distinction of his name and by the very real interest and enterprise of his plays, probably did more than any other writer to establish verse drama as a living part of the modern English-language theatre.

Of those who came after him, with few exceptions, little need be said. The first generation of the 'revival of religious drama' included one major figure, Charles Williams, and he shows his real quality less in the relatively conventional historical dramas he wrote for festival performance, *Thomas Cranmer of Canterbury* for production in the same circumstances as *Murder in the Cathedral*, and *Judgment at Chelmsford* to celebrate the twenty-fifth anniversary of Chelmsford diocese, than in his shorter plays on religious themes, such as *Seed of Adam* and *The House by the Stable*. Both the pageant plays are works of some imaginative distinction, but Williams's peculiar vision of the world, so vividly conveyed in his novels, which have been described as metaphysical thrillers, comes out more clearly in plays with no necessary historical connection. In *Seed of Adam* (1939), a nativity play, the action ranges freely in time, using as its unifying idea the constant search of Adam (i.e. man) for a way of return to Paradise, and letting its characters change and redefine themselves in a dreamlike progression which seems extremely complex and obscure in reading but makes perfect sense in performance. *The House by the Stable* (1938) is also a nativity play, but very different, and much simpler, with the story of Christ's birth retold in terms of its effects on the man in whose stable it took place, and allegorical figures such as Pride and Hell mingling unconcerned with mortals and angels. Williams's last completed stage play, *The House of the Octopus* (1945), is extremely curious, a symbolic drama set on a remote island, the background of the action vaguely suggesting the Japanese invasion of the Pacific in the Second World War, though in his introduction to the printed text Williams disclaims any topical allusion. The drama is, as ever in Williams's work, a battle between good and evil, both conceived in very concrete terms; the play was written at the request of the United Council for Missionary Education, and one cannot help wondering what, precisely, they made of it.

The revival, such as it was, continued during and after the war, and a number of young poets were drawn to verse drama, more or less religious in theme, often with the encouragement of E. Martin Browne, whose season of new verse plays at the Mercury Theatre in 1945–6 defined the group and their aims in the minds of critics and public. Among the plays then staged were Norman Nicholson's *The Old Man of the Mountains* and Anne Ridler's *The Shadow Factory*, both rather earnest and sober plays of ideas (the first based on the story of Elijah and Ahab, the second a sort of modern nativity play), Christopher Fry's sparkling comedy *A Phoenix Too Frequent*, and Ronald Duncan's showy fantasy about a saint's life and its incongruous aftermath *This Way to the Tomb*. Duncan's play, and Peter Yates's *The Assassin*, about the flight of Booth, Lincoln's murderer, also produced in 1945, had a considerable, if shortlived, success. But in general the work of these dramatists survives today, if at all, as of largely period interest, unlikely to be staged again but still offering quiet rewards for the patient reader. The great exception, of course, is Christopher Fry. Though, as we have noted, his first play, *The Boy with a Cart*, a fresh and simple religious parable retelling the life of St Cuthman set in the legendary past, was first produced as long ago as

1938, it was not until after the war that he surprised everyone by becoming the most extravagantly, consistently successful of all British dramatists on the commercial stage, and that with, of all things, a series of fantasticated plays in evident, self-advertising verse. Not for him the deviousness and discretion of an Eliot: his characters seem to burst on to the stage, full of bubbling excitement at the wonder of it all, that the sun rises every morning and one and one usually makes two. There was seldom much more to his message than that, but in a theatre starved of eloquence it was for some years enough.

Fry's London career began with one of his best plays, the witty one-act fantasy *A Phoenix Too Frequent* (1946); two years later he really established himself with *The Lady's Not for Burning*, a romantic comedy set in vaguely medieval times about a girl who does not want to be burnt as a witch and a soldier who thinks he does want to be hanged. There was little plot and hardly any noticeable characterization, but the talk went with a swing, in a constant fizz and glitter of metaphor, and the powerful advocacy of John Gielgud in the leading role did not exactly do harm to its commercial chances. After *The Lady's Not for Burning* came in rapid succession *Thor, with Angels* (1948), written for the Canterbury Festival; *The Firstborn* (1948), an uncharacteristically sober piece of dramaturgy about the early life of Moses; *Venus Observed* (1950), an autumnal comedy about a duke who invites his son to choose a stepmother from among three of his former mistresses, written for Laurence Olivier; and *A Sleep of Prisoners* (1951), a religious allegory, written for performance in a church, during which four sleeping soldiers dream their own versions of four Old Testament stories. All of these plays had in common Fry's ebullient way with language, and if they showed some extension of his range of subject matter they suggested little deepening, though *The Firstborn* indicated that he could manage to tell a strong story plainly if he had a mind to and *A Sleep of Prisoners* was more soberly worded and more persuasively argued out on the level of ideas than any of his earlier work, perhaps because Fry's powerful feelings against war impelled him to write with closer attention to what he actually wanted to say.

During this period Fry also did some effective translation-adaptations, notably *Ring Round the Moon*, from Anouilh's *L'Invitation au Château* (1950), and could seemingly do no wrong with critics and public. But after *The Dark is Light Enough* (1954), a winter play written for Edith Evans, who played a countess upholding traditional standards of civilization during the troubled time of the 1848 Hungarian revolt against Austrian rule, there came a period when the inevitable reaction set in, and suddenly he could do no right. Consequently, during the first vital years of the new British drama, Christopher

Fry retired entirely from the stage, and the next new play by him to appear, *Curtmantle* (1961), was produced in Holland a couple of years before it arrived in London. It is a sober study, rather in the line of *The Firstborn*, of the life of Henry II of England, and was greeted with respect rather than enthusiasm. Subsequently, Fry wrote the 'summer' play of his seasonal cycle, *A Yard of Sun* (1970) and a group of television plays about the Brontës, but he has devoted himself largely to film scriptwriting, awaiting, perhaps, the inevitable moment when his plays will be revalued and – perhaps – he will regain in critical estimation something of the commanding stature he once held in the twentieth-century English theatre.

8 The war years and after

Following Fry's career, and the later developments of the verse-drama movement, we have come on already to the era of *Look Back in Anger* and the new drama. But its arrival is premature: there are still writers of interest in the 1930s and 1940s who call imperatively for attention. We may brush aside such shortlived vogues as that which swept the pre-war theatre (perhaps latterly on the strength of the film *The Private Life of Henry VIII*) for historical drama, serious or extravagantly iconoclastic. Who now remembers *Richard of Bordeaux* (1932), a lightweight vehicle for John Gielgud as Richard II by Gordon Daviot (Elizabeth Mackintosh), or Laurence Housman's charmingly irreverent, episodic *Victoria Regina* (1934), or others in the same vein? We do, it is true, remember Rudolph Besier's *The Barretts of Wimpole Street* (1930), which has entered, in the mysterious way these things happen, into popular mythology without being, fundamentally, any more than a superficial piece of stage carpentry. And Ashley Dukes's *Man with a Load of Mischief* still returns to haunt us from even further back (1924), though why this particular piece of cunning pastiche (mainly of eighteenth-century sentimental comedy) should show such staying power is really rather mystifying. The charms of the long succession of triumphant musical romances by Ivor Novello (1893–1951), which kept Drury Lane happily occupied for many years, have now faded, perhaps beyond recall, though the scores of *Glamorous Night* (1935), *Careless Rapture* (1936), *The Dancing Years* (1939), *Perchance to Dream* (1945) and *King's Rhapsody* (1949), assisted by the lyrics of Christopher Hassell, still exert some nostalgic appeal.

But two writers refuse to be brushed aside: Terence Rattigan (1911–77) and Peter Ustinov (b. 1921). Both really emerged in the 1940s, both were extremely precocious. They differ primarily in that whereas Rattigan, after a period of uncertainty near the beginning of his career, very soon settled down into a reliable theatrical pro, progressing comfortingly with each play he wrote, seldom writing a failure and never achieving a success which was not squarely based on craftsmanship, intelligence and extreme technical efficiency as well as the more elusive, arguable qualities of imagination and personal vision, Ustinov has always remained, almost wilfully, the *enfant terrible*, the ragbag of undisciplined talents who is always expected, exhorted, hoped to be about to write a fully achieved play which will bring his work satisfactorily into focus but never quite does, or at least has never yet quite done so.

Rattigan's career began with a bang in 1936, when he was twenty-five (thereby just beating Coward and Osborne, who were both twenty-six when they first hit the jackpot). He had already had another play written in collaboration briefly staged in London (*First Episode*, 1934), but *French Without Tears*, the lightest of light comedies, made him instantly the most successful young man around, the dramatist from whom most might be most eagerly expected in the years to come. Not that *French Without Tears* was all that extraordinary. It had no very high aims, but what it aimed at it hit with consistent expertise. Three young men and one not so young swotting up their French on the Riviera; the sister of one a *femme fatale* for the other three, and a discreet romance blooming between a reticent French girl and one of the adorable Diana's slaves who has had the sense to disengage himself from her. Nothing much to that except consummate craftsmanship and a light touch: no pretension to psychological penetration, to flights of verbal wit. And yet the play hit the taste of the moment and went on to run for 1039 performances. If the young man was promising, it was hard to say what he promised.

Then for six years only one flop, quickly withdrawn and not even permitted the permanence of print. A drama, it would seem (*After the Dance*, 1939), with a suicide and a managing young woman who takes the hero in hand; the critic of *The Times*,[1] perhaps significantly, evoked the shade of Sardou in his notice. Next, in 1942, *Flare Path*, an emotional drama about the lives of the

[1] 22 June 1939.

RAF and their womenfolk; topical, adroit, not cutting very deep but showing some extension of range. Followed by a farce, *While the Sun Shines* (1943), and a light comedy, *Love in Idleness* (1944), both successes in their way, neither particularly memorable. Then suddenly, with *The Winslow Boy* (1946), all that changed. *The Winslow Boy* was in almost every respect a surprising play: surprising for its date, surprising from its author. What Rattigan set out to do in it was nothing less than a full-dress revival of the complete well-made play, with revelations, reversals, *scènes à faire*, big speeches and all. And considering the hazardousness of the enterprise, it is quite remarkable how extraordinarily well he did it. The story concerns a naval cadet who is expelled after being accused of stealing. His father takes his word that he is innocent, and hires a leading KC to get the case a proper hearing. The big scene is that of the boy's interrogation by the KC, at the end of which, having apparently broken him down completely, the KC announces that he will take the case, as the boy is plainly innocent. In the end the boy is vindicated, though the family is ruined in the process. All the pieces of the classic well-made play, the realistic drawing-room problem play, all fall here perfectly into place, and the play does work. Perhaps a trifle stiffly; perhaps it has too much the air of a demonstration about it to carry complete conviction. But all the same it established Rattigan firmly as not only the best light entertainer of his generation, but an intelligence worth taking seriously in the theatre as well.

After *The Winslow Boy* he wrote other comedies, some of them – *Who is Sylvia?* (1950), *The Sleeping Prince* (1953) – rather pleasing. But most of his work was in the field of drama, and here, even when fashion seemed to be passing him by, he never ceased to explore and deepen his talent, to find new things to say with almost everything he wrote. Themes and characters recur, modified or transformed, from play to play: humiliation, the role of the neurotic, possessive woman who often brings it about. In *The Browning Version* (1948), a long one-act play, an unsuccessful, emotionally frozen schoolmaster finds the strength at last to make a small gesture of defiance when he is touched by one tiny sign that perhaps his years of teaching have not been entirely wasted. In *The Deep Blue Sea* (1952) the neurotic heroine, caught between two suicide attempts, shows up the insufficiency of the two men in her life, her chilly husband and hearty lover, even while they show up her complete impossibility as a human being. The heroine of *Variation on a Theme* (1958) is a modern equivalent of *la dame aux camélias*, marrying her men instead of being kept by them, and a centre of considerable, if destructive (and finally self-destructive) energy. The hero of the second play in the bill *Separate Tables* (1954) is profoundly humiliated by life, and in his despair finds a sort of comradeship with another born loser.

All these plays (except *Variation on a Theme*, which is rather a muddle) deal strongly and intelligently with their subjects while never breaking loose from the confines of comfortable middle-brow realism in the theatre. Their dialogue is always clear and precise, yet natural-seeming; they are clearly situated in time and place, as their characters are clearly situated in class and background, and all these elements of the plays are observed acutely and conveyed economically to audiences. There is seldom if ever any feeling that the limitations of the genre are restricting the author in anything he wants to do, or that he chafes against them; on the contrary, the plays frequently seem positively to benefit from the disciplines imposed on them, particularly *The Deep Blue Sea*, with its claustrophobic setting for the study of the impossible Hester and, especially, her ex-RAF lover, a character common enough in life at the time, but never otherwise studied seriously and in depth by a playwright.

But two of Rattigan's later stage plays, *Ross* (1960) and *Man and Boy* (1963), do something more. *Ross* is a dramatic biography of T. E. Lawrence, or rather it is a psychological inquiry into his career which comes to the conclusion that the key to his personality was his humiliation at the hands of the homosexual Bey of Deraa. *Man and Boy*, suggested vaguely by the career of the match-king Kreuger, is another study in humiliation. Antonescu, an international financier now on his last go-round, faces ruin and has holed up in the flat of his none-too-friendly son. In a last, desperate bid to recoup his fortune he passes himself off to another snobbish businessman as a fellow homosexual, and suggests that his son is a conceivably available lover. But even that does not work, and suicide is the only way out. In both plays Rattigan moves beyond the powerful but essentially prosaic style of his earlier work to a richer, more suggestive style which seems to imply more than it ever says, to leave some of the mystery of its characters intact. After *Man and Boy* Rattigan wrote for television and the cinema screen, but less directly for the stage. Indeed, his most effective later play, *Bequest to the Nation* (1970), began life as a television script four years earlier. With its disenchanted picture of a blowsy, middle-aged Lady Hamilton and its Nelson a national hero cut down to size as a puzzled, tormented would-be private man torn between two difficult women, it is a compelling redefinition of the themes which had haunted him for much of his career, and uses its impeccable craftsmanship as a functional aid to expressing its substance rather than, as so often in drama of Rattigan's generation, so much sleight-of-hand to disguise a lack of substance. In his maturity Rattigan became a dramatic thinker, something still rare enough in the British theatre to command our attention, in whatever unlikely circumstances we may find it.

After the reliability of Rattigan, Ustinov's quicksilver quality can be both a delight and an irritation. He began, while still in his teens, by contributing sketches to revues, mostly written for himself to perform, and came before West End audiences as a fully fledged dramatist at the age of twenty-one with *House of Regrets* (1942), a sad comedy about a crew of eccentric White Russians washed up in a Kensington boarding house. This was followed by *The Banbury Nose* (1944), a comedy which took us backwards through the career of a scion of a great military family, from his irascible old age to his youth as a defiant young subaltern, determined to break free of the family tradition. Both were full of ideas; neither really worked. His next play, *The Indifferent Shepherd* (1948), was quieter, more sober: a study of a saintly but ineffectual parish priest which confirmed that Ustinov was not confined to being a joker on stage. Nor, indeed, has he been, though probably his happier efforts have been those, like *The Love of Four Colonels* (1951) and *Romanoff and Juliet* (1956), where the joker has been uppermost. The first uses a slip of a plot about a four-power commission and a Sleeping Beauty as an excuse for a virtuoso exercise in parody, as each colonel woos the lady in terms of a national fantasy, the Englishman in Shakespearian style, the American like something from a gangster movie, the Russian Chekhovianly, and the Frenchman in witty Marivaudage. The second dresses a cold-war love story in Ruritanian fantasy which is extravagantly enjoyable for its parodic elaborations of national protocol and the character of the wild, scheming prime minister, written for Ustinov himself to play, even though the lovers, nominal centrepiece of the play, count for very little. Ustinov's more 'serious' plays such as *The Moment of Truth* (1951) – the later life of Pétain seen in terms of *King Lear* – and *The Empty Chair* (1956) – a personal view of the French Revolution – have been considerably less compelling, and his later comedies, such as *Photo-Finish* (1963) and *Half Way Up the Tree* (1967), at best patchy, assembling their casts of amiable eccentrics and putting them through their paces with no very apparent purpose in view beyond keeping us lightly amused from moment to moment. And yet, and yet . . . Even if Ustinov seems destined to be a perennial *enfant terrible* of the English stage, at least he continues to keep us guessing, and none of his work is merely respectable.

'Merely respectable' would fairly describe much of the other drama of the later 1930s and 1940s in Britain. There are a few plays which rise above that level, of course. Among all the lightweight plays with which Dodie Smith (b. 1895) has kept the West End amused, *Dear Octopus* (1938) cuts rather deeper, both in its now nostalgically appealing depiction of a sort of middle-class English life which has gone for ever, and, in its strangely elegiac atmosphere, reflecting the mood of Munich year. Gerald Savory (b. 1909) produced in *George and Margaret* (1937) a perennial repertory favourite of light comedy; some of his post-war work, such as *A Likely Tale* (1956) and *Come Rain, Come Shine* (1958), shows a delicate, poetic temperament at work within the framework of conventional West End comedy. Wynyard Browne (1911–64) had his major success with *The Holly and the Ivy* (1950), a quiet, sensitive piece about the relations of a clergyman with his grown-up children. N. C. Hunter (1908–71) began writing plays in 1934, but his first success was the sub-Chekhovian *Waters of the Moon* (1951), followed by *A Day by the Sea* (1953), *A Touch of the Sun* (1958) and *The Tulip Tree* (1963), all in much the same style, and perhaps stronger in their own right than the independent strength of their star-studded casts led us to suppose.

But whatever the quiet merits of all these plays and writers, they are all inescapably minor, parochial, and indeed none of them would claim to be anything else. The one possibly major dramatist to make his début in these years was no youngster, but the novelist Graham Greene (b. 1905), who was nearly fifty when his first original play, *The Living Room*, was staged in 1953. This was a tense, gloomy view of a suicide, a recognizable part of Greene's world chopped off and shaped for the stage. So was *The Potting Shed* (1957), about the recovery of faith, though that was never quite satisfactory, either in the first version, staged in New York, or in the somewhat rewritten version seen in London. *The Complaisant Lover* (1959) is a comedy about adultery with serious undertones, and *Carving a Statue* (1964) is a tragical farce about a sculptor with an obsession but no talent. Idiosyncratic, personal and, in a measure, genuinely dramatic as these plays are, they remain very evidently the byproducts of a talent whose most important manifestations are to be found elsewhere. The same could be said of another senior novelist, Enid Bagnold (b. 1896), whose most successful play, *The Chalk Garden* (1955), was a classic anachronism, a surprisingly successful attempt to write a glitteringly epigrammatic high comedy in the manner of Wilde, which, alas, her later works in a similar genre, *The Last Joke* (1960) and *The Chinese Prime Minister* (1963), have failed to match. *Call Me Joey* (1968), a weird allegory of the state of modern Britain, seen very much from the right of the political spectrum, managed to be taken seriously even by critics fiercely opposed to everything it was saying, and did also give Sybil Thorndike a real virtuoso role; in 1976 a rewritten version called *A Matter of Gravity* gave the same role to Katharine Hepburn, with similarly spectacular results.

By the middle of the 1950s there was no escaping the fact that the British theatre was in the doldrums. Fry's reputation was fading fast, and apart from him no indisputably major dramatist had appeared in Britain since Rattigan – if, indeed, his standing as a major dramatist was altogether beyond dispute. But happily revolution was just around the corner, and its flag was first planted on the barricades, in no uncertain fashion, by *Look Back in Anger* at the Royal Court Theatre in May 1956. It is normal for historians to declare, after the event, that no revolution comes from nothing, that there are always forerunners, straws in the wind, and so on. But in this case the explosion, when it came, does genuinely seem to have appeared like a bolt from the blue. Before Osborne there was really only one new talent in the British theatre whose work seemed to look decisively towards the future rather than the past; and he, though a centre of controversy, had received relatively little recognition until the 'new drama' came along with new standards by which it might be judged. His name was John Whiting.

Whiting (1915–63), as a precursor of the new drama, certainly suffered for his convictions, and for the originality of his talent. His first play to be staged, *Penny for a Song* (1951), was a whimsical period comedy about a lot of odd characters awaiting a threatened Napoleonic invasion, conceived somewhat in the manner of Fry, though in prose, which enjoyed a *succès d'estime*. His second to be staged, though written earlier, *Saint's Day* (1951), was the centre of a controversy which now seems almost inconceivable. It was chosen as one of the three finalists in an Arts Council drama competition for the Festival of Britain, produced to almost universal critical incomprehension, and then, amid a storm of disapproval, awarded the first prize. Looking at the play again now it is hard to see quite why it was thought so difficult. It is highly coloured, admittedly: the central character, an old and rather mad writer, gradually sweeps all about him into a succession of violent actions and sudden deaths, all dictated by his obsession that people are plotting to kill him. But though its meaning may not be simple to paraphrase, and there are moments when it comes perilously near to the ridiculous, there should be no doubt about the theatrical power of the piece if its audience will only allow itself to be swept along without asking too many questions.

Whiting's third play, *Marching Song* (1954), a cool, intellectual examination of a failed general's situation on the eve of his suicide, was less difficult, and arguably his most satisfactory work as a whole, but too passionless to appeal widely; his fourth, a bitter comedy called *The Gates of Summer* (1956), never even reached London. In 1961 he was lured back to the theatre by a commission from the Royal Shakespeare Company to write a play based on Aldous Huxley's book *The Devils of Loudun*, about a case of demonic possession and/or mass hysteria in a seventeenth-century French convent. This he did in *The Devils*, an intelligent, richly patterned piece which, though it suffered a little from Whiting's tendency to chilling rationalization in his plays – he never came anywhere near to wearing his heart on his sleeve – and seemed a little too selfconscious, almost to the point of pastiche, in its rhetorical style of writing, still achieved a considerable success with the public, a measure, perhaps, of the change in public taste wrought by the first years of the new drama. But Whiting died prematurely, before he could take full advantage of the new climate of opinion, and he remains the author of several puzzling, not quite satisfactory plays which yet had the honour of first striking the new note in British drama that was very soon to be heard on all sides.

Before the day of the 'new drama' actually dawned in Britain, though, there was one other significant novelty: *Waiting for Godot*, which arrived in London in 1955, first for a club showing only at the Arts Theatre Club, but then for an extended run in the public theatre. It is, admittedly, problematical how far Samuel Beckett can be claimed for the British theatre at all: *Waiting for Godot* itself and a number of his other plays were actually written in French and first staged in France. But then, in view of Beckett's importance to the whole international drama scene, merely national boundaries have little relevance anyway, so perhaps on the basis of his nationality, background and literary origins we may claim at least a significant part of him for British theatre.

Beckett was born in Dublin in 1906 of Protestant, Anglo-Irish parents (like Shaw, Wilde and Yeats), and during a distinguished academic career made a particular study of French. He spent 1928–9 in Paris as a *lecteur d'anglais* and while there became closely associated with Joyce and his circle – an experience which was to prove significant in his own later work. His first produced dramatic work was actually written in French: a 'Cornelian nightmare' called *Le Kid*, staged by the Dublin University Modern Language Society in 1930. But this was a small, incidental work, never published, and for the next few years most of his energies were expended on writing fiction and a little poetry – nearly all in English. In 1937 he settled permanently in Paris; the following year his first novel, *Murphy*, was published in English. But from then on he chose to write entirely in French, largely in order to write without style, which is always easier in a language one has acquired than in one's own native language, with its complex web of associations.

Fiction still claimed most of his time until 1949, when he wrote *En attendant Godot*, though in 1947 he had written *Eleutheria*, another play long unpublished and unperformed. It was the production of *Godot* in 1953 in Paris which began the international spread of Beckett's reputation, previously confined to a small minority readership. Largely this was on the strength of the play itself, but it gained incidentally from the date it appeared, since in the early 1950s a number of dramatists had already come forward – Ionesco, Adamov and Genet among them – whose works lent themselves to critical arrangement within a theoretical structure of 'Theatre of the Absurd'. They did not regard themselves as a coherent group or school, but all seemed to share certain attitudes towards the predicament of man in the universe. Essentially they were those summarized by Camus in his essay *The Myth of Sisyphus* (1942), which diagnoses humanity's plight as purposelessness in an existence out of harmony with its surroundings. Awareness of this lack of purpose in all we do – the situation of Sisyphus, for ever rolling a stone up a hill, for ever aware that it will never reach the top, is a perfect metaphor here – produces a state of metaphysical anguish which is the central theme of writers in the Theatre of the Absurd. In their work, as distinct from the plays of Camus himself, for instance, the idea is allowed to shape the form as well as the content: all semblance of logical construction, of the rational linking of idea with idea in an intellectually viable argument, is abandoned, and instead the irrationality of experience is transferred to the stage.

All this is true of *Waiting for Godot*. The two principal characters, tramps called Vladimir and Estragon, wait endlessly for a Mr Godot, though they do not know quite why, or quite who he is, or quite where and when they will meet him. They consider hanging themselves, but do not; messages come, apparently from Godot, but only to say that he will come later than they think, and even so he never does come. There is a subplot involving a sadistic master, Pozzo, and his servant, Lucky, whom he tyrannizes mercilessly in the first act and says he intends to sell, and whom he still keeps on a tight rein in the second, even though he has meanwhile gone blind. Everything can be understood as a metaphor for the human situation at its most 'absurd': Godot could be anything or nothing, and in Vladimir's and Estragon's journey through time it is pointless to consider whether it is better to travel hopefully than to arrive, because arrival is never seriously in question and even hope is scarcely possible. Maybe it is marginally better to travel than not to travel, to keep on keeping on because there is nothing better to do, but even that is arguable. On the other hand, while these are associations the action of the play undoubtedly carries for most spectators, and it is not illegitimate to read it in this way, the play is not limited by such interpretations, it cannot be confined neatly and completely to them. Hence its strength in the theatre: it works first of all, and without qualification, as a story that unfolds on a stage, and beyond that what, if anything, it 'means' is problematical and at best a matter for quite subjective judgement.

Indeed, Beckett himself has made gentle fun of spectators eager to know what his plays mean: in his third full-length play, *Happy Days*, written in English and first produced in New York in 1961, he has his heroine, Winnie, who is throughout the play largely buried in a mound of earth, first up to her waist, then up to her neck, take exception to the comments of a couple of passers-by who want to know 'What's the idea? . . . stuck up to her diddies in the bleeding ground? What does it mean? What's it meant to mean?' To herself obviously, she does not *mean* anything, she just is. And in all Beckett's plays we find a similar avoidance of exact definition, no doubt because Beckett himself does not know, or is not willing to define for himself, who Godot is, what Winnie means, what is the significance of the master–servant relationship sketched in *Waiting for Godot* and fully developed in *Endgame* (written in French, as *Fin de partie*, and first performed in the French version in London, 1957), or any other of the questions which arise while watching his plays. And there is, anyway, something that tends to get overlooked in Beckett's plays: a teasing sense of humour which makes even the blackest of them often very funny. Beckett himself seems to be forbidding us to take him quite as solemnly as we are inclined to.

Beckett's influence on drama in general has been considerable, if fairly shortlived. In Britain the most obvious influence he has exerted is on Harold Pinter, an avowed admirer of his work, and then only in his very early plays and – perhaps – a couple of his shortest and most mysterious, *Landscape* and *Silence*, which drain away external drama and play entirely on their characters' memories and their functional isolation from one another very much as Beckett does in his later plays. These have been getting progressively shorter and shorter and more and more drained of action. In *Play* (1963), which is run through twice in twenty minutes, there are three characters, heads protruding from urns, and each speaks only when a shaft of light hits his or her face. In *Come and Go* (1965), which runs for only three minutes, there are three women and only 121 words of dialogue. In *Breath* (1968) there is nobody visible, only a pile of dirt and the sound of heavy breathing, and the whole thing is over in a few seconds. Beckett himself seems to be tired of drama, or at any rate to have reached in his constant refinement and concentration of his art a sort of *ne plus ultra*. More tiny dramatic fragments have followed, but the only logical progression beyond *Breath* is into silence.

But the influence exerted by Beckett in his time goes considerably beyond what can be observed in the plays of other dramatists. *Waiting for Godot* played an enormously important role in familiarizing audiences with a new kind of drama, and changing their expectations of what they would and would not be likely to see in the theatre. Its drastic reduction of the plot element obviously made it a novel experience in 1955, but not, after all, a disagreeable one. So did its steadfast refusal to explain anything, to give clear, unequivocal answers in the second act to the questions it had raised in the first. Though in the British theatre Beckett began as and has remained an exotic, his example, both in his stage plays and in his radio and television plays (*All That Fall*, 1957; *Embers*, 1959; *Eh Joe*, 1965), has not been lost on other writers or on audiences; and though *Waiting for Godot* did not have any appreciable direct influence on most of the 'new drama' which was to invade the British theatre the following year – least of all on *Look Back in Anger* – its influence in creating a receptive climate of opinion should certainly not be underestimated.

9 The new drama

Whiting and *Waiting for Godot* notwithstanding, it was *Look Back in Anger* which marked the decisive turning point. Not so much for the play in itself, but for the success it enjoyed and the consequence this had for a whole generation of writers; writers who fifty, fifteen, or even five years before would probably have adopted the novel as their chosen form but now, all of a sudden, were moved to try their hand at drama and, even more surprisingly, found companies to stage their works and audiences to appreciate them. *Look Back in Anger* had a *succès d'estime*, a *succès de scandale* and finally just a *succès*. It was revived at the Royal Court, went on tour, was staged all over the world, made into a film, and in the end even turned up in a novelized version as the book of the film of the play. It was not just another play by another young writer, staged in a fit of enterprise by a provincial rep and then forgotten; it was something much more, something suspiciously like big business, and for the first time the idea got around that there might be money in young dramatists and young drama. And with a new willingness to consider staging new plays by new and unknown writers came, not surprisingly, the new and unknown writers to supply the plays.

Not all the plays were good, of course, or even interesting, and the relative youth of the dramatists who emerged during the next ten years or so could hardly be regarded by even the most optimistic as a guarantee of quality. But during those years there was suddenly an extraordinary amount of exciting new writing in the theatre, almost entirely from writers under forty, and quite often from writers under thirty. They had, moreover, two further distinguishing features: their tremendous variety and patent unwillingness to fall neatly behind any one standard or one leader; and the fact that the great majority of them were of working-class origin. The first quality is striking enough: with the great commercial success of *Look Back in Anger* one would have expected a host of imitations to follow, but, in fact, there has never been any 'School of Osborne', and Anger in his special sense has on the whole been conspicuous by its absence.

Nor has there been any clear overriding influence from any other source, native or foreign. N. F. Simpson's rigidly logical brand of linguistic fantasy may owe something to his admiration of the Rumanian-French Ionesco's fantastic elaborations on phrasebook formulas in *The Bald Prima Donna*, but owes quite as much to *The Goon Show*. Harold Pinter's admiration for the Beckett of *Waiting for Godot* may be appreciable in *The Caretaker*, but only as one thread in an intricate fabric of wholly personal creation. The admiration of John Arden for Brecht seems to betoken likemindedness rather than direct influence, while the influence of Brecht on the John Osborne of *The Entertainer* and *Luther* or the Robert Bolt of *A Man for All Seasons* resolves itself largely into the superficial imitation of a few obvious tricks of organization. And as for an influence of the American 1930s social drama of Clifford Odets on Wesker, that seems historically so improbable that one can only guess it to derive from a chance resemblance in the situation and attitudes of two working-class Jewish intellectuals at the same period in their respective careers. In any case, the extreme diversity of these influences, real or imaginary, tells its own tale: a 'movement' which can encompass, say, *Roots*, *The Caretaker*, *A Taste of Honey*, *The Knack*, *Afore Night Come*, *One Way Pendulum*, *Serjeant Musgrave's Dance*, *Nil Carborundum*, *Black Comedy*, *The Narrow Road to the Deep North* and *Rosencrantz and Guildenstern are Dead* can be accused of many things (including being too incoherent to merit the name of the movement at all), but hardly of conformity or readiness to follow the easy line of the established popular success.

Even stranger in the context of British dramatic history, however, is the second fact about these writers – their predominantly working-class origin. For many years the West End stage has been a middle-class preserve: middle-class writers wrote for mainly middle-class audiences. But since *Look Back in Anger* there has been a significant change. Few of the new writers went to university – John Arden and John Mortimer are exceptional in this respect – though whether they could any of them hope to escape the university net were they aged about ten now is another matter. Arnold Wesker is the son of a Jewish tailor in the East End, and Harold Pinter, too, comes from an East End Jewish family; Shelagh Delaney, as all the world knows, comes from Salford and did not even manage to scrape into the local grammar school; Alun Owen is Liverpool-Welsh, an ex-Bevin boy turned straight-man to music-hall comics at the time he wrote his first play; he and several others, John Osborne and Harold Pinter among them, have worked their way up from the ranks, as it were, after periods spent with varying degrees of success as humble repertory actors. This reversal of a pattern accepted almost with out question for several generations is remarkable enough in itself to suggest some of the distinctive new quality this generation of dramatists brought to the English theatre.

All this, of course, is to anticipate slightly. When *Look Back in Anger* opened there was no reason (except the hope that springs eternal) to suppose that it was anything more, or stood for anything more, than just another new play, by another new playwright. John Osborne was young, only twenty-six, and this was his third play to be produced, though the first in London and the first written alone. It was, as Osborne himself was quick to observe, in many ways a rather oldfashioned play, never trying to step outside the bounds of elementary theatrical realism. The story, too – a rebellious young man of working-class origin quarrels constantly with his middle-class wife, has an affair with her best friend when she leaves him, but goes back to her after she has lost their baby – was nothing very out of the ordinary. What was remarkable was the rhetorical force of the tirades given to the central character, Jimmy Porter. The rest of the characters are hardly more than sounding-boards for Jimmy's diatribes against his surroundings, society, life (significantly, the only exception, Jimmy's father-in-law, is never brought into head-on collision with him), but the power of his eloquence is sufficient to carry the play, and at the time obviously found a quick response in a whole generation of young people scornful of Britain's attempts at old-world imperialism in the Suez fiasco, disillusioned with the organized Left after the Hungarian revolution, vaguely dissatisfied with the world as they saw it even if, like Jimmy Porter, they had no very clear alternative in mind.

The play became, in a month or two, a major talking point, the centre of a lot of solemn theorizing about the 'angry young man' and his place in society. More important, its success ensured the survival of the enterprising company which had staged it, the English Stage Company, and kept the Royal Court

Theatre (once before, under the Barker–Vedrenne management, a permanent home for the best in new drama) open as a platform for young writers with something new to say and a variety of dubiously commercial ways of saying it. As things turned out, it did not limit itself to becoming the home of 'angry' drama – only one play anyone remembers, Willis Hall's overheated war drama *The Long and the Short and the Tall* (1958), could be fairly categorized thus – and even Osborne himself did not stick at the position adopted in *Look Back in Anger*. *Epitaph for George Dillon* (1957), written earlier, in collaboration with Anthony Creighton, was technically similar, though it managed to give more of a fair hearing to other points of view besides that of the unsuccessful writer hero. But with *The Entertainer* (1957) Osborne broke away from realism, to encase the story of a run-down comedian's relations with his family, quite realistically told, in a framework of fantastic music-hall numbers which generalized the personal drama into some sort of allegory of the state of Britain in decline. A similar use of an 'endistancing' framework was to be seen in the television play *A Subject of Scandal and Concern* (1960), about Jacob Holyoake, the last man to be tried and imprisoned for blasphemy in England, which suggested some influence from Brecht, and the idea was confirmed by *Luther* (1961), an epic drama very much on the lines of Brecht's *Galileo*. Even here, though, it was noticeable that Luther made a hero very much in line with Osborne's own invented heroes, a Renaissance angry young man railing against the way things were and most effective when given the stage to himself to deliver a sermon; the usual thrust-and-parry of historical drama, even as defined by Brecht, is virtually nonexistent in *Luther*.

Though all of these plays achieved considerable success (Osborne's only notable failure has been in a satirical musical, *The World of Paul Slickey*, 1959), Osborne still seemed in them to be looking for a style which would enable him to move beyond the subjective outpouring of *Look Back in Anger* towards a broader, more objective statement. But curiously enough it was a more completely subjective approach to drama than anywhere else in his work which brought his next major success, and in the opinion of many critics his best play, *Inadmissible Evidence* (1964). In this the central character, Bill Maitland, is a drunken, disreputable lawyer of around forty, a Jimmy Porter some years on who finds that the world has ceased to listen to him, that his tirades, brilliant though they are, move no one, change nothing. The play is written almost as a monologue, with the other characters presented unmistakably as projections of Maitland's own neurotic, guilt-racked mind. This makes complete sense, and gives the play a unity and coherence lacking in Osborne's previous work.

Inadmissible Evidence ushered in a period of great fertility in Osborne's work. The next year another major play, in terms of length and scope Osborne's most ambitious to date, *A Patriot for Me*, was produced. It tells the history of the homosexual double agent Alfred Redl and his spying activities for both Austrians and Russians in the years preceding the First World War. The play attempts to place Redl and his problems in a larger social and moral context, but the overall balance is unsatisfactory, and finally Redl's character and motivation are obscured rather than illuminated by the elaboration of the context. An adaptation from Lope de Vega, *A Bond Honoured* (1966), done for the National Theatre, proved highly personal but more like a parody of Osborne than the real thing. In 1968 came two more new plays, *Time Present* and *The Hotel in Amsterdam*, the first notable as the first occasion of which Osborne has taken a woman as his central character (even if she does carry on rather like a Jimmy Porter in skirts) and the second an uncharacteristic attempt to broaden his talent and increase his technical resources by writing a play dependent on a balanced ensemble of six major characters rather than on a magnetic central character surrounded by an attentive chorus; opinions are sharply divided on the question of how far either of them in fact succeeds.

In recent years Osborne's writing has continued to follow much the same lines as his earlier plays, predictable in its content and its attitudes but often unexpected in the precise form it takes. He seems, for instance, to have had second thoughts about the hard words he once had for television, and has written a series of major television plays, including *The Right Prospectus*, a wildly comic story of school life, and two studies of a new topic in his repertoire, the problems of fame and distinction, and how the famous and distinguished deal with them, in *Very Like a Whale* and *The Gift of Friendship*. Indeed, as Osborne has progressed in his own life from being an angry young unknown to being an angry middle-aged institution, his interests and sympathies have shifted more towards the problems of middle age, of fame and money and power. *West of Suez* (1969), perhaps the most substantial of Osborne's later stage plays, is a muddled panorama of family life in an outpost of the collapsing empire in which the older characters seem to come in for most of the playwright's sympathy. Other Osborne plays of this period, such as *A Sense of Detachment* (1972) and *The End of Me Old Cigar* (1975), are satirical charades which some thought significant and some merely messy, but *A Place Calling Itself Rome* (1973), a modern reworking of *Coriolanus* as a sober political drama, suggested, like his adaptations of *Hedda Gabler* and *The Picture of Dorian Gray*, that Osborne was taking a new practical interest in his craft as such, the how as well as the why of what he was saying.

In all these plays Osborne has shown a large-scale, unruly talent. His attempts to extend it have been more successful than his attempts to discipline it; he remains a splashily effective, untidy dramatist, whose work seems almost infallibly to capture the attention of a more broadly based public than that of any of his contemporaries. He is, indeed, the nearest that the whole new drama in Britain has come to producing a genuinely popular dramatist, a dramatist with the sort of shameless theatrical effectiveness which alone can get over to some sort of mass audience in the theatre today. It seems unlikely that we can expect any great change in his dramatic attitudes, which have remained remarkably consistent from the first; deep distress, which apparently he continues to feel about the way things are, shows little sign of humanizing his soul. But the expressions of the distress, if not always profound, are seldom less than striking in their instant effect, and his best plays remain remarkably fresh in revival: *Look Back in Anger*, though already a period piece and a social document of the disorientated mid-1950s, does not date, but if anything seems better today, when a more balanced view is possible, than it did at the time, as a centre of excited controversy.

Once *Look Back in Anger* had started things off, there was for some time no stopping the new dramatists. Almost at once another writer of importance emerged in another part of London – Brendan Behan (1923–64). His first play, *The Quare Fellow*, had actually been staged in Dublin in 1954 without attracting much notice, but when it was put on in London by Joan Littlewood's company, Theatre Workshop, it went through the process of communal revision and improvisation normal with the group to emerge as a powerful, concentrated piece of tragicomedy evoking the strange atmosphere in a prison while an execution is being prepared and carried out. Behan himself attracted a lot of attention as a personality, as a result of his picturesque background as a Borstal boy and political prisoner, and all this reflected back on his second play, *The Hostage* (1958, originally written in Gaelic as *An Giall*), a more strongly comic account of the goings-on at a decrepit brothel turned into a centre of IRA activities, in which a British soldier is held as a hostage and finally, almost accidentally, shot. The play itself, though lively enough as an excuse for the colourful staging effects in which Joan Littlewood specialized, is much thinner and weaker than *The Quare Fellow*, and Behan, whose forte was lively invention rather than rigorous construction, never managed to complete his long-announced third play, *Richard's Cork Leg* (after his death the sketches were edited for staging by Alan Simpson).

The Quare Fellow, however, remains impressive – almost the only play to come out of Ireland in recent years which in any way challenges comparison with Sean O'Casey, both in the density and power of its dialogue and in its intensity of feeling.

Though Theatre Workshop was for several years one of the vital forces in new British theatre, it was very much an actors' and directors' theatre, and not to any important degree a platform for writers. In fact, of all the other writers who contributed material to its shows, only one other, Shelagh Delaney (b. 1939), calls for individual mention. Her first play, *A Taste of Honey* (1958), was written when she was seventeen and had had little direct contact with theatre of any sort (curiously enough, she wrote it after seeing Rattigan's *Variation on a Theme* during its pre-London tour and deciding that, if that was all there was to drama, she could do better herself). It is a largely subjective picture of its young heroine's drifting life, her relationship with her tarty mother and with a couple of men, a negro sailor who fathers her baby and a homosexual art student who mothers her. The point of view gives the play coherence, since we are never asked to believe in the characters who surround the heroine as more than her partial view of them, and the whole thing has a strange, casual grace and charm. Shelagh Delaney's second play, *The Lion in Love* (1960), was more ambitious, taking as its central character a middle-aged woman whose drinking makes her impossible to live with and yet impossible for her husband to leave. There was a definite development shown here, but the subject, if truly felt, was inadequately dramatized. Subsequently, Shelagh Delaney has written stories and film scripts, but seems to have deserted the theatre.

The Lion in Love was finally staged at the Royal Court under the aegis of the English Stage Company; and it was to the Royal Court that those in search of exciting new dramatists would first look. Looking, they found a remarkable but encouraging variety. During the next two years, for instance, they might encounter in rapid succession playwrights as different as Ann Jellicoe and N. F. Simpson, John Arden and Arnold Wesker. Each had his or her very distinctive style; none of them had anything noticeable in common with John Osborne, angry theatre, or indeed anything else worth mentioning in the recent past of the English-speaking stage.

The most traditional of the quartet is undoubtedly Arnold Wesker (b. 1932). Of an East End Jewish, working-class background, he began by writing plays which reflected his own early experiences of Jewish family life, working in a restaurant kitchen, and so on, and which did so in a fairly straightforward, realistic manner. His first play to be produced, *Chicken Soup with Barley* (1958), is a quiet, episodic piece tracing the history of one family, the Kahns, through the years from the 1930s to the 1950s. The central character, the mother, is a lifelong Communist with a vision to hold on to and live for; but the father drifts from apathy into premature senility and the children lose faith in simple political solutions, or finally in solutions of any sort. The play is written simply, directly, and is a little inclined to preach. The following year, however, when Wesker took up the history of the same family again in *Roots*, the second of what was to become the 'Wesker Trilogy', his scope had broadened slightly. The play is about the girlfriend of one of the Kahn children, and her attempt, paving the way for his first visit to her family (which never comes off), to make them – obscurantist country folk – see something of what she thinks she has seen in literature and 'good' music under the careful tuition of her fiancé. To dramatize this, Wesker uses the same rather pedestrian naturalistic style as in *Chicken Soup with Barley*, except that here there is a tendency in climactic moments to leave words aside altogether, as in the heroine's ecstatic dance at the end of the second act, trying to convey the feelings a record of *L'Arlésienne* arouses in her. The very end of the play, though, returns ploddingly to words as Beatie breaks free of Ronnie's influence to speak out on her own behalf.

The third part of the trilogy, *I'm Talking about Jerusalem*, followed in 1960, staged, like the other two, first in Coventry and then at the Royal Court, where eventually the three were played together in succession. This pushes rather further Wesker's experiments with a sort of 'drama of the unspoken': the plot concerns the unsuccessful attempt of the Kahn daughter and her husband to begin life again in Morrisian terms as self-supporting craftsmen in a rural community, but the most effective sections of the play are those, like the 'creation myth' acted out by the family, which relegate words, with which Wesker never seems altogether happy, to a secondary position. The tendency is pushed further still in his 1961 revision and expansion of his short play *The Kitchen*, originally staged privately in 1958. Here what was originally a naturalistic piece about the personal dramas of a group of characters working in a restaurant kitchen, set against the external tensions of a lunchtime rush, becomes in revision an almost balletic fantasy, a nightmare vision interrupted by the happier dreams of some of the employees.

Clearly Wesker was progressing towards a liberation from naturalism, and many felt that he achieved it completely with his next play, *Chips with Everything* (1962), based explicitly on his new realization that 'the theatre is a place where one wants to *see* things happening'.[1] As it happens, *Chips with Every-*

'Art is Not Enough', *The Twentieth Century* (February 1961), p. 192.

thing is decidedly muddled in what it wants to say – more so than any of Wesker's other plays – but in compensation it handles the purely physical side of its action far more expressively. Though obviously service life is presented here as a sort of microcosm of the world at large (like the kitchen), it is far from clear what Wesker intends by his central character's initial opting-out of authority (he is a scion of the officer class determined to stay in the ranks), or his final capitulation and elevation, but scenes of wordless action like the raid on the coal store or the final ceremonial in the course of which the hero returns to his class have an infallible theatrical effect, making the sticky question of what paraphrasable content, if any, they have seem for the moment at least quite irrelevant.

Similarly, Wesker's next play, *The Four Seasons* (1965), seems fated to be remembered as the play in which the heroine is required to make an apple strudel on stage, though in this two-character love story Wesker also essayed, none too successfully, a more elaborate, half-poetic dialogue style to convey his characters' thoughts and feelings in a way beyond the narrower limitations of stage realism. In *Their Very Own and Golden City* (1966) he sets about breaking down the bounds of stage realism in another way, by adopting a complex structure in which the young architect hero's vision of the co-operatively owned golden cities he will build is intercut with episodes showing how the vision fades and achieves only partial realization during his life. Again, the trouble is too many, too explicit words; but this is not matched on the whole with compensating advantages, in that we never really see things happening, we never see the hero actually at work. Much the same judgement applies also to *The Old Ones* (1972). *The Friends* (1970) is entirely a talk-piece, using the withdrawal of a group of leading lights of the 'swinging sixties' into a small private world of personal relationships as a sort of allegory of the state of modern Britain – and, incidentally, disastrously confirming that words are not Wesker's forte as a dramatist. However, Wesker's seems still to be a developing talent, hard though it is to guess where it will finally lead him.

N. F. Simpson (b. 1919) is, if not so traditionally based a writer as Wesker, at least fairly easy to fit into a fashionable pigeonhole: the Theatre of the Absurd. But even here, though some influence from Ionesco in particular seems likely, it is not absolutely necessary: Simpson could just as well be seen as a latterday exponent of the English nonsense tradition, his plays imbued with the home-grown surrealistic inconsequence of *The Goon Show* and developed sometimes with the sort of doggedly logical reduction to absurdity we find in the writings of Lewis Carroll. Opinion divides on Simpson largely

in terms of what meaning his plays are meant to have beyond being elementary farcical fun. The point of Theatre of the Absurd, after all, is supposed to
be that it brings man face to face with the cosmic absurdity of his own situation in the universe, for ever striving to do what he knows to be impossible,
to bridge the unbridgeable gaps between himself and fellow human beings by
his feeble and inconclusive attempts at communication.

It is rather doubtful whether Simpson does, or intends to do, any of this in
his plays. In the first to achieve notice, *A Resounding Tinkle*, which won a new
drama award in 1956 and was staged in a shortened version by the English
Stage Company in 1968, the main plot, if such it can be called, giving
glimpses of the dottily inconsequential home life of a couple called Paradock,
is constantly interrupted by interludes from cross-talk comedians, direct
addresses to the audience on the subject of what may and may not be
expected of the drama, and slightly Pirandellian moments when the actors
are supposed to step aside from their roles to comment on them. *One-Way
Pendulum* (1959) is somewhat less overtly experimental. Here we meet a
group of characters each with a comic *idée fixe*. The father of the house is
busy building a do-it-yourself Old Bailey, in which, when he has completed
it, he is instantly brought to trial; the son's great aim in life is to train a group
of speak-your-weight machines to sing the 'Hallelujah Chorus'; the old aunt
in a wheelchair lives in the permanent fantasy that she is touring the Outer
Hebrides; and so on. The whole play is constructed according to a sort of
Alice-through-the-looking-glass logic, whereby, for example, the son of the
house has to murder lots of people in order to indulge his passion for wearing
black, and the judge installed in his father's do-it-yourself courtroom lets him
go, on the grounds that if he were executed right away the law would be cheated
of exacting due penalty for all the crimes he might subsequently commit.

Simpson has explored similar territory later in another full-length play,
The Cresta Run (1965), a halfhearted send-up of a spy-thriller, and various
one-act plays, television comedy scripts, etc. It is hard, despite high claims
made for his work in early days, to see in it much more than the agreeable but
modest ambition to make us laugh without *arrière pensée*. Whether it succeeds in that aim is very much a matter of taste, though *One-Way Pendulum*
had a successful West End run and an extensive career in repertory – which
is at least some indication of the widespread change of taste in the popular
theatre brought about by and since the advent of the 'new drama'.

Ann Jellicoe (b. 1928) is one of the most extraordinary and individual
dramatists to emerge in these years. She came to playwriting by an unusual
path – from play-direction – and her first major play, *The Sport of My Mad*

Mother (1958), was written partly under the misapprehension (as it proved) that a playwright might have more chance of directing in the professional theatre. Consequently the play itself is conceived less as a literary artefact, a text which would make rewarding reading in itself, than as a sort of blueprint for production. Of course, any play seriously intended for performance must be that to some extent, but *The Sport of My Mad Mother* went considerably further in this direction than any previous British play, seeking to express the feelings of its cast of illiterate teddy-boys and layabouts not so much by words, indeed hardly at all by words used as a coherent means of self-expression, as by an intricate pattern of sounds and actions. Quite a lot of the dialogue, in fact, is merely 'sound' – cries and ejaculations, repeated monosyllables shorn of any associative effect and used entirely for their tonal qualities.

On the page it looks as intimidating and uncommunicative as the hieroglyphics of some unknown tongue; in the theatre it surges over and around one, a strange, disturbing pattern of sights and sounds that produces a corresponding series of emotional reactions from which gradually a total picture of a violent, instinctive way of life emerges. Hopeless to ask what this or that 'means', how we should interpret the actions of the teddy-boys, full of a purely arbitrary spirit of violence, and of their spiritual leader, Greta, a legendary figure of destruction and in the end, when she gives birth to a child, of creation too, who corresponds presumably to Kali, the Indian goddess of creation and destruction who is the 'mad mother' of the title ('All creation is the sport of my mad mother Kali'). Instead, the play's audience is asked to leave its critical intellect at the door and simply to react, instinctively, to the total experience the play in performance has to offer.

Similar techniques are used in *The Rising Generation*, a pageant-play commissioned (but not performed) by the Girl Guides Association, and *The Knack* (1961), a four-character comedy about sex. In *The Knack* we meet four apparently quite intelligent, articulate people caught in the very situation where they are most completely ruled by their elementary emotions. Into a house occupied by three bachelors comes a girl, a strange innocent who acts as a catalyst by provoking competition between the sexual athlete of the group and the sexually timid landlord, with the mild and balanced third party acting as referee. Again, the play is a happening rather than a piece of verbal communication. Whole sections of the text make no noticeable sense in themselves, because it is always what is going on, and what the audience apprehends from participating in what is going on, that counts. Often the dialogue is simply a series of non sequiturs or uncomprehending repetitions, and in one key scene, when two of the men gradually draw the girl into their fantasy that a bed in the room is actually a piano, of 'pings' and 'plongs' variously distributed and extending virtually uninterrupted over some three pages of script. The result is very funny, a vivid theatrical image which tells the spectator forcefully what the play is about even if he would find it impossible to formulate, stage by stage, exactly what it 'means'.

Ann Jellicoe's two later plays, *Shelley* (1965) and *The Giveaway* (1969), are somewhat more conventional, or at any rate are unconventional in different and less obvious ways. *Shelley* is a documentary biography of the poet, sober, highly intelligent and with some individual touches, but largely the sort of play in which the playwright deliberately keeps the expression of his or her personality under a tight rein, placing the given subject matter very much to the fore. *The Giveaway* is an interesting attempt, none too well served by a lackadaisical production, to inject Ann Jellicoe's own personal brand of non-verbal comedy into a more conventional low farce about a family whose lives are dominated by the ten-year supply of breakfast cereal they have won in a competition. Possibly she has wanted to demonstrate that she is not confined to one limited way of writing plays, and in these two plays she has done so; but in the process she has lowered quite considerably the level of creative intensity appreciable in *The Sport of My Mad Mother* and *The Knack*.

John Arden (b. 1930) is again very different from any of his fellow dramatists brought forward by the English Stage Company in these years. He has in common with Osborne a certain expansiveness of utterance, a taste for the broad canvas and an urge to reach a large public in the most immediate way possible (an urge which has not as yet been altogether realized), and with Wesker he shares a preoccupation with social issues and an attraction to sociopolitical subject matter. But his creative personality is far remote from those of Osborne and Wesker, and his plays come out with little or no even passing resemblance to the work of either. Perhaps the really radical difference is that Arden is an intellectual, in a way that very few other modern British dramatists are. He has had a university education (for what little that may guarantee), but more importantly he has made his own literary and dramatic studies, he has ideas about the forms he uses, can, if pressed, analyse his own dramatic procedures and indicate the intended significance of his recurrent symbols, the roots of his style not only in Brecht – the most obvious influence – but in popular melodrama, opera, folk plays and the ballad tradition.[1]

[1] See, for instance, the interview in Charles Marowitz and Simon Trussler (eds), *Theatre at Work* (London, 1967), pp. 36–57.

This in itself does not of course make his plays necessarily better – often, after all, the writers who most effectively do are precisely those who have the least clear idea of how they do it – but it does give them a very individual flavour, quite unlike anything else in current British drama. This is noticeable even in the very earliest of his plays to survive, the radio play *The Life of Man* (1956), which tells of a fatal voyage in an unpredictable mixture of verse and prose, with strong mythical overtones. But then in something which unmistakably inhabits the same mental world as *The Ancient Mariner* and *Moby Dick* that is acceptable enough. Where Arden's eccentric approach creates more of a problem for an audience is in plays set in modern times, immediately recognizable surroundings, and with apparently clear-cut social themes – plays like *The Waters of Babylon* (1957) and *Live Like Pigs* (1958), both produced, to fairly general incomprehension, at the Royal Court. The first is about prostitution and local government corruption, but the hero – rightly so called, in that he is the most generally sympathetic character – is a pimp and ruthless slum landlord who was once a guard at Buchenwald. To make matters worse, all the characters are liable to shift without warning from colloquial prose to ornate verse or burst into song. *Live Like Pigs*, though somewhat conventionalized in a fairly naturalistic production, is essentially much the same mixture, this time exploring the uncomfortable relations between neighbouring families, one stolid, respectable and middle-class, the other untamable vagrants settled in the other half of their suburban semidetached.

The problem audiences found with these plays was only partly technical. More puzzling still was Arden's steadfast refusal to tell them what they ought to think, to single out one character or group as 'right', and the rest as 'wrong'. As it has normally been understood in the British theatre, social drama is always expected to put a clear point of view on the issue in question, to propagandize. This is what Wesker's plays do, for instance, and also most of the Manchester School plays and their 1930s derivatives like Walter Greenwood's *Love on the Dole* (1933). (To find something radically different one must look back as far as Galsworthy, a dramatist with whom Arden has one or two unexpected affinities.) But Arden, wherever his own sympathies lie, is in his plays scrupulously fair to every side. Few people, after all, are villains to themselves. The conflict between the two families in *Live Like Pigs* is not the result of malevolence or blind prejudice or anything of the sort, but arises because each of them has its own perfectly coherent, even honourable way of life but the two ways of life cannot coexist. Even Herod, as Arden indicates in his nativity play *The Business of Good Government* (1959), was in his own eyes doing his duty, arranging things for the best, and to appreciate the position we must fairly balance his concept of the best against God's.

Once one appreciates that fair hearing for all shades of opinion is an essential of Arden's dramatic method, his plays are not so hard to approach. Though *Serjeant Musgrave's Dance* (1959) mystified many on its first appearance, publication and a number of amateur performances, plus a television presentation, rapidly familiarized it and confirmed it as one of the most substantial and telling plays of its time. It concerns, though in an oblique and rather riddling way, the rights and wrongs of war and of pacifism. A serjeant arrives in a mining town with a small group of men, apparently recruiting, but gradually it emerges that he is really there with some crazy scheme to bring home the horrors of war and killing by killing a number of the locals in a kind of expiation for the death of five natives, killed in reprisal for the death of one soldier, a local boy. This scheme goes awry because his followers are fatally divided among themselves about their aims, and in the end the status quo (a highly unsatisfactory one for everybody) is restored by the arrival of the military in force. A strange, bitter, haunting play, it refuses to give up its secrets to logical analysis of plot and character; it is, like the plays of Ann Jellicoe, first and foremost an experience in the theatre, working through our instincts rather than our intellects.

Since *Serjeant Musgrave's Dance*, Arden's career has been scarcely more predictable, nor have his plays grown any easier, though to some extent audiences have gradually got on to his wavelength. *The Happy Haven* (1960) is a quirky comedy set in an old folks' home, with a serious point about our tendency to dehumanize the elderly. *The Workhouse Donkey* (1963) takes up some characters from earlier plays, particularly *The Waters of Babylon*, and is an expansive farce, with plot in operatic profusion, about hanky-panky in local politics and the rise of the niggling, book-keeping middleman at the expense of both the inflexible idealists and the old freebooting robber barons of the community. *Ironhand* (1962), a very free adaptation from Goethe, finds something of the same pattern in *Goetz von Berlichingen*. *Left-Handed Liberty* (1965), commissioned for the 750th anniversary of Magna Carta, carries Arden's scrupulous fairness to all sides so far that King John finally emerges as something like the hero of the piece. *Armstrong's Last Goodnight* (1964) is something of a *tour de force* verbally, being written in an extraordinary pastiche of Middle-Scottish which somehow manages never to seem precious or merely antiquarian; it is also a direct and powerful drama on Arden's favourite theme of the conflict of incompatible codes and standards of conduct, in this case between Armstrong, the robber baron, and Lindsay, the devious courtier sent to deal with him.

Armstrong's Last Goodnight, produced by the National Theatre, has been Arden's nearest approach yet to a popular success. Since then he has concentrated almost entirely on work at the fringes of the normal commercial theatre, writing children's plays, supervising the improvisations of amateurs, experimenting in free-admission theatre, lunchtime theatre, and so on. At least one of the texts so produced, *The Hero Rises Up* (1968), a play about Nelson and the Nelson myth, is a work of more than passing interest. Most of his later writings have been in collaboration with his wife Margaretta D'Arcy, though they retain his strong individuality. This collaborative and for the most part aggressively anti-commercial work seems to give him great satisfaction, but perhaps we may hope that his return to the professional theatre, and his wider acceptance by ordinary, non-specialist audiences, will not be indefinitely delayed.

Naturally, not everything exciting that happened in the years of the 'new drama' happened at the Royal Court. At least one of the major playwrights, Harold Pinter (b. 1930), began in the commercial theatre and made his way (not without some initial setbacks) entirely there and in the mass media of television and radio. Pinter's career, in fact, presents the best single index for the changes of taste which have come about in the years since *Look Back in Anger*. When his first play to be professionally produced, *The Birthday Party* (1958), arrived in London hardly any of the critics understood it, or for that matter seemed to feel any sort of sympathy for it, and the public stayed away in droves. Two years later Pinter's second full-length play, *The Caretaker*, a work no easier to take by the standards of what had been normal in the West End theatre, received almost universally favourable notices and went on to become a major commercial success.

What had brought about this surprising shift of opinion? Partly, of course, it was the mere passage of time and the increasing familiarity with Pinter's style and way of thought this had brought. Partly it was the slowly felt effect of a whole lot of new drama, departing in all sorts of different directions from any familiar norm and, in the aggregate, gradually changing the average theatregoer's expectations of what he might see in the theatre. But, perhaps most important of all, it was the intervention of television, which brought new and unfamiliar forms of drama into homes where no sort of drama was familiar, to audiences who had no clear preconceptions of what they could and could not expect from a play. *The Birthday Party* itself had been televised successfully, and Pinter's first original television play, *A Night Out*

(1960), had gained an all-time record viewing figure for drama, which remained unchallenged for several years. In the theatre a couple of successful revues had included sketches by Pinter which audiences with no specialist pretensions found simply funny or appealingly odd, and thought no more about it than that. The 'new drama' was already well on the way to becoming acclimatized, as drama *tout court*.

It is curious, but encouraging, that Pinter's rapid progress from Britain's most misunderstood dramatist to one of her most popular and sought-after should have made no perceptible difference to his work. He has always followed his own line of development with ruthless logic and sublime disregard for outside circumstances. From his very first play, the one-act *The Room* (1959), to his latest at time of writing, *No Man's Land* (1975), an entirely consistent and coherent development of ideas and techniques is apparent – so much so that probably an observant student, faced with the mass of them shuffled, could rearrange them in their correct chronological order entirely from internal evidence. Within this sequence, however, they fall into three roughly defined groups. The first, up to and including *A Slight Ache* (1959), is concerned mainly with the pervasive symbol of the room, representing security, and with menace of various sorts from without; the tone of these plays, despite their sinister undertones, is primarily comic, hence the term coined for them,[1] 'comedy of menace'. The second, from *A Night Out* to *The Basement* (written 1963), is more psychological, and shows an increasing preoccupation with personality and the impossibility of formulating any reliable notions of its nature and even its very existence. The third, from *Tea Party* (1965) to date, is more firmly objective and external in its viewpoint, and increasingly concerned with the subject of memory – as something which brings people together or holds them apart, weakens or strengthens them.

The style in which Pinter follows out his preoccupations is difficult to categorize briefly. He has been assigned, mainly on the strength of his earlier work, to the Theatre of the Absurd, but though a certain relationship with the Beckett of *Waiting for Godot* may be seen here and there, the connection is only superficial. In an important sense Pinter is a realistic dramatist: it is simply that he happens to see reality from an unfamiliar aspect, his ear picks up and his art transmutes into dramatic dialogue another sort of English than that we are used to hearing on the stage. But the fact remains that he captures the rhythms of English as it is really spoken more accurately than anyone else, taking into account especially the interplay almost incvitable in con-

[1] Apparently by Irving Wardle, drama critic of *The Times*, in a 1958 article for *Encore* magazine.

versation between the quicker and the slower, the more and less intelligent, those eager to find out and those determined to give away nothing. Examples of this gift can be found all over Pinter's work, down to the tiniest examples, like his revue sketches *The Black and White* and *The Last to Go*. And the essential truth of his writing in this respect is recognizable as soon as we have got over the initial shock of hearing it instead of the more usual tidy formulations of the stage.

Similarly with the structural problems presented by his early plays. It has been observed, for instance, that *The Birthday Party*, which shows the terrorization of an out-of-work pianist by two mysterious strangers who finally dominate him completely and take him away with them, is really a well-made play from which the exposition and dénouement are omitted: we get process and conclusion without explanation or revelation. We never know what, if anything, Stanley has done to be hounded in this way, or who has sent Goldberg and McCann to get him. It is not to Pinter's purpose that we should – both because the less tightly defined the menace is, the wider its range of possible applicability and because, after all, life is like that: when, except on the stage, do people explain everything to each other or to themselves, when do they produce complete and unarguable credentials? As Pinter himself put it in a programme note to the Royal Court production of *The Room* and *The Dumb Waiter*:

> There are no hard distinctions between what is real and what is unreal, nor between what is true and what is false. The thing is not necessarily either true or false; it can be both true and false. The assumption that to verify what has happened and is happening presents few problems, I take to be inaccurate. A character on the stage who can present no convincing argument or information as to his past experiences, his present behaviour or his aspirations, nor give a comprehensive analysis of his motives, is as legitimate and as worthy of attention as one who, alarmingly, can do all these things . . .

In all the earlier plays the menace comes from outside in some way. But already in *The Birthday Party* Pinter suggests that it is as much Stanley's fears as the threats of the outsiders that bring about his breakdown. In *The Dumb Waiter* (1960) two men in a room suddenly find themselves in the position of menacing each other: in *A Slight Ache* the 'menace', a mute matchseller, does nothing, but his mere presence brings about a breakdown in the owner of the house outside which he has mysteriously stationed himself. The stage is set for Pinter's second phase, in which the central subject is the interrelation of characters, their communication or avoidance of communication with each other, their manifold understandings or misunderstandings of each other. *The Caretaker* shows a manœuvring for position of three men in one room, two brothers and a strange vagrant brought in by one of them, a mental case who is leading a vegetable existence after electric-shock treatment. There is no real menace, no insoluble problem: the play is a psychological drama which simply leaves a lot more to our imagination than most. We can, of course, interpret the three men and their relations with one another in all sorts of ways, some of which do demonstrable violence to the play (such as that which sees them as God the Father, God the Son and God the Holy Ghost), but most of which are valid as far as they go. The play, however, refuses to be confined: it always retains something of its mystery, and can be explained but never explained away.

From here to *The Dwarfs* (1960), *The Collection* (1961) and *The Lover* (1963) there is a gradual development of concentration on the nature of personality itself. The central character in *The Dwarfs* meditates on whether the two others really exist as coherent entities at all, or are merely 'the sum of so many reflections'. In *The Collection* the plot turns on the (unsuccessful) attempts of one of the characters to find out what, if anything, happened between his wife and another designer during a fashion show in Leeds, thwarted at every turn because no one tells the same story twice running and in any case a thing may, as Pinter has pointed out, be true, or untrue, or both simultaneously. In *The Lover* the effective fragmentation of human personality is accepted as a fact of life: a husband and wife keep their marriage alive by giving full play to their alternative characters as mistress and lover, and being willing to envisage, beyond the major division, a number of possible subdivisions. In *The Basement* not only the people, but their settings, vary constantly from moment to moment, in a world where no appearances are any longer to be relied on as the life around us disintegrates into an incoherent collection of subjective impressions.

This would seem to be a very shaky basis for a dramatist to work on, since drama above all depends on what Len in *The Dwarfs* calls 'the joint pretence [that there is an objective truth beyond mere appearances] we depend on to continue'. In *Tea Party* Pinter extracts himself from the impasse by withdrawing himself, and us, from the character who cannot make sense of the appearances around him: there is an objective reality, and if he cannot apprehend it this is because he is going mad. *The Homecoming* (1965), Pinter's third full-length play, moves further into total objectivity. It tells its story in an absolutely clear, direct fashion: a young man comes back home unannounced, with his wife, presumably to set the record straight, or at any rate to impose on his terrible family his own view of himself in place of theirs. He does not succeed, he stands no chance of succeeding – but his wife manages without difficulty to impose her will on them all, and is last seen arranging a neat set-up whereby she will function as a high-class whore, aided by the family, but ruling the roost herself. Here Pinter's drama has moved beyond mystification, beyond the point where it makes any sense to ask what does it mean. It is a story, told with complete, unquestioning conviction, as a fairy tale should be, for the audience to take or leave as they will, but not to question.

Incidentally, *The Homecoming* raises the question which is to dominate Pinter's next two plays, *Landscape* (1968) and *Silence* (1969): the role of memory in life. Teddy, the son who comes home, is shackled to the past, to memory, and is rendered impotent by it; Ruth, his wife, succeeds because she has no such ties. In *Landscape* two old people seem to exchange recollections, but actually go on living in their own independent worlds, sublimely unaware of each other; in *Silence* two men and a woman muse, mostly in separation, about a mysterious triangular relationship they have, haunted by fleeting glimpses of an almost forgotten past. In both the tone is meditative yet uneasy; emotion is recollected, but by no means in tranquillity.

Pinter's two more recent full-length plays, *Old Times* (1971) and *No Man's Land* (1975), both develop further the theme of memory and the power struggle involved in who accepts whose version of the past and who can more effectively create and re-create the present. In *Old Times* it is a husband, a wife and the wife's old friend who comes to stay; in *No Man's Land* it is two old men, one seemingly unassailable in his riches and his power, the other apparently frail and transparent in his half-truths, whose roles vary and redefine themselves considerably in the course of a brief relationship. It is impossible to guess where Pinter will go from there. But one may be sure that in his obsessive concern for structure, for exactly the right word in the right place, and not one word too many, his plays are built to last; he has created his own private world in the theatre, and it is one from which, once entered, it is impossible to emerge entirely unchanged, unaffected by the author's compelling personal vision of things.

10 The situation today

The 'new drama' was already solidly established in the work of several leading figures – Osborne, Simpson, Jellicoe, Wesker, Arden, Pinter – by the end of the 1950s. But before we go on to consider what else was happening at the time, and what was to happen next, we should look briefly at some of the external conditions that shaped the careers of these new dramatists and dictated to some extent what they wrote. One thing noticeable, even so far, in describing the careers of dramatists who emerged in the 1950s is the frequency with which radio, television especially, and the cinema crop up. Radio had provided an outlet – in the 1940s and early 1950s virtually the only outlet – for advanced drama of various kinds, and with the setting-up of the Third Programme in 1946 it became, for the dramatist, a force to reckon with. There were writers of older generations, such as Louis MacNeice, who developed the dramatic side of their talents almost entirely in terms of radio, while of slightly younger writers there were several, most notably Giles Cooper (1918–66), whose most significant achievements were in the field of radio drama and who never quite managed to seem so at home in any other medium (Cooper's television plays were mostly slight and obviously simplified for mass consumption, while of his stage plays perhaps only *Happy Family* (1966), a strange piece about a middle-aged family who still maintain at home a full range of nursery disciplines, achieved a density and richness comparable with his best radio work).

Even in the early days of the 'new drama' radio was still playing its part. John Arden's first professionally produced play was for radio, and two of Pinter's early works, *A Slight Ache* and *A Night Out*, were first designed for radio. But already the coming thing was television. BBC Television had started up again, after a wartime break, in 1946, and in 1954 it was joined by a second, commercial channel. Between them, even allowing for a considerable percentage of adaptations at the start, these two channels created an enormous new market for plays, as well as requiring a large number of dramatic scripts for serials and series. At first the norm for an original television play was about 50 minutes – the equivalent, roughly, of that one-act play the professional theatre has given such short shrift since the demise of the curtain-raiser – but before long 90-minute and even two-hour plays were fitted into the schedules as well. And as television is organized the speed with which it gobbles up material is alarming, since few plays get repeated, and fewer still are given more than one production. However, while the here-today-and-gone-tomorrow side of television is something of a drawback to dramatists with a taste for permanence, it does also mean that the market is ever open for fresh material, ever tempting to the writer, especially if he is not yet established in any other medium.

It was inevitable, therefore, that most of the newer writers should write at least occasionally for television. But it was also inevitable that television, with its vast audiences – unthinkably vast in terms of a West End theatre run – should have some effect in its turn on the drama at large and audience's responses to what they saw elsewhere, especially in the theatre. And here the effect has not been all bad, and has certainly not been so bad for the live theatre as gloomy prophets held during television's first wildfire spread. As it happens, television played an important role in the very beginning of the new drama. *Look Back in Anger* had opened to generally interested and sometimes enthusiastic notices, but was not doing business anything out of the ordinary. It had been introduced in a repertory season, and had excited sufficient interest to justify a solo run thereafter, but for eight weeks it played at just below a break-even figure. Then an act was shown on BBC television, and at once the takings jumped, while in two weeks they had nearly doubled. Obviously it was the television exposure which had made the difference: a new audience had been offered a free sample, liked what it saw, and decided to buy. Television was already helping to bypass the traditional channels by which information and opinion on live drama were passed on to the possible ticket-buying public, and for the first time had made a significant contribution to the shaping and definition of public taste. It did so again, as we have seen, by familiarizing a mass audience with Pinter's style and approach to dramatic storytelling between the *débâcle* of *The Birthday Party* and the triumph of *The Caretaker*.

And there were other ways that television could and did act as a mediator between the theatre and the public. It had the initial advantage (at least, in many ways it was an advantage) of a public almost completely lacking in sophistication where the drama was concerned, and therefore – an important point, this – remarkably unprejudiced about what they did and did not expect of the drama. They required to be held, interested, and that was all; how and why what held and interested them worked, and whether it was the sort of thing that they would expect to hold and interest them, mattered not a jot. Now in many ways this is an ideal situation for an enterprising young dramatist to work in. It may mean that many of his subtleties and refinements go unnoticed, though it does not necessarily preclude their use. But it does mean that he is free from the usual battle to manœuvre audiences out of their preconceptions about drama and into the right receptive frame of mind for his own particular interpretation of the genre.

Hence, it is hardly surprising to find that many dramatists of the 1960s made their first appearance and/or first significant effect on television. So it was, for instance, with John Mortimer (b. 1923), whose first play and first success, *The Dock Brief* (1957), a Dickensian legal extravaganza about a hopeless client and his fantasy-prone solicitor, began life on radio, went on to television, stage and the cinema, and many of whose better later works have been designed specifically for television. His gifts are in fact particularly suited for television because he seems happiest in the one-act form: his best stage play, *What Shall We Tell Caroline?* (1958), is a one-acter, and when he launches into more elaborate and lengthy stage plays, as with *The Wrong Side of the Park* (1960), *Two Stars for Comfort* (1962) and *The Judge* (1966), the results tend to seem inflated or artificially 'constructed' from smaller units. Alun Owen (b. 1926) also owes most of his fame to his television work, particularly the trilogy of plays with Liverpool connections *No Trains to Lime Street* (1959), *After the Funeral* (1960) and *Lena, Oh My Lena* (1960), which firmly established him as a lively exponent of regional exoticism and, more important, as a writer with a superb gift of the gab. On stage he has exploited similar backgrounds in a loosely organized Liverpool Romeo-and-Juliet story, *Progress to the Park* (1959), and a Lionel Bart musical, *Maggie May* (1964), but his best work is to be found elsewhere, in his historical play with a Latin American background *The Rough and Ready Lot* (1959) or his drama of redbrick university life *A Little Winter Love* (1963).

The tendency of dramatists is to gravitate as soon as possible from television to the stage, though most continue occasionally to write for television even after some stage success (the reasons for this progression have something to do with a persisting snobbery about the superiority of a West End presentation to anything else, something to do with critical reputation, and something to do with money). One exception is Clive Exton (b. 1930) who became a top-ranking television dramatist in the early 1960s but never had a stage play produced until *Have You Any Dirty Washing, Mother Dear?* (1969), a witty satirical fantasy about the deliberations of a parliamentary committee regulated by an intricate structure of absurd rules and conventions. But in television alone Exton has managed to make an enviable reputation as an individual writer, first in plays of loving surface realism like *No Fixed Abode* (1959), a story of doss-house life, and *I'll Have You to Remember* (1961), about two old people brooding over the fate of their son, who killed himself ten years earlier, then with black comedies like *The Trial of Doctor Fancy* (1963), about a doctor who persuades all his patients to have their legs needlessly amputated, and *The Boneyard* (1966), about a policeman who has a vision while on the beat. A dramatist who has, exceptionally, moved in the opposite direction is David Rudkin (b. 1936), whose name was first made with *Afore Night Come* (1962), a mysterious piece about the dark gods and human sacrifice in the modern English countryside, first produced by the Royal Shakespeare Company. Since that, however, he seemed for some years to have deserted the theatre entirely, and written instead a series of major television plays, the best of which, *Children Playing* (1967), a funny-sinister picture of life in a youth hostel with particularly fresh and vivid characterization of the younger children, and *Blodwen Home from Rachel's Wedding* (1969), a devious, sidelong study of a neurotic spinster and her relations with the unpredictable outside world, are in every way comparable with full-scale stage plays, while gaining considerably from television's flexibility in time and place. His return to the theatre in 1975 with *Ashes*, a lengthy and agonizing marital drama with a background of the present troubles in Northern Ireland, proved that he had lost nothing of his dramatic power and individuality in his time out.

Another dramatist who has done much of his best work in television is David Mercer (b. 1928). A recurrent theme in his work, almost *the* recurrent theme, is social alienation expressed in terms of psychological alienation. This has been stated, in various guises, in several television plays, including

A Suitable Case for Treatment (1962), *For Tea on Sunday* (1963) and *In Two Minds* (1967), as well as in his stage play *Ride a Cock Horse* (1965), all of which turn on the incursion of unreason, in the form either of insanity or of apparently unmotivated violence, into everyday life. His early television trilogy, *The Generations* (1961–3), showed him gradually throwing off the shackles of realism and of close political commitment, but the political theme has continued to play a prominent part, albeit variously disguised, in his later stage plays *Belcher's Luck* (1966) and *After Haggerty* (1970), as well as in a sequence of television plays which began with *The Parachute* (1968). Though his stage plays demonstrate that he has a big talent, as yet not directed with complete certainty, it is probably true to say that his best work is still to be found in television.

Given the tremendous economic importance of the television market to the modern dramatist, we should probably be surprised, not that nearly all of them have written for television at least once or twice, but that so many have managed to keep relatively aloof, and certainly remain very much of the theatre, theatrical. The most remarkable of these is undoubtedly Henry Livings (b. 1929), the only one of the new arrivals in the 1960s who seems unarguably to take his place, by virtue of the power and variety of his output, the striking individuality of his means of dramatic expression, alongside the major figures of the heroic days. Livings has chosen up to now to work almost entirely within the framework of farce, which may perhaps have hampered his rapid recognition as a leading figure in modern British drama, but it is evident from even a very cursory examination of his work that he has a lot of serious things to say in the guise of farce, and a totally fresh and in-dividual way of saying them. Fundamentally his plays are constructed in units of about ten minutes, which he takes to be the longest span an audience can hold a new situation clearly and totally in mind. Within these units the action is conceived entirely in terms of objectives, of what each of the characters wants to do. Thus his plays are farces of character rather than of situation, and this has to be understood if they are to be produced to maximum effect: the humour, and the sense, of them resides primarily in what is not said, in the mental processes of the various characters as they criss-cross, speed up and rush ahead or lag behind, only catching hold of an idea minutes after everyone else has moved on to something else.

The first impact of Livings on the London theatre came with *Stop It, Whoever You Are* (1961), a quirky comedy about a lavatory attendant who gets into trouble with an under-age girl, tries to humiliate his detested land-lord (in vain), goes mad, dies, and returns in a seance to get his own back before the assembled cast is blown up in an explosion from a leaky gas-main. This puzzled critics so much that one or two toyed with the idea that the whole thing was meant as a malicious parody of the new drama. Hardly anybody, except a few of the audience, appeared to find it funny, or to accept that being funny was its immediate and most important aim, any serious point it might have to make about the human dignity of the underdog being quite incidental. In general, it has been Livings's misfortune to be produced mainly in circumstances where audiences are liable to look first for significance rather than a good laugh – which is starting at the wrong end for him. Still, *Big Soft Nellie* (1961), a seemingly random collection of unfortunate incidents in the life of one of nature's butts, a worker in an electrical appliances shop, had its admirers, and so, even more, did *Nil Carborundum* (1962), a sharp-edged picture of life in a peacetime National Service RAF where fantasies run riot because the whole pattern of life is founded in fantasy.

This was produced by the Royal Shakespeare Company in an experimental season; Livings's next comedy, and in many ways his best-known play so far, *Eh?* (1964), was produced by the Company as part of its normal season at the Aldwych Theatre. Despite a curiously unsympathetic production it did manage to reach a wider and more appreciative audience than Livings's earlier plays: its theme, the ability of an obsessed individual (a man who gets a job minding a factory boiler so that he can continue growing hallucinogenic mushrooms) to throw a spanner into the works of even the largest, most impenetrably efficient organization, is very characteristic, and very happily developed by Livings in a succession of zany comedy scenes. A similar approach is used, rather less effectively, in *Honour and Offer* (1969), but Livings also has another side to his talent, represented in the theatre chiefly by *Kelly's Eye* (1963), a tragic tale of a stupid man and an inexperienced girl whose love is overshadowed by a crime committed by the man three years before they met; this shows that when he wants to he can step outside his chosen farcical form and lose nothing of his individuality.

Livings is, technically speaking, an eccentric, but his methods are undeniably adventurous; he belongs unmistakably to the new drama, however we may choose to define that term. But not all the dramatists who have emerged since 1956 have any sort of experimental leanings at all, and there are several who would quite conceivably have written much as they do if Osborne, Pinter, Arden *et al.* had never disturbed the theatrical scene as Rattigan left it. Foremost among these more technically conservative writers is Robert Bolt (b. 1924), who had considerable success with his Chekhovian *Flowering Cherry* (1957) and his mildly Brechtian historical drama *A Man for All Seasons* (1960); in general, his plays, though neatly crafted and providing reassuringly meaty parts for large-scale theatrical stars of the old school, seem rather short on individuality or real urgency, and in recent years Bolt has devoted most of his energy to film-scriptwriting, though a new historical piece *Vivat, Vivat Regina* (about Queen Elizabeth I and Mary Queen of Scots) was produced in 1970. Peter Shaffer (b. 1926) made his name with a neat but unexpectedly intense family drama, *Five Finger Exercise* (1958), and went on to impress critics with his dignified, intelligent, spectacular play about the Spanish Conquest of Peru, *The Royal Hunt of the Sun* (1964); perhaps too much so, in that shorn of its spectacle the intelligence comes to look a trifle thinly spread. Shaffer has another side to his talent, though, a more engaging one represented most brilliantly by his one-act farce *Black Comedy* (1965), which plays with the utmost virtuosity on the simple idea of reversing light-values so that when the stage is in darkness for all the characters we can see perfectly what is going on. This is one kind of powerful theatrical image. Another is at the centre of *Equus* (1973), with its magical imaging of the god-like horses which haunt the dreams of the troubled young man who shares the play with the emotionally repressed psychiatrist put in charge of his case. Powerfully verbal, powerfully visual, the play represents a newly satisfying fusion in Shaffer's work, one that augurs well for the future.

Of the other technical conservatives of these years the most notable and noted are Frank Marcus (b. 1928) and Joe Orton (1933–67), who have in common chiefly the fact that the biggest success of each is a comedy prominently involving homosexuality. In Marcus's case it is *The Killing of Sister George* (1965), which deals sympathetically and perceptively with a lesbian relationship between an ageing radio actress and the tiresome young woman she lives with. In Orton's it is *Entertaining Mr Sloane* (1964), in which an apparently harmless, vulnerable suburban couple, brother and sister, turn the tables on their menacing, homicidal guest, Mr Sloane, and end up sharing his sexual favours for alternate half-years. Orton had a particular gift for expressing outrageous ideas in language of tortured primness and refinement, but his humour needed a firm grounding in some sort of believable humanity, and *Entertaining Mr Sloane*, appreciably a comedy, remains far superior to his two later plays, *Loot* (1966) and *What the Butler Saw* (1968), which slip well over into farce.

Somewhat more advanced in their ideas are a number of dramatists who have been influenced temporarily or permanently by the Theatre of the

Absurd. David Campton (b. 1924) used its forms, unusually, for directly political themes in his sets of linked one-act plays *The Lunatic View* (1957) and *Four Minute Warning* (1960). James Saunders (b. 1923) wrote a classic piece of Theatre of the Absurd in his most successful play *Next Time I'll Sing to You* (1962), a partly analytic, partly poetic, partly farcical consideration of a modern English hermit; his other plays are extremely eclectic in style, ranging from the muted poetic fantasy of *A Scent of Flowers* (1964) to the satirical extravagance of *The Borage Pigeon Affair* (1969). Tom Stoppard (b. 1932) provides in *Rosencrantz and Guildenstern Are Dead* (1967) a sort of plain-man's-introduction to the genre by dramatizing in terms of *Waiting for Godot* the lives of Rosencrantz and Guildenstern between their appearances in *Hamlet*; he too is an eclectic, and his next two plays to be produced in the West End, *Enter a Free Man* (1968) and *The Real Inspector Hound* (1968), could have been written by two other people, though the family comedy-drama of the first and the fantasy of the second, which imagines two rival theatrical critics becoming involved in the action of a play they are watching, are both effective in their different ways. His major later plays, *Jumpers* (1973) and *Travesties* (1974), are both intricate intellectual games, frenziedly comical, arguably serious, in which a lot of university wit and many bright ideas lead eventually to self-defeating aridity.

Other writers go more wilfully their own way. David Turner (b. 1927) offers us in *Semi-Detached* (1962) a spirited modern equivalent of Jonsonian comedy of humours set in a middle-class Northern suburb. Edward Bond (b. 1935) is interested in the drama of extreme situations, but the notoriety achieved by the baby-stoning scene in *Saved* (1965), the fantasy of Queen Victoria's lesbianism and the final cannibal feast in *Early Morning* (1968) and the succession of horrors in *Narrow Road to the Deep North* (1968), set in medieval Japan, has rather obscured the passages of quiet good writing all these plays contain. *Lear* (1971), Bond's variation on themes from Shakespeare, and *The Sea* (1973), a not very comical symbolic comedy, suggested a maturing in his talents, though as *Bingo* (1974), a wild and wayward piece about the physical and spiritual death of Shakespeare, made clear, no matching tendency to retreat into conventionality and respectability. Charles Wood (b. 1932) has written a number of plays exploiting in a highly personal way themes from military life, notably the triple bill *Cockade* (1963) and *Dingo* (1967), as well as writing an odd comedy about life in tatty provincial theatre, *Fill the Stage with Happy Hours* (1966), and a comedy with a film-making background, *Veterans* (1972), which gave John Gielgud one of his best recent roles. John Hopkins (b. 1931), a prolific and variable television dramatist, made a remarkable stage début with an intricate and subtle drama about mental breakdown, *This Story of Yours* (1969).

In the 1970s another generation of dramatists made their mark in the London theatre. Or rather one should say another group, since in terms of age there was a considerable spread between the very young indeed, like David Hare, who was twenty-two when his all-woman play *Slag* was staged at the Royal Court in 1970, and contemporaries of Pinter and Osborne who had taken longer to establish themselves or turned late to drama from other kinds of writing. The most notable of these latter is David Storey (b. 1933), who had achieved great distinction as a novelist before the extraordinary outpourings of plays which made him a dominating figure in the theatre from 1970 on. *In Celebration* (1969) was an elaborate essay in stage naturalism, a drama of agonized family relations, but his two plays of 1970, *The Contractor* and *Home*, developed a more specifically theatrical form of discourse, *The Contractor* being built round an action – the raising of a marquee for a party – which is at once actual and symbolic, and *Home* round a mysterious dialogue among the inmates of a mental hospital which says everything by seeming to say nothing. The most interesting of several later plays are *The Changing Room* (1972), a fine-spun, almost documentary evocation of rugby life, and *Cromwell* (1973), an out-and-out symbolic drama which did not really work but suggested new dimensions to Storey's dramatic talents.

The other outstandingly successful new British dramatist of the 1970s could hardly be further removed from Storey. The speciality of Alan Ayckbourn (b. 1939) is farcical comedy, developed in all kinds of technically and sometimes emotionally ingenious ways. His first popular hit was *Relatively Speaking* (1967), an intricate and finally rather desperate development of one basic misunderstanding joke. Since then he has been very prolific, always more or less within the comic conventions of the traditional West End stage. His most substantial, and in many ways his best, work has been the sequence of three plays under the general title *The Norman Conquests* (1975), all covering different aspects of the same happenings in the same house during the same overcrowded weekend and designed to be played in repertory. Here Ayckbourn's extreme technical ingenuity serves the purpose of illuminating human character; elsewhere, for all its frequent entertainment value, it has sometimes tended to betray him into something rather too arid and mechanical to bear close scrutiny.

There are many more. Simon Gray (b. 1936), after several muffed attempts, hit his dramatic stride with two ironic comedy-dramas of life among the intellectuals, *Butley* (1971) and *Otherwise Engaged* (1975), which achieved the interesting feat of making West End theatregoers find human interest in people who talked about Ibsen and T. S. Eliot as though they really cared. Peter Terson (b. 1932) turned out stage and television scripts in profusion, most strikingly individual when working closely with the kids of the National Youth Theatre on lively, improvisatory shows like *Zigger Zagger* (1967) and *The Apprentices* (1968). Other dramatists, like Howard Brenton (b. 1942), chose to work consistently in fringe theatrical circumstances, using improvisation, directing happenings, exploring the possibilities of very topical drama, and so on. But the most extraordinary work to emerge from this area of activity has been *AC/DC*, by Heathcote Williams (b. 1941), a weird, obsessive picture of life among some crazy, drugged and generally peculiar people which, for all its extreme violence of language, has clearly been written with a care and precision and sense of words which persuaded its first director, William Gaskill, to compare Williams, alarmingly but on consideration with some justice, to Congreve.

Nor is everything of interest in British drama necessarily centred in London or even Britain. The arrival in London of Ray Lawler's strong emotional drama about the city interludes of a couple of Australian sugar-cane cutters *Summer of the Seventeenth Doll* in 1957, together with the production of Richard Beynon's *The Shifting Heart*, a prizewinner in the 1956 *Observer* play competition, served to draw attention to the existence of a native school of Australian playwrights whose work benefited from a specifically local flavour in its dialogue and backgrounds without being weakly dependent on mere exoticism for its effect. Unfortunately no more has been heard of Richard Beynon, Ray Lawler's later plays have not matched *Summer of the Seventeenth Doll*, and most young Australian dramatists seem to come to London anyway and busily set about losing their local accent. The major exception is the novelist Hal Porter, whose play *The Professor*, a picture of an expatriate Australian academic and his life in Japan, written in a solid literary manner, had a considerable, if unfashionable, critical success when presented in London in 1965.

In the other dominions and ex-dominions, there are varying amounts of theatrical activity, but those where the live theatre seems strongest, India and South Africa (probably because in neither has television made any real progress yet), there is little playwriting of any significance. The most interesting dramatist to emerge yet from Africa is the Nigerian poet Wole Soyinka, whose simple, seemingly naïve parable plays such as *A Dance of the Forest*, *The Lion and the Jewel* and *Kanje's Harvest* vibrate powerfully in the memory after performance. The West Indies have little theatre on the spot, but again they have sent interesting talents to London, the best known being two dramatists produced at the Royal Court, Errol John, whose picturesque drama of life among the Caribbean poor, *Moon on a Rainbow Shawl*, won first prize in the *Observer* play competition, and Barry Reckord, whose writing is at its most effective when dealing with the British scene, as in *You in Your Small Corner* (1960), about snobberies and rivalries among London's black population, and *Skyvers* (1963), a sympathetic and impeccably accurate account of life in a London secondary modern school.

There are still more dramatists, of very varied backgrounds and very various talents, but it would be pointless to go on. Evidently, even from the examples cited, the English stage has had a great and unexpected revival since 1956 – all the more unexpected in that during the same period the theatre as we have known it has seemed to be in a state of disastrous decline almost everywhere else, except perhaps Russia, and even there new writing talent has been conspicuously lacking. Inevitably critics and audiences are spoilt by an apparently unending flow of new writing talents to the stage, and when the flow showed signs of diminishing after five or six years at once the question started to be posed: is the 'new drama' dead? The answer, of course, is that as long as the writers who emerged since 1956, or a significant proportion of them, continue to write worthwhile plays the new drama will continue to exist. Naturally, it will not always remain 'new'. Already the generation of dramatists born since 1920, or especially since 1930, have become familiar fixtures of our theatre, taking their places beside Coward, Rattigan and other survivors of older, more settled days. Which is as it should be. New dramas may come and go, revolutions overthrow the established order to become themselves the basis of a new establishment. But the drama itself goes on, and as long as these cycles of rebellion and consolidation continue, as new blood supplements old in the veins of the theatre, it will never die.

Bibliography

I The social and literary context

(a) SOCIAL

(i) *General*

G. M. Trevelyan, *English Social History*, Vol. IV (London, 1944), provides an invaluable introduction to the period up to the end of the Victorian age. Thereafter the student will find a variety of useful reference books on social change. I would particularly recommend Raymond Williams, *Culture and Society 1780–1950* (London, 1958), as a penetrating study of the relationship between artistic and social development. For an overall survey of the political history, William L. Langner, *An Encylopedia of World History* (London, 1968), provides a comprehensive reference. For general reference to social attitudes to the theatre, I would refer the student to George Rowell, *The Victorian Theatre* (London, 1967), and J. C. Trewin, *The Edwardian Theatre* (Oxford, 1976). *The Stage Year Book*, 38 vols (London, 1908–69), contains much useful information.

(ii) *The Arts Council of Great Britain*

The reports and accounts of the Council are published annually, and can be obtained from the Arts Council of Great Britain, 105 Piccadilly, London W1. They provide factual information on the activities of the subsidized theatres, together with grants and subsidies. *Theatre Today* (London, 1970), also published by the Council, is a report on an inquiry into the state of the theatre – provincial, West End, touring and subsidized. Also a report on the operation of British Actors' Equity and a recommendation for the setting-up of the Theatre Investment Fund. The early work of CEMA is critically examined in Charles Landstone, *Off-Stage* (London, 1953). More recent criticism is contained in publications mentioned below.

(iii) *Social and economic problems*

Richard Findlater, *The Unholy Trade* (London, 1952), John Elsom, *Theatre Outside London* (London, 1971), and Ronald Hayman, *The Set-Up* (London, 1973), contain chapters on the Arts Council's policy. The latter has useful chapters on Equity, the role of the agent and audience attitudes. The changing role of the modern actor in society, his training and the effect of television on his livelihood are discussed in Michael Billington, *The Modern Actor* (London, 1973).

(iv) *Censorship*

Richard Findlater, *Banned* (London, 1967), is a full and well-informed history of theatrical censorship in Britain, to which I would add John Elsom, *Erotic Theatre* (London, 1973). This traces the history of pornography in the theatre from the nineteenth century onwards, and its later manifestations since the abolition of censorship.

(v) *Educational*

The case for the teaching of drama in universities is well argued by Glynne Wickham, *Drama in a World of Science* (Bristol, 1952). Drama as an educational subject in schools and colleges is under continuing review in John Hodgson and Martin Banham, *Drama in Education* (London, 1973–). The case for young people's theatre is argued in *The Provision of Theatre for Young People* (London, 1967), an Arts Council report on a Commission of Enquiry.

(b) LITERARY

(i) *General*

Una Ellis-Fermor, *The Frontiers of Drama* (London, 1954), contains a valuable insight into the relationship between form and content. Theodor Shank, *The Art of Dramatic Art* (California, 1969), is thoroughly recommended as a thought-provoking treatise on theatre as a distinct and unified art form. The case for theatre art, as opposed to the written drama, is of course argued with picturesque force by Edward Gordon Craig, *On the Art of the Theatre* (London, 1924); no student of theatre should fail to read this. Eric Bentley, *The Life of the Drama* (London, 1965), poses this question of what gives life to drama. Particularly valuable is his defence of farce and melodrama as non-literary forms. Ronald Peacock, *The Poet in the Theatre* (London 1946; rev. ed. 1960), examines the relationship between poetry and drama, as does W. B. Yeats in a number of his essays. A selection of these can be found in *Essays* (London, 1924). Both these writers argue the case for the poet as against the actor.

(ii) *Literary influences on the theatre*

E. G. Craig, *On the Art of the Theatre* (London, 1924) and his earlier publication *The Art of the Theatre* (London, 1905), did much to revive interest in theatre as an art as opposed to 'show-business'. Shakespearian production was revolutionized by Harley Granville Barker in his Savoy Theatre seasons (1912–14). His *Prefaces to Shakespeare* (London, 1927–47) are now available in paperback. Constantin Stanislavsky, *My Life in the Theatre* (London, 1924) and *An Actor Prepares* (London, 1937), have had a vast influence on the actor's approach to his art. Play direction, too, has been influenced by literary and critical works. Michel Saint-Denis, *Theatre: The Rediscovery of Style* (London, 1960), is a powerful plea for the classical as against the realistic tradition. Brecht's work is studied in John Willett, *The Theatre of Bertolt Brecht* (London, 1959), and Martin Esslin, *Brecht: A Choice of Evils* (London, 1959). Antonin Artaud, Jan Kott and Jerzy Grotowski have all had considerable influence, more especially on Peter Brook and the productions of the Royal Shakespeare Company. The student should refer to Antonin Artaud, *The Theatre and Its Double* (London, 1970), Jan Kott, *Shakespeare Our Contemporary* (London, 1964), and Jerzy Grotowski, *Towards a Poor Theatre* (London, 1969).

II Actors and Theatres 1880 to Present Day

(This bibliography is highly selective and excludes some books and all articles referred to in the notes.)

(a) GENERAL

Indispensable general studies are Allardyce Nicoll's two volumes, *Late Nineteenth Century Drama 1850–1900*, Vol. V of his *A History of English Drama 1660–1900* (Cambridge, 1962) and *English Drama 1900–1930* (Cambridge, 1973). J. P. Wearing's *The London Stage 1890–1899 : A Calendar of Plays and Players* (Metuchen, 1976) is a valuable reference work, and James Ellis and Joseph W. Donohue, Jr, have a full calendar in preparation, *The London Stage 1800–1900*. George Rowell's authoritative *The Victorian Theatre : A Survey* (Oxford, 1956) includes the period to the First World War, and Rowell has edited a valuable collection of critical writings, *Victorian Dramatic Criticism* (London, 1971). Richard Southern has provided a brief illustrated account, *The Victorian Theatre : A Pictorial Survey* (London, 1970), and a concise overview is given by G. Lunari, *Henry Irving e il teatro inglese dell'800*, Documenti di teatro 22 (Bologna, 1962). The introductions and notes to Michael Booth's *English Plays of the Nineteenth Century*, 4 vols (Oxford, 1969–73), have much of relevance to theatres and acting in the period. W. Macqueen Pope gives a lively and personal account of the Edwardian theatre in his entertaining *Carriages at Eleven* (London, 1947), A. E. Wilson has written a useful survey, *Edwardian Theatre* (London, 1952), and the period has been reconsidered in a fine recent study by J. C. Trewin, *The Edwardian Theatre* (Oxford, 1976). For the inter-war period, J. C. Trewin, *Theatre in the Twenties* (London, 1958) and *Theatre in the Thirties* (London, 1960), provide valuable coverage. For the period from 1950 onwards, there are many critical works. A brief list would be: Arnold P. Hinchliffe, *British Theatre 1950–70* (Oxford, 1974); Lawrence Kitchin, *Mid-Century Drama* (London, 1960) and *Drama in the Sixties* (London, 1966); John Russell Taylor, *Anger and After* (London, 1962) and *The Second Wave* (London, 1971). Political engagement in the theatre is examined by Eric Bentley, *The Theatre of Commitment* (New York, 1954; London, 1968), and by Robert Brustein, *The Theatre of Revolt* (New York, 1962; London, 1965). Experimental and 'fringe' theatre are briefly examined in James Roose-Evans, *Experimental Theatre* (New York, 1970), and in Ronald Hayman, *The Set-Up* (London, 1973).

(b) ACTORS AND DIRECTORS

(i) *General*

Bertram Joseph has a good discussion of the tragic acting styles of the major players in his *The Tragic Actor* (London, 1959). The Coquelin–Irving debate is documented in *Actors and Acting* (Publication of Drama Museum of Columbia University, 1926). Two useful studies of late nineteenth-century acting are Percy Fitzgerald, *The Art of Acting* (London, 1892), and J. A. Hammerton, *The Actor's Art* (London, 1897). Frederic Whyte's *Actors of the Century* (London, 1898) has short comments and a good gallery of portraits, and profusely illustrated are *Edwardian Actors* (London, 1901) and *The Stage in the Year 1900* (London, 1901). Sir George Arthur has an interesting personal account, *From Phelps to Gielgud* (London, 1936). General studies of the actor-managers include Hesketh Pearson, *The Last Actor-Managers* (London, 1950), an entertaining and informed survey including much personal reminiscence; Richard Findlater, *The Player Kings* (London, 1968); and Frances Donaldson, *The Actor-Managers* (London, 1970).

(ii) *Henry Irving and Ellen Terry*

The standard biography of Henry Irving is Laurence Irving's massive and excellent *Henry Irving* (London, 1951); also indispensable are Edward Gordon Craig's *Henry Irving* (London, 1930), which contains some of the finest descriptions penned of Irving's playing, and Ellen Terry's inside account of work at the Lyceum, *The Story of My Life* (London, 1908). Among important early studies are Austin Brereton, *The Life of Henry Irving*, 2 vols (London, 1908); William Archer, *Henry Irving, Actor and Manager* (London, 1883); Bram Stoker, *Personal Reminiscences of Henry Irving*, 2 vols (London, 1906); P. Fitzgerald, *Henry Irving* (1893) and *Sir Henry Irving* (London, 1906); Joseph Hatton, *Henry Irving's Impressions of America* (New York, 1884); Walter Calvert, *Souvenir of Sir Henry Irving* (London, 1895); and Edward R. Russell, *Irving as Hamlet* (1875). There is detailed discussion of Irving's stage delivery in Edwin Drew, *Henry Irving, On and Off the Stage* (1889). Clement Scott's *From 'The Bells' to 'King Arthur'* (1897) is a collection of his reviews of major Irving productions; a vigorously critical comment is provided by Henry Arthur Jones, *The Shadow of Henry Irving* (London, 1931); and a varied collection of essays is to be found in H. A. Saintsbury and C. Palmer (eds), *We Saw Him Act: A Symposium on the Art of Sir Henry Irving* (London, 1939). (See also (viii).)

Ellen Terry wrote one of the most sensitive and entertaining auto-biographies of the period, *The Story of My Life* (London, 1908); it was edited with additional material by Edith Craig and Christopher St John (London, 1933). The most substantial modern biography is Roger Manvell, *Ellen Terry* (London, 1968), and Gordon Craig wrote a fine personal study, *Ellen Terry and Her Secret Self* (London, 1931). Earlier studies include Charles Hiatt, *Ellen Terry and her Impersonations* (London, 1898), and Clement Scott, *Ellen Terry* (New York, 1900). *Ellen Terry and Bernard Shaw: A Correspondence* was edited by Christopher St John (London, 1931).

(iii) *Herbert Beerbohm Tree*

The most detailed account of Tree is Hesketh Pearson, *Beerbohm Tree* (London, 1956); Max Beerbohm edited a varied collection of critical essays and reminiscences, *Herbert Beerbohm Tree* (London, n.d.), and there is an account by Mrs G. Cran, *Herbert Beerbohm Tree* (London, 1907). Among Tree's own writings are the books *Thoughts and Afterthoughts* (London, 1913) and *Nothing Matters* (London, 1917), and occasional lectures and essays like *Hamlet, from an Actor's Prompt Book* (London, 1897), the substance of a lecture to the Wolverhampton Literary Society and reprinted from *The Fortnightly Review* (1895), and the prefatory remarks to his arrangement for the stage of Shakespeare's *The Tempest* (London, 1904).

(iv) *From the Bancrofts to Alexander*

Squire and Marie Bancroft wrote entertaining reminiscences in their *Mr and Mrs Bancroft On and Off the Stage*, 2 vols (London, 1888), and *The Bancrofts: Recollections of Sixty Years* (London, 1909). T. Edgar Pemberton wrote a study of *The Kendals* (London, 1900), and Madge Kendal published an autobiography, *Dame Madge Kendal* (London, 1933). There is a biography of Wyndham by T. Edgar Pemberton, *Sir Charles Wyndham* (London, 1904), another account by F. T. Shore, *Sir Charles Wyndham* (London, 1908), and a very perceptive essay-length study by George Rowell, 'Wyndham of Wynd-hams', in Joseph W. Donohue, Jr (ed.), *The Theatrical Manager in England and America* (Princeton, NJ, 1971). The career of John Hare is traced by T. Edgar Pemberton, *John Hare, Comedian 1865–1895* (London, 1895). A. E. W. Mason's *Sir George Alexander and the St James's Theatre* (London, 1935) is an engaging life that provides much information about the financial side of Alexander's management.

(v) *Other actors, actresses and actor-managers*

The best study of Benson is J. C. Trewin's *Benson and the Bensonians* (London, 1960). *The Autobiography of Sir John Martin-Harvey* (London, 1933) is entertaining and informative, George Edgar wrote a study of the actor, *Martin Harvey: Some Pages of His Life* (London, 1912), and M. W. Disher an authorized biography, *The Last Romantic* (London, n.d.). Forbes-Robertson wrote an autobiography, *A Player Under Three Reigns* (London, 1925), as did Mrs Patrick Campbell, *My Life and Some Letters* (London, 1922), and there is a good modern biography of the latter player, Alan Dent, *Mrs Patrick Campbell* (London, 1961). Particularly valuable is the same writer's edition *Bernard Shaw and Mrs Patrick Campbell: Their Correspondence* (London, 1954). There is an early account of the career of Toole in Joseph Hatton, *The Reminiscences of J. L. Toole*, 2 vols (London, 1889), and of Terriss in Arthur J. Smythe, *The Life of William Terriss* (London, 1898). Among other autobiographies and reminiscences may be noted: Bransby Williams, *An Actor's Story* (London, 1909) and *Bransby Williams: By Himself* (London, 1914); Sir Frank Benson, *My Memoirs* (London, 1930); Constance Benson, *Merely Players* (London, 1926); *Behind the Scenes with Cyril Maude* (London, 1927); *Oscar Asche: His Life by Himself* (London, 1929); Seymour Hicks, *Between Ourselves* (London, 1930); Elizabeth Robins, *Both Sides of the Curtain* (London, 1940); and Irene Vanbrugh, *To Tell My Story* (London, 1948).

(vi) *1919 onwards*

Daphne du Maurier, *Gerald: A Portrait* (London, 1934), is a lively biography of Gerald du Maurier and provides an impression of his style of acting. Anthony Curtis (ed.), *The Rise and Fall of the Matinee Idol* (London, 1974), has contributions on such stage personalities as Lewis Waller, Gladys Cooper, Gertrude Lawrence, Jack Buchanan, Ivor Novello and Noël Coward. There are a number of biographies of contemporary actors and actresses including: John Casson, *Lewis and Sybil* (London, 1972), the story of the devoted partnership of Sybil Thorndike and Lewis Casson; J. C. Trewin, *Edith Evans* (London, 1954); Ronald Harwood, *Sir Donald Wolfit* (London, 1971); Ronald Hayman, *John Gielgud* (London, 1971), which throws useful light on his working method; Logan Gourlay (ed.), *Olivier* (London, 1973), a collection of studies and reminiscences by many who have worked with him; Kenneth Tynan, *Alec Guinness* (London, 1953), which traces his development as a film and stage actor; and Richard Findlater, *Michael Redgrave* (London, 1956), a description of his development and style. Peter Brook's biography has been written by J. C. Trewin, *Peter Brook* (London, 1971), but his ideas are better expressed in his own book, *The Empty Space* (London, 1968). Tyrone Guthrie has written two important books on his working method, *A Life in the Theatre* (London, 1960) and *In Various Directions* (London, 1963). Michael Billington, *The Modern Actor* (London, 1973), has useful chapters on acting schools and theories of acting.

(vii) *Shakespearian production*

G. D. Odell's *Shakespeare from Betterton to Irving*, 2 vols (London, 1920), discusses some Shakespearian productions of the late nineteenth century. J. C. Trewin, *Shakespeare on the English Stage 1900–1964* (London, 1964), provides a thorough and highly readable survey, and W. Moelwyn Merchant's *Shakespeare and the Artist* (Oxford, 1959), although of much broader compass, gives a detailed account of selected stagings. Robert Speaight's *Shakespeare on the Stage* (London, 1973) is a concise and excellently illustrated international overview.

(viii) *Grein and Poel*

The most systematic and exhaustive study of the work of J. T. Grein is N. Schoonderwoerd, *J. T. Grein, Ambassador of the Theatre 1862–1935* (Assen, 1963). Michael Orme, *J. T. Grein* (London, 1936), contains much valuable information on the Independent Theatre Society; there is a good examination of the plays produced by the Society in John Stokes, *Resistible Theatres* (London, 1972). A more general study is Anna Irene Miller, *The Independent Theatre in Europe* (New York, 1931).

The standard full-length study of Poel is Robert Speaight, *William Poel and the Elizabethan Revival* (London, Society for Theatre Research, 1954); Arthur Colby Sprague has an important chapter on Poel in his *Shakespearian Players and Performances* (London, 1954).

(ix) *Granville Barker*

The standard biography of Granville Barker is C. B. Purdom, *Harley Granville Barker* (London, 1955); Purdom also edited *Bernard Shaw's Letters to Granville Barker* (London, 1956). The Barker seasons at the Court Theatre are discussed by Desmond MacCarthy, *The Court Theatre 1904–*

1907 (London, 1907), and by Irving Zucker, *Le Court Théâtre (1904–1914) et l'évolution du théâtre anglais contemporain* (Paris, 1931). W. Bridges Adams has a good short essay, *The Lost Leader* (London, 1954), and Margery M. Morgan's *A Drama of Political Man: A Study in the Plays of Harley Granville Barker* (London, 1961) has some excellent things to say on Barker's approach to acting and direction.

(x) *Edward Gordon Craig*

Edward Craig has written an excellent critical biography of his father which includes much material not available elsewhere, *Gordon Craig* (London, 1968). Denis Bablet's *Edward Gordon Craig* (London, 1966) is a detailed study. Perceptive and well illustrated is Ferruccio Marotti's *Gordon Craig*, Documenti di teatro 20 (Bologna, 1961), and there are valuable essays on Craig's work in the same author's *Amleto o dell'oxymoron* (Rome, 1966). A good, short account with many illustrations is Janet Leeper, *Edward Gordon Craig: Designs for the Theatre* (Harmondsworth, 1948). The introduction by George Nash to the 1967 Victoria and Albert Museum exhibition of Craig's work is a useful, short overview, *Edward Gordon Craig 1872–1966* (London, 1967). Craig's own writings are indispensable: among them *The Art of the Theatre* (1905), *On the Art of Theatre* (1911), *Index to the Story of My Days* (London, 1957), the studies of Irving and Ellen Terry cited above, and of course the issues of *The Mask*. For further reference see Ifan Kyrle Fletcher and Arnold Rood, *Edward Gordon Craig, A Bibliography* (London, 1967).

(c) THEATRES

(i) *General*

Invaluable studies of London theatres are R. Mander and J. Mitchenson, *The Theatres of London* (London, 1961) and *The Lost Theatres of London* (London, 1968). A good reference work is Diana Howard, *London Theatres and Music Halls 1850–1950* (London Library Association, 1970). An important contemporary account of some mid- and late nineteenth-century theatres is Edwin Sachs, *European Theatres and Opera Houses*, 3 vols (1887–97). Studies of individual theatres include: A. E. Wilson, *The Lyceum* (London, 1952); Barry Duncan, *The St James's Theatre: Its Strange and Complete History* (London, 1964); T. Edgar Pemberton, *The Criterion*

Theatre 1875–1903 (London, 1903); W. Macqueen Pope, *The Theatre Royal, Drury Lane* (London, 1945) and *The Haymarket: Theatre of Perfection* (London, 1948). D. Forbes-Winslow, *Daly's, The Biography of a Theatre* (London, 1944), W. Macqueen Pope, *Gaiety, Theatre of Enchantment* (London, 1949), and Alan Hayman, *The Gaiety Years* (London, 1973), are general accounts of important musical theatres. The variety and musical stages have their own extensive bibliography, but particularly recommended are the excellently illustrated overviews by Mander and Mitchenson: *British Music Hall: A Story in Pictures* (London, 1965), *Musical Comedy: A Story in Pictures* (London, 1969), *Revue: A Story in Pictures* (London 1971) and *Pantomine: A Story in Pictures* (New York, 1973). A richly illustrated reference work is R. Busby, *British Music Hall* (London, 1976).

(ii) *Repertory and little theatres*

Two early general studies are P. P. Howe, *The Repertory Theatre* (London, 1910), and Basil Dean, *The Repertory Theatre* (London, 1911). Among many accounts of the early repertory companies may be noted: Grace W. Goldie, *The Liverpool Repertory Theatre 1911–1935* (Liverpool and London, 1935); J. C. Trewin, *The Birmingham Repertory Theatre 1913–1963* (London, 1963); Cicely Hamilton and Lilian Baylis, *The Old Vic* (London, 1926). Miss Horniman's repertory in Manchester is fully discussed in Rex Pogson, *Miss Horniman and the Gaiety Theatre, Manchester* (London, 1952).

Kathleen Barker, *Theatre Royal, Bristol, 1766–1966* (London, 1974), contains a comprehensive account of the Bristol Old Vic Company, but students should also read Audrey Williams and Charles Landstone, *The Bristol Old Vic: The First Ten Years* (London, 1957). Nigel Playfair, *Hammersmith Hoy* (London, 1930), contains an informative chapter on the influential revival of *The Beggar's Opera*. Norman MacDermot, *Everymania* (London, 1975), provides an account of this hitherto neglected example of an early little theatre. Norman Marshall, *The Other Theatre* (London, 1947), is a standard work on the repertory theatres of the inter-war and immediate post-war period. John Elsom, *Theatre Outside London* (London, 1971), gives a concise and comprehensive study of all the major regional repertory companies, together with a critical study of Arts Council policy.

(iii) *Irish Theatre*

The bibliography of the Irish National Theatre movement is substantial. A good overview is provided by Una Ellis-Fermor, *The Irish Dramatic*

Movement (London, 1939), and a concise account is given in Micheal O'hAodha, *Theatre in Ireland* (Oxford, 1974). A good, short history is G. Lunari, *Il movimento drammatico irlandese (1899–1922)*, Documenti di teatro 33 (Bologna, 1964). Perhaps the most valuable early history is Lady Gregory's *Our Irish Theatre*, available in the Coole Edition, Vol. IV (Bucks., 1972). Two studies of the Abbey Theatre are Lennox Robinson, *Ireland's Abbey Theatre* (London, 1951), which gives cast lists of many productions, and Gerard Fay, *The Abbey Theatre* (London, 1958); the latter is particularly useful for its discussion of the contribution of the Fays. James W. Flannery has an interesting survey of Miss Horniman's involvement with the Abbey, *Miss Annie F. Horniman and the Abbey Theatre* (Dublin, 1970), and Frank Fay's *Towards a National Theatre: Dramatic Criticism* has been edited by Robert Hogan (Dublin, 1970). Among W. B. Yeats's writings, particularly relevant are *Autobiographies*, *Dramatis Personae*, *Explorations* and *Plays and Controversies*. Hugh Hunt, *Ireland's National Theatre* (Dublin, 1979), is the authorized history of the Abbey Theatre from its inception as the Irish Literary Theatre to the present day.

(iv) *The Old Vic, the Royal Shakespeare Company, the English Stage Company and the National Theatre Company*

The history of the Old Vic up to 1950 can be followed in Harcourt Williams, *Old Vic Saga 1914–1949* (London, 1949), which provides a useful list of productions with producers and designers, and Lionel Hale, *The Old Vic 1949–1950 Season* (London, 1950). R. Ellis and M. C. Day, *The Shakespeare Memorial Theatre* (London, 1948) and *The Royal Shakespeare Theatre Company 1960–63* (RSC publication), provide sketchy information of productions. A useful chapter on the Royal Shakespeare and National Theatre companies can be found in Ronald Hayman, *The Set-Up* (London, 1973). This also contains critical chapters on the West End, the Royal Court, the Memorial Theatre, British Actors' Equity, the Arts Council and the actors' agent. Terry Browne, *Playwrights' Theatre* (London, 1973), traces the history of the English Stage Company.

(d) SCENIC DESIGN AND NEW THEATRE FORMS

Among accounts of scene design, effects, etc., are Percy Fitzgerald, *The World Behind the Scenes* (London, 1881); Jospeh Harker, *Studio and Stage* (London, 1924); Charles Ricketts, *Pages on Art* (London, 1913) and *Self-*

Portrait: Letters and Journals of Charles Ricketts, collected and compiled by T. Sturge Moore, ed. Cecil Lewis (London, 1939). John Stokes, *Resistible Theatres* (London, 1972), has a good, detailed account, with illustrations, of the ideas and productions of E. W. Godwin and Hubert von Herkomer.

Stage scenery is discussed by Sybil Rosenfeld in her excellent overview, *A Short History of Scene Design in Britain* (Oxford, 1974). More detailed general studies are Fuerst and Hume, *Twentieth Century Stage Decoration*, 2 vols (London, 1928), and Denis Bablet, *Le Décor de théâtre de 1870 à 1914* (Paris, 1965).

Theatre buildings and stages are examined in detail by Richard Leacroft, *The Development of the English Playhouse* (London, 1973), and Victor Glasstone's *Victorian and Edwardian Theatres* (London, 1975) is lavishly illustrated. New theatre forms are also discussed in Richard Southern, *The Open Stage* (London, 1943), and Stephen Joseph, *Theatre in the Round* (London, 1967).

(e) CRITICISM

For the writings of the major critics of the period, the following collections are but a selection: George Bernard Shaw, *Our Theatres in the Nineties*, 3 vols (London, 1931); E. J. West (ed.), *Shaw on Theatre* (New York, 1958); Clement Scott, *The Drama of Yesterday and Today*, 2 vols (1899); Henry James, *The Scenic Art*, ed. Allan Wade (London, 1949); A. B. Walkley, *Playhouse Impressions* (1892); William Archer, *The Theatrical World 1893–7* (London, 1894–8); J. T. Grein, *Dramatic Criticism* (1899); C. E. Montague, *Dramatic Values* (London, 1910); Max Beerbohm, *Around Theatres* (London, 1953), *More Theatres, 1898–1903* (London, 1969) and *Last Theatres* (London, 1973); and Desmond MacCarthy, *Theatre* (London, 1954). James Agate, dramatic critic of *The Sunday Times* from 1923 to 1947, is the leading commentator on theatrical performances up to and including the Second World War period. His criticisms are published in *Those Were the Nights* (London, 1946), *The Contemporary Theatre*, 6 vols (London, 1923–45) and *My Theatre Talks* (London, 1933). Less waspish than Agate is Ivor Brown, dramatic critic of *The Observer* from 1928 to 1954. His kindly but perceptive criticisms are published in *Masques and Phases* (London, 1926), *First Player* (London, 1927) and *Parties of the Play* (London, 1928). *The Encore Reader* (London, 1965), edited by Charles Marowitz, Tom Milne and Owen Hale, contains a selection of articles and criticisms of the period 1956–65.

Important periodicals include *The Theatre* (1877–97), *The Era* (1868–1919), *The Playgoer* (1901–4), *Playgoer and Society Illustrated* (1909–13), *Play Pictorial* (1902–39), *Theatre World* (1925–65) and *Plays and Players* (1953–). *The Stage Year Book*, 38 vols (London, 1908–69), has cast lists of all London productions, together with articles on matters affecting the theatre and obituaries. Among current scholarly journals including articles on nineteenth- and early twentieth-century theatre are *Theatre Notebook, Victorian Studies, Nineteenth Century Theatre Research* and *Theatre Research International* (formerly *Theatre Research/Recherches théâtrales*). *Drama*, published quarterly by the British Drama League, has well-informed criticisms of current productions. *Theatre 54 to 55* and *Theatre 55 to 56* (London, 1956 and 1957), edited by Ivor Brown, *Theatre 71 to 74* (London, 1971–4), edited by Sheridan Morley, 4 vols, are comprehensive annuals containing criticism, checklists of London first nights and informative articles, as well as honours and awards and obituaries. Also highly recommended for recent theatre is the magazine *Theatre Quarterly*. In addition to criticisms of contemporary productions from 1971 onwards, including the leading 'fringe' theatres and educational theatres, it contains a comprehensive reference section of theatre events throughout the world, and an invaluable bibliography of all books published on the theatre from 1970 onwards.

III Plays and playwrights since 1880

(a) PLAYS

Most of the important plays staged since 1880 have been published in some form, if only in acting editions. The grander playwrights were often treated to collected editions of their works, or extensive selections. For most of the writers concerned, during the first half of the period, most editions of both sorts are long out of print. There are still available many collected editions of the Gilbert texts for the Savoy operas; otherwise the standard edition is *Original Plays by W. S. Gilbert*, 4 vols (London, 1876–1911), with J. W. Stedman's more accessible collection *Gilbert Before Sullivan* (Chicago, Ill., 1967). There is really no presentable collection of Robertson's plays; James Albery, surprisingly, fares better with *The Dramatic Works of James Albery*, 2 vols (London, 1939). Henry Arthur Jones and Pinero have both been the subject of four-volume collections in the twentieth century, Jones with *Representative Plays* (London, 1926) and Pinero with *The Social Plays of A. W. Pinero* (New York, 1917–22). Wilde and Shaw, on the other hand, are very readily available. The standard edition of Wilde is *The Complete Works* (London, 1949 and 1966), but humbler volumes like the Penguin editions of the major plays are perfectly acceptable. For Shaw there are the 36-volume *Works* (London, 1931–50), *The Bodley Head Bernard Shaw: Collected Plays with their Prefaces* (London, 1970–) and *The Complete Plays of Bernard Shaw* in one volume (first really complete edition London, 1950).

In addition, there are several useful anthologies of nineteenth-century drama which include plays of our period. Notably Michael R. Booth's *English Plays of the Nineteenth Century*, 4 vols (Oxford, 1969–73), and *'The Magistrate' and Other Nineteenth-Century Plays* (London, 1974), and George Rowell's *Late Victorian Plays* (London, 1968).

Once we arrive decidedly in the twentieth century, and are speaking more of current literature than of more or less scholarly texts, there is an embarrassment of riches. It is, naturally, a sign of having arrived in critical and public estimation when a writer's works are collected. There are, for example, *Plays by W. Somerset Maugham*, 6 vols (London, 1931–4; reprinted in 3 vols, 1952), *Play Parade* by Noël Coward, 6 vols (London, 1934–62), and *The Collected Plays of Terence Rattigan*, 4 vols to date (London, 1953–). *The Plays of J. M. Barrie in One Volume* (London, 1928) was the first such lectern-size tribute to a living dramatist, followed rapidly by *The Plays of John Galsworthy* (London, 1929). Another contemporary, Harley Granville Barker, has had to wait until a recent revival of interest for his *Collected Plays* to appear (London, 1967–). J. B. Priestley had his plays collected in 3 vols (London, 1948–50); Emlyn Williams's *Collected Plays* (London, 1961–) are still in progress. *The Collected Plays* of T. S. Eliot appeared in one volume (London, 1962); the *Plays* of the other most familiar figure in the post-war revival of verse drama, Christopher Fry, have recently been gathered in, up to now, 3 vols (London, 1972–).

The Irish dramatic renaissance has also been represented very extensively in print. The editing and explication of Yeats texts has become a minor scholarly industry. There are *The Collected Plays of W. B. Yeats*, plain text version (London, 1952), and *The Variorum Edition of the Plays of W. B. Yeats* (New York, 1965), not to mention *Selected Plays of W. B. Yeats* (London, 1964) and many variously annotated individual texts. The *Plays* of J. M. Synge constitute Vols 3 and 4 of *The Collected Works* (London, 1968). Lady Gregory's *Collected Plays* take up four volumes in the Coole

Edition (Gerrards Cross and New York, 1970), and there is a one-volume *Selected Plays* (New York, 1962). Many, though by no means all, of Sean O'Casey's dramatic works are included in *The Collected Plays*, 4 vols (London, 1949–51). Beckett's plays, though their brevity seems to lend them to convenient collection, still have to be sought out in more than a dozen books and booklets.

The arrival of the 'new drama' in Britain in the mid-1950s was accompanied by an enormous increase in the willingness of the general reading public to read the texts of plays, and so by a greater readiness on the part of publishers to bring out new plays in reading editions rather than merely acting texts. The two publishers in Britain most involved were Methuen (latterly Eyre Methuen) and Faber and Faber. Fabers have published all of John Osborne's plays and the work of some other new dramatists, notably Ann Jellicoe and N. F. Simpson, as well as the English texts of most of Beckett's plays. Methuen, in their 'Modern Plays' series, have published Pinter, Arden, Behan, Delaney, Livings, Alun Owen, John Mortimer, Charles Wood, Edward Bond and many more. Pinter has even – the first of his generation – been collected in, to date, 3 vols (London, 1975–). And then there is a long series of relevant anthologies in the Penguin 'New English Dramatists' volumes. Nearly all the new English plays of quality since 1956 have been published one way or another and are readily available.

(b) PLAYWRIGHTS

Anyone seeking a reliable general outline of theatrical history and how the plays and playwrights fit into it during the later nineteenth century could hardly do better than George Rowell's *The Victorian Theatre* (Oxford, 1956), supplemented by the indispensable Allardyce Nicoll *History of Late XIXth Century Drama 1850–1900* (Cambridge, 1946). For determined and provocative oddity the latter parts of G. Wilson Knight's very personal 'Study of the British Drama', *The Golden Labyrinth* (London, 1962), take some beating. George Bernard Shaw's *Our Theatres in the Nineties*, his reviews collected in 3 vols (London, 1932), gives a vivid contemporary picture as well as throwing a lot of light on Shaw himself and his attitudes. Martin Meisel's *Shaw and the Nineteenth-Century Theatre* (Oxford, 1963) brings it all together within a larger context.

An enormous literature has gathered round Shaw himself – more, certainly, than around any other single figure. Stanley Weintraub has compiled

An Autobiography, 2 vols (New York, 1969 and 1970), from Shaw's own scattered writings. The best general studies remain Hesketh Pearson's journalistic, anecdotal *Bernard Shaw: His Life and Personality* (London, 1942), which still has the vividness of close personal knowledge, and Eric Bentley's *Bernard Shaw* (Norfolk, Conn., 1947), the most balanced general critical assessment. There are many books on Shaw's ideas and various aspects of his intellectual development, far fewer centred on his drama as such. Louis Crompton's *Shaw the Dramatist* (Lincoln, Nebr., 1969), though selective, dealing with only eleven plays, is an honourable exception; Bernard F. Dukore's *Bernard Shaw, Director* (London, 1971) throws a lot of light on Shaw's theatre practice from an unexpected angle. Alick West's *A Good Man Fallen Among Fabians* (London, 1950) is an excellent introduction to Shaw's imagination which still takes adequate account of his special qualities as a dramatist; likewise Richard Ohmann's *Shaw: The Style and the Man* (Middleton, Conn., 1962), which approaches Shaw through analysis of his language. For basic information on the what, when, where and who of Shaw's plays in production Mander and Mitchenson's *A Theatrical Companion to Shaw* (London, 1954) is indispensable.

None of Shaw's seniors or contemporaries has been so well served. There are more or less solid biographies of most of them, such as Doris Arthur Jones's *The Life and Letters of Henry Arthur Jones* (London, 1930), H. V. Marrot's *The Life and Letters of John Galsworthy* (London, 1935), H. Montgomery Hyde's *Oscar Wilde* (London, 1975) and C. B. Purdom's *Harley Granville Barker* (London, 1955), only the last of which concerns itself centrally with the theatrical career. Then there are a few primarily critical books, fewer still to be taken very seriously. W. D. Dunkel's *Sir Arthur Pinero* (Chicago, Ill., 1940) is rather uncritical, but Walter Lazenby's *Arthur Wing Pinero* (New York, 1972) offers a more modern judgement, and Pinero's *Collected Letters*, edited by J. P. Wearing (Minneapolis, Minn., 1974), also contain useful material. K. Beckson's anthology *Oscar Wilde: The Critical Heritage* (London, 1971) and Richard Ellmann's collection of critical essays *Oscar Wilde* (Englewood Cliffs, NJ, 1969) fill the gap on Wilde quite well, though the fascination of his personal history has tended to inhibit full-length purely critical study. Robert Lorin Calder's *W. Somerset Maugham and the Quest for Freedom* (London, 1972) is a rare attempt to put this embarrassingly popular writer in a reasonable critical perspective.

Early twentieth-century Irish theatre has been as productive of biographical and critical studies as it has of scholarly editions of the texts. The

Abbey Theatre, Dublin, and its writers have been exhaustively written about: the most interesting books are Lennox Robinson's *Ireland's Abbey Theatre* (London, 1951), Gerard Fay's *The Abbey Theatre, Cradle of Genius* (London, 1958) and *Joseph Holloway's Abbey Theatre* (Carbondale, Ill., 1967), a selection covering the years 1899 to 1926 from the 25-million-word diary of an obsessive Dublin theatregoer. The later history of the Irish theatre is well covered in Robert Hogan's *After the Irish Renaissance: A Critical History of the Irish Drama since 'The Plough and the Stars'* (Minneapolis, Minn., 1967). Useful studies of specific dramatists are Peter Ure's *Yeats the Playwright* (London, 1963), D. R. Clark's *W. B. Yeats and the Theatre of Desolate Reality* (Dublin, 1965), L. E. Nathan's *The Tragic Drama of William Butler Yeats: Figures in a Dance* (New York, 1965), J. R. Moore's *Masks of Love and Death: Yeats as Dramatist* (Ithaca, NY, 1971) and James W. Flannery's *W. B. Yeats and the Idea of a Theatre* (New Haven, Conn., 1976); Elizabeth Coxhead's *Lady Gregory* (London, 1961) and *J. M. Synge and Lady Gregory* (London, 1962); Robin Skelton's *The Writings of J. M. Synge* (London, 1971), Howard K. Slaughter's *George Fitzmaurice and his Enchanted Land* (Dublin, 1972) and David Krause's *Sean O'Casey: The Man and His Work* (London, 1960).

English drama between the wars still awaits any kind of serious revaluation, and tends still to be scurried over in elementary outlines of dramatic history as an unworthy prelude to the 'new drama' of the 1950s. John Russell Taylor's *The Rise and Fall of the Well-Made Play* (London, 1967) deals with this particular strain in English drama from Robertson to Rattigan. J. C. Trewin's *Dramatists of Today* (London, 1953) is a sensible, hopeful picture of the dramatic situation immediately before the new drama. There are a couple of acceptable popular biographies of Noël Coward, Sheridan Morley's *A Talent to Amuse* (London, 1969) and Cole Lesley's *Remembered Laughter* (London, 1976); Frances Donaldson's well-written biography of her father *Freddy Lonsdale* (London, 1957); and Ben Travers's illuminating autobiography *Vale of Laughter* (London, 1957). The revival of verse drama is sensibly considered in Denis Donoghue's *The Third Voice: Modern British and American Verse Drama* (Princeton, NJ, 1959); on Christopher Fry there are two versions of Derek Stanford's *Christopher Fry: An Appreciation* (London, 1951, 1962); and on T. S. Eliot, owing largely to his eminence in fields other than drama, a whole slew of books, among which may be mentioned E. Martin Browne's *The Making of T. S. Eliot's Plays* (London, 1969), David E. Jones's *The Plays of T. S. Eliot* (London, 1960), C. H. Smith's *T. S. Eliot's Dramatic Theory and Practice* (Princeton, NJ,

1963) and Grover Smith's *T. S. Eliot's Poetry and Plays: A Study in Sources and Meaning* (Chicago, Ill., rev. ed., 1974). Mander and Mitchenson have written *Theatrical Companions*, uniform with their Shaw volume, on Maugham (London, 1955) and Coward (London, 1957).

From the opening of *Look Back in Anger* in 1956 things have changed considerably. There have been many studies of the whole dramatic scene, among them John Russell Taylor's *Anger and After* (London, rev. ed., 1968) and its sequel *The Second Wave* (London, 1971), and Arnold Hinchliffe's *British Theatre 1950–70* (Oxford, 1974). Many of the most influential original reviews of the plays are to be found in Kenneth Tynan's various collections, particularly *Curtains* (London, 1961). Martin Esslin's *The Theatre of the Absurd* (London, 1961) is the classic formulation of ideas on this group of dramatists, who include for Esslin's purposes (and ours) Beckett and Pinter.

The scholarly examination and elucidation of Pinter has proliferated vastly of late. The best books, out of many, remain Martin Esslin's *The Peopled Wound* (London, 1970) and Arnold Hinchliffe's *Harold Pinter* (New York, 1967). There are monographs on *Arnold Wesker, Robert Bolt, John Arden, John Whiting* and others in a series by Ronald Hayman (London, 1970–1), by Simon Trussler on John Osborne (London, 1969), by Simon Trussler and Glenda Leeming on Arnold Wesker (London, 1971) and by Albert Hunt on John Arden (London, 1975). The British Council's 'Writers and their Work' series includes essays on many twentieth-century British dramatists, among them Christopher Fry, Shaw, O'Casey, Osborne, Pinter, Wesker, David Storey and Peter Shaffer. There are also many dispatches from the front line, keeping pace as far as possible with happenings in recent British drama. Two anthologies edited by Charles Marowitz and others are revealing: *The Encore Reader: A Chronicle of the New Drama* (London, 1965) and *Theatre at Work: Playwrights and Productions in the Modern British Theatre* (London, 1967). Even more recent are Terry Browne's *Playwright's Theatre: The English Stage Company at the Royal Court* (London, 1975) and Peter Ansorge's *Disrupting the Spectacle: 5 Years of Experimental and Fr nge Theatre in Britain* (London, 1975).

Index

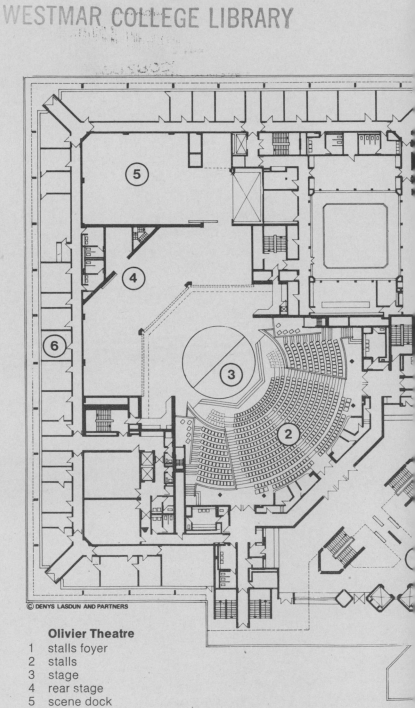

© DENYS LASDUN AND PARTNERS

Olivier Theatre
1 stalls foyer
2 stalls
3 stage
4 rear stage
5 scene dock
6 offices